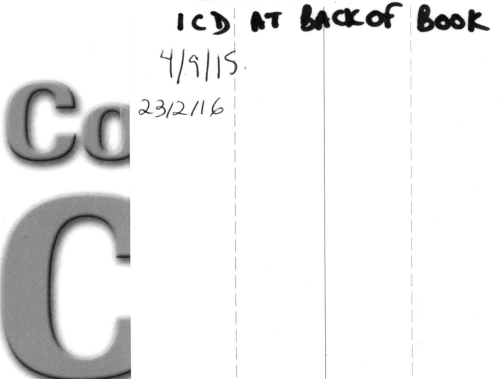

Student's Book *with answers*

Guy Brook-Hart and Simon Haines

CAMBRIDGE UNIVERSITY PRESS

Cambridge, New York, Melbourne, Madrid, Cape Town,
Singapore, São Paulo, Delhi, Mexico City

Cambridge University Press
The Edinburgh Building, Cambridge CB2 8RU, UK

www.cambridge.org
Information on this title: www.cambridge.org/9780521698436

First published 2009
8th printing 2013

Printed in Dubai by Oriental Press

A catalogue record for this publication is available from the British Library

ISBN 978-0-521-69843-6 Student's Book with answers with CD-ROM
ISBN 978-0-521-69842-9 Student's Book without answers with CD-ROM
ISBN 978-0-521-69845-0 Teacher's Book
ISBN 978-0-521-69847-4 Class Audio CDs (3)
ISBN 978-0-521-69844-3 Student's Book Pack (Student's Book with answers, CD-ROM and Class Audio CDs(3))
ISBN 978-0-521-69849-8 Workbook with answers with Audio CD
ISBN 978-0-521-69848-1 Workbook without answers with Audio CD

Contents

Unit title	Reading	Writing	Use of English
1 Our people	Reading Part 1: The subject of a book, Starting a conversation, My choice of career	Writing Part 1: A letter	Use of English Part 4
2 Mastering languages	Reading Part 2: Kenneth Hale, Master Linguist	Writing Part 2: A report	Use of English Part 3: The naming of products
Vocabulary and grammar review Units 1 and 2			
3 All in the mind	Reading Part 3: The next step in brain evolution	Writing Part 1: An article	Use of English Part 2: Nature vs Nurture
4 Office space	Reading Part 4: Is there an architect in the house?	Writing Part 1: A report	Use of English Part 1: Friends benefit firms
Vocabulary and grammar review Units 3 and 4			
5 Dramatic events	Reading Part 1: A night of fear, An unpleasant night, A night among the trees	Writing Part 2: A competition entry	Use of English Part 5
6 Picture yourself	Reading Part 3: Teenage self-portraits	Writing Part 2: A review	Use of English Part 2: Art for offices
Vocabulary and grammar review Units 5 and 6			
7 Leisure and entertainment	Reading Part 2: How to get the life you really want	Writing Part 2: An informal letter	Use of English Part 1: The changing face of Bollywood
8 Don't blame the media	Reading Part 3: The ethics of reality television producers	Writing Part 1: A proposal	Use of English Part 3: Broadcasters must find ways to regain public trust
Vocabulary and grammar review Units 7 and 8			
9 At top speed	Reading Part 2: Bugatti Veyron	Writing Part 2: An essay	Use of English Part 4
10 A lifelong process	Reading Part 4: What our students say about us	Writing Part 1: A report	Use of English Part 1: Why do we need lifelong learning?
Vocabulary and grammar review Units 9 and 10			
11 Being somewhere else	Reading Part 3: Disappearing into Africa	Writing Part 2: A contribution to a longer piece	Use of English Part 2: Island wanted
12 The living world	Reading Part 2: Alex the African Grey	Writing Part 2: An information sheet	Use of English Part 3: Species loss accelerating
Vocabulary and grammar review Units 11 and 12			
13 Health and lifestyle	Reading Part 4: Unusual national sports	Writing Part 1: A letter	Use of English Part 4
14 Moving abroad	Reading Part 1: The Atlantic passage, When talent goes abroad, Getting a student visa or permit	Writing Part 2: An article	Use of English Part 5
Vocabulary and grammar review Units 13 and 14			

Listening	Speaking	Vocabulary	Grammar
• Listening Part 4: Unusual occupations • Two students doing Speaking Part 1	Speaking Part 1	Collocations with *give*, *do* and *make*	Verb forms to talk about the past
• Listening Part 1: *Khalkha*, Spelling reform, Job interviews • Opinions about language • A university student talking about two photos	Speaking Part 2	Collocations with *make*, *get* and *do*	Expressing purpose, reason and result
• Listening Part 2: A psychological condition • Two people discussing photographs	Speaking Part 3	Formal or informal?	• *No*, *none*, *not* • The passive
• Listening Part 2: A skills shortage • Two people giving opinions	Speaking Part 4	Adjective/noun collocations (1)	Expressing possibility, probability and certainty
• Listening Part 1: Dramatic past experiences • A student speaking about the photos	Speaking Part 2	Idiomatic language	Verbs followed by *to* + infinitive or the *–ing* form
• Listening Part 3: An interview with artist Liam Carolan • Talking about self-portraits • Two pairs of students doing Speaking Part 3	Speaking Part 3	Adjective/noun collocations (2)	Avoiding repetition
• Listening Part 4: Talking about music • Two people doing Speaking Part 2	Speaking Part 2	• Prepositional phrases • Money verbs	Ways of linking ideas
• Listening Part 3: An interview with journalist Harry Cameron • Two people doing Speaking Part 3	Speaking Part 3	'Talking' verbs	• Transitive verbs • Reported speech
• Listening Part 1: Rail travel, Olympic records, Spaceships • A student doing Speaking Part 2	Speaking Part 2	*Action*, *activity*, *event* and *programme*	Tenses in time clauses and time adverbials
• Listening Part 2: Studying Arabic in Egypt • Two people doing Speaking Part 3	Speaking Part 3	*Chance*, *occasion*, *opportunity* and *possibility*	Modal verbs expressing ability, possibility and obligation
• Listening Part 1: Travelling on a river, A sponsored walk, An interview with a traveller • Three people doing Speaking Part 1	Speaking Part 1	*At*, *in* and *on* to express location	Conditionals
• Listening Part 2: Climate change and the Inuit • Two people doing Speaking Part 3	Speaking Part 3	• Word formation • Prepositions following verbs	Nouns and articles
• Listening Part 3: Allergies • Two people doing Speaking Part 2	Speaking Part 2	Prepositions after adjectives	• Ways of contrasting ideas • The language of comparison
• Listening Part 4: Migration • Migrants talking about their experiences • Two people doing Speaking Part 4	Speaking Part 4	*Learn*, *find out* and *know* *Provide*, *offer* and *give*	• Comment adverbials • Emphasis

Introduction

Who this book is for

Complete CAE is a stimulating and thorough preparation course for students who wish to take the **Certificate in Advanced English** exam from **Cambridge ESOL**. It teaches you the reading, writing, listening and speaking skills which are necessary for the exam as well as the grammar and vocabulary which, from research into the **Cambridge Learner Corpus**, are known to be essential for exam success. For those of you who are not planning to take the exam in the near future, the book provides you with skills and language highly relevant to an advanced level of English (Common European Framework (CEF) level C1).

What the book contains

In the **Student's Book** there are:

- **14 units for classroom study**. Each unit contains:
  - one part of each of the five papers in the CAE exam. The units provide language input and skills practice to help you deal successfully with the tasks in each part.
  - essential information on what each part of the exam involves, and the best way to approach each task.
  - a wide range of enjoyable and stimulating speaking activities designed to increase your fluency and your ability to express yourself.
  - a step-by-step approach to doing CAE Writing tasks.
  - grammar activities and exercises for the grammar you need to know for the exam. When you are doing grammar exercises you will sometimes see this symbol: ⊙. These exercises are based on research from the **Cambridge Learner Corpus** and they deal with the areas which are known to cause problems for students in the exam.
  - vocabulary necessary for CAE. When you see this symbol ⊙ by a vocabulary exercise, the exercise focuses on words which CAE candidates often confuse or use wrongly in the exam.
  - a unit review. These contain exercises which revise the grammar and vocabulary that you have studied in each unit.
- A **Grammar reference section** which clearly explains all the main areas of grammar which you will need to know for the CAE exam.

- **Speaking and Writing reference sections**. These explain the possible tasks you may have to do in the Speaking and Writing papers, and they give you examples together with additional exercises and advice on how best to approach these two CAE papers.
- A complete **CAE exam supplied by Cambridge ESOL** for you to practise with.
- A **CD-ROM** which provides you with many interactive exercises, including further listening practice exclusive to the CD-ROM. All these extra exercises are linked to the topics in the Student's Book.

Also available are:

- **Three audio CDs** containing listening material for the 14 units of the Student's Book plus the Listening Test supplied by Cambridge ESOL. The listening material is indicated by different coloured icons in the Student's Book as follows: ∩ CD1, ∩ CD2, ∩ CD3.
- A **Teacher's Book** containing:
  - **step-by-step guidance** for handling all the activities in the Student's Book.
  - a large number of suggestions for **alternative treatments** of activities in the Student's Book and suggestions for **extension activities**.
  - **extra photocopiable materials** for each unit of the Student's Book to practise and extend language abilities outside the requirements of the CAE exam.
  - **complete answer keys** including recording scripts for all the listening material.
  - **four photocopiable progress tests** at regular intervals throughout the book.
  - **14 photocopiable word lists** (one for each unit) containing vocabulary found in the units. Each vocabulary item in the word list is accompanied by a definition supplied by a corpus-informed Cambridge dictionary.
- A **Student's Workbook** containing:
  - **14 units for homework and self-study**. Each unit contains **full exam practice** in one part of the **CAE Reading Paper** or in two parts of the **CAE Use of English Paper**.
  - **full exam practice** in one part of the **CAE Listening Paper** in each unit.
  - further practice in the **grammar and vocabulary** taught in the Student's Book.
  - exercises for the **development of essential writing skills** such as paragraph organisation, self-correction, spelling and punctuation based on the results from the **Cambridge Learner Corpus** ⊙.
  - an **audio CD** containing all the listening material for the Workbook.

CAE content and overview

Part/timing	Content	Test focus
1 **READING** 1 hour 15 minutes	**Part 1** Three texts on one theme from a range of sources. Each text has two multiple-choice questions. **Part 2** A text from which six paragraphs have been removed and placed in a jumbled order, together with an additional paragraph, after the text. **Part 3** A text followed by seven multiple-choice questions. **Part 4** A text or several short texts preceded by 15 multiple-matching questions.	Candidates are expected to show understanding of attitude, detail, implication, main idea, opinion, purpose, specific information, text organisation features, tone and text structure.
2 **WRITING** 1 hour 30 minutes	**Part 1** One compulsory question. **Part 2** Candidates choose one task from a choice of five questions (including the set text options).	Candidates are expected to be able to write non-specialised text types such as an article, a contribution to a longer piece, an essay, information sheets, a proposal, a report, a review, or a competition entry, with a focus on advising, comparing, evaluating, expressing opinions, hypothesising, justifying, and persuading.
3 **USE OF ENGLISH** 1 hour	**Part 1** A modified cloze test containing 12 gaps and followed by 12 multiple-choice items. **Part 2** A modified cloze test containing 15 gaps. **Part 3** A text containing 10 gaps. Each gap corresponds to a word. The stems of the missing words are given beside the text and must be changed to form the missing word. **Part 4** Five questions, each one containing three discrete sentences. Each sentence contains one gap, which must be completed with one word which is appropriate in all three sentences. **Part 5** Eight separate questions, each with a lead-in sentence and a gapped second sentence to be completed in three to six words, one of which is a given 'key word'.	Candidates are expected to demonstrate the ability to apply their knowledge of the language system by completing a number of tasks.
4 **LISTENING** Approximately 40 minutes	**Part 1** Three short extracts, from exchanges between interacting speakers. There are two multiple-choice questions for each extract. **Part 2** A monologue with a sentence completion task which has eight items. **Part 3** A text involving interacting speakers, with six multiple-choice questions. **Part 4** Five short themed monologues, with 10 multiple-matching questions.	Candidates are expected to be able to show understanding of agreement, attitude, course of action, detail, feeling, function, gist, interpreting context, main points, opinion, purpose, specific information, etc.
5 **SPEAKING** 14 minutes	**Part 1** A conversation between the interlocutor and each candidate (spoken questions). **Part 2** An individual 'long turn' for each candidate with a brief response from the second candidate (visual and written stimuli, with spoken instructions). **Part 3** A two-way conversation between the candidates (visual and written stimuli, with spoken interaction). **Part 4** A discussion on topics related to Part 3 (spoken questions).	Candidates are expected to be able to respond to questions and to interact in conversational English.

Unit 1 Our people

Starting off

1 Work in small groups. How do you think these things reflect our personality? (Give examples.)

- the job we choose
- the subject(s) we choose to study
- our free-time interests
- the clothes we wear
- the friends we choose
- the place where we choose to live

2 Work alone. Choose one of the things above and spend a few minutes preparing a two-minute talk on how it reflects your personality.

3 Work in small groups and take turns to give your talks. While you are listening to your partners, think of one or two questions to ask them when they finish.

Listening Part 4

1 Work in pairs. The photos show people with interesting or unusual occupations.

1 Look at the list of occupations (**A–H**) in Task One on the right and match each occupation with one of the photos.
2 What do you think attracts people to these occupations?
3 Which do you think is easiest and which is the most difficult to learn?

2 **You will hear five short extracts in which people are talking about a member of their family who they admire. Before you listen, work in pairs.**

Which of these phrases would you associate with each job? (You can associate some of the phrases with more than one job.)

- a few of his/her recordings
- complete dedication to his/her craft
- perform a new trick
- his/her underwater adventures
- out in all weathers
- the first person to set foot in a place
- what it would be like tomorrow
- digging at some excavation or other

Now think of one more phrase you might associate with each job.

3 **Look at the list of qualities (A–H) in Task Two and explain what each of them means in your own words. Which quality would you associate with each job?**

Task One

For questions **1–5**, choose from the list **A–H** the person who each speaker is talking about.

A a deep-sea diver

B a fisherman/fisherwoman

C a glass-blower

D a magician

E a musician

F a weather forecaster

G an archaeologist

H an explorer

Speaker 1	1
Speaker 2	2
Speaker 3	3
Speaker 4	4
Speaker 5	5

Task Two

For questions **6–10**, choose from the list **A–H** the quality the speaker admires about the person.

A a positive outlook on life

B ability to anticipate problems

C an enquiring mind

D attention to detail

E calmness under pressure

F readiness to explain things

G kindness to children

H originality and inventiveness

Speaker 1	6
Speaker 2	7
Speaker 3	8
Speaker 4	9
Speaker 5	10

4 **🎧 Now listen to the five speakers and do the two tasks.**

Exam information

In Listening Part 4,

- you hear five short monologues and you have to do two listening tasks.
- in each task you have to choose one answer for each speaker from a list of eight options.
- you hear each speaker twice.

5 **Work in pairs. Tell each other about someone interesting or unusual in your family.**

- What do they do?
- What are they like?
- What is your relationship with them like?

Grammar
Verb forms to talk about the past

❶ Look at these extracts from Listening Part 4. Match the underlined verb forms with their names (a–h).

a   past simple
b   past continuous
c   past perfect simple
d   past perfect continuous

e   present perfect simple
f   present perfect continuous
g   *used to* + infinitive
h   *would* + infinitive

1   We loved his stories of … the strange creatures he'd seen.   *c*
2   It was a real eye-opener to see her at work. I mean, she <u>was doing</u> what many people think is a man's job.
3   She <u>invited</u> me to come out on one of her trips …
4   We'<u>ve listened</u> to them so many times …
5   He'<u>d drop</u> whatever he was doing …
6   She never <u>used to panic</u> …
7   … even if he was tired because he'<u>d been working</u> all day.
8   He'<u>s been getting</u> this new show ready recently.

❷ Which of the verb forms in Exercise 1 is used to do the following?

1   refer to something that happened at a specific time in the past: ....*past simple*........
2   refer to a repeated action or habit in the past which doesn't happen now: .... and ....
3   refer to an activity which started before and (possibly) continued after an event in the past:
....
4   indicate that we are talking about something which happened before another activity or situation in the past which is described in the past simple: ....
5   indicate that we are talking about something which happened before another activity or situation in the past simple, but focusing on the length of time: ....
6   refer to something that started in the past and is still happening now and emphasises the activity rather than the result: ....
7   refer to something that started in the past and still happens now and often says how many times something has been repeated: ....

▶ page 148 *Grammar reference: Verb forms to talk about the past*

❸ Put the verbs in brackets in the following sentences into the simple or continuous forms of the past, past perfect or present perfect. (In some cases more than one answer is possible.)

1   Chen *has been working* (work) in Singapore since he .... (leave) university two years ago, but next year he expects to be transferred to Hong Kong.
2   Sven takes university life very seriously. He .... (study) here for six months and he still .... (not go) to a single party!
3   Maria .... (come) round to dinner last night; she .... (start) telling me her life story while I .... (make) the salad and .... (continue) telling it during dinner.

4   Ivan .... (have) a splitting headache yesterday evening because he .... (work) in the sun all day and he .... (not wear) a hat.
5   I .... (grow) up in a house which .... (belong) to my great-great-grandfather. We .... (sell) it now because it is too big for our small family.

❹ Circle the correct alternative in *italics* in each of the following sentences.

a   My teachers (1) *were often getting /* (*often used to get*) annoyed with me when I was at school because I (2) *never used to bring / had never brought* a pen with me and I (3) *would always ask / have always asked* someone if I could borrow theirs.
b   The village (4) *used to be / would be* very quiet and remote until they (5) *built / had built* the motorway two years ago. In those days everybody (6) *would know / used to know* everyone else, but since then, a lot of new people (7) *came / have come* to live in the area and the old social structures (8) *gradually changed / have gradually been changing.*
c   When I was a child, both my parents (9) *used to go / were going* out to work, so when they (10) *would be / were* out, my grandmother (11) *was looking / would look* after me.

5 ⦿ CAE candidates often make mistakes with present perfect, past and past perfect tenses. In the sentences below, circle the correct alternative in *italics*.

1 In recent times people *had /* (*have had*) more contact with their friends through email and mobile phones than they did in the past.

2 The feedback we received from our clients meant we *have been / were* able to provide excellent advice to the people developing the product which they then acted on.

3 The party was great and the best bit for me *has been / was* the jazz band.

4 We should have had a really good holiday for what we paid, but unfortunately we discovered that they *didn't organise / hadn't organised* anything very much so it was rather a disappointment.

5 While I was studying in England, I *haven't taken / didn't take* an examination because it was not offered to me or to any of my fellow students either.

6 Are you going to the dinner on Saturday? A lot of my other friends *were invited / have been invited* and I know they'd love to meet you.

7 I *have only lived / have only been living* in Geneva for the past few months, though Madeleine, who you met yesterday, *lived / has lived* here all her life.

8 Petra looks after my children very well. I *haven't noticed / didn't notice* any weaknesses in her character, so I'm sure you'll be happy to offer her a job.

Reading Part 1

1 Work in pairs. You are going to read three short texts about people, their activities and their relationships. Before you read, discuss this question:

If you were going to write a short text about one of your activities or relationships, what or who would you write about? Why?

2 Read the three texts quite quickly. Which text comes from:

a a novel?   b a biography?   c an autobiography?

3 Now read each text again and answer the two questions which follow each one in your own words.

The subject of a book

I spent hours listening to the bookseller's stories about his battles against the different regimes and their censors. How he launched his personal fight, hiding books from the
5 police, lending them out to others and finally going to prison for it. He was a man who had tried to save the art and literature of his country, while a string of dictators did their best to destroy them. I realised that he was
10 himself a living piece of his country's cultural history: a history book on two feet.

One day he invited me home for an evening meal. His family – one of his wives, his sons, sisters, brother, mother and a few cousins –
15 was seated on the floor round a sumptuous feast. Sultan recounted stories, the sons laughed and joked. The atmosphere was unrestrained and a huge contrast to the simple meals I'd shared with the people in the
20 mountains.

When I left I said to myself: 'How interesting it would be to write a book about this family.' The next day I called on Sultan in his bookshop and told him my idea.

25 'Thank you,' was all he said.

'But this means that I would have to come and live with you.'

'You are welcome.'

From *The Bookseller of Kabul* by Åsne Seierstad

1 In line 11, what does the writer want to show by using the phrase *a history book on two feet*?

2 What do we understand from the writer's use of the word *unrestrained* in line 18?

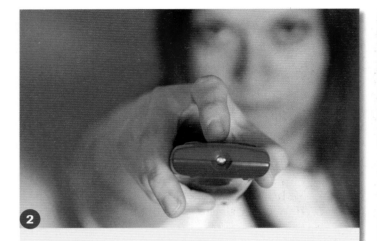

Starting a conversation

'Have I missed something here?'

It was an ordinary Thursday evening in January – at least I thought so. I was round at my girlfriend Mel's flat and it was to her that I'd aimed my question, as for some unknown reason she'd just turned off the TV even though I'd quite clearly been watching it. What really wound me up, however, was the fact that she'd used the remote control to do it, adding insult to injury. It was an unofficial rule of ours that I looked after all TV channel-changing duties – in the same way that Mel got first grazing rights on the top layer of any box of chocolates that came into our possession. We'd arrived at these and other rules through a process of trial and error over the course of our four-year relationship. These rules made me happy. I always knew where I stood. But when you abandon rules there's bound to be chaos, and right now what I had on my hands was a serious case of anarchy.

My obviously deranged beloved pursed her perfect full lips together and blew into the end of the remote haughtily as if she'd just battled the TV for my attention and won. There's no need for you to be quite so pleased with yourself, I thought. After all, it was only a repeat of Star Trek.

'So what is it?' I asked carefully.

'It's us.'

'Us?'

'Us,' she said calmly. 'Let's talk about us.'

From *Mr Commitment* by Mike Gayle

3 What particularly upset the writer?
4 What impression do we have of the writer from reading this text?

My choice of career

I am a woman. I am a fisherman. Neither abused nor neglected, I am the product of a blissful and unique childhood, a rare claim these days. Like all young children, I believed wholeheartedly in the words of my mother and father. It was only natural that I took seriously the assertions of my parents that I could do whatever I liked with my life, become anything I wanted. Although the advice they gave was well intentioned, my parents never dreamed that it might come back to haunt them when I decided that what I liked and wanted to become was a fisherman.

One day, when I was just 12, my sister asked, 'Aren't you going to play in the woods today?'

'No.' I smiled. 'Today I'm going to sea.'

And go to sea I did, every chance I got for the next twenty years. Rarely did a day leave me ashore. Fishing my way through college, I made my first deep-sea trip at the age of nineteen aboard the Walter Leeman. My primary job was cooking, and although I disliked the galley chores, I liked the money. It wasn't until a fellow crew member hit the bunk with a back injury that I was allowed to work on deck, work I enjoyed for years. By the time I graduated from college I had outlasted the original crew members I had started with, most of whom moved on to boats of their own, and became captain of the boat by attrition. Promising my parents that I would postpone law school for just one year, I became a full-time fisherman.

Adapted from *The Hungry Ocean*
by Linda Greenlaw

5 How did the writer's parents feel about her becoming a fisherman?
6 How did she become captain of the *Walter Leeman*?

Text 2

3 The writer was particularly upset because his girlfriend had
  A eaten all the chocolates.
  B interrupted his favourite TV programme.
  C scored a victory over him.
  D used something that normally only he used.

4 What impression do we have of the writer from reading this text?
  A He dislikes talking about relationships.
  B He's dominated by his girlfriend.
  C He likes clearly defined relationships.
  D He's highly sensitive to insults.

Text 3

5 How did the writer's parents feel about her becoming a fisherman?
  A They encouraged her to join the profession.
  B They thought that it was a normal thing for her to do.
  C They hadn't expected her to make this choice.
  D They felt that her education had been wasted.

6 How did she become captain of the *Walter Leeman*, instead of the other crew members?
  A She studied harder.
  B She worked harder.
  C She stayed on the boat for longer.
  D She found the work more enjoyable.

> **Exam information**
>
> In Reading Part 1, you
> - read three short texts on the same theme.
> - answer two multiple-choice questions, each with four options, about each text.
>
> In the exam you have approximately 18 minutes for this part.

4 Now, for questions 1–6 below, choose the answer (A, B, C or D) which you think fits best according to the text.

Text 1

1 In line 11, the writer uses the phrase *a history book on two feet* to show that
  A the bookseller was working to conserve his country's cultural heritage.
  B the cultural life of the country was very fragile.
  C the bookseller had to move from place to place frequently.
  D the bookseller could teach her a lot about the country.

2 What do we understand from the writer's use of the word *unrestrained* in line 18?
  A Other people the writer had eaten with had been more reserved with her.
  B The family was more relaxed when they were with the writer.
  C Family members were always ready to express themselves openly.
  D The family was keen to feature in the writer's book.

5 Work in small groups. Discuss these questions.
- Which of the people in the texts would you be most interested to meet?
- What questions would you ask that person?

Vocabulary
Collocations with *give*, *do* and *make*

❶ Look at this sentence from Reading Part 1, Text 3. Write the correct verb A–D in the gap.

Although the advice they .... was well intentioned, my parents never dreamed that it might come back to haunt them …

A made **B** gave **C** said **D** expressed

❷ ⊙ CAE candidates often use the wrong verb when they should use *give*, *do* or *make*. In most of the sentences below, the underlined verb is wrong. Replace the underlined verb with either *give*, *do* or *make*, or write *correct* if you think there is no mistake.

1 When you print the article, we also expect you to ~~give~~ an apology. *make*
2 Carla always <u>gives</u> her best, even if she does not always manage to get very high marks.
3 Her report on the trip <u>did not show</u> accurate information so we were quite confused.
4 I have some suggestions to <u>give</u> before the forthcoming trip.
5 I hope your company will <u>give</u> me at least a partial refund.
6 I'm so grateful that you have <u>made</u> me the chance to attend the course.
7 In my boss's absence, I <u>give</u> telephone calls to customers, clean desks, and write emails.
8 Installing modern technology will <u>give</u> a good impression of the college.
9 Our evening lectures were <u>made</u> by 'experts' who knew nothing about the subject.
10 There is another recommendation I would like to <u>give</u> concerning the club.

❸ Words which are often used together (e.g. *make an apology*) are called collocations. Which verb often forms a collocation with these nouns? Write *give*, *do* or *make* in each gap.

1 ....*give*...... a speech, lecture, talk or performance
2 .... someone information, details, advice or instructions
3 .... a recommendation, comment, apology, suggestion
4 .... someone a chance, opportunity
5 .... someone a refund, their money back
6 ...*Do*..... your best, the best you can
7 .... a telephone call
8 .... an impression on someone
9 .... someone an impression

Use of English Part 4

❶ Many words have several different meanings. Look at this sentence from Reading Part 1, Text 2. Which of the four definitions (a–d) from the *Cambridge Advanced Learner's Dictionary* (*CALD*) do you think the word *missed* matches?

'Have I *missed* something here?'

a to arrive too late to get on a bus, train or aircraft
b to fail to hit something or to avoid hitting something
c to regret that a person or thing is not present
d to not notice someone or something

❷ What meanings does *missed* have in the three sentences below? Match the sentences with the definitions in Exercise 1.

1 Dani overslept and *missed* the bus, so she arrived really late for class.
2 I enjoyed going on holiday with my friends though I *missed* my family to start with.
3 The ball *missed* the goalmouth completely and flew harmlessly into the crowd.

❸ Look at the groups of three sentences below. What sort of word is needed for each group (noun, verb or adjective)?

1 My friends gave me a really .... welcome when I got back from holiday.
Take a .... coat if you're going out tonight because it's absolutely freezing outside.
Cindy decided to decorate the hallway using .... colours to make it feel friendlier.

2 It's a good .... the police didn't see you driving so fast!
Paola's desperate to work, but unfortunately she never manages to hold down a .... for long.
They didn't make a very good .... of printing out the leaflet, did they?

3 The new traffic regulations will come into .... on 1 January.
He's persuaded the Council to adopt his ideas by sheer .... of personality.
Magda is thinking of joining the police .... after she graduates.

4 Sofia has been in the same company all her working ...., so it's quite surprising that she's leaving.
You would expect the ocean floor to be dead, but in fact it's full of ....
Careful use will prolong the .... of your machine.

④ For questions 1–4 in Exercise 3 on page 14, which word from the box will fit all three gaps?

bright	career	effect	force	friendly	heavy
job	life	thick	time	warm	work

Exam information

In Use of English Part 4, there are five questions. Each question consists of three sentences, each with a gap. You have to think of one word which fits the gaps in all three sentences.

The word will:

•   be the same type of word, e.g. noun, verb, etc., and have the same form in all three gaps

•   have a different meaning in each sentence.

⑤ For questions 1–5, think of one word only which can be used appropriately in all three sentences.

1   I entirely agree with the government's .... on free medicine for pensioners.
I'm feeling very stiff because I slept in a really uncomfortable .... last night.
Najib has applied for the .... in our company that was advertised in the paper.

2   Stella has been .... the business almost single-handed since her assistant left.
I never knew you were interested in politics and now I see you're .... for parliament!
We'd better stop at a filling station soon as we're .... out of petrol.

3   If you think you need a bit more exercise, why don't you .... up tennis?
If you find the gadget doesn't suit your needs, ... it back to the shop.
I .... it you'll be at the meeting tomorrow – it's really vital that you are.

4   The place where I study has a very .... policy towards time-keeping and you can't be late for class.
Candela is a .... vegetarian and refuses to eat meat or poultry.
We need a very .... translation of the report so as to avoid any misunderstandings.

5   I wasn't enjoying studying law at university, so I .... to history at the end of the first year.
I found his speech very boring so I'm afraid I .... off before the end.
The weather has been so mild that we haven't .... the heating on yet this winter.

Speaking Part 1

Exam information

You do the Speaking Paper in pairs. In Part 1, the examiner asks each of you questions about your lives, your interests, your activities, your experiences, your background, etc. You discuss these things with the examiner and the other candidate.

This part of the exam lasts three minutes.

① Work in pairs. Read the questions below from Speaking Part 1. Which questions are:

a mainly about the present? **b** mainly about the past?

How would you answer each question?

1   What do you most enjoy doing with your friends?
2   Have you ever had the opportunity to really help a friend? How?
3   Would you prefer to spend your holidays with your family or your friends?
4   What is the best way for people visiting your country to make friends?
5   Who do you think has had the most influence on your life so far? Why?
6   What's your happiest childhood memory?
7   Who is the best teacher you've ever had?
8   Tell me about a friend of yours and how you got to know him or her.

② ③ Listen to two students, Nagwa and Carlos. Which question does each of them answer?

Nagwa .... Carlos ....

③ ④ Now listen to them again, with the examiner's questions, and say if the following statements are true (T) or false (F).

1   They both give very brief answers.
2   They give a few details to support their answers.
3   They use a variety of tenses appropriately.
4   They speak in a relaxed, natural way.

④ Work alone. Think about how you could answer each of the questions in Exercise 1. Then work in pairs and take turns to ask and answer the questions.

▶ page 175 *Speaking reference: Speaking Part 1*

Writing Part 1 A letter

① Work in pairs. Read the writing task below and answer the questions which follow.

You are studying at an international college for a few months. Your friend, Elena, is thinking of studying at the same college this summer and has written to you asking about it. Read the extract from her email and your notes. Then write her a letter saying whether you think she should study at the college or not and giving your reasons.

Should come because ...

Our teacher is great because ...

It would be very good for me to improve my English, but I'll be living abroad for the first time. I'm worried about feeling lonely and wonder how easy it'll be to make friends. Also, I'd be doing this in my summer holiday, so I want to have time off to enjoy myself as well. It's quite expensive: are the teachers good?

Best wishes,

Elena

Tell her about the friend I made the first day

Must mention our free-time activities

1 Who will read your letter?
2 So should you write in a formal or informal style?
3 What things must you deal with in your letter? Underline them in the task above.
4 What things can you say to persuade Elena to come to the college? Make some notes.

② Read Toni's letter on the right and answer the questions.

1 Has he dealt with all the points in the task?
2 Has he written in a formal or an informal style?
3 What has he said to persuade Elena to come to the college?

Dear Elena,

Thanks for your letter asking about coming to Millwall College. I think it's a really good idea because you'll learn so much English. And don't worry about loneliness at all because you'll make plenty of friends.

One really good friend (1) *I made* / (I've made) is Martyna, who I (2) *actually met* / *have actually met* before I even arrived! It was quite a coincidence because we (3) *sat* / *were sitting* next to each other on the bus and we got chatting and discovered we (4) *have been* / *had been* on the same plane coming here and were going to the same college! Anyway, she's really good fun and (5) *we've been doing* / *we did* lots of things together.

That brings me to free time. We get plenty of it, by the way, and (6) *I've already visited* / *I already visited* quite a few places round about. Last week Martyna and I (7) *have joined* / *joined* a local sports club and (8) *we've played* / *we've been playing* tennis there several times. I know it's your summer holiday, but, speaking for myself, (9) *I've been having* / *I've had* a really good time!

As for your last worry: yes, the college is expensive, but my teacher, Jackie, is excellent. (10) *She's taught* / *She's been teaching* in several different countries, so she's pretty experienced and interesting. Apparently, her first teaching job (11) *has been* / *was* in Thailand, where she (12) *actually used to teach* / *has actually taught* some members of the royal family!

Do come if you can – you won't regret it!

Best wishes,

Toni

③ Read the letter again and circle the correct verb form from the alternatives in *italics*.

④ Read the letter again and write in your notebooks any words or phrases you think may be useful to use in your writing.

⑤ Work alone and write your own answer to the Writing task in Exercise 1.

▶ page 173 *Writing reference: Letters*

Unit 2 Mastering languages

Starting off

❶ Work in pairs. Read the following remarks and write a word or phrase from the box in each gap.

> a bit rusty   accurately   an excellent command   ~~bilingual~~
> fashionable loanwords   mother tongue   persuasion
> pick up   switch   fluency   highly articulate

Living in the country, you just (6) .... the language naturally and that's just about the best way to learn it.

People tend to be (1) ...... *bilingual* ...... – they speak the regional and the national language and they (2) .... between languages with ease.

I aim to achieve (7) .... of English, which means becoming (8) .... and being able to use the language (9) ....

Lots of (3) .... are coming into the language, particularly from English, so my (4) .... is not at all the same as it was, say, fifty years ago.

I wouldn't consider accuracy to be as important as (10) .... when learning a foreign language.

My English has got (5) .... because I don't use it very often.

We should be teaching young people to use language for (11) .... rather than self-expression.

❷ ⑤ Check your answers by listening to the speakers.

❸ Work in pairs. Which opinions do you agree with? Which do you disagree with? Why?

Reading Part 2

1 Work in small groups. You will read an article about a linguist called Kenneth Hale. Before you read: what do you think is the best way to go about learning a new language?

2 Read the main part of the article quite quickly. (There are six missing paragraphs.) What advice did Kenneth Hale give about learning new languages?

Summary of:

Kenneth Hale, Master Linguist

1st para:

B

SOMETIMES Kenneth Hale was asked how long it would take him to learn a new language. He thought ten or fifteen minutes would be enough to pick up the essentials if he were listening to a native speaker. After that he could probably converse; obviously not fluently, but enough to make himself understood. To those whose education, however admirable in other respects, had provided only rudimentary language skills, he seemed a marvel.

> 1

2nd para:

As many of these languages had no written grammar or vocabulary, and indeed were spoken by few people, Kenneth picked them up orally. His tip for anyone who pressed him for advice on learning a language was to talk to a native speaker. Start with parts of the body, he said, then common objects. After learning the nouns, you can start to make sentences and get attuned to the sounds.

> 2

3rd para:

This is all the more confusing as language is much more complex than, say, simple arithmetic, which often takes years to master. It is often hypothesised that language is an innate human faculty, with its own specialised system in our brain.

> 3

4th para:

He spent his childhood on a ranch in Arizona and started his education in a one-roomed school in the desert. Many years later, lecturing at MIT, he still felt most comfortable in cowboy boots. On his belt was a buckle he had won at a rodeo by riding bulls, and he had the slightly bowed legs of a horseman. His students were impressed that he could light a match with his thumbnail.

> 4

5th para:

One Indian language at its last gasp was spoken by the Wopanaak, the tribe that greeted the Pilgrim Fathers in 1620. It is now spoken again by several thousand people around Cape Cod. A Wopanaak who studied under Kenneth is preparing a dictionary of her language. 'Ken was a voice for the voiceless,' said Noam Chomsky. And he worked tirelessly to learn endangered languages.

> 5

6th para:

Despite these setbacks, Ken did contribute to an understanding of the apparently innate human capacity for speech. He made a number of what he called 'neat' discoveries about the structure of language, and had an instinctive sense of what all languages had in common. After his retirement from MIT, he said he would 'really get down to work', an ambition he was unable to achieve, though his other achievements were considerable.

> 6

7th para:

And these people are often particularly upset by a scholarly argument which surfaces from time to time about the desirability of keeping alive languages that have little chance of survival. Occasionally the argument turns nationalistic. For example, is what Kenneth called the 'revitalisation' of Welsh merely a nuisance in Britain where, obviously, English is the working language? Kenneth Hale had an indignant answer to that question. 'When you lose a language,' he told a reporter, 'you lose a culture, intellectual wealth, a work of art. The damage that's done is irreparable. It's like dropping a bomb on a museum, the Louvre.'

Adapted from *The Economist*

3 Read the article again and match the paragraph summaries from the box below with each paragraph.

A	A language Ken helped save
B	~~Ken's ability to learn languages quickly~~
C	How Ken learnt languages
D	Ken's origins
E	Reasons for protecting languages under threat
F	Ken's involvement in language theory
G	The biological basis of language

4 Now choose from the paragraphs A–G the one which fits each gap in the text. There is one paragraph which you do not need to use.

Exam information

In Reading Part 2, you read a text with six gaps where paragraphs have been removed and placed after the text.
- You have to decide which paragraph goes in each gap.
- There is one extra paragraph which you do not need.

5 Work in small groups.
- In your country, how many languages do most people learn? Which are the most useful and why?
- Do you think learning to speak one foreign language helps you to learn another?
- Are any languages in your country under threat? (Why?) Do you think it's important to protect endangered languages?
- Should there be a world language which everyone speaks? Why (not)?

A And he had discovered his talent for language when playing with Indian friends who taught him Hopi and Navajo. Learning languages became an obsession. In Spain he picked up Basque, in Ireland he learnt Gaelic, and he mastered Dutch within a week. He sought to rescue languages that were dying out.

B And so he was. He had a gift. But he was also an academic, a teacher of linguistics at the Massachusetts Institute of Technology (MIT). He was aware that many otherwise clever people find learning a second language extremely hard. He sought to find laws and structures that could be applied to all languages and the search took him into many linguistic byways, to the languages of native Americans and Australian aborigines and the Celtic fringes of Europe.

C However, for Kenneth bilingual dictionaries were an anathema and banned in his classes. He held that meanings were too fluid to be captured and readily translated word-for-word from one language to another. He always told his students that meaning was intuitive: you either grasped it, or you didn't.

D In addition to his feat of learning so many languages, he is likely to be remembered by *The Green Book of Language Revitalisation*, which he helped to edit. It was warmly welcomed, especially by those who may be a touch aggrieved by the spread of English, which is blamed for brutally sweeping other languages aside.

E Kenneth could converse in about 50 languages, perhaps a world record. He was the last person on earth to speak some languages. Hundreds are disappearing, he said. 'They became extinct, and I had no one to speak them with.'

F Some students of linguistics believe that such an ability, if it exists, is normally lost at the age of 12. But for Kenneth it was around this age that his interest in language was just starting.

G Still, there is much more to language than that. Noam Chomsky, like Kenneth a teacher of linguistics at MIT, wrote: 'Language is really weird. There is nothing else in the natural world that even approaches its complexity. Although children receive no instruction in learning their native language, they are able to fully master it in less than five years.'

Vocabulary
Collocations with *make*, *get* and *do*

1 Form collocations with the words in bold by writing *make*, *get* or *do* in the correct form in the gaps in these sentences from Reading Part 2. Then copy the complete collocation into your notebook.

After that he could probably converse; obviously not fluently, but enough to (1) ....*make*.... **himself understood**.

After learning the nouns, you can start to (2) .... **sentences** and (3) .... **attuned** to the sounds.

He (4) .... a number of what he called 'neat' **discoveries** about the structure of language ...

The **damage** that's (5) .... is irreparable.

2 CAE candidates often use the wrong verb with the words and phrases in the box. Copy the table below into your notebook and write each word or phrase in the correct column. Two words/phrases can be written in more than one column.

> a comment a course a decision a mistake a job
> an effort a point a proposal a qualification
> a suggestion activities an apology business
> complaints changes exercise friends
> further information harm money back one's best
> some shopping sport household chores the cooking
> the right choice use of something an improvement

make	get	do
a comment	a job	a job

3 ⊙ Each of the sentences below contains a mistake made by CAE candidates with a collocation of *make*, *do* or *get*. Correct the mistakes.

1 Before working in our shop you first ~~make~~ a one-week course in developing photos. *do*
2 A lot of my time was wasted, so I do think I should receive some of my money back.
3 I have some suggestions to give before we start the trip.
4 She did everything possible to turn the trip more pleasant.
5 We were made to work very hard at school and that certainly didn't make me any harm.
6 We need to reduce the time taken to achieve all the tasks mentioned above.

7 We'd be very grateful if you'd make your best to solve this problem.
8 You can spend lots of time at this holiday camp practising exercise and having a great time!

Listening Part 1

1 You will hear three different extracts. Before you listen, work in pairs. Read questions 1–6 below and on page 21 and discuss the following.

a What do you think Khalkha is?
b Which answer would you give to question 2?
c What do you think is meant by 'spelling reform'?
d In question 4, how are options A, B and C related to spelling reform?
e How would you answer question 5?
f In question 6, which option, A, B or C, would be most helpful for non-native speakers looking for jobs?

Extract One

You hear an interview on a travel programme with a writer who has been to Mongolia.

1 How did Colin first start learning Khalkha?
  A He taught himself before starting his journey.
  B He took lessons with a teacher in London.
  C He learnt it while he was in the country.

2 Colin thinks that adults wanting to learn a new language must
  A have a talent for language learning.
  B be prepared to work hard.
  C be ready to take risks.

| through | thorough | **though** |
| plough | rough | |

Extract Two

You hear two teachers, Rajiv and Susan, discussing the need for English spelling reform.

3 Rajiv became interested in spelling reform
 A when he was learning the language himself.
 B when he started teaching the language.
 C when he read about the subject.

4 What do Rajiv and Susan agree about?
 A Children would have fewer problems learning to read and write.
 B Foreign learners would know how to pronounce new words.
 C It would lead to considerable economic savings.

Extract Three

You hear an interview with Peggy, a researcher who has studied job interviews conducted in English.

5 What does she consider the main problem for non-native speakers?
 A Their English is not good enough.
 B Their body language gives the wrong message.
 C Their answers are unsuitable.

6 She suggests improving the recruitment process by
 A replacing interviews with practical tests.
 B training interviewers to ask clearer questions.
 C changing interviewers' expectations.

2 🔘 **Now listen, and for questions 1–6, choose the answer (A, B or C) which fits best according to what you hear. There are two questions for each extract.**

3 **Work in pairs.**

- What are the main difficulties for people wanting to learn your language?
- What, for you, are the main difficulties of doing an interview for an exam or for a job in English?

Use of English Part 3

1 **Work in small groups. How many words can you form from each of these base words?**

| govern | care | critic | child | break | occasion |
| force | deep | fragile | friend | | |

Example:

govern – government, governmental, governable, ungovernable, ungovernably, governing, governor, governability

2 **Look at your answers to Exercise 1. Which of these suffixes did you use?**

-ion, -ment, -less, -ise, -ally, -hood, -able, -ly, -ful, -en, -ity, -ship

Which of the suffixes above are used to form:

1 verbs? **2** nouns? **3** adjectives? **4** adverbs?

3 **Can you think of other suffixes which are used in each of the categories 1–4 in Exercise 2? For each suffix, write one word as an example, e.g.** *nouns: -ness: kindness.*

4 **Which of the words in the box are spelled correctly? Correct the words which are spelled incorrectly.**

occurrence	happenning	developement	statement
reference	opening	realy	factually	beautifuly
truthfull	disappointed	disatisfied	iregularrity
reliable	undenyable	useable	refuseing
basicaly	arguement		

▶ page 151 *Grammar reference: Spelling rules for affixes and inflections*

5 🔘 **Find and correct the spelling mistakes in the sentences below, made by CAE candidates in the exam.**

1 As you can see in the ~~advertisment~~, the holiday is quite cheap. *advertisement*
2 People are begining to get tired of being promised things it's impossible to give them.
3 I'm sure you're going to be as succesful as your predecessor was.
4 He was sent to prison for expressing his disagreement with the goverment.
5 By implementing these proposals we will be doing more to protect the enviroment.
6 The family I stayed with was realy kind and helpful.

6 Work in pairs. You are going to read a text about names for new products. Before you read:

- Are there any products produced by international companies whose names sound strange or funny in your language?
- What do you think each of the following products are?

  | Gold Blend | Lego | Ka | Macintosh | Brut |

- How much does a product's name influence you when deciding whether to buy or not?

7 Read the text below quite quickly to find out:

1 how companies name products
2 what problems they have when naming products.

Ka or car?

The Naming of Products

International companies are finding it (0) ......*increasingly*...... important to develop brand names that can be used in a wide range of countries. A product with a single, universally recognised name can lead to major (1) .... in production and promotion costs – especially now that world advertising is a (2) .... in such contexts as major sporting events.

It is said that more time is (3) .... spent deciding the name of a product than on its (4) .... Thousands of possible names may need to be investigated to find one that is internationally (5) ....

An indication of the scope of the problem can be seen from the experience of Dunlop, who spent over two years (6) .... researching a name for a new tyre. They then launched an international (7) .... amongst their employees, receiving over 10,000 entries. Around 30 names were selected from the enormous number (8) .... – but not one was found to be legally available in more than a small number of countries. Often companies end up with a name that is (9) .... for legal or linguistic reasons. For example, a word may be unpronounceable in some languages; and there is always the danger of the name being the same as a word which is either (10) .... or taboo.

	INCREASE
	SAVE
	REAL
	ACTUAL
	DEVELOP
	ACCEPT
	SUCCEED
	COMPETE
	SUBMIT
	USE
	RELEVANT

Adapted from *The Cambridge Encyclopaedia of Language* by David Crystal

8 For questions 1–10, read the text again. Use the word given in capitals at the end of some of the lines to form a word that fits in the gap in the same line. There is an example at the beginning (0).

Exam information

In Use of English Part 3, there is a text with ten gaps. You have to write the correct form of the word given IN CAPITALS at the end of the line in the gap.

9 Work in pairs.

- How do people in your country choose names for their children?
- Are fashions in children's names changing?
- In Britain, people also name their pets and sometimes their houses. What things do people in your country name, and what sorts of name do they choose?

Grammar
Expressing purpose, reason and result

1 **Match the beginnings of the following sentences (1–8) with their endings (a–h).**

1 I thought I should pick the language up while I was there, **so** *c*
2 It might be better to set up a simulation of the job in question **so as**
3 The candidate often lacks the sort of cultural background that would stand them in good stead in these situations **with the result that**
4 They used to give us dictations in class **to** make sure
5 I always write new vocabulary down in my notebook **in case**
6 Pavla is studying languages at university **with the intention of**
7 We found the lecturer difficult to hear **due to**
8 You'll need to use a microphone, **otherwise**

a eventually working as an interpreter.
b I forget it.
c I immersed myself in the neighbourhood.
d the people at the back won't hear you.
e the poor acoustics in the hall.
f their responses take the interviewer by surprise.
g to see whether the candidate has the skills and attitude they're looking for.
h we knew things like putting a double 'p' in 'approve' …

2 **Answer the following questions.**

1 Which of the **bold** phrases in Exercise 1 express:
   a a purpose?   b a reason?   c a result?

2 Which of the words/phrases are followed by:
   a an infinitive?   b a noun / verb + *-ing*?
   c a sentence?

▶ page 150 *Grammar reference: Expressing purpose, reason and result*

3 **⊙ CAE candidates often make mistakes with words and phrases to express reason, purpose and result. Circle the correct alternative in *italics* in each of the following sentences.**

1 My Italian is excellent (*because*) / *due to* I lived in Italy for four years.
2 *By / For* technical reasons, the flight was delayed for several hours.
3 Over the last decade, our lives have changed a lot *because of / by* computers.
4 Could you please send us a brochure *so as / so that* we can see exactly what you are offering?
5 I hope the organisation's efficiency will improve *for not to / in order not to* waste people's time and money.

Speaking Part 2

1 **Work in pairs. Follow the examiner's instructions below.**

> Now in this part of the test I'm going to give each of you three pictures. I'd like you to talk about them on your own for about a minute.
>
> Here are your pictures. They show people explaining things. I'd like you to compare two of the pictures and say what they might be explaining and which situation is the most difficult for the speaker.

② 🎧 **Listen to Bethia, a university student, talking about two of the photos on page 23.**

1 Did she answer all parts of the examiner's instructions?
2 What ideas did she express? (Take notes.)

③ 🎧 **Listen again. Which of the adverbs in the box did she use?**

actually	almost certainly	clearly	obviously
perhaps	possibly	probably	really

Work in pairs. Make your own sentences about the photos using some of the adverbs in the box.

④ The examiner used the word *difficult* in his question. Which two words meaning *difficult* did Bethia use in her answer?

⑤ Change partners and take turns to talk for a minute about the photos using your ideas. Follow the instructions in Exercise 2. Try to use words from Exercise 4 and try to avoid repeating the words from the question too often.

⑥ Work in pairs. Look at the photos below and read the examiner's instructions.

> I'd like you to talk on your own for about a minute. Here are your pictures. They show adults and children talking to each other. I'd like you to compare two of the pictures and say why they might be talking to each other and how they might be feeling.

Student A: Follow the examiner's instructions above.
Student B: When Student A has finished, follow the examiner's instructions above using the photo Student A didn't use and one of the others.

▶ page 176 *Speaking reference: Speaking Part 2*

Writing Part 2 A report

Exam information

In Writing Part 2 there are four questions numbered 2–5, from which you choose one to answer.

- Questions 2–4 may ask you to write an article, a competition entry, a contribution to a longer piece (such as a brochure), a letter, an information sheet, a report, an essay, a proposal or a review.
- Question 5 is based on a set book (reading the set book is optional).
- You must write between 220 and 260 words and you have about 45 minutes to do this.

① Work in pairs. Read the following writing task and answer the questions below.

> An international media company is investigating the influence that television programmes imported from English-speaking countries have on different countries around the world. You have been asked to write a report on English-language TV programmes in your country. In your report you should address the following:
>
> - how popular these programmes are and why.
> - the effect they are having on local culture.
> - any changes you would recommend.
>
> Write your **report**.

1 Who is expected to read this report?
2 Should you use a formal or informal style?
3 What are the four main points you should deal with?
4 In what order would you deal with them?

2 Read the sample report on the right and write one word/phrase from the box in each gap.

accounted for	~~the aim~~	as a consequence
due to	means	meant	resulted	so as
the effect	the result			

3 Work in pairs. Read the report again and answer these questions.

1 How is the layout of a report different from other types of writing?
2 Has the writer included all the points in the writing task? Where are they dealt with in the report?
3 Is the style appropriate for the target readers?

4 Work in pairs. Read the following writing task and:

1 underline the points you must deal with
2 identify who will read the report
3 decide what style you will need to use
4 decide what title to give your report and what sections and section headings you will need.

> A leading educational publisher is interested in language learning in different countries. You have been asked to write a report on foreign language learning in your country. In your report you should deal with
>
> • the languages people learn, who learns them and where they learn them.
>
> • recommendations for improving language-learning in your country.
>
> Write your **report**.

5 Work alone and write the report. Use the sample report in Exercise 2 as a model.

▶ page 171 *Writing reference: Reports*

English-language TV programmes in my country

Introduction

(1) ....The aim........ of this report is to comment on the popularity of imported English-language television programmes in my country, to explain how they are affecting local culture and to recommend changes that could be made in the way these programmes are shown.

Popularity of imported programmes

Approximately fifty percent of the programmes shown on TV in this country have been made in an English-speaking country and were originally in English. The popularity of these programmes can be (2) .... by their larger budgets, which (3) .... they are generally more spectacular than locally made programmes and may include internationally famous stars in their casts. On most channels, viewers can choose which language they wish to watch the programme in, with (4) .... that people with a good command of English tend to watch programmes in their original versions.

Effects on local culture

The popularity of English-language programmes has (5) .... that it is hard for local programme-makers to compete, given their limited budgets. (6) .... , local culture has been heavily influenced by American values of consumerism. Moreover, exposure to mistranslations of English-language films has (7) .... in words in our languages being used with new or wrong meanings. However, a positive effect has been that people have become more open and ready to change (8) .... the fact that they see other ways of living and thinking.

Recommended changes

I would recommend the government to subsidise national television companies (9) .... to encourage them to make more quality programmes. This would have (10) .... of reducing our reliance on imported programmes while at the same time promoting local values and culture.

Unit 1 *Vocabulary and grammar review*

Vocabulary

❶ Complete each of the sentences below by writing the correct form of *give*, *do* or *make* in each gap.

1 The minister ....*gave*........... a rousing speech at the end of the conference.
2 Carrie sat through the entire meeting without .... a single suggestion to solve the problem.
3 Although she's been .... her best, I know she's finding it hard to cope.
4 Fergus .... a pretty bad impression in Saturday's match, so the manager is .... him just one last chance or he'll be dropped from the team.
5 If you'd just .... me the details, I'll take a note of them and pass them to the person responsible.
6 I never expected to see you at the concert because the last time we met, you .... me the impression that you didn't like classical music.
7 If you're not completely satisfied with the result, we'll .... you a full refund.
8 Patsy is just .... a phone call at the moment, so she'll be with us in a sec.

❷ For questions 1–5, think of one word only which can be used appropriately in all three sentences.

1 Where do you .... on the issue of student loans to pay for university education?
I can't .... the sound of her voice – I find it so irritating!
You don't .... a chance of passing the exam if you don't work harder.

2 Ivan .... what he was doing and ran to help the accident victims.
He's been playing so badly lately that they've .... him from the team.
Sergei was disappointed with his course, so he .... out of university and found a job instead.

3 It's only .... for young people to want to leave home and become independent.
It's a delicious, healthy drink made entirely from .... ingredients.
There's little that can be done to prevent .... disasters such as earthquakes and hurricanes.

4 If you're .... , could I see you in my office in about ten minutes?
Please feel .... to ask me any questions during my talk.
We've managed to enrol on the course completely .... of charge.

5 I'm going to need a holiday at home after all this travelling – it's .... me out.
I expect everyone will be .... something formal to go to the Parkinsons' party.
These boots are .... out, so I'll have to buy some new ones.

Grammar

❸ Circle the best alternative in *italics* in the sentences below.

1 We got to the park quite soon after lunch and fortunately the rain *stopped* / *(had stopped)* by then.
2 *We'd stood* / *We'd been standing* in the rain for at least twenty minutes before the bus arrived, by which time we *were feeling* / *had been feeling* pretty cold and wet, as you can imagine.
3 *I've driven* / *I've been driving* along this road a thousand times – I could almost do it with my eyes shut!
4 You'd expect Fran to be looking tired because *she's studied* / *she's been studying* for her final exams for the last three weeks.
5 Maisie *ate* / *had been eating* sweets all evening so it was not surprising she didn't want any supper!
6 I think people *used to work* / *would work* much harder in the past than they do nowadays.
7 So much noise *had come* / *had been coming* from our flat all afternoon that eventually the neighbours complained and we had to explain that we *repaired* / *were repairing* the heater and that we'd be finishing soon.
8 We always used to go to the Mediterranean for our holidays when I was a child. I think we *went* / *used to go* to Ibiza at least five times.

Unit 2 *Vocabulary and grammar review*

Vocabulary

❶ Complete this crossword using words related to language.

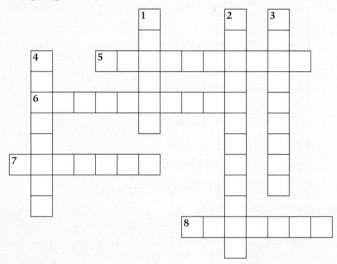

Across

5 You've got to be able to write .... for this job. We can't afford to have people making mistakes. (10 letters)

6 Amina expresses her ideas very clearly – but then she's a highly .... young woman. (10)

7 Having lived in Chile for seven years, Philippe has a perfect .... of Spanish. (7)

8 It takes a great deal of practice to achieve .... in a language. (7)

Down

1 I'm not too keen on going to classes. I prefer to just .... the language while I'm in the country. (4, 2)

2 Maria's English is virtually perfect although her .... is Greek. (6, 6)

3 With a Japanese father and a French mother, Motoko grew up completely .... (9)

4 *Tattoo* is a .... in English. It was originally a Polynesian term. (8)

❷ Complete each of these sentences by writing the correct form of *make, get* or *do* in the gaps.

1 Lee has been working hard because he needs to ....*get*........... better professional qualifications.

2 The new principal is planning on .... quite a few changes to the way this college is run.

3 How long have you been .... your current job?

4 It was a difficult decision, but I think you .... the right choice.

5 I don't understand you. What point are you trying to .... ?

6 It wouldn't .... you any harm to take a bit more exercise!

❸ Each of the sentences below contains one or two spelling mistakes. Find and correct them.

1 Carol played the piano ~~beautifuly~~ at the openning concert of the festival. *beautifully*

2 Brenda had a highly successfull career as editor of a London daily.

3 There are strong arguements in favour of giving permission to the company to proceed with the new housing developement.

4 Basically, I just felt embarrassed at the begining of the lecture because I thought people were laughing at me.

5 Patricia has been studing really hard and she's becoming extremely knowledgable on the subject as a result.

6 Gaby and Jean felt extremely dissapointed about the flight cancelation because they thought they were going to miss their honeymoon.

Grammar

❹ Complete each of the sentences below by writing a word or phrase from the box in each of the gaps.

due to	in case	otherwise	so as	so that
~~with the intention of~~				

1 I caught an earlier train this morning .....*with the intention of*..... finishing the report before my boss arrived in the office.

2 Natalie delivered the parcel herself .... to make sure it arrived safely.

3 If I were you, I'd take your bank card .... your money runs out.

4 You really should write new vocabulary in your notebook, ... you'll forget it.

5 Services on North-East Trains were cancelled today .... a train drivers' strike.

6 Amin covered his face as he left the building .... no one would recognise him.

Unit 3 All in the mind

Starting off

1 Work in pairs.

- Do you believe it is possible to measure a person's intelligence fairly and accurately? Why (not)?
- Even if you believe it is possible, do you think we *should* measure intelligence?

2 Now consider what type of a thinker you are. Read through the nine types of thinker below and choose which type describes you best. Give yourself a score between 0 and 5 for each statement. (0 = completely untrue for me / 5 = absolutely true for me)

Compare yourself with other students. How similar or different are you?

Type of thinker	Characteristics	Score 0–5
Logical/ Mathematical	You like to understand patterns and relationships between objects or actions.	....
	You are good at thinking critically, and solving problems creatively.	....
Linguistic	You think in words and like to use language to express complex ideas.	....
	You are sensitive to the sounds and rhythms of words as well as their meanings.	....
Interpersonal	You like to think about and try to understand people.	....
	You make an effort to cultivate good relationships with family, friends and colleagues.	....
Intrapersonal	You spend a lot of time thinking about and trying to understand yourself.	....
	You understand how your behaviour affects your relationship with others.	....
Naturalistic	You like to understand the natural world, and the living beings that inhabit it.	....
	You have an aptitude for communicating with animals.	....
Existential	You like to think about philosophical questions such as 'What is the meaning of life?'	....
	You try to see beyond the 'here and now' and understand deeper meanings.	....
Musical	You tend to think in sounds, and may also think in rhythms and melodies.	....
	You are sensitive to the sounds and rhythms of words as well as their meanings.	....
Spatial	You tend to think in pictures and can develop good mental models of the physical world.	....
	You think well in three dimensions and have a flair for working with objects.	....
Kinaesthetic	You think in movements and like to use your body in skilful and expressive ways.	....
	You have an aptitude for working with your hands.	....

❸ What type of thinkers do you think these famous people are/were? (Focus on their occupations.)

Louise Bourgeois, sculptor, France

Charles Darwin, scientist, Britain

Chinua Achebe, novelist, Nigeria

Judit Polgár, chess grandmaster, Hungary

Ayn Rand, philosopher, Russia

Maria Callas, opera singer, Greece

Antoni Gaudí, architect, Catalonia, Spain

Zinedine Zidane, footballer, France

❹ What is your opinion of attempts like this to categorise people?

Listening Part 2

Exam information

In Listening Part 2 you listen to a talk or lecture and you have to complete eight sentences with a word or short phrase you hear on the recording.

- There will be no more than three words missing from each sentence.
- The sentences on the question paper are not exactly what you will hear on the recording.

❶ Work in pairs. How good are you at recognising people you have only met once or twice before?

❷ Now look at this painting by the surrealist artist René Magritte. Do you find it amusing, disturbing, interesting, mystifying or just pointless? Compare your reaction with a partner.

3 (8) You are going to listen to part of a radio programme about a psychological condition known as *prosopagnosia*. What is the more common name for this condition? Listen to the first part of the programme to find the answer.

4 (9) Listen to the whole programme and say if the following statements are true (T) or false (F).

1 The speaker compares face-blindness to the inability to hear.
2 Scientists do not understand how normal people remember faces.
3 The face-blind subjects could not distinguish between the faces or the objects.

5 Read the sentences below. How many of the gaps can you already fill?

According to the speaker, the painting by René Magritte (1) ...*perfectly illustrates*... the idea of face-blindness.

People with face-blindness have no memory of a person's face once the person (2) .... their sight.

Some people with this condition are so (3) .... that they cannot recognise members of their own family.

It would help scientists to understand (4) .... if they knew more about face-blindness.

Scientists do not yet know whether the ability to recognise faces has a (5) .... of its own or whether it is part of an individual's general ability.

In an experiment, a number of (6) .... were shown images of people, places and objects.

The experiment proved that the human brain processes (7) .... differently from faces.

Other experiments have shown that people with this condition can improve their (8) ....

6 (9) Listen to the whole programme again and complete gaps 2–8 with the information you hear.

7 Discuss these questions.

1 How good are you at remembering people's names? What about their phone numbers?
2 How easily do you recognise places you have been to before?
3 Have you ever experienced *déjà vu*? How do you explain this phenomenon?

Grammar
No, none, not

1 Complete these extracts from the recording with *no, none* or *not*.

1 The subjects were shown images of ... houses and landscapes, and also black-and-white pictures of faces with .... hair on their heads.
2 .... of the face-blind subjects could recognise the faces in the series well.
3 It is still .... known what prosopagnosia sufferers are missing.
4 This is .... to say that prosopagnosia has .... advantages.

▶ page 151 *Grammar reference:* No, none, not

2 ⊙ Correct the seven sentences which contain negation errors of the types made by CAE candidates. (One sentence is correct.)

1 It was difficult to get around last weekend as there was ~~not~~ public transport. *no*
2 Most students were no satisfied with the standard of food in the school canteen.
3 We've had hardly no communication from management for over a week.
4 As far as I can see, there's not much difference between the grammar of Spanish and Italian.
5 I'm afraid I don't know nothing about human psychology.
6 I usually have not problems when I talk to someone in English on the phone.
7 All the students did not hand their homework in on time.
8 We couldn't get treated for two hours because none doctors were available.

Grammar

The passive

1 <u>Underline</u> the passive verbs in these extracts from the recording.

a The subjects <u>were shown</u> images of cars, tools, guns, houses and landscapes, and also black-and-white pictures of faces with no hair on their heads.

b The subjects were asked to indicate, as quickly as possible, whether each image they saw was new or repeated.

c … faces are handled differently by the brain from other objects.

d It has been shown in experiments that people with face-blindness can be taught to improve their face recognition skills, …

2 Work in pairs to discuss these questions.

1 In which of these kinds of writing would you be more likely to find passive verbs used?

- an academic essay
- the description of a scientific process
- an email to a close friend
- a job application
- a magazine story
- a personal anecdote
- a report for a committee

2 The passive is frequently used to bring known information to the beginning of a sentence. In which of the extracts **a–d** in Exercise 1 is this true?

3 Answer these questions about the agent in the passive.

1 In which extract, **a–d**, is the doer of the action (the 'agent') mentioned?

2 Who or what could be the agents in the other extracts?

3 Why is the agent not mentioned in these extracts? (There are several possible reasons.)

4 In formal writing we often begin sentences with *It* + passive, especially if we want to focus attention on ideas and arguments, e.g. *It has been shown* in extract d above. Work in pairs to complete these beginnings with your own ideas. Choose any subject you find interesting.

1 It is commonly believed that …

2 It has been reported in the last few days that …

3 It has been proved beyond doubt that …

▶ page 152 *Grammar reference: The passive*

5 Rewrite this article using passive verbs to replace the <u>underlined</u> active verbs. Only include the agent if it is important. Start at least one sentence with *It* … .

Example:

I … intelligence could be tested …

The concept that we (1) <u>could test</u> intelligence began with a nineteenth-century British scientist, Sir Francis Galton. People (2) <u>knew</u> Galton as a man with many interests, including biology and psychology. After publishers (3) <u>published</u> Darwin's The Origin of Species, in 1859, Galton (4) <u>spent</u> most of his time trying to discover the link between heredity and human ability. People (5) <u>thought</u> at that time that the human race had a few geniuses and a few idiots, while the majority were equally intelligent people. Whatever a person achieved in their life was the result of hard work and willpower. This idea did not (6) <u>satisfy</u> Galton. He believed that physical factors (7) <u>determined</u> mental characteristics.

Reading Part 3

Exam information

In Reading Part 3 you have to answer seven multiple-choice questions, each with four options, on a text of 550–850 words.

- The answers to the questions appear in the text in the same order as in the questions.
- You have about 18 minutes for this part.

1 You are going to read an article about how digital technology is affecting people's lives. Before you read: how does it affect your life? Make a list of digital technology that you use, then compare your ideas with a partner and discuss how important it is in your lives.

Example:

email, downloading music, films or podcasts, creating a website …

2 Read *The next step in brain evolution* quickly and decide whether you are more like Emily Feld or her mother, Christine.

The next step in brain evolution

Emily Feld is a native of a new planet. While the 20-year-old university student may appear to live in London, she actually spends much of her time in another galaxy – in the digital universe of websites, e-mails, text messages and mobile phone calls. The behaviour of Feld and her generation, say experts, is being shaped by digital technology as never before. It may even be the next step in evolution, transforming our brains and the way we think.

'First thing every morning I check my mobile for messages, have a cup of tea and then check my e-mails,' says Feld. 'I look at Facebook.com, a social networking website, to see if anything has been written on my "wall". I'm connected to about 80 people on that. I'll then browse around the Internet, and if a news article on Yahoo catches my eye, I'll read it.'

'The other day, I went to meet a friend in town, and realised I'd left my mobile phone at home. I felt so lost without it that I panicked and went back to collect it. I need to have it on me at all times. Technology is an essential part of my everyday life. I don't know where I'd be without it.'

That's what makes Emily a 'digital native', someone who has never known a world without instant communication. Her mother, Christine, on the other hand, is a 'digital immigrant', still coming to terms with a culture ruled by the ring of a mobile and the zip of e-mails. Though 55-year-old Christine happily shops online and e-mails friends, at heart she's still in the old world. 'Children today are permanently multitasking – downloading tracks, uploading photos, sending e-mails. It's non-stop,' she says. 'They find sitting down and reading, even watching TV, too slow and boring.'

Are digital natives like Emily charting a new course for human intelligence? Many parents fear that children who spend hours glued to computer screens will end up as zombies with the attention span of an insect. Cyberspace is full of junk, they worry, and computer games are packed with mindless violence. But it need not be like that, say some experts, and increasingly it isn't, as users exert more control and discrimination.

The sheer mass of information in the modern world is forcing digital natives to make choices that those who grew up with only books and television did not have to make. 'Younger people sift more and filter more,' says Helen Petrie, a professor of human–computer interaction. 'We have more information to deal with, and we pay less attention to particular bits of information, so it may appear that attention spans are shorter.'

The question, then, is how do digital natives learn to discriminate, and what determines the things that interest them? Parents who hope that skills, values and limits are instilled at school may be fighting a losing battle. According to some educationalists, the reason why many children today do not pay attention in school is that they find teaching methods dull compared with their digital experiences. Instead, parameters are increasingly set by 'wiki-thinking', peer groups exchanging ideas through digital networks. Just as the online encyclopaedia Wikipedia has been built from the collective knowledge of thousands of contributors, so digital natives draw on the experience and advice of online communities to shape their interests.

Where is this all leading? Only one thing seems clear: changes propelled by the digital world are just beginning. Indeed, apart from age, one of the differences between the natives and the immigrants is the intuitive acceptance of rapid digital change. Parents may use the Internet as much as their children, but what they are not used to doing is upgrading. The younger generation are much more used to replacing old technology. Faster broadband speeds, smaller hardware – innovation is happening at such a pace that what was science fiction a few years ago will soon be fact.

Anecdotally, it seems, a lot of natives in this digital culture are adept at multitasking, doing several things simultaneously. But nobody knows exactly what the effect will be. 'In a sense, we are running a grand-scale experiment. We're bringing up a whole generation in this totally new environment – without any firm evidence of how they will be affected.'

Adapted from The Times online

3 Read the article again and for questions 1–7, choose the answer (A, B, C or D) which you think fits best according to the article.

1 Why are the first three paragraphs of the article devoted to Emily Feld?
   A She is particularly interested in technology.
   B She is a typical university student.
   C She is a representative of people of her age.
   D She is studying the effects of digital technology on students.

2 How would you sum up Emily's relationship with digital technology?
   A She is completely dependent on it.
   B She uses it mainly to support her academic studies.
   C It provides her with a meaningful social life.
   D It's useful but she could live without it.

3 The term 'digital native' is used to refer to someone who
   A is inexperienced in using digital technology.
   B has always inhabited a digital environment.
   C is interested in using digital technology whenever possible.
   D has yet to come to terms with digital technology.

4 How is Emily's mother different from her daughter?
   A She is very uncomfortable using digital technology.
   B She rarely uses digital technology.
   C She is still adjusting to digital technology.
   D She prefers reading or watching TV.

5 Some parents worry that continued exposure to digital technology will result in children
   A becoming uncontrollable and violent.
   B having lower life expectancy.
   C being unable to discriminate between right and wrong.
   D losing the ability to pay attention for more than a few seconds.

6 Educationalists believe that digital natives may be developing their ideas and interests from
   A older family members.
   B online encyclopedias like Wikipedia.
   C internet contacts of their own age.
   D schools and teachers.

7 What, according to the writer, is the only certainty with regard to the future of digital technology?
   A Children will always be happier with digital technology than their parents.
   B Everybody will need to become accustomed to multitasking.
   C The world is at the start of the digital age.
   D People will accept that digital technology is changing their world.

4 Discuss these questions in small groups.

1 How do you feel about the idea expressed in the following extract?

> The behaviour of Feld and her generation … is being shaped by digital technology. It may even be the next step in evolution, transforming our brains and the way we think.

2 Do you find sitting down and reading or watching TV too slow and boring?

3 The writer says *Many parents fear that children who spend hours glued to computer screens will end up as zombies.* Are parents right to be worried?

4 The article concludes with this sentence: *We're bringing up a whole generation in this totally new environment – without any firm evidence of how they will be affected.* How do you think this generation will be affected?

Vocabulary
Formal or informal?

1 Work in pairs. Which of the following examples would you be more likely to find in formal writing and which in informal writing? Pay particular attention to the words in bold type.

- **asap**
- **They've** phoned to say **they're** coming tomorrow.
- **What on earth are you doing?**
- **We will** be leaving as soon as **the fog has** lifted.
- We have never **contemplated residing** in any other **neighbourhood**.
- I can't **put up with** this situation for much longer.
- 'Community' can be defined as any individual or organisation **with whom** we interact.
- A teenager **is believed** to have started the fire.
- **Grub's up.** Come and get it.
- That's the girl I go to school **with**.

2 Look at the article in Reading Part 3 again and answer these questions.

1 Which language features in the list in Exercise 1 can you find?
2 Is the language formal, informal or a combination?
3 How would you explain the style used in the article?

Use of English Part 2

1 You are going to read an article which considers the extent to which we inherit our personalities as well as our physical characteristics from our parents.

1 What is your opinion on this issue? Are we born with a ready-made personality, or does our personality develop from our experiences? Think about yourself and people you know.
2 Read *Nature vs Nurture* quickly, ignoring the missing words. What conclusion does the article come to?

Exam information

In Use of English Part 2 there is a text with 15 gaps. You have to write one word in each gap. Most missing words are 'grammar words', e.g.

- articles (*the, a*)
- auxiliary verbs (*are, is, can*)
- pronouns (*he, us*)
- conjunctions (*but, although*).

A few may be 'meaning' words, for example nouns, verbs, adjectives. You must spell your answers correctly.

2 Before completing the article, try to work out what kinds of word are missing, for example:

- Is the word a noun or verb?
- Should it be singular or plural?

Read the sentences with gaps carefully, looking especially at the words before and after each gap.

3 Now do the exam task. For questions 1–15 read the text and think of the word which best fits each gap. Use only one word for each gap. There is an example at the beginning (0).

4 Discuss these questions in pairs.

1 What physical characteristics have you inherited from your parents?
2 Where do your likes, dislikes, tastes and interests come from – your genes or your experience?

Nature vs Nurture

You got your blue eyes from your mother, and your ears from your father. But (0) ...*where*... did you get your adventurous personality or your talent (1) .... singing? Did you learn these from (2) .... parents or were they predetermined (3) .... your genes? While it's clear that physical characteristics are hereditary, things are a little (4) .... clear when it comes to an individual's behaviour, intelligence (5) .... personality. Ultimately, the old argument of nature vs nurture (6) .... never really been won. We (7) .... not yet know exactly how much (8) .... what we are is determined by our DNA and how much by our life experience. But we do know that both (9) .... a part.

Some scientists think that people behave (10) .... they do according to genetic predispositions or even 'animal instincts'. This (11) .... known as the 'nature' theory of human behaviour. (12) .... scientists believe that people think and act in certain ways (13) .... they are taught to do so. This is the 'nurture' theory.

Our growing understanding (14) .... the human genome has recently made it clear that both sides are partly right. Nature endows us (15) .... inborn abilities and traits; nurture takes these natural tendencies and moulds them as we learn and mature.

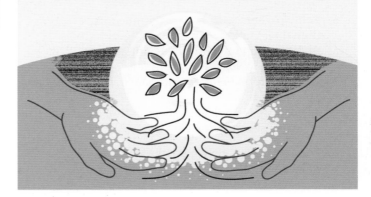

Speaking Part 3

1 There are many causes of irritation and stress in today's society. Do the following tasks.

1 Make a list of everyday irritations – things people complain about, for example, noisy neighbours, barking dogs, nagging parents, traffic jams.
2 Compare lists with a partner. How many irritating situations are in both your lists? Which of these situations can lead to stress?

2 🔟 **Listen to two people discussing these six photographs. How do they answer these questions?**

1 How can stress affect people in these situations?
2 Which of these situations is the most stressful for most people, in your opinion?

3 🔟 **Listen again. How do the speakers use the words and phrases in *italics* in these extracts from their conversation? Match a word or phrase with one of the uses below.**

1 Stress *can* affect people in many ways.
2 The first one *looks like* an exam situation. / It *looks like* they can't communicate ...
3 The second one, someone in hospital – *could* be a relative ...
4 ... traffic jams because they're so commonplace, whereas *perhaps* personal illness or something doesn't happen so often.

a so as not to sound too certain
b to describe how something appears
c to express a general possibility
d to suggest a possibility

4 **Now discuss the questions in Exercise 2 in pairs. Try to use words and phrases from Exercise 3 above as well as other expressions of opinion.**

5 **Work in pairs. Is life more stressful today than it was in the past? What are the best ways of dealing with stress? Can it ever be useful?**

▶ page 177 *Speaking reference: Speaking Part 3*

Writing Part 1 An article

1 **Work in pairs.**

1 What is an *article*? Which of the following would you be most likely to find in a typical article?
   • an eye-catching title
   • informative sub-headings
   • factually accurate detailed information
   • a first paragraph that arouses your interest
   • a formal language style
   • interesting content
   • the writer's opinions or ideas
   • content aimed at a specialist readership

2 Do you often read articles in your own language or in English? Do you prefer reading articles in print or online?

3 What kinds of article do you enjoy reading? What makes a good article?

▶ page 166 *Writing reference: Articles*

2 **Read the Part 1 writing task on the right, and answer these questions in pairs.**

1 Who will read the article you write?
2 What is the main purpose of the article?

3 **Work in pairs.**

1 Choose one of these titles for your article or think of one of your own. You need to arouse readers' interest.
 • Proven techniques for overcoming stress and passing exams
 • Revision without stress
 • Don't let nerves ruin your chances of exam success
 • Exams and mental health

2 If you were a reader, which of these beginnings would most make you want to continue reading an article about exams? Discuss the reasons for your choice.
 a To tell you the truth, I don't care whether I pass the end-of-year exams or not. That's what I always try to convince myself as exams approach!
 b I'll never forget the first exam I ever did. I was eight years old and nobody had told me I ought to revise. Nobody had told me I ought to be nervous, either. Of course, I passed!
 c Are you one of the millions of people all over the world who consider exams to be a kind of torture dreamed up by bored academics intent on causing as much mental anguish as possible to their potential students?

4 **Think about the style that would be appropriate for an article like this. Look back at the article in Reading Part 3.**

1 Which part(s) could be written in an informal style?
2 Which part(s) would be better in a formal style?

An international English-language magazine has asked readers to submit articles on ways of preparing for important exams. Read the extract from a letter that the magazine received from a student asking for advice and the notes you made in response to this. Think of your own ideas as well. Then write your article, making suggestions and giving general advice. You may include personal experience.

Make a timetable and keep to it.

So, with important exams coming up in the next few months, I need practical tips to help me revise. I know from experience that as the time gets nearer, I will get more and more nervous, so I'd be particularly grateful for advice on dealing with stress.

Don't miss any sleep.
Do physical exercise.

5 **Plan your article.**

1 Note down as many ideas as you can under these headings.

Practical tips	Dealing with stress
Make a timetable and keep to it.	Don't miss any sleep. Do physical exercise.

2 Plan your article paragraph by paragraph. Here is a possible plan.

Paragraph 1	Grab your readers' attention. Look back at the three beginnings a–c in Exercise 3 for ideas.
Paragraphs 2 & 3	Practical tips 1 and 2: Advice and example(s)
Paragraphs 4 & 5	Dealing with stress 1 and 2: Suggestions
Paragraph 6	Concluding paragraph. End on an optimistic note.

For paragraphs 2–5, choose the best ideas from the table above.

6 **Write your article in 180–220 words. Use the title you chose in Exercise 3 or think of a new one. Remember to include features of both formal and informal styles.**

Unit 4 Office space

Starting off

1 **Work in pairs. Match these work environments with the photos.**

a open-plan office with individual workstations
b office overlooking warehouse or factory
c office/studio outside the city
d individual office in a high-rise office block
e room converted into an office for working from home

2 **Which of the work environments are good for the following?**

working under pressure   being creative
impressing clients   saving money
working in teams   working independently
providing quality of life   supervising staff

3 **Which work environment would suit you? Why?**

Reading Part 4

1 Work in pairs. What things contribute to a bad working environment, e.g. poor lighting?

2 Work in pairs. You are going to read an article about problems of office design and their solutions. Before you read the article, read the statements 1–15 in Exercise 3 below. Which do you think refer to …

a problems? 2, 8, …
b solutions?
c either problems or solutions?
d neither problems nor solutions?

3 Now, for questions 1–15, choose the appropriate section (A–F) in the article opposite. The sections may be chosen more than once.

Changing the lighting will give this office a more spacious appearance. **1** [ ]

The problems of this office do not provide enough challenge for the architect. **2** [ ]

Employees in this office are prepared to accept poor working conditions. **3** [ ]

This office requires an area where informal discussions can take place. **4** [ ]

Some problems in this office can be solved by changing the way work is organised. **5** [ ]

We would like our staff to benefit from a more varied routine. **6** [ ]

The atmosphere of this office could be improved by repainting it. **7** [ ]

The directors do not want the office to be perceived as very formal. **8** [ ]

This office would work better if each department was clearly labelled. **9** [ ]

The situation in this office is likely to get worse. **10** [ ]

There's a limit to what is acceptable in this office. **11** [ ]

This office has been given a different title from other similar offices. **12** [ ]

This office only needs one big architectural modification. **13** [ ]

This organisation cannot afford better premises. **14** [ ]

These offices may give visitors a false impression when they first arrive. **15** [ ]

Is there an architect in the house?

We took three offices, each in dire need of improvement, and paired them with three workplace design experts. Tom Dyckhoff watched their theories put to the test.

The multimedia company

A The problem: The reception at Channelfly.com is crammed with 'new office' design features: the bashed-up sofas, the table football, the spike-haired staff, Daft Punk on the stereo. But it's all front. Behind, it's crowded and confusing, with strip lighting, hotch-potch furniture and thirsty spider plants. Not exactly the image of a young multimedia music company.

'We get top musicians like Cerys from Catatonia coming here,' says the Managing Director, Jeremy Ledlin. 'We don't want it to look like an office.' But it just looks ugly. 'Well, we don't want it to look like that either.' The company has long working hours and a wide range of activities, so it's hard to keep coordinated. The claustrophobic, labyrinthine layout doesn't help either.

B The solution: Architect Ralph Buschow says, 'The office should be like a city. You need ugly areas too. What they need right now is somewhere to talk, not just the street or the photocopier. Otherwise, people only talk to the same people all the time. There was another office we went to where we put a bar next to the lift and it immediately became a hotbed of idea-swapping. And they need signposts. People want easy clues about how everything connects, or they go crazy.'

The charity

C The problem: Dreariness, cramped space, stifling ventilation, nasty lighting, carpet tiles, utilitarian furniture – Jim Devereux has it all and the deep dissatisfaction that goes with it. The trouble is money: 'In a charity, it's tight.' His office, a housing aid centre combined from two shops in Fleetwood, Lancashire, is threadbare, with only a clock, clutter, posters on benefit rates and the like for decor. 'But our biggest bother is there's nowhere to go for a break, so everyone has lunch at their desks, and we've got six new staff starting soon. Mind you, you should have seen where we used to work.'

D The solution: 'Hmm,' sighs architect Mervyn Hill. 'Sometimes the answer isn't design, but rethinking how you work, like how to work flexibly in the space you have: think of computers as workstations, do different jobs in different parts of the office, and keep mobile: not one person tied to a desk all day.' But what about the ambience? 'The people here are so committed, they'd work in a cellar with two candles. A charity shouldn't be luxurious, but it needs to be warm. This is spartan. The bare fluorescent strip lights have to go. Up-lights will lift the ceiling, make it sparkle.'

The call centre

E The problem: Account manager Sally Stapleton insists this isn't a call centre. In fact, she calls where she works in Edinburgh a contact centre. 'Compared with other contact centres it's light and airy, with plants, fresh decor.' But a call centre's a call centre, even when it's a contact centre – with similar problems, such as noise, and mundanity. 'We need to alleviate the repetitive tasks of the agents, so they can enjoy what they're selling. We don't mind a more casual space. But we'd draw the line at lots of fluffy animals cluttering up the desks.'

F The solution: 'I've seen a lot worse,' says Julian Frostwick. He sounds disappointed. 'But there's lots to get my teeth into. They need to humanise the space. It's very bland and anonymous. They can kill a few birds with one stone by putting in a beautiful new ceiling, a big wave, maybe, and this would break up the space into defined areas. Keep the rest cosmetic, treating the windows for glare, a few colours. A bit of bright red will make it more exciting.'

Adapted from *The Guardian*

Exam information

In Reading Part 4, you have to match 15 questions or statements with parts of a text or a number of short texts. In the exam you will have about 18 minutes to do this.

4 Work in pairs. Discuss this question.

Some people believe that companies are more successful if their staff enjoy their work. Other people don't think this is so important. What is your view?

Vocabulary
Adjective/noun collocations (1)

❶ Look at these two sentences from Reading Part 4. Which of the words in *italics* form correct collocations with the words in **bold** that follow them?

1 The company has *many* / *long* working **hours** and a *wide* / *long* **range** of activities.
2 Jim Devereux has it all and the *deep* / *big* **dissatisfaction** that goes with it.

❷ **⊙** CAE candidates often make mistakes forming collocations with the words in **bold** in the following sentences. Which adjective from each set of three is incorrect?

1 Karl has ~~wide~~ / *extensive* / *vast* **experience** of repairing computers.
2 Gustav's report made a(n) *huge* / *extreme* / *powerful* **impact** on the Board of Directors.
3 Our staff enjoy a *high* / *big* / *great* degree of **flexibility** in their working hours.
4 People working here have to work under *heavy* / *constant* / *high* **pressure**.
5 The company I work for has a(n) *excellent* / *big* / *unrivalled* **reputation** for quality.
6 There has been *high* / *fierce* / *intense* **competition** for the manager's job.
7 We have had a *high* / *large* / *great* **number** of applicants for this job.
8 There's been a *strong* / *huge* / *considerable* **increase** in the number of job applicants.
9 With her *expert* / *high* / *specialist* **skills**, Suzy is bound to get the job.
10 With Marianne's *vast* / *extensive* / *strong* **knowledge** of statistical theory, I'm sure she'll get the job.

Listening Part 2

❶ Work in small groups. You will hear an economist talking about a skills shortage (when there are not enough skilled workers for the jobs available). Match these things happening in modern workplaces with the photos.

a offices relocating to the countryside
b perks such as career breaks and sabbaticals for key staff
c telecommuting – working from home
d people from different parts of the world collaborating on the same projects
e working on past retirement age
f longer working hours

❷ Which of these things would help companies to attract and retain skilled workers? Which would skilled workers find unattractive?

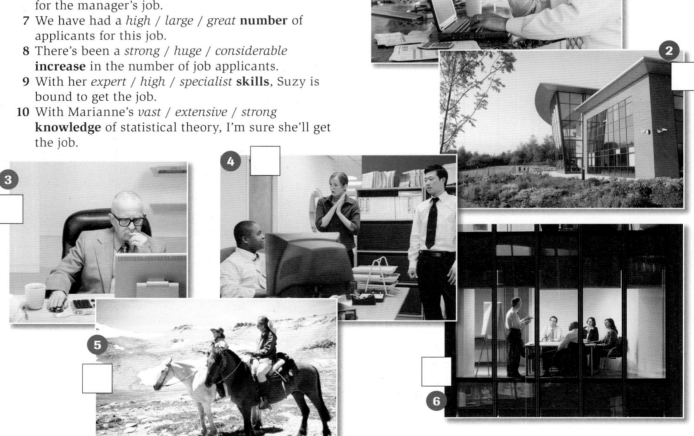

③ Work in pairs. What sort of information do you think you will need to fill each of the gaps in the notes below?

Example: (1) *highly qualified staff or successful graduates or something similar*

The Skills Shortage

In order to compete successfully, companies in many sectors try to attract workers (1) ....

The competition to recruit good workers is strongest in (2) .... companies.

This is a feature of both (3) .... and Western economies.

By one estimate, Bangalore is expected to have a shortage of 200,000 (4) ....

Many European countries have smaller (5) .... than in the past.

Also, too many university students are tending to study the (6) ....

The biggest shortage in international organisations is people with (7) .... skills.

Some companies have been considering (8) .... to attract staff, but this leads to other problems.

④ (11) Now listen and for questions 1–8, complete the sentences.

Exam advice

Before you listen, look at the gaps to check:
*   what type of information you need
*   what types of word will fit the gaps.

Then, when you listen:
*   write words you actually hear
*   make sure you spell them correctly.

⑤ Work in small groups.

*   Is there a skills shortage in your country?
*   Some people believe that it is not necessary to have a university qualification in order to get highly paid work. What is your view?
*   Which subjects would you recommend university students to study in your country in order to get interesting or well-paid jobs? Which would you recommend students to avoid?

Grammar
Expressing possibility, probability and certainty

① Read these pairs of sentences. Which sentence in each pair expresses a stronger possibility?

1   a   … soon there *may well* be vacancies for thousands of software engineers.
    b   … soon there *may* be vacancies for thousands of software engineers.
2   a   In fact, many of us *could easily* find ourselves working on well into our 70s.
    b   In fact, many of us *could* find ourselves working on well into our 70s.
3   a   Raising salaries *could possibly* be an option for some employers …
    b   Raising salaries *could* be an option for some employers …

○ page 152 *Grammar reference: Expressing possibility, probability and certainty*

② What do you think you will be doing in five years' time? Write five sentences about yourself, using the words and phrases in *italics* from Exercise 1.

Example: *In five years' time I may well be working for an international company.*

When you have finished, compare and discuss your sentences in pairs. Give reasons for your statements.

③ ⊙ The sentences below all contain mistakes made by CAE candidates. Find and correct the mistakes.

1   By reaching an advanced level of English, I am more ~~probably~~ to succeed in business. *likely*
2   If you come here for your holiday in July, you bound to enjoy it.
3   If you also watch television and films, then you're most likely to learn the language faster.
4   I've studied the three posible options to try to solve the problem.
5   I'd like to recommend Grey's Academy as one of the possibly best schools in Barnsley.
6   Probably you will want to go to another country to learn another language.
7   This was the worst trip I probably have ever experienced.
8   That may be the possible reason why you're having such problems.

Use of English Part 1

1 **Work in pairs. How far do you agree with each of the following statements?**

1 My best friends are the ones I've met through my work/ studies.

2 I'd never consider going on holiday with someone I work/ study with.

3 What I find most motivating about my work/studies are my colleagues.

4 My friendships with colleagues help me to cope with my work/studies.

2 **Quickly read the text on the right. Which of the ideas in the statements above are reflected in the text?**

3 **For questions 1–12, read the text again and decide which answer (A, B, C or D) best fits each gap. There is an example at the beginning (0).**

- Use the clues to help you (in the exam there are no clues).
- Some of the words are collocations (see the vocabulary exercise on page 40).

Exam information

Use of English Part 1 is a text with 12 gaps.

- You have to choose the best option, A, B, C or D, for each gap.
- In the exam you will have about ten minutes for this.

4 **Work in pairs.**

- How important to you are the people you work/study with? Why?
- Do you think people find it easier or more difficult to make friends than they did in the past? Why?

Friends benefit firms

We have all heard tales about difficult people at work, usually managers, but the office is also where many people make friends, and friends (0) ...... *C* ...... us to feel that bit more enthusiastic about the job we do. Research has found that more than half of British workers (1) .... their best friends in the office and more than a third say that they go on holiday with (2) .... workers.

The changing nature of work – more flexibility, more multi-tasking – means that people (3) .... stability from their workmates. Friendships bring (4) .... in a changing world. A collaborative working environment (5) .... the way to make job-sharing and expansion of roles more of an (6) .... for employers and employees.

So fun workplaces, where friendships flourish, (7) .... workers who can handle changing job roles. This is not (8) .... surprising although it may have been when Elton Mayo (9) .... experiments in human behaviour with workers at the Western Electric Company in Chicago in the 1920s. By fiddling with the factory lighting levels, Mayo found that productivity and morale were (10) .... more by cohesion levels among staff than by physical (11) .... The conclusion he (12) .... from these experiments was that work is a social affair.

From The Times

0 A enliven   **B** influence   **C** inspire   **D** stimulate

1 A meet   **B** make   **C** find   **D** know
Clue: this word means 'to see and speak to someone for the first time'.

2 A peer   **B** colleague   **C** companion   **D** fellow
Clue: this word can be used as an adjective to describe someone who has the same job or interests as you, or is in the same situation as you.

3 A desire   **B** search   **C** seek   **D** wish
Clue: a word which means 'look for' and is not followed by a preposition.

4 A basis   **B** support   **C** assistance   **D** backing
Clue: a word which means 'agreement with' or 'encouragement'.

5 A leads   **B** finds   **C** shows   **D** paves
Clue: If something … the way for/to something else, it makes the other thing possible.

6 A option   **B** opportunity   **C** opening   **D** occasion
Clue: a word which means 'one thing which can be chosen from a set of possibilities'.

7 A appeal   **B** attract   **C** lure   **D** engage
Clue: these workplaces are pleasant and enjoyable, so people want to work there.

8 A extremely   **B** thoroughly   **C** entirely   **D** utterly
Clue: this word forms part of a phrase which means 'not completely' and is often used with 'surprising'.

9 A practised   **B** conducted   **C** ran   **D** administered
Clue: this verb collocates with 'experiments'.

10 A altered   **B** adapted   **C** varied   **D** affected
Clue: this word means 'influenced, causing them to change'.

11 A states   **B** conditions   **C** situations   **D** requirements
Clue: the correct answer refers to the physical environment surrounding staff.

12 A arrived   **B** jumped   **C** leapt   **D** drew
Clue: to .... a conclusion means 'to consider the facts of a situation and make a decision about what is true, correct, likely to happen, etc'.

Speaking Part 4

1 🎧 **Listen to two people, Frances and Sally, being asked their opinions about issues connected with work. Write down the three questions you think they have been asked.**

Now look at Exercise 5 below and compare your questions with the questions there.

2 🎧 **Listen again. Say if the following statements are true (T) or false (F).**

Sally and Frances:
1 suggest several different ideas to answer each question T
2 help each other with ideas and encouraging comments
3 treat each question very seriously
4 answer some questions by talking about their personal situation
5 speak in quite a formal style.

3 🎧 **Complete these extracts from Speaking Part 4 by writing an adverb from the box in each space. Then listen again to check your answers.**

| actually completely fairly generally horrifically |
| just sort of ~~necessarily~~ obviously quite |

1 You don't ...... *necessarily* ...... have to deal with in-line work colleagues.
2 The disadvantages are that it might be .... difficult to separate work and home life, because you can .... see your office as you walk past and think, oh, I'll just check my emails again.

3 You might need more self-motivation to .... do things and not just go to the kitchen every five minutes and get something.
4 Some things, yes, because some very basic manual work is going to be .... boring … but then .... you're losing lots of your workforce and creating more unemployment, but .... it would be great.
5 .... the opposite of my boss now. I'd look for somebody who's a good communicator, that tells you what's going on, that doesn't yell at you, that doesn't smell, that has, sets like boundaries, that helps you prioritise your workload and doesn't give you half their workload without giving you any support. That's all .... negative.

4 **Work in pairs. How do the adverbs affect the meanings of the sentences above?**

Example:

1 'Necessarily' tells us that you don't have to work with in-line colleagues in every situation, or in every case.

5 **Work alone. Think about your answers to the questions below. How could you use some of the adverbs in Exercise 3 in your answers?**

1 The world we live in is changing faster than ever before. How do you think our working lives will be different in the future?
2 Many people dream of being able to work from home. What do you think are the advantages and disadvantages of working from home?
3 Some people believe that we should all continue working as long as we are able to, while other people believe that we should all retire at 60 or 65. What is your view?
4 In the future, many jobs we do nowadays may be done by robots or machines. Do you think this is a good thing? Why (not)?
5 How have computers changed the way people work?
6 Many people complain about their bosses. What qualities would you look for in a perfect boss, and why?

6 **Work in pairs. Take turns to ask and answer the questions in Exercise 5.**

⏵ page 178 *Speaking reference: Speaking Part 4*

Writing Part 1 A report

1 Work in pairs. Read the exam task below and answer the questions which follow.

You have been working for an international company. Your manager has told you that there is a sum of money available for making improvements to the office. He has asked you to write a report saying how your work colleagues feel about working conditions in the office and recommending changes.

You have carried out a survey of your colleagues' opinions. Here are some of their comments:

'The furniture's fine but we need more space for relaxation – not just two hard chairs by the water cooler!'

'Yes, somewhere to talk over ideas.'

'Some sofas!'

'The office is too hot in the winter and too cold in the summer – what about global warming?'

'Quite!'

'I'm suffering from eye strain.'

'Me, too – is it the lighting?'

Write your **report**. Write between 180 and 220 words.

1 Should you write the report in a formal or an informal style? Why?
2 When you write the report, should you use the same structures and vocabulary as in the comments? Why (not)?
3 What sections do you think your report should include, and what section headings?
4 What changes should you recommend in your report? What reasons will you give for your recommendations?
5 Write a plan for your report: note down what you will put in each section.

2 Read the sample report below. Compare the contents of the report with your plan.

Report on office working conditions

Introduction

The aim of this report is to (1) *sum up /* (*outline*) employees' attitudes to working conditions in the office and to (2) *make recommendations / give ideas* for improvements.

The office environment

A number of people (3) *talked about / mentioned* the temperature in the office. They feel that the heating system should not be kept so high in the winter and that the air conditioning could be turned down in the summer. They suggested that a policy change here could (4) *play a part in / contribute towards* protecting the environment.

Some people also complained of eye strain which they feel could easily be due to the lighting. I would suggest that we (5) *ask / consult* an expert to (6) *ensure / make sure* that every employee works with comfortable, healthy lighting.

Office furniture

The furniture is generally considered to be (7) *fine / satisfactory*. However, the relaxation area could be (8) *improved / made better* with more comfortable seating such as sofas. This would (9) *create / lead to* a space for informal discussions and (10) *exchanges / swapping* of ideas which might well be (11) *helpful / beneficial* to the company.

Conclusion

I would recommend (12) *implementing / making* all the changes outlined above as they will help to retain staff and improve their productivity.

▶ page 171 *Writing reference: Reports*

3 Read the report again and choose the more formal alternatives from the options 1–12 in *italics*.

4 Work in pairs. Writing Part 1 often asks students to persuade the reader about something.

1 Why is using a suitable style essential to persuading the reader?
2 Underline words and phrases in the sample report which are used to persuade the manager.

5 Work in pairs. Read the writing task on the right.

1 Who will read your report?
2 What would be a suitable style?
3 Write a plan for your report.
4 What words, phrases and structures from the sample report above could you use in your answer?

6 Work alone and write your report.

You and a number of students from different countries have been working in an international company for a month as part of a work experience programme. The human resources manager of the company has asked you to write a report saying how useful the programme has been for the participants and including recommendations for future programmes. Write a report on the programme using the comments below which you collected from the students' feedback forms.

Team work:

- Great international mix.
- Some of the students need more language training.
- Pity we couldn't finish the project!
- Not enough time.
- I didn't always understand everything.

Working in different departments:

- Very interesting. Staff very helpful and friendly.
- Would like more time in fewer departments.
- I learnt a lot about office work.

In general:

- Well organised.
- Not enough time for us to compare ideas and experiences.
- Made some really good friends.

Write your **report**. Write between 180 and 220 words.

Unit 3 *Vocabulary and grammar review*

Vocabulary

1 Match these formal words with their more informal equivalents.

1 adept
2 contemplate
3 food
4 generation
5 neighbourhood
6 rapid
7 reside
8 tolerate

a grub
b area
c live
d put up with
e quick
f think about
g age group
h clever

2 Complete these sentences with the correct form of the expressions in the box.

> cultivate good relationships   exert control
> express ideas   run an experiment   win an argument

1 One of the main functions of office managers is to
   ...cultivate good relationships.... between members
   of their staff.
2 I really enjoy .... but it doesn't
   matter much to me whether I ....
   or not.
3 One of the most difficult jobs an army officer has
   to do is .... over his men when
   morale is low.
4 Researchers are .... to find out
   how children learn and use new vocabulary.

Grammar

3 The words *no*, *not*, *none* are used incorrectly in some of these sentences. Correct the mistakes.

1 I've searched everywhere for my passport but there
   is ~~not~~ sign of it. *no*
2 Most of my family love all kinds of sport, but no
   my sister – she thinks all sport is a waste of time.
3 The exam was so difficult that I didn't get none of
   my answers right.
4 Humans are basically no different from any other
   animal.
5 I thought we had plenty of coffee but I've just
   looked in the cupboard and there's no left.
6 Not one of Patrick's friends remembered his
   birthday.
7 Our rate of pay is no the point – it's the actual
   working conditions that are so awful.
8 The group left for the North Pole three weeks ago
   and, so far, we've had none news of their progress.

4 Rewrite these short texts replacing active verbs with passive verbs where possible. You do not always need to include the agent in your answer.

Example:

I *The term 'amnesia' is used to refer to a partial or complete loss of memory. Amnesia can ...*

1 We use the term 'amnesia' to refer to a partial or
   complete loss of memory. It is usually a temporary
   condition which only affects a certain part of a
   person's experience. Specific medical conditions
   can cause amnesia.

2 We all know very well that our real experiences
   form our memory. But could someone put a false
   memory into our heads? Could they persuade us
   that we had experienced something that never
   actually took place?

3 We use our semantic memory to store our
   knowledge of the world. Everyone has this
   knowledge base, and normally we can access
   it quickly and easily. Our semantic memory
   includes the meanings of words and the names of
   people and places.

4 Our working memory is a very important part
   of our memory system, which we need in order
   to survive in the world. You can think of it as the
   ability to remember and use a limited amount
   of information for a short amount of time. Our
   working memory can help us to perform a task,
   like following a set of instructions. However, this
   information is erratic. If someone distracts you,
   you can lose the information and you have to start
   the task again.

5 Although we may find it annoying, forgetting
   is a part of how normal memory functions.
   Researchers are now studying forgetting and
   think of it not as a failure of memory, but as a
   more active process. They even believe that a
   specific biological mechanism may drive it.

5 Complete these sentences with your own ideas.

1 It used to be thought that ...
2 As a child, I was led to believe that ...
3 Within the next few years, it is expected that ...

Unit 4 *Vocabulary and grammar review*

Vocabulary

❶ Complete each of the sentences below by writing an adjective from the box in the gap to form a noun/adjective collocation. In some cases more than one answer is possible, and you can use the same adjective more than once.

constant	excellent	extensive	fierce	huge
powerful	specialist	~~vast~~		

1 Malik's positive attitude and ....vast............ experience make him the best man for the job.
2 Almodóvar's film has made a .... impact on audiences throughout the country.
3 This is a highly stressful job and we're under .... pressure to meet our targets.
4 The Paradise Hotel has a(n) .... reputation in this town.
5 I want to join the football team but there's extremely .... competition for places.
6 The .... increase in house prices has made it very difficult for young people to buy a first home.
7 Ivan's .... knowledge of the market is invaluable to our operations.
8 We need someone with .... language skills to work as part of our expert team.

❷ Choose the best option, A, B, C or D, to complete each of the sentences below.

1 Jan is under huge pressure from people in his .... group to dress differently.
   A peer   B colleague
   C companion D fellow

2 Before taking your lawyers to court, you ought to .... legal advice.
   A desire   B search
   C seek   D wish

3 He got the job on the .... of his excellent qualifications.
   A basis   B support
   C assistance D backing

4 This job won't .... to you unless you're a highly organised person.
   A appeal   B attract
   C lure   D engage

5 You'll have plenty of .... to travel when you've been working here for a while.
   A options   B opportunities
   C openings   D occasions

6 It's difficult to .... to working in a different cultural environment from the one you're used to.
   A alter   B adapt
   C vary   D affect

7 Scientists have been .... a series of experiments to see how effective the new drug is.
   A practising   B administering
   C making   D conducting

8 The news of Magda's failure was not .... unexpected, considering how ill she had been.
   A extremely   B thoroughly
   C entirely   D utterly

Grammar and vocabulary

❸ Circle the correct alternative in *italics* in each of the sentences below.

1 It's by far the best film of the festival so far. I think it *must / could* easily win first prize.
2 The weather forecast isn't too good so the outing *might not / could not* take place tomorrow.
3 Jay had a sprained ankle so he *mightn't have / couldn't have* run very far!
4 It's just about *probable / possible* that the train has been delayed.
5 We're *highly / strongly* likely to see Fran at the concert tonight.
6 You're looking exhausted! You *mustn't / can't* have had a very relaxing holiday.
7 Why don't you call Marcos? He's *bound to / can* have the information you need.
8 There's a *slight / little* possibility that you'll receive the money tomorrow.
9 I don't know where they are. I suppose they could *probably / conceivably* be waiting by the post office.

Unit 5 Dramatic events

Starting off

1 You receive a letter telling you that you have won an adventure holiday competition. Which of these three holidays would you choose? (You can refuse them all, but there is no alternative money prize!)

2 Compare and discuss your choice of holidays with other students.

3 Work in pairs.

- Do you think dangerous activities like these can be good for you? Why (not)?
- What is the attraction of these kinds of experience?

HYDROSPEEDING

Hydrospeeding in Morzine, Switzerland, is not for everyone but the more extreme will love it. Equipped with a float, helmet, flippers and wetsuit you will float, plunge and scream your way down the River Dranse!

Interested? Click here >>>

York Skydiving Centre

Ready to skydive!! We offer tandem skydiving, parachuting and freefalling at York Skydiving Centre. Come and experience the exhilaration of jumping from an aeroplane at 4,000 metres at the closest full-time Parachute Centre to York.

Interested? Click here >>>

Wilderness Husky Safari

Quite simply, we love this and, judging by the feedback, so do our clients.

You will be provided with all the necessary equipment, including thermal clothing, and then taken to meet the dogs. You will be taught how to handle your team and the sled, and then you depart into Pallas-Ounas National Park in Western Lapland, one of Europe's few remaining wilderness areas. **Interested?**

Click here >>>

Listening Part 1

Exam advice

Before you listen to the recording, read the questions and options, and infer as much information as possible from them about the topic. This should help you to understand the recording when you hear it for the first time.

1 You will hear three extracts in which people are talking about dramatic past experiences. Before you listen, choose one of the topics below and tell your partner a true story about yourself.

1 A dramatic event that took place while you were travelling, e.g. you got lost or were caught in a storm.
2 A mysterious experience you could not explain, e.g. seeing a UFO or experiencing telepathy.
3 A situation when a machine or technological device went wrong, e.g. a car you were in broke down.

2 Which of the expressions from the box might be associated with each of the topics 1–3 in Exercise 1? (Some may be associated with more than one topic.)

> I was scared to death   I felt as if I wasn't alone
> a strange whirring noise   it all happened so quickly
> I've always been very cynical about the supernatural
> it didn't stop for nearly six hours
> there was an explosion and all the lights went out
> the engine was flooded

Think of another phrase that could be associated with each of the three topics.

3 Before you listen, read the questions and options in Exercise 4. At this stage, think about what you can work out from the question and answers. Ask yourself questions like these.

1 In Extract One, what are we told about Harry? For example, where has he been? What has happened to him? Whose fault might it have been?
2 In Extract Two, what do we know about what happened to the motorist? Why do you think the police were involved?
3 In Extract Three, why might the person have to leave her home and why might moving back be a problem?

4 ⑬ Now listen and for questions 1–6, choose the answer (A, B or C) which fits the best according to what you hear.

Extract One

You hear two people, Harry and Jasmine, talking about an incident at a gym.

1 What condition is Harry in now?
  A His leg is still very painful.
  B He sometimes relives the experience.
  C He has recovered completely.

2 What is Harry planning to do in relation to the incident?
  A He is trying to forget the whole thing.
  B He is taking legal action against the gym company.
  C He hasn't made his mind up yet.

Extract Two

You hear part of an interview between a police officer and a motorist who has been involved in a driving incident.

3 How well can the driver remember the incident?
  A He can remember every detail.
  B He can remember certain parts of the incident clearly.
  C His memory of the whole incident is vague.

4 What was the driver's state of mind after he was hit by the stone?
  A He was convinced he was going to die.
  B He was confused but still able to steer the car.
  C He was optimistic that the trees would slow the car down.

Extract Three

You hear a radio reporter interviewing someone who has had to leave her home.

5 How do the interviewee and her neighbours feel about being out of their homes?
  A They resent having to sleep in the school hall.
  B They're trying to stay positive.
  C They're expecting to move back quite soon.

6 How does she feel about the whole incident?
  A She realises that it could have been much worse.
  B She can't stop thinking about the problems she faces.
  C She is afraid she'll never be able to move back.

5 Discuss these questions about words and phrases from the conversations. You may want to check your ideas in a dictionary.

1 Are *flashbacks* pleasant or unpleasant? What kinds of event cause *flashbacks*?
2 How do people use a treadmill at the gym? How does a treadmill work? What is the more negative meaning of the word here: *There were days when child-rearing seemed like an endless treadmill of feeding and washing*?
3 What would normally happen if you *put your foot on the accelerator*? What other controls are there in a car?
4 What might cause a memory to be *a blur*?
5 What does the speaker mean by *I was sure we'd had it*?

Vocabulary
Idiomatic language

Discuss the meaning of these idioms, which all include parts of the body.

1 The speaker on the out-of-control treadmill said, 'In the end all I could do was jump off and *keep my fingers crossed*.' Why do people *keep their fingers crossed*?
2 I'm really scared of heights but if you *twist my arm*, I suppose I'll go climbing with you.
3 It really *makes my blood boil* when I see people driving too fast.
4 James may seem friendly, but he's likely to *stab you in the back* when he has something to gain.
5 Lots of people use their work computers for personal reasons, but managers usually *turn a blind eye to it*.
6 He told me I'd won the lottery but I knew he was just *pulling my leg*.

Grammar
Verbs followed by *to* + infinitive or the *-ing* form

1 Look at these extracts from the conversations you have heard. Circle the verb form the speakers used in each extract, then compare your choices in pairs.

1 Then I decided (*to run*) / *running* fast for ten minutes.
2 I'm considering *to take* / *taking* the company that runs the gym to court.
3 I keep *to think* / *thinking* how disastrous it could have been.
4 I was frantically trying *to stop* / *stopping* it by digging ditches.
5 In the end, I just gave up *to dig* / *digging* and got out as quickly as possible.

2 Are the verbs in the box followed by the *to* infinitive or the *-ing* form? Make two lists of verbs then check your answers in the Grammar reference.

admit afford agree avoid can't help choose deny enjoy expect finish hope involve keep on mind offer pretend promise put off refuse resent risk suggest

verbs followed by *to* + infinitive	verbs followed by *-ing*
afford	admit

▶ page 153 *Grammar reference: Infinitives and verb + -ing forms (Part 1)*

3 Some verbs have different meanings depending on whether they are followed by the *-ing* form or the infinitive. Discuss the differences in meaning between the verbs in *italics* in these pairs of sentences.

1a I *remember* waking up on the grass verge.
1b *Remember* to wake me up early tomorrow morning.

2a I *tried* putting my foot on the brake, but the car simply went faster.
2b I *tried* to hold on to the steering wheel, but it slipped out of my hand.

3a While we were driving along the motorway, we *saw* planes taking off.
3b When we went to the airport to meet my brother, we got there in time to *see* his plane land.

4a I *regret* saying anything now.
4b I *regret* to say that I won't be able to come to your wedding.

5a Being a careful driver *means* paying attention to other road users.
5b I'm sorry. I didn't *mean* to offend you.

▶ page 153 *Grammar reference: Infinitives and verb + -ing forms (Part 2)*

④ ⊙ The following sentences each contain one or two mistakes made by candidates in the CAE exam. One of the mistakes can be corrected in two different ways. Correct the mistakes.

1 First of all, I suggest ~~to take~~ the overnight train to Vienna. *taking*
2 Part of my job is to help maintaining the machinery in good working order.
3 I would strongly recommend to sail rather than going by plane.
4 I hope you won't need phoning me, but if you do, you needn't to worry about the cost. I'll pay.
5 I never considered to do anything except being a teacher.
6 I told my department manager that I objected to work at weekends.

⑤ Work in small groups. Discuss some of these topics.

- what I'm looking forward to
- things I'd like to give up
- things I put off doing
- jobs I'd refuse to do
- something I've tried to do without success
- something dramatic I saw happen recently
- something I regret having done

Use of English Part 5

Exam information

Use of English Part 5 consists of eight items. For each item:

- you are given two sentences and one key word
- you have to fill a gap in the second sentence using between three and six words
- you **must** include the key word, unchanged
- the completed sentence must have a similar meaning to the first sentence and be grammatically correct.

❶ Work in pairs. In this sample task, the second sentence has to be completed to mean the same as the first sentence, using the word given and between three and six words. Discuss the questions.

Sentence 1   We only felt safe when we were on dry land again.
Key word   **UNTIL**
Sentence 2   It *was only after we had finally got* on dry land again that we felt safe.

1 Does the completed second sentence have a similar meaning to the first?
2 Is it grammatically correct?
3 Would this answer be correct in the exam?
4 If not, what should the answer be?

❷ Now read these lead-in sentences and discuss the clues under each one. (You do not have clues in the CAE exam.) Then complete the second sentence with between three and six words, using the word given.

NB contractions = two words

1 I have absolutely no interest whatever in adventure holidays.
APPEAL
Adventure holidays ....
in the least.
Clue: What preposition do you need after the verb 'appeal'?

2 They had offered him a .38 gun for his own protection.
PROTECT
They had offered him a .38 gun so
.... himself.
Clue: Which word can follow 'so' to mean 'for the purpose of'?

3 Having an unlicensed gun in your possession is illegal.
LAW
It ....
have an unlicensed gun in your possession.
Clue: Which phrase which includes 'law' means 'illegal'?

4 People generally think of tennis as a safe sport.
CONSIDERED
Tennis ....
a safe sport.
Clue: How does starting with 'Tennis' affect the grammar of the second sentence?

5 Our surroundings became more primitive as we travelled further inland.
THE
The further we travelled ....
our surroundings became.
Clue: What comparative structures include the word 'the' twice?

6 It is advisable not to climb mountains after a heavy snowfall.
AVOID
You ....
mountains after a heavy snowfall.
Clue: Which modal verb is normally associated with advice?

7 You can't control the weather; all you can do is keep your fingers crossed.

HOPE

You can't control the weather; the only thing to do .... the best.

Clue: What preposition follows 'hope'?

8 At the last minute her courage failed her, and she pulled out of the competition.

NERVE

At the last minute she .... and pulled out of the competition.

Clue: Which verb could be used with 'nerve', which means courage here?

❸ Use of English Part 5 tests how accurately you are able to use a wide range of words and phrases. Some questions test your knowledge of idiomatic expressions and phrasal verbs, such as those in *italics* below. Match each of the expressions in 1–8 to a phrase with a similar meaning, a–h.

1	The match *took place* yesterday.	**a**	very busy
2	After the meal we *settled up* and left.	**b**	look forward to
3	It's *a wonder* that you got here at all.	**c**	begin an argument
4	I *can't wait* for the weekend	**d**	get better
5	*Keep an eye on* the weather	**e**	happen
6	I'm *tied up* until this afternoon.	**f**	surprising
7	Thank goodness, she's *on the mend*.	**g**	watch carefully
8	He's always trying to *pick a fight*.	**h**	pay what you owe

❹ Write sentences of your own using these eight expressions.

Reading Part 1

❶ You are going to read three texts about potentially dangerous situations. Read the texts (on pages 52 and 53) very quickly. Which text …

a describes a location which feels threatening?

b describes a situation where someone knows that they are in danger?

c describes a situation which caused extreme discomfort?

❷ Read the texts again and for questions 1–6, choose the answer (A, B, C or D) which you think fits best according to the text.

❶

A night of fear

Cal turned over to go to sleep. But it was too quiet. Now and again he raised his head off
5 the pillow and listened. Once a dog barked in the distance. Then another and another, from different farms.
10 Just as suddenly they stopped and the silence returned. He listened so hard there was a kind of static in his ears – like listening to the sea in a shell. He expected whispering voices, the squeak of a rubber-soled shoe on the
15 concrete path. He lay on his back and listened to the echoes waiting for his window to explode.

The first threat had been posted the same way and written in the same crude felt-tip printing. His father had been worried and angry and had told some of his workmates
20 about it, including Crilly. The very same night Crilly had arrived at the house with a friend of his. Cal had been out at the time but later heard the story from his father. They had offered him a .38 for his own protection and he had accepted it. He was happy to know that in the house he had
25 the means to frighten off a mob that some night he knew would march up to his door. Or to get a doorstep killer before the killer got him.

From Cal by Bernard MacLaverty

1 The writer uses the phrase *Then another and another* in lines 7–8 to

A indicate that there are a lot of dogs in the area.

B suggest that someone could be moving around outside.

C emphasise the silence of the night once the dogs stop.

D suggest that it will soon be morning.

2 How did Cal receive the first threatening message?

A The postman delivered it through his letterbox.

B A schoolchild delivered a note to the house by hand.

C His father heard it from one of his work colleagues.

D It came through the window, tied to something heavy.

② An unpleasant night

Last night was desperately uncomfortable. A fierce wind blew, occasionally gusting with such ferocity that I feared it might tear the windows out. I lay awake, mouth dry despite regular swigs of water, listening to the village dogs and detritus in the yard being flung about by the wind. As soon as I dropped off to sleep my breathing slowed and within moments I was wide awake, gasping for breath. I needed to sleep so much, but I found myself fighting it, forcing myself to stay awake and breathe slow and deep.

One advantage of the wind is that when daylight comes it is clear and pristine. The summit of the mountain trails a plume of spindrift, blown off the mountain by winds which, at that height, must be in excess of a hundred miles an hour. The rest of the mountain, including the long flanking shoulders below the arrow-head peak, is crystal clear.

We had hoped to move up to Base Camp today, but with the wind still strengthening the decision is taken to stay down here and acclimatise. With atmospheric pressure about half that at sea level, everyone is suffering to some degree and Mr Yang, our minder, and John Pritchard, our sound recordist, are particularly uncomfortable.

From *Himalaya* by Michael Palin

③ A night among the trees

Woods are not like other spaces. Their trees surround you, loom over you, press in from all sides. Woods choke off views, and leave you muddled and without bearings. They make you feel small and confused and vulnerable, like a small child lost in a crowd of strange legs. Stand in a desert or prairie and you know you are in a big space. Stand in a wood and you only sense it. They are a vast, featureless nowhere. And they are alive. So woods are spooky. Quite apart from the thought that they may harbour wild beasts and armed, genetically challenged fellows named Zeke and Festus, there is something innately sinister about them – some indescribable thing that makes you sense an atmosphere of pregnant doom with every step and leaves you profoundly aware that you are out of your element and ought to keep your ears pricked. Though you tell yourself it's preposterous, you can't quite shake the feeling that you are being watched. You order yourself to be serene – it's just a wood for goodness' sake – but really you are feeling jumpy. Every sudden noise – the crack of a falling limb, the crash of a bolting deer – makes you spin in alarm and stifle a plea for mercy. Whatever mechanism within you is responsible for adrenalin, it has never been so sleek and polished – so keenly poised to pump out a warming squirt of adrenal fluid. Even asleep you are a coiled spring.

From *A Walk in the Woods* by Bill Bryson

3 What made the night particularly uncomfortable for the writer?
   A He found it difficult to breathe normally.
   B He was continually thirsty.
   C He found it impossible to fall asleep.
   D The noise of the dogs and objects in the wind.

4 Why did the group decide not to move to Base Camp?
   A They needed to get used to the weather conditions first.
   B The wind was getting stronger.
   C Everyone was feeling stressed.
   D Everyone in the group was feeling ill.

5 What is the writer describing?
   A The memory of a past experience which frightened him.
   B A past situation in which he was attacked by a wild animal.
   C Feelings anyone might experience in a particular situation.
   D A childhood experience which made a great impression on him.

6 How does the writer react to the kind of feeling he describes?
   A He persuades himself there is nothing to fear.
   B He thinks of a logical explanation for his reactions.
   C He succeeds in staying completely calm.
   D He realises that his feelings are irrational.

③ Work in small groups. Discuss these questions.

1 In Text 1, why might someone be threatening Cal and his father?

2 In Text 2, why do you think the writer forced himself *to stay awake and breathe slow and deep*?

3 Text 3 describes a situation which makes people feel *jumpy*. What other situations can have the same effect on people?

Speaking Part 2

1 **Read the examiner's instructions and look at the three photos below.**

> Here are your pictures. They show dangerous occupations. I'd like you to compare two of the pictures and say what makes each occupation dangerous and why people choose to do them.

Work in pairs. Take turns to compare only two of the three photos. You should each talk for about a minute. Time your partner, but don't interrupt them while they are speaking.

2 🔊14 **Listen to a student speaking about the photos.**

1 Which two is he comparing?
2 Why does he use these words and phrases?

almost certainly	obviously	I don't know	It must be
he seems to be	probably	I'd say	perhaps

3 **Now read these examiner's instructions and look at another set of three photos.**

> Here are your pictures. They show people doing dangerous activities. I'd like you to compare two of the pictures and say what different skills each activity involves, and how these activities make people feel.

Continue working in pairs.

Student A: Choose photos 1 and 2.
Student B: Choose photo 1 or 2 and photo 3.

Now prepare what you are going to say about your two photos.

- Listen very carefully to the instructions you are given by the examiner, so that you answer the specific question you are asked rather than talking vaguely or generally about the pictures.
- The question may have two separate parts – make sure you answer both of them.
- You shouldn't try to describe the photos in detail.
- If you have time before starting to speak, spend a few seconds planning what you want to say.

4 **Take turns to speak for one minute about your photos. Incorporate some of the words and phrases from Exercise 2 above.**

5 **After your partner has spoken, ask him/her a question related to his/her photos.**

Writing Part 2
A competition entry

Exam advice

In Part 2 of the Writing paper, you may be asked to write a competition entry. This is written for a judge or a panel of judges who will expect you to nominate someone or propose yourself for selection for something.

You should use persuasive language and give reasons for your choice. Formal language is appropriate for this task.

1 **Work in pairs. Read the announcement on the right from an international student magazine. Who would you nominate?**

You could choose:
- a person you know or have heard of
- a well-known example from history
- a fictional character from a play or novel.

Make notes about the person and the event they were involved in. Give at least two reasons for your nomination.

2 **Take turns to tell your partner about the person you have chosen. Answer your partner's questions about your nomination.**

Competition –
Heroes like you and me

We are planning a series of profiles of ordinary members of the public who have selflessly risked their own lives to successfully rescue others from danger.

Do you know anyone who you think should be included in this series?

Write to us describing the dramatic event and the person's part in it, and give reasons why you believe this person should be one of our 'Heroes like you and me'.

3 Read this entry to the competition. How does this person compare with the people you and your partner talked about?

To whom it may concern

I am writing in response to your 'Heroes like you and me' competition announcement. The person I wish to nominate is from my town. I do not know her personally, but I have known about her for six months.

My nominee is 32-year-old Helen Keane, who, until one Friday last August, was an ordinary working mother. That afternoon, Helen was driving home from work along the motorway, looking forward to a relaxing weekend. Suddenly, a lorry ahead of her swerved and crashed into a bridge. Without thinking, Helen pulled over and went to help. When she reached the lorry, flames were coming from the engine, but without a thought for herself, Helen opened the cab door and struggled to free the driver. After several minutes, she succeeded in dragging the unconscious man out of his smoke-filled cab and onto the grass verge. Helen herself suffered serious burns which kept her in hospital for several weeks.

My main reason for nominating Helen is that she was an ordinary person going about her daily life. She could easily have driven home, leaving the emergency services to deal with the accident. But she stopped and helped, saving a man's life in the process.

My second reason for choosing Helen is that she is an example to people who think that training is needed to deal with events like this. Helen showed us that anyone can make a difference.

I hope you will agree that Helen Keane deserves to be included in your series of profiles.

Yours faithfully,

4 Underline the *-ing* forms in the competition entry, then work in pairs to discuss how the *-ing* forms are used. Choose from this list:

a as an adjective
b as part of a participle phrase
c as part of a main verb
d after a preposition
e instead of a relative clause (with who, which, etc.)
f as a noun

5 ⊙ Most of the following sentences contain one or more mistakes made by candidates in the CAE exam. Correct all the mistakes you can find.

1 We think we can solve this problem by opening the museum to the public and ~~charge~~ them an entrance fee. *charging*
2 In addition to keep up with their studies, university students often have to cope on very low budgets.
3 Within the next few weeks a new sports centre will be opening in the north of the city.
4 A hardwork committee has recently put forward a set of interested proposals for improve the food and service be offered in the college canteen.
5 To bring in new health and safety regulations, the government has shown that it is concerned with improving the wellbeing of the whole population.
6 I knew my decision to work abroad would mean to leave my friends and family.

▶ page 154 *Grammar reference: Infinitives and verb + -ing forms (Part 3)*

6 Write a competition entry in response to the announcement below which appeared in another international student magazine. Write 220–260 words.

- Use the example letter above as a model.
- Try to include *-ing* forms to link ideas in your letter.
- You can write about a real person or your entry can be fictional.

Heroes and Heroines at Work

We are planning a series of profiles of people who have shown great bravery at work. Who would you nominate to be included in the series? Write to us, describing this person's achievements, and give two reasons why you believe he or she should be included in our series.

▶ page 168 *Writing reference: Competition entries*

Unit 6　Picture yourself

Starting off

1 Work in pairs. *The Times* newspaper and the Tate Gallery in London held a drawing challenge recently. They asked 11 to 18 year olds to submit a self-portrait. Look at the results.

- Which do you like best?
- What can you tell about the personality of each artist?

2 🔊15 You will hear three of the artists speaking. Which do you think are their self-portraits? Why?

Speaker A: ....
Speaker B: ....
Speaker C: ....

3 Work in pairs. If an artist were to paint a portrait of you, how would you like to be painted? Talk about:

- your pose (standing, sitting etc.)
- the clothes you would wear
- the expression on your face and your mood
- the background.

Reading Part 3

1 You will read an article about the Tate *Times* Drawing Challenge. Read the article quite quickly and note down the different phrases the writer uses to describe the entrants and their drawings e.g. *ruthless honesty, ways of deceiving* (lines 16 and 17).

Teenage self-portraits

When The Times *invited anyone aged 11 to 18 to submit a self-portrait, the response was phenomenal.*

You were interested in how your face and hair
5 looked. We were interested in honesty, courage
and lack of self-consciousness. And on Monday
our mutual concerns met. A panel of judges that
included a professor of drawing, Stephen Farthing;
the Turner prize-winning artist Grayson Perry;
10 and myself, an art critic, assembled to assess the
entries for the Tate *Times* Drawing Challenge. The
competition invited anyone from 11 to 18 to pick up
their pencils and submit a self-portrait, the best of
which would be displayed in the Tate. There were
15 more than 1,000 entries.

A self-portrait can be about ruthless honesty. But,
equally, it can be all about ways of deceiving. Artists
can rival actors when it comes to obscuring or
making themselves look better. Think of the
20 difference between that public face that you practise
in the mirror and that embarrassing grimace in the
camera snap. The construction of an image involves
dozens of decisions. To study a self-portrait is to
understand how an artist wants to be seen. In the
25 case of young people it would seem that for every
pretty-faced teenager who would like to imagine
themselves as some soft-focus fashion model there
is another who is keen for the world to know that
they are lurking alone and misunderstood in their
30 rooms. Despite all the worst intentions, a self-
portrait reveals how its sitter sees the world.

The judges were looking for a vision that
seemed enlivening or truthful, courageous or
unselfconsciously fresh. Sometimes the panel burst
35 out laughing at the sheer exuberance – though that
was mostly in the work of the younger entrants
before the toothy grins gave way to grimacing
teenage angst. There were pictures of young people
doing anything from brushing their teeth, to
40 donning funny hats to listening to iPods. But the
most interesting images were less self-consciously
presented: it was as if the sitters had been caught
unprepared.

The judges tended to prefer the pictures in which
45 the artist had really tried to look in a mirror
rather than copy the surface of a photograph. 'The
best images,' says Stephen Farthing, professor of
drawing at University of the Arts, London, 'are
those done by someone who has spent time
50 drawing from life, not just trying to make pictures
that look as if they are finished.' Most of the most
obviously perfect images were passed over by the
panel. 'The distortions and quirks are where the
subconscious leaks out,' Grayson Perry says.
55 It was notable how many entrants mapped out the
spots on their faces. Clearly this matters a lot to
a teenager. Hair was another obsession, though
several got so caught up that their images were
more like advertisements for L'Oréal. They weren't
60 worth it. Most judges preferred the bad-hair days
of entrants such as 13-year-old Daniel Adkins, in
whose self-portrait the hair took on a character all
of its own.

Drawing may be unfashionable – and not least in
65 our art colleges – but it was heartening to see not
only how naturally talented so many of the entrants
were, but also how naturally drawing could be
taught. Three of the self-portraits were by pupils of
the English Martyrs Sixth Form College, Hartlepool.
70 Where some schools submitted work that arrived
in cloned clumps, here, it seems, is a teacher who
knows how to tease out and develop innate talent.
And that matters.

Drawing is a means of expression as much as
75 writing and mathematics. It's a tool to be sharpened
so that you can take it out when you need it and do
whatever you want. But what does this competition
tell us about the entrants? It offered a portrait of
young people who are engaged, enthusiastic and
80 eager. Once, young people aspired to be bankers
and doctors and lawyers. But who wants to go to
the office when they could be an artist?

From *The Times*

2 Read the text again and underline where it answers questions 1–7 below. Then work in pairs and summarise your answers in your own words.

1 What did the panel of judges discover when they met?
2 According to the writer, what do all self-portraits have in common?
3 How did the children's work generally differ from that of the adolescents?
4 Which self-portraits interested the judges least?
5 How did the judges generally feel about the way the competitors drew their hair?
6 According to the writer, what is the English Martyrs Sixth Form College an example of?
7 According to the writer, what do we learn about contemporary young people from the competition?

3 Now, for questions 1–7, choose the answer (A, B, C or D) which you think fits best according to the text.

1 When the panel of judges met, they discovered that
  A they shared the same objectives as the competitors.
  B both entrants and judges were equally satisfied with the results.
  C the entrants' and the judges' differing objectives were achieved.
  D the winning entries combined good looks with other positive qualities.

2 According to the writer, what do all self-portraits have in common?
  A They reflect exactly what the artist sees.
  B They are used to improve the artist's image.
  C They deceive both the artist and the viewer.
  D They reflect the artist's attitudes and concerns.

3 How did the children's work generally differ from that of the adolescents?
  A It was livelier.
  B It was more honest.
  C It was more humorous.
  D It showed more self-awareness.

4 The judges were least interested in the self-portraits which
  A showed spontaneity.
  B concentrated on excellent drawing technique.
  C produced unintended results.
  D were incomplete.

5 How does the writer feel about the way competitors drew their hair?
  A It was better when it was untidy.
  B It deserved more attention from the artists.
  C It was more attractive than their spots.
  D It took up too much time for some artists.

6 The English Martyrs Sixth Form College is an example of
  A how schools can help pupils to develop their natural abilities.
  B why schools should teach unfashionable subjects.
  C how some schools teach all their pupils to draw in the same style.
  D why only naturally gifted pupils should be taught how to draw.

7 What impression does the writer have of those who took part in the competition?
  A They suffer from the typical anxieties of teenagers.
  B They are extremely interested in what they are doing.
  C They generally prefer drawing to writing or mathematics.
  D They are more artistically talented than previous generations.

Exam advice

- First read the text quickly to get a general idea of what it is about.
- Read the first question, find where it is answered in the text and underline the words in the text which answer the question.
- Read each of the options, A, B, C or D, carefully and choose the one which matches what the text says.

4 Work in small groups. Discuss the questions.

But who wants to go to the office when they could be an artist? (lines 81–82)

1 What are the attractions of a creative or artistic career?
2 What are the drawbacks?
3 In what ways are you artistic or creative?

Grammar
Avoiding repetition

❶ Look at these sentences from the text and write one word in each gap. Then check your answers by looking back at the text.

1 The competition invited anyone from 11 to 18 ... to submit a self-portrait, the best of ....*which*........... would be displayed in the Tate. (lines 11–14)

2 In the case of young people it would seem that for every pretty-faced teenager who would like to imagine .... as some soft-focus fashion model there is .... who is keen for the world to know that .... are lurking alone and misunderstood in their rooms. (lines 24–30)

3 'The best images ... are .... done by someone who has spent time drawing from life, not just trying to make pictures that look as if .... are finished.' (lines 46–51)

4 It was notable how many entrants mapped out the spots on their faces. Clearly .... matters a lot to a teenager. (lines 55–57)

5 Most judges preferred the bad-hair days of entrants such as 13-year-old Daniel Adkins, in .... self-portrait the hair took on a character all of its own. (lines 60–63)

6 Here, it seems, is a teacher who knows how to tease out and develop innate talent. And .... matters. (lines 71–73)

▶ page 154 *Grammar reference: Avoiding repetition*

❷ ⊙ CAE candidates often make mistakes when using pronouns and determiners to avoid repetition. Each of the following sentences contains one wrong word. Delete the wrong word and write the correct one. In some cases there is more than one possible correct word.

1 The heating wasn't working and I said ~~it~~ to the manager but nothing was done about it. *so*

2 There are several umbrellas in the stand in the hall. I'd advise you to take it if you're going for a walk.

3 I wasn't happy about the size of the classes. I said it to the director but nothing was done about it.

4 I'd always wanted a portable DVD player and when I was given it as a birthday present, I thought it was wonderful.

5 Some of the machines broke down quite often, but when things like these happened we just called a technician.

6 The lecturers will give you a detailed explanation of the subject. You may not be able to understand all, but you should be able to get a general idea.

7 There were hundreds of CDs on sale in the shop and most of the children wanted it.

8 We're looking for a new accountant and it is why I'm writing to you.

9 You should aim to arrive at any time that's convenient for yourself.

❸ Rewrite the following to reduce the number of words and phrases and avoid repetition.

1 I've been to two exhibitions at the National Gallery this year. The two exhibitions focus on 17th-century painters.
   I've been to two exhibitions at the National Gallery this year. Both focus on 17th-century painters.

2 Fewer and fewer people listen to classical music. The fact that fewer and fewer people listen to classical music means that less classical music is being recorded.

3 I have to read lots of books for my Business Studies course. The books I enjoy most are the books on management theory.

4 I'm hoping to be given a pay rise. Being given a pay rise will mean I can buy a better car.

5 I want Karl, Pau, Ludmila and Mar to come to the meeting. I've told Karl. Can you tell Pau, Ludmila and Mar?

6 Marina doesn't like spending a lot of money on books, so she tends to buy second-hand books.

7 My mother asked you to help her and she'd have been so happy if you'd helped her.

8 When Raul feels strongly about something, he says he feels strongly about something.

9 She didn't do the shopping because no one asked her to do the shopping.

10 Someone left a message on the answering machine but the person didn't leave the person's name.

Listening Part 3

❶ You will hear an interview with the artist, Liam Carolan. Before you listen, work in pairs.

1 Do you have any pictures at home? Did you choose them? What do you like about them?

2 Look at Liam's two paintings on page 61. What do you think of them? What do they reveal about the sitters' personalities?

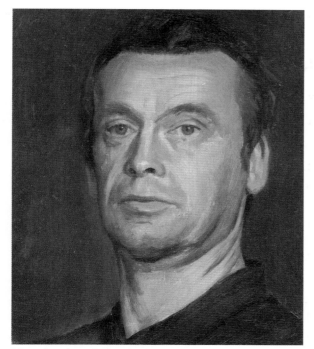

Liam Carolan: Self-portrait

② **Work in pairs. Before you listen, read multiple-choice questions 1–6 below and answer these questions.**

a For Question 2, which comment do you think people would make about his paintings?

b How would you answer Question 3?

c For Question 4, what do you think is the main advantage of painting with the sitter?

d For Question 5, what do you think reveals the sitter's personality?

e For Question 6, what problem do you think artists have when painting a self-portrait?

1 What does Liam say about his father's career?
  A He taught portrait painting.
  B He didn't paint portraits professionally.
  C His portraits were influenced by abstract artists.
  D He exhibited his portraits together with other famous artists.

2 What comment do people sometimes make about Liam's painting?
  A It's old-fashioned.
  B It lacks formal training.
  C It's too intellectual.
  D It lacks individuality.

3 According to Liam, people generally prefer to have paintings in their home to photos because
  A paintings look more pleasant than photos.
  B they suit the design of most houses.
  C they are not produced by machine.
  D they don't look as modern as photos.

4 Why does Liam prefer painting portraits with the sitter in front of him?
  A He thinks the final result is more interesting and alive.
  B He enjoys working with other people in the room.
  C He finds the work more challenging.
  D He receives instant feedback from his sitters.

5 According to Liam, the sitter's personality is revealed in portraits as a result of
  A good artistic technique.
  B artistic interpretation.
  C the artist's acute observation.
  D the way people look at portraits.

6 What problem does Liam have when he is painting a self-portrait?
  A He lacks time to practise painting self-portraits.
  B He has difficulty staying in the same position while painting.
  C He cannot make himself look as relaxed or as handsome as he would like.
  D He cannot get close enough to the image he is painting.

Liam Carolan: Portrait of Catherine Bonser

③ **⟨16⟩** **Now listen to the interview. For questions 1–6, choose the answer (A, B, C or D) which fits best according to what you hear.**

Exam information

Listening Part 3:
• is a conversation between two or more speakers
• lasts about four minutes
• has six multiple-choice questions, each with four options.

④ **Work in pairs.**

• Would you prefer to have a painted portrait or a photograph of yourself in your house? Why?
• How big would it be and where would you put it?

Vocabulary
Adjective/noun collocations (2)

1 **Look at this sentence from Listening Part 3.**

He had a **fair number** of exhibitions in London before the war …

One of the adjectives below <u>cannot</u> be used with *number* to form a collocation. Which one?

fair	large	huge	big	small	limited

2 ⊙ **CAE candidates often make the mistake of using *big* with the nouns in bold in the sentences below. Which of the adjectives in the box can be used with each noun to form collocations? (In all cases several adjectives are possible.)**

amazing	considerable	endless	good	great
heavy	high	huge	large	loud	satisfactory
terrible	tremendous	valuable	wide

1 Pascual is very busy: he spends a ......*large /*...... ......*considerable / huge / tremendous*...... **amount** of time studying.

2 Our local supermarket sells a(n) .... **range** of coffees, so you should find what you're looking for.

3 I found it difficult to concentrate on the conversation because of the .... **noise** coming from the neighbours' television.

4 Your decision about whether to go to art school or study economics is of .... **importance**, so think it over carefully.

5 Magda was very late for the meeting because of the .... **traffic** on the motorway.

6 Seeing elephants in the wild was a(n) .... **experience** and quite unforgettable.

7 Quite a(n) .... **percentage** of our students go on to become professional artists – in the region of 60%.

8 I think Jaroslaw has made .... **progress** with his drawing and is showing real talent.

9 Colin is a teacher with .... **experience** of teaching both adults and children.

10 The paintings in this gallery show a(n) .... **variety** of different styles.

3 **Work in pairs. Where there was more than one possibility in Exercise 2, do the different alternatives change the meaning of the sentence? If so, how?**

Speaking Part 3

1 **Work in pairs. What does each of these pictures show?**

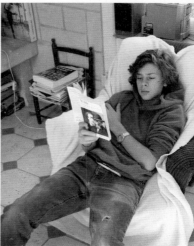

- How do these pictures show the role books play in our lives?
- Which activity is the most demanding?

2 (17) **Listen to extracts from recordings of two pairs of students doing Speaking Part 3 and talking about the photos above. Write *Pair A*, *Pair B* or *Both pairs* to answer these questions.**

Which pair:

1 doesn't start working on the task immediately?
2 deals with each photo in order?
3 deals with the photos in a random order?
4 gives a short description of each photo?
5 relates photos to themselves personally?
6 shows most interest in their partners' reactions to the photos?
7 follows the instructions most closely?
8 uses synonyms to avoid repeating the word *demanding* from the question?

3 **Work in pairs.**

1 Which pair do you think deals with the task better? Why?
2 What synonyms did Pair B use instead of the word *demanding*?

4 (17) **In each sentence below the students are using phrases to refer to a photo / photos or to avoid repeating something already said. Write one word or phrase from the box in each gap. Then check by listening to the candidates again.**

| ~~one here~~ | that would be | the one | this one |
| was doing that | which | which others | |

1 This ....*one here*....... looks quite demanding – there's a librarian putting books back on the shelves.
2 I think if I .... , I'd probably feel a bit frustrated.
3 And there's .... with someone just relaxing and reading a novel probably.
4 But again, you'd have to be very methodical, ... you say you aren't …
5 … so I imagine for you .... pretty demanding.
6 I think this one with the diary would probably be .... I'd find the hardest.
7 And .... do you think are really challenging?

5 **Work in pairs. Which of the activities in the photos do you think is most demanding?**

6 **Work in pairs. Do the task below in about three minutes.**

- How can young people benefit from doing the artistic activities in the pictures on the right?
- Which of the activities do you think would be most popular with young people?

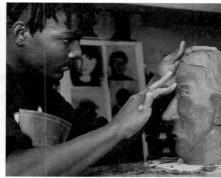

Exam advice

When you discuss the first part of the task:

- talk about each of the things shown in the pictures
- make suggestions, ask your partner's opinion and respond to your partner's ideas.

When you discuss the second part of the task:

- discuss several of the options and give reasons for your opinions
- try to reach a decision.

Use of English Part 2

1 You will read a text about art in offices. Before you read, work in pairs. Is it important for work or study places to have art on the walls? Why (not)?

2 Read the text quite quickly without paying attention to the gaps.

   1   What are the benefits of having art in the workplace?
   2   How has the role of art in the workplace changed?

3 For questions 1–15, read the text again and think of the word which best fits each gap. Use only one word in each gap.

Exam advice

- Read the text quite quickly to get a general idea of what it is about.
- Look at the words before and after the space and decide what type of word you need (an article, pronoun, preposition, etc.).
- Look to see whether the word you need refers to some other part of the text.
- Words may be part of fixed phrases or phrasal verbs, e.g. *instead of, go along with*, etc.

Art for offices

(0) ......*As*...... a professional photographer and environmental psychologist, Wayne Hill knows (1) .... needs to be (2) .... with bland-coloured offices and windowless conference rooms: hang art on the walls. It (3) .... down on stress and raises productivity and creative thinking. 'Our vivid experience of a place (4) .... usually be a wonderful memory, a magic moment at (5) .... of the sweet spots of the world. Realistic landscape photographs help us reconnect with (6) .... places.'

When questioned, most employees say good original art is more (7) .... to 'stimulate and inspire' them than an endless supply of the finest coffee. Fully 98 per cent of workers want (8) .... form of art at work. More surprisingly, perhaps, nearly two-thirds of office workers say they have never been consulted about the décor in (9) .... office.

Peter Harris, (10) .... has been taking art into workplaces for more than 20 years, has seen a great change (11) .... company attitudes: 'The kind of image companies try to project through art is no (12) .... just aimed at visitors and customers. Now art is spread (13) .... the building and the image (14) .... projects is related to employees.' He believes art fulfils an important need in offices. People spend (15) .... much time working in them that they need to feel cared for.

Adapted from *The Observer*

4 Work in small groups. Imagine you work together in the same bland-coloured office. Your office manager has asked you how you would like to see the office made a more pleasant place to work. Below are some of her suggestions. Discuss each of the suggestions.

- How would they improve the office atmosphere?
- Which two would be most suitable?

Writing Part 2 A review

1 Work in pairs. Read the writing task below, then discuss your answers to the questions which follow.

> An international magazine for learners of English has asked its readers to submit a review of a novel they've particularly enjoyed and which they think other learners would also enjoy. Write a review for the magazine including:
>
> - the name of the novel
>
> - a brief summary of the plot and main characters
>
> - what you particularly enjoyed about it
>
> - what other readers may find interesting about it.
>
> Write your **review**.

1 Should you do the following? Why (not)?
  - **a** explain the whole plot including how the story ends
  - **b** give detailed character descriptions
  - **c** include a comment on the writing style
  - **d** make a general recommendation to your readers
  - **e** make some criticisms of the book
  - **f** say what you most enjoyed about the book
  - **g** say why you decided to read the book
  - **h** include a general synopsis of the plot and characters
2 In what order would you mention each of the elements you chose?
3 Is there anything else you should include?

2 Read the review on the right. Which of the elements listed above are included?

3 Read the review again. Which paragraphs deal with:
  - **a** the plot?
  - **b** the main characters?
  - **c** what the writer enjoyed about it?
  - **d** what other readers may find interesting?

4 Find words and phrases in the review which show the writer's reaction to the novel, e.g. *drew me into.*

5 Find adjectives and phrases in the review which describe:
  - characters, e.g. Inman: ***army deserter***
  - places, e.g. ***war-torn***.

Where necessary, check their meanings in a dictionary.

▶ page 169 *Writing reference: Reviews*

Cold Mountain *by Charles Frazier*

Cold Mountain is set in North Carolina during the American Civil War. What drew me into the novel from the outset was the main character, Inman, who makes a hazardous journey across a war-torn country to join Ada, the woman he loves. As an army deserter, he is pursued by armed groups sent to kill traitors. Meanwhile, after her father's death, Ada struggles to survive on her farm.

I was fascinated by the vivid descriptions of American rural life at the time. During his journey, Inman comes across a series of people scratching an insecure living in wild, isolated places in extraordinary ways. I was spellbound by the detail and at the same time horrified and caught up in the suspense from the dangers he and Ada have to survive.

The novel contains a whole gallery of unusual characters: Inman, the thoughtful and observant hero who is desperate to escape the war and survive, and who is motivated by love yet capable of extreme violence; Ada, the heroine, who develops from a well-off, sheltered background, incapable of surviving in the harsh conditions of a lost war, to someone who becomes self-sufficient and decisive, with the help of Ruby, the brash but lovable country girl.

You will really love this book with its detailed observations and descriptions of life in nineteenth-century America and its wonderful ear for styles of speech in a rural backwater. You will be transported into a contrasting world of love, kindness and horror which is unlike any novel you have read before.

6 Work in pairs. Which novel(s) could each of you write about? Tell each other about:
  - the plot
  - the characters
  - what you enjoyed about the novel.

Say why you think your partner would find the novel interesting.

7 Write your own answer to the task in Exercise 1 above.

Exam advice

When you write a review:
  - identify who your readers will be and what style will be suitable for them
  - consider what information will be of interest to your readers
  - express your opinions of the different elements you decide to include in your review so that your readers have a clear idea whether you are recommending what you are reviewing or not.

Unit 5 Vocabulary and grammar review

Vocabulary

1 **Find ten words for parts of the body in this wordsearch puzzle.**

B	L	O	O	D	M	F	L	U
U	F	I	N	G	E	R	S	D
T	K	C	H	E	S	T	F	N
B	N	E	Y	E	I	I	O	L
R	E	A	O	B	C	P	O	E
E	E	S	W	A	A	U	T	G
X	A	E	E	C	A	R	M	A
R	I	N	F	K	H	E	A	D

2 **Complete these idioms with six of the body words you found in the wordsearch, then match each idiom with the correct meaning a–f below.**

1 keep your .... crossed
2 turn a blind .... to something
3 pull someone's ....
4 make someone's .... boil
5 twist someone's ....
6 stab someone in the ....

a make someone angry
b persuade someone to do something
c be disloyal to someone
d hope for good luck especially if you are doing something difficult
e pretend not to notice something / ignore something you would prefer not to know about
f tease or make fun of someone

3 **Write sentences using these sets of words.**

1 dream / flashback / accident
2 gym / fit / treadmill
3 windscreen / break / stone

Grammar

4 **Complete these sentences with the correct form (infinitive or -ing form) of the verbs in brackets. One verb is in the passive.**

1 I considered ...._joining_......... (join) the police or the fire service, because I wanted .... (help) other people in some way. In the end I decided .... (train) .... (be) a paramedic.

2 Three of the people trapped on the third floor managed .... (climb) out on to the roof of the hotel, where they jumped to safety. The other two refused .... (leave) their room and waited .... (rescue).

3 The manager admitted .... (wait) for 20 minutes before .... (phone) the fire brigade. He claimed that he had attempted .... (put out) the fire himself before .... (realise) the seriousness of the situation. He apologised to his colleagues for .... (put) their lives at risk.

4 The climbers refused .... (take) the weather forecast seriously and ended up .... (get) lost when it started .... (snow). Despite this, they went on .... (climb), but were eventually forced .... (admit) defeat. It was then that they tried .... (telephone) mountain rescue .... (ask) for help. Because there was no phone signal on the mountain, they could not .... (contact) the team and spent the night on the mountain, ... (regret) their decision .... (ignore) the forecast.

5 **Complete the second sentence so that it has a similar meaning to the first sentence, using the word given. Do not change this word. Use three to six words including the word given.**

1 I can't wait to start my new job.
FORWARD
I'm really _looking forward to starting_ my new job.

2 Thank goodness we avoided the floods.
LUCKY
We .... the floods.

3 I wish I hadn't phoned my sister.
REGRET
I .... that phone call to my sister.

4 We can't buy a new car – we don't have enough money.
AFFORD
We .... a new car.

5 He says he's never seen her before.
DENIES
He .... her before.

Unit 6 *Vocabulary and grammar review*

Vocabulary

❶ In each of the sentences below, cross out the adjective in *italics* which does not collocate with the noun in bold.

1 A *high / big / significant* **percentage** of accident victims coming to hospital have been doing DIY at home.
2 For me, visiting Paris is always a *great / wide / tremendous* **experience** – it really is my favourite city.
3 Giovanni attaches *considerable / great / large* **importance** to the way he dresses, so he always gets up extra early.
4 If you want to do a gap year before going to university, there is a(n) *endless / huge / deep* **range** of possibilities for you to choose from.
5 Martina is showing a lot of promise and she's made *high / considerable / satisfactory* **progress** with her English this term.
6 My brother has spent a *huge / heavy / considerable* **amount** of money renovating an old farmhouse – I don't know how he can afford it.
7 They're doing road works in the street and the **noise** is so *loud / terrible / big* that I can hardly hear myself think!
8 One of the attractions of this job is the *endless / high / wide* **variety** of different tasks I have to perform.

Grammar

❷ Rewrite the following sentences in order to avoid repetition of words and phrases.

1 'Do you think you'll get a holiday in July?' 'I hope I get a holiday in July!'
   'Do you think you'll get a holiday in July?'
   'I hope so!'
2 When a child feels unhappy, the child will ask for the child's mother more often than the child will ask for the child's father.
3 Gustav bought a large house by the sea about ten years ago. Buying a large house by the sea turned out to be a good investment.
4 Leonardo lived in Canada as a child. The fact that he lived in Canada is the reason why he speaks such fluent English.
5 Svetlana spent several months trying to decide which car to buy and she finally bought a car last week.

6 Three runners entered the race, but only one runner finished because one runner twisted her ankle and one runner stopped to talk to her friends among the spectators.
7 Matthew likes reading novels. Matthew especially likes reading romantic novels.
8 Violeta bought apples in the market. Violeta put some of the apples in the fruit bowl. Violeta used the other apples to make an apple pie.
9 Narayan has had two jobs. The two jobs were in a bank. Unfortunately the two jobs were not well paid.
10 There are five official languages in Spain. Manolo speaks all of the five official languages of Spain.
11 Pete had never spoken to Ann although Pete had often wanted to speak to Ann.
12 Maria often invites me to go with Maria on Maria's business trips to New York. I have never been with Maria on Maria's business trips to New York.

❸ Using expressions from the text in Reading Part 3, complete the second sentence so that it has a similar meaning to the first sentence, using the word given. Do not change the word given. You must use between three and six words, including the word given.

1 To me, he looks exactly the same in the photo as he does in the portrait.
   DIFFERENCE
   I can't see ....*any difference in the*.... way he looks in the photo and in the portrait.
2 The judges were generally less keen on portraits painted from photos than portraits painted from life.
   TENDED
   The judges .... on portraits painted from life than portraits painted from photos.
3 This painting does not appear to be finished.
   LOOK
   This painting .... is finished.
4 Several of the applicants were not considered because of their age.
   PASSED
   Several of the applicants .... to their age.
5 For many teenagers, their looks are their highest priority.
   MATTERS
   Appearance is .... many teenagers.

Unit 7 Leisure and entertainment

Starting off

1 How do you spend your leisure time? Which of the following activities do you do or have you done? Tick or cross the boxes.

At Home

- [ ] watch TV (*What are your favourite programmes?*)
- [ ] surf the Internet (*What are your favourite websites?*)
- [ ] play computer games (*Do you play alone or with other people?*)
- [ ] listen to music (*How do you listen – radio, Internet, MP3 player?*)
- [ ] play a musical instrument (*What kind of music / what instrument do you play?*)
- [ ] read (*What do you read – books, magazines, newspapers?*)
- [ ] chat to friends (*Do you speak on the phone or in a chat room?*)
- [ ] spend time in a virtual world, like *Second Life*?

Away from home

- [ ] go to the cinema (*How often do you go? What is your favourite type of film?*)
- [ ] go to the theatre (*What was the last play or show you saw?*)
- [ ] go to live music events (*What kinds of music do you enjoy most?*)
- [ ] watch or play sports (*What are your favourite sports – to watch or play?*)
- [ ] other outdoor activities (*What do you like most about being outside?*)
- [ ] meet friends (*Where do you meet? What do you do together?*)

Other activities

Make a list of other things you do in your leisure time.

2 Work in pairs.

1 Compare your leisure-time activities then discuss the questions in brackets in the list above.
2 Are there any other leisure-time activities you would like to do in the future?
3 Discuss the best and/or worst ways for the following groups of people to spend time together:
   - ten university students
   - a family of four (for example, two parents and two children)
   - a class of 30 nine-year-old children.

Listening Part 4

1 (18) You are going to hear ten snippets of music. Listen and match each with one of the types of music in the box. Which of these types of music do you enjoy listening to?

classical	disco	folk	jazz	Latin	opera
pop	rock	soul	world		

Exam advice

Before you listen,

- read both tasks, underlining the key ideas in each option.

While you listen,

- listen for words and phrases which mean the same as the key idea you have underlined
- listen for the answers to both tasks. You may hear the answer to Task Two before the answer to Task One.

2 **You will hear five short extracts in which people are talking about an aspect of music which is or has been important to them.**

1 First look at the five photos and discuss with a partner what the people are doing in each one.
2 Read through the ten questions you will have to answer for Tasks One and Two. Can you match the people listed in Task One (**A–H**) with any of the photos you've been discussing?

3 (19) **Now listen to the five speakers and do the two tasks.**

Task One

For questions **1–5**, choose from the list **A–H** the person who is speaking.

A a composer	Speaker 1	**1**
B a festival-goer		
C an orchestra member	Speaker 2	**2**
D a young folk musician		
E a keen listener	Speaker 3	**3**
F a rock musician		
G a jazz trombone player	Speaker 4	**4**
H a novice dancer	Speaker 5	**5**

Task Two

For questions **6–10**, choose from the list **A–H** the feelings or ideas expressed by the speakers.

A an admission of a near addiction	Speaker 1	**6**
B disappointment at a failure		
C planning an ambitious project	Speaker 2	**7**
D gratitude to musicians		
E satisfaction from involvement with music	Speaker 3	**8**
F relief that a project has succeeded	Speaker 4	**9**
G surprise at a new enthusiasm		
H pride in a family tradition	Speaker 5	**10**

4 **Work in pairs.**

1 What do the phrases in *italics* in these extracts from the recordings mean?
   a He sang at *family gatherings* ...
   b ... was in a band that performed at weddings and other *local functions*.
   c I love my iPod and quite frankly *I'd be lost without it*.
   d So at the moment *it's just a dream*.

2 Now finish these sentences with your own ideas.
   a My favourite *family gatherings* are ...
   b *Local functions* I've been to recently include ...
   c *I'd be completely lost without my* ...
   d I'd really like to ... , but at the moment *it's just a dream*.

Vocabulary
Prepositional phrases

❶ Sometimes prepositional phrases have three parts. Look at these examples from the recording.

I've travelled all over the world and played *in front of* audiences of thousands.

As well as having normal tango instruments …

I'll be listening to them *from now on* …

❷ Complete the phrases in these sentences with some of the words from the box.

account	addition	~~aid~~	anticipation	keeping
means	pains	start		

1 Last night's concert was performed **in** ....*aid*............. **of** a charitable trust.
2 These remarkable sounds were produced **by** .... **of** magnetic waves.
3 His grandfather played music very much **in** .... **with** folk traditions.
4 **In** .... **to** reproducing high-quality digital sounds, portable MP3 players can store vast amounts of information.
5 I really didn't like The Killers **to** .... **with** but now actually they've kind of grown on me.

Reading Part 2

Exam advice

- First, read the main body of the text carefully to familiarise yourself with the contents of each paragraph and how the text is structured.
- Then read each of the missing paragraphs one by one. Pay close attention to the content and place each paragraph in a gap after you have read it.

❶ Work in pairs. You are going to read an article about the online virtual world, *Second Life*. Before you read, discuss these questions.

1 What do you know about virtual worlds?
2 Why do you think people create avatars in virtual worlds? (An *avatar* is an image or virtual representation of a person.)

❷ Read the main part of the article (but not the missing paragraphs A–G).

1 What kinds of real-life entertainment are mentioned as being available to *Second Life* 'residents'?
2 How can people whose virtual characters misbehave be punished?

How to get the life you really want

In a loft in New York City the singer Regina Spektor is performing songs from her new album. People wander in, sit down and discuss the music. Everything seems normal. But then so did life for people in the film *The Matrix*.

1

This is *Second Life*, an internet-based virtual world 'inhabited' by ordinary people from all over the world, as well as politicians and other celebrities, and rivalling MySpace for worldwide popularity. By 2007, 20 million people had registered accounts with *Second Life*, with thousands of new members joining every day.

2

These different activities are played out in a sprawling virtual country, with its own simulated cities, streets and open spaces. Participants choose their avatar's identity – potentially changing sex and ethnicity – then guide it wherever they choose: down streets, into nightclubs, gatecrashing weddings. When they meet another avatar, they can start a conversation. And so friendships, love affairs and entire subcultures develop.

3

Second Life, however, is not a game. It is an internet community, where people can flirt, do business, or go off and build their own virtual cities. Women make up 43 per cent of the residents, and the average age

is 32. According to Justin Bovington, 'It's the best combination of social networking, chatrooms and a 3D experience.'

4 _____

Regina Spektor's album was the first virtual record release by a major company. A British radio station 'rented' a tropical island within *Second Life* for a year, where the world's biggest virtual music festival was staged in parallel with a real-life event. While people attended the real concert, the music by Franz Ferdinand, Pink and others was streamed live into *Second Life*, where 6,000 avatars crowded around a virtual stage, hosted by an avatar of a well-known DJ.

5 _____

Second Life is built from user-generated content: its software provides the tools to design a dress, construct a building or carry out a range of other real-world activities. Its population includes a pet manufacturer, a nightclub owner, a car maker, a fashion designer, an architect, a tour guide, and a property speculator. There is a detective agency, which can be hired to check whether your virtual spouse is cheating – such cases are reported to have caused marital rows over whether online cheating counts as real-life cheating.

6 _____

Normal commercial activities such as these are an acceptable part of this virtual world, but Linden Lab, the San Francisco company which launched *Second Life* in 2003, has rules against overtly offensive behaviour in public, such as racial slurs. Its punishment is unique. 'If someone is regularly abusive, we have a prison,' said Vice-president Dave Fleck. 'They are put in a cornfield and made to watch black-and-white public service television announcements from the 1950s in a constant loop.'

Adapted from *The Observer*

❸ **Read the paragraphs that have been removed from the article, and note down a word or phrase that summarises the purpose of each paragraph.**

Example: Paragraph A – *suggested reasons for the appeal of Second Life*

❹ **Now choose from the paragraphs A–G the one which fits each gap in the text. There is one paragraph which you do not need to use.**

A
The chief executive of Rivers Run Red, a branding agency which has helped to shape *Second Life*, continues, 'It's such an immersive experience that people get into it quicker than anything else. We'd been looking for the broadband killer application, and *Second Life* is it.'

B
If any serious 'first life' politicians are considering crossing over into *Second Life*, they may find that they are not the first to take politics seriously. Take avatar Smoke Wijaya, the founder and leader of a virtual communist party which is committed to kicking fascism and racism out of *Second Life*.

C
From these and other services, an entire economy has developed, based around *Second Life's* currency, Linden Dollars. This is not so virtual, as Linden Dollars can be converted into US dollars and back again at fluctuating exchange rates. Just as thousands of people now earn a living from online auction sites, many are doing the same by buying and selling virtual goods and services on *Second Life*. Anshe Chung, the avatar of a Chinese-born language teacher in Germany, has a virtual land development business with holdings worth an estimated £135,000.

D
In a similar way, the premiere of *X-Men 3: The Last Stand* at the Cannes Film Festival was also streamed into *Second Life*. And it has been rumoured that a senior US politician is planning to set up a campaign office within *Second Life*, using a virtual town hall to address voters.

E
Like the world inside the Hollywood hit, the loft is a 3D-computer animation – but in this case it exists only on the Internet. The audience is made up of virtual representations of real people. The real people sit at their computer screens around the world, living their lives through avatars, their screen characters. Regina Spektor and her music are real people selling themselves in a virtual world.

F
Some of these demonstrate their talents in designing virtual buildings or fashions. Some form mutual support groups because in the real world they have a disability. Some run businesses and convert the profits into money in the real world, and some do the same for charity. They do this chatting and trading under an assumed identity – their second life.

G
Virtual worlds, in which relationships like this can flourish, are not new. Games, in which thousands of people play simultaneously, are known in the industry as Massively Multiplayer Online Role-Playing Games. The most popular is a fantasy of swords and sorcery.

Leisure and entertainment 71

5 Work in pairs. What do you think the words and phrases in *italics* from the article mean? What clues did you use to guess the meanings?

1 Participants choose their avatar's identity … then guide it wherever they choose: down streets … *gatecrashing* weddings. And so friendships, love affairs and entire *subcultures* develop.
2 Second Life is built from *user-generated* content.
3 We'd been looking for the broadband *killer* application, …

6 Discuss these questions.

1 If you could build a virtual city, what would it be like? List its main features.
2 Do you think online cheating is the same as real-life cheating?
3 Would you be impressed by a politician who talked to you in a virtual world?

Grammar
Ways of linking ideas

1 These extracts from Reading Part 2 have words or phrases missing. Fill the gaps with the correct missing words and phrases a–e below.

1 .....*e*..... people attended the real concert, the music by Franz Ferdinand, Pink and others was streamed live into *Second Life*.
2 Anshe Chung, ... , has a virtual land development business.
3 The real people sit at their computer screens around the world, ... through avatars, …
4 Virtual worlds, ... , are not new.
5 Linden Lab, ... has rules against overtly offensive behaviour in public.

a in which relationships like this can flourish
b living their lives
c the avatar of a Chinese-born language teacher in Germany
d the San Francisco company which launched *Second Life* in 2003,
e while

2 Choose grammatical descriptions to fit the missing words or phrases a–e above.

- a relative clause
- a participle clause
- a conjunction
- a descriptive noun or noun phrase (sometimes called *apposition*)

▶ page 155 *Grammar reference: Ways of linking ideas*

3 Work in pairs. Find other sentences in the article which link ideas in these ways.

4 Combine the ideas in these short texts using the linking ideas in Exercise 2.

1 The novel *Snow Crash* was written in 1992. The novel foresaw a futuristic virtual world. This world was called the metaverse. In the metaverse, characters controlled digital representations of themselves. These representations were known as avatars.
2 Players can convert their 'play money' into US dollars. To do this, they use their credit card at online currency exchanges.
3 A player's real-world personal reputation may be affected by their virtual representation in the virtual social world. For this reason, they are even more likely to spend real money on their avatars.
4 *Second Life* participants pay 'Linden dollars'. 'Linden dollars' are the game's currency. They use this currency to rent or buy apartments from Chung. Chung is the property developer. They buy apartments so they have a place to build and show off their creations.

Use of English Part 1

Exam advice

First read the whole text quickly to get a general idea of what it is about.

When choosing options, think about the meanings of the options and look for clues in the text including:
- collocations
- dependent prepositions.

Narrow your choice by eliminating options which are obviously incorrect.

1 Work in pairs. Discuss these questions.

1 What is your favourite type of film?
2 What is the best film you've seen in the last twelve months?
3 How is going to the cinema different from watching a film on DVD at home?
4 What do you know about Bollywood films? How are they different from Hollywood films?

2 Quickly read this article about Bollywood films. Does it confirm or contradict any of the ideas you have just discussed?

3 For questions 1–12, read the article again and decide which answer (A, B, C or D) best fits each gap. There is an example at the beginning (0).

The changing face of Bollywood

Bollywood is the informal name (0) ......C..... to popular Mumbai-based Indian films in the Hindi language. Bollywood films are generally musicals and are expected to contain catchy music in the (1) .... of song-and-dance numbers woven into the script. A film's success often depends on the quality of such musical numbers. Indeed, a film's music is often (2) .... before the movie itself as this is an effective way of (3) .... advance publicity.

Indian audiences expect full (4) .... for their money from their films, which must include a famous actor in the (5) .... Songs and dances, romance and daredevil thrills – all are mixed up in a three-hour-long extravaganza with an intermission.

The (6) .... of Bollywood films have tended to be melodramatic. They frequently employ formulaic ingredients such as star-crossed lovers and angry parents, love triangles, family (7) .... , corrupt politicians, kidnappers, long-lost relatives and siblings (8) .... by fate, and convenient coincidences.

There have always been Indian films with more artistic aims and more sophisticated stories, inside and outside the Bollywood tradition, but

these often (9) .... at the box office to movies with more mass (10) .... Bollywood conventions are changing, however. Large Indian (11) .... in many English-speaking countries, and increased Western influence at home, have nudged Bollywood films closer to Hollywood films. Plots now tend to feature westernised urbanites dating and dancing in discos rather than the more traditional (12) .... marriages.

	A		**B**		**C**		**D**
0	assigned		donated		given		conferred
1	way		form		look		shape
2	published		issued		released		emitted
3	growing		generating		constructing		developing
4	worth		value		price		appear
5	crew		staff		team		cast
6	accounts		plots		scenes		plays
7	feuds		wars		hostilities		complaints
8	divided		separated		lost		detached
9	fell		failed		missed out		lost out
10	popularity		appeal		attraction		lure
11	people		residents		populations		inhabitants
12	arranged		organised		planned		set up

Vocabulary
Money verbs

❶ Complete these sentences with the correct 'money verbs' from the box.

buy	earn	hire	~~rent~~	sell (x2)	spend

1 A British radio station ...*rented*... a tropical island within *Second Life* for a year.
2 There is a detective agency, which can be .... to check whether your virtual spouse is cheating …
3 Just as thousands of people now .... a living from online auction sites, many are doing the same by .... and .... virtual goods and services on *Second Life*.
4 Regina Spektor and her music are real people .... themselves in a virtual world.
5 Alayne Wartell met her real-life husband in *Second Life* and now works full-time within it, making a living from the money other characters .... in her virtual shoe and flower shop.

❷ Complete the questions below with some of the verbs in the box, then discuss them in pairs.

afford	borrow	buy	cost	cover	make
pay	raise	~~sell~~	shop		

1 If you went for a job interview, how would you ....*sell*............ yourself?
2 What would you do if you wanted to .... a quick buck?
3 Do you believe that money can .... happiness?
4 When you go shopping, for example for clothes, how do you .... ?
5 Is there anything you can't .... because it .... a fortune?

❸ ⊘ Correct these sentences, which contain errors made by CAE candidates.

1 I'm sure you'll enjoy the job – and don't forget, you'll be ~~gaining~~ good money.   *earning*
2 As you will be using your own car and staying in hotels, the company will afford all your expenses and spend you a daily meal allowance.
3 You can pay your ticket here or on the bus.
4 We went along with hundreds of other people to buy at the market.
5 You can rent all the books you need from the college library – at no cost.
6 Save time and money if you buy more than $200.
7 In the last month we have earned over £2000 for charity – most of it from public donations.

Speaking Part 2

❶ Look at the three photographs and discuss these questions in pairs.

1 Do you know people who regularly spend some of their free time doing these activities? Maybe you do them yourself.
2 What abilities do people need to do these activities successfully?
3 Why do people enjoy doing these things?

❷ (20) You are going to hear two people talking about the photographs.

1 First, read the examiner's instructions.

> Here are your pictures. They show different indoor leisure activities. I'd like you to compare two of the pictures and say what skills and abilities each activity requires and what participants enjoy about each activity.

2 Now listen to two people talking separately about two of these photos.
 a Which two photos are they comparing?
 b Which speaker gives a better response to the instructions? How?
 c What is the problem with the other speaker's response?

3 (21) **Listen carefully to the second speaker again. Complete some of the things she says.**

What does the speaker say:	Finish her answers.
to start her answer?	*I'm going to* ....
to introduce what she says about chess?	*To play chess* ....
to change the subject from chess to cookery?	*As far as* .... , *I think* ....

4 **Work in pairs. Think of some appropriate replacements for the adjectives in *italics* in these phrases from the second speaker's talk.**

1 To play chess you need a very *logical* mind, ...
2 ... you need *endless* patience.
3 Being a successful cook is probably more to do with *creative* instinct than just *practical* skills.
4 Chess players like solving *complex* problems.

Exam advice

It is more important to show that you can speak fluently than to be 'correct' about the content of the photos. This may mean coming up with different interpretations of what you can see. If you change your mind about a previous idea, tell the examiner your new idea.

5 **Now look at another set of three photos and read the examiner's instructions.**

> Here are your pictures. They show places people visit in their leisure time. I'd like you to compare two of the pictures and say what people can see and do at each place and why these places attract so many visitors.

a Continue working with a partner.
  Student A: Work with photos 1 and 2.
  Student B: Choose photo 1 or 2 and photo 3.
  Prepare what you are going to say about your two photos.
b Take turns to speak for one minute about your photos. Try to include some of the phrases the second speaker used to introduce different parts of your answer.
c After your partner has spoken, ask them an extra question related to their photos, for example:
  • Do you think these leisure activities are aimed at particular groups of people?
  • Why do you think certain people would not enjoy these activities?

Writing Part 2 An informal letter

1 **Answer these questions individually. Then compare your answers with a partner.**

1 How often do you write letters (not including emails)?
2 Why would you write a letter rather than an email?
3 Who would you write an informal letter to? And a formal letter?

2 **Read the extracts A–E from five letters. Number them 1–5 according to how formal they are.**
(1 = very informal, 5 = very formal)

1 What is the purpose of the letter each extract is from?
2 What can you deduce about the writers and recipients of each letter?
3 What features of informal language does each extract include?

A

... so am looking for a family of masochists to put me up for a few days. As you seemed sorry we didn't manage to meet up last time I was over, I thought I'd give you first option this time. I'll be around from 7–11 November. Don't worry if it's inconvenient, there are loads of other people I can ask, but it'd be good to see you all.

B

We can now confirm that we have taken 1,490 euros from your credit card account, that being the total cost of your forthcoming vacation. Any agreed deductions for extras, breakages, cleaning, etc. will be debited from your credit card the week following your departure.

C

Secondly, we would like to try to get everyone together before they start their summer break – we're asking all the trainees and course tutors over for a barbecue in Junko's garden on 15 June. It's a Friday evening, so hopefully people shouldn't be going to work or doing anything too serious the next day.

D

Just a short note to thank you for the music on Saturday. Everyone seemed to have an excellent time and we have had some nice emails and notes back. Everyone really liked the dancing as well – I thought it set the evening up very nicely.

E

Please accept my apologies for this. We do make every effort to pack the CDs well and always use the best available courier company. Unfortunately, the CD cases themselves are quite fragile and it only needs one employee in any of the various depots across the country to drop one of the boxes or to throw it into the back of a van and the whole batch can be damaged.

Exam advice

When you write an informal letter, think carefully before you start about the following:

- the purpose of the letter – this will be stated in the question itself
- who the reader will be; what this person will expect to hear from you
- what exactly the question asks you to include in your letter
- how informal the language can be. (This will depend on your relationship with the reader.)

3 **Rewrite these formal expressions from the extracts in more informal English.**

1 We can now confirm that
2 your forthcoming vacation
3 will be debited from your credit card
4 the week following your departure
5 Please accept my apologies for this
6 We do make every effort

▶ page 173 *Writing reference: Letters*

4 **Work in pairs. Read the following writing task, then discuss and list some indoor and outdoor activities in your town that you could suggest in your reply to the letter.**

An Australian penfriend is attending a language course in your town next month. Read this extract from the email your friend has sent you and write a reply making useful suggestions.

My classes are on weekday mornings, so my afternoons and weekends are free. I'd be really grateful if you could suggest how I could spend my free time. I can't rely on good weather, so could you suggest indoor and outdoor activities, please? Don't forget, I'm not keen on any kind of sport!

5 **Discuss the beginning and end of your letter. Which of these ideas would you include at the beginning and which at the end?**

- say you're looking forward to seeing your penfriend
- comment on the fact that your friend is planning to learn your language
- give some general information about your town
- suggest meeting during the friend's stay
- ask about the language course your friend is attending

6 **Write your answer to the task in 220–260 words. Remember to use informal language.**

Unit 8 Don't blame the media

Starting off

1 Work in pairs. How many of the following sources of information do you use regularly?

- local and national newspapers
- local and national radio
- local, national and satellite television
- public and educational libraries
- the Internet
- news bulletins and sports results direct to a mobile phone

2 How has your use of these sources of information changed in recent years? How do you think it will change in the future?

3 Where would you look for information about the following if you did not have access to the Internet?

1 a breaking news story about a serious fire in your local area
2 the result of an important sporting event
3 the economic situation, for example the inflation rate in your country
4 technical information about your computer
5 biographical information about your favourite actor or singer
6 information about the side effects of medicine you are taking
7 today's main national and international news
8 the history of your language
9 the departure and arrival times of flights at an airport

Reading Part 3

1 Discuss these questions in pairs.

1 Which reality TV shows do you watch or have you watched in the past? Which are the best and worst reality TV shows you have seen? Give your reasons.

2 What do you think about reality TV shows in general? Choose **one** of these statements.

a "I don't watch them, but I don't have any moral objections to them."
b "I watch them and I don't have any moral objections to them."
c "I don't watch them because I am worried by the ethics of some shows."
d "I watch them, but the ethics of some shows worry me."
e "I don't know / don't care."

3 Some people object to reality TV for ethical or moral reasons. Why is this? Discuss these ideas:

- the way in which people are chosen for reality TV programmes
- the way contestants are treated on the show
- the way in which programmes are edited
- the short- and long-term effects on contestants of being in the media spotlight.

2 Read the article on the right about the ethics of reality TV quickly, and answer these questions.

1 What is the source of most of the ideas in this article?
2 What general conclusion does the writer come to about TV companies' motives for putting on reality TV shows?
3 Is this text written in British or American English? How do you know?

3 Now read the article. For questions 1–7, choose the answer (A, B, C or D) which you think best fits according to the text.

1 Who did the writer interview for his research into reality television?
   A a random selection of television company employees
   B the production team of a particular reality TV show
   C a number of people who had once worked for him
   D the top executives of a TV network

2 What does the case of the 1997 Swedish reality TV show contestant demonstrate?
   A that reality TV shows should be banned
   B that reality TV show contestants don't like being voted off
   C that contestants should have psychological tests before being accepted
   D that reality TV programmes need tighter control

3 One of the main tasks of the executive producer interviewed was to
   A select compatible contestants for the show.
   B help contestants to cope with rejection by the public.
   C tape and edit the show accurately.
   D advise contestants during the show.

4 According to television network representatives, audiences enjoy
   A shows in which there are personality clashes.
   B a wide variety of personalities involved in the shows.
   C seeing contestants who have consumed too much alcohol.
   D watching a well-directed drama.

5 If a show is not dramatic enough, producers are expected to
   A replace less interesting contestants.
   B provoke tension between contestants.
   C ask contestants to improve their performance.
   D arrange for certain contestants to be voted off.

6 Producers can use technology to show how contestants really feel by
   A showing interviews which have had words removed.
   B showing face-to-face interviews with them.
   C filming them secretly without their knowledge.
   D mixing private conversations with separately filmed material.

7 The writer concludes that the unethical treatment of reality TV contestants is
   A unfortunate but accidental.
   B standard policy of TV networks.
   C a result of the drive for high audience figures.
   D something audiences want to see.

4 Work in pairs.

1 Why do you think reality TV programmes have become so popular in recent years?
2 What effects do you think these programmes can have on participants?

The Ethics of Reality Television Producers
– Richard Crew

After producing television documentaries for 14 years, I closed my production company to begin doctoral studies. One year later, *Survivor* was broadcast. As the 'reality television' fad snowballed, I became curious about the ethical principles producers apply when they create 'reality' television.

I decided to examine 'reality' shows for two reasons. First, I was intrigued by this new generation of programs that fall at the 'fiction' end of a fact/fiction continuum for viewers. And second, several of my former employees have been working on these shows, providing a cooperative and candid sample of reality television production personnel. I interviewed four producers at various levels of reality television production – an executive producer, a field producer, a supervising producer, and a story editor. They were not working on the same reality show when interviewed, so the picture formed here is not representative of a specific show.

My questions were framed by two ethical concerns. First, that non-professional actors be treated in a fair and responsible manner, and second, that program makers present the stories of ordinary people and their experiences in an ethical manner.

Failing to treat non-professional actors fairly can have serious consequences, especially for psychologically unsuited participants. In 1997 the first contestant banished from a Swedish reality show threw himself under a train. Richard Levak, a consulting psychologist, believes that many reality TV shows would not be allowed to take place if they were overseen by the same regulations that guard volunteers' rights in psychological experiments.

This was a priority, however, for the executive producer that I interviewed. An important part of his job was to prepare participants for what would happen to them, as well as to help them deal with the situation if they were voted off the show. Furthermore, he claimed, he makes it very clear to his employees that cast members should be accurately portrayed, both in taping and editing. When I talked with production personnel below the executive producer level, however, I heard a different story.

The supervising producer and the story editor I interviewed both told me that ethical direction had never been given to them by their executive producers. Rather, they were directed to 'create entertaining stories'. According to the supervising producer, this direction comes from the TV networks. Specifically, network representatives insist that reality shows be 'cast' with characters that, when put together, will create conflict. This leads to compelling drama, they say, and the resulting drama should deliver the escape and entertainment that viewers seek. Some ex-reality show participants informed me that producers made alcohol freely available during the tapings, significantly affecting their behavior.

It appears that the 'create entertainment' directives from the networks carry messages that contribute to show producers' ethical behavior. For example, since 'conflict' is a network requirement, producers accordingly cast their shows with a volatile mix of characters. But if the casting doesn't produce the desired conflict and drama, producers know they may have to manipulate the conditions under which the cast members perform. Producers can vary the tasks and games required of show participants to build friction, or they can simply open the bar during recordings.

Also, producers can always heighten drama during the editing process. This 'cheating footage', according to the story editor, is necessary because cast members don't always demonstrate on camera how they really feel. They can, however, usually verbalize their feelings when interviewed one-on-one by producers. So producers can manufacture scenes out of surveillance footage to visually portray the feelings discussed in the interviews.

One of the tools used for 'cheating footage' is an editing technique termed the 'Franken bite'. This is production jargon for 'Frankenstein bite', something which all the producers I interviewed admitted having used. To them, this practice is acceptable if it depicts the character's point of view. A female cast member from a well-known show claimed that she was victimized by this technique, through the creative editing of her words, which were taken from the many different days on which she was taped, and then cut into a single embarrassing scene. The field producer I interviewed was actually present during this taping and confirmed that the event did not happen as shown.

My interviews suggest that ethical standards to protect non-professional cast members' psychological well-being are in place. But since producers are required to make myriads of decisions during the production process, they mostly operate without ethical direction from their superiors. The networks want entertainment on these programs, so the opportunity exists for an individual's ethical standards to be crowded out by pragmatic considerations for audience stimulation and successful ratings. The ultimate portrayal of cast members on a reality show appears to be left to the discretion of different production personnel going about their work to 'create interesting stories.'

Adapted from *Media Ethics*

Vocabulary
'Talking' verbs

1 Students often confuse the different 'talking' verbs. Complete the gaps in this summary with the verbs in the box in the correct form. In some cases more than one answer is possible.

comment	~~discuss~~	say	speak	talk	tell

In this article, Richard Crew (1) ....*discusses*.......... the ethics of reality TV shows. He explains that he (2) .... to an executive producer of reality TV shows, who (3) .... him that adequate ethical guidelines concerning the treatment of participants were in place. However, when Richard (4) .... to those actually making the programmes, they (5) .... that the most important factor in these shows is to produce exciting TV. Richard (6) .... at the end of the article that the ethics are really down to the discretion of people trying to produce 'interesting stories'.

2 ⊙ CAE candidates sometimes make mistakes when using 'talking' verbs. Choose the correct verbs in these sentences.

1 Many people believe that the mass media do not always *say* / (*tell*) the truth.
2 When I'm in China, I can understand what people are *speaking* / *saying* to me, but I can hardly *speak* / *talk* any Chinese myself.
3 This morning's newspaper doesn't even *say* / *mention* the economic crisis.
4 The spokesperson for the authorities *expressed* / *spoke* his thanks for people's understanding.
5 There's an article in my newspaper which *says* / *writes* that people absorb information more quickly from the Internet than from printed material.
6 When asked about the latest rumours, the minister refused to *comment* / *say*.
7 After Ben had used Wikipedia he *said* / *told* everyone how great it was. He didn't *mention* / *tell* the fact that it had taken him an hour to find what he wanted.
8 If you feel strongly about something, you should *express* / *speak* your mind.

Grammar
Transitive verbs

1 It is important to include the object after transitive verbs. Underline the transitive verbs and their objects in these extracts from the text. Verbs may have two objects.

1 The supervising producer and the story editor both told me that their executive producers had never given them ethical direction.
2 Some ex-reality show participants informed me that …

2 ⊙ CAE candidates often miss out objects after transitive verbs, especially in the case of verbs with a complex structure. Correct the mistakes in the sentences below.

1 I can assure that we will do everything to resolve your case as quickly as we can.
   I can assure you that we …
2 I'd be very grateful if you could tell where to look for the information I need.
3 Do you like my new painting? Maria gave to me.
4 We have been taught special techniques that will allow to do well in our exams.
5 I didn't know anyone at Jo's party, so she introduced to some of her friends.
6 I don't know why Helen called a liar. I've always been very honest with her.
7 Your new job starts on Monday, doesn't it? We all wish the best of luck.
8 It's two years since I had a pay rise. I really think my employer should give more money for the work I do.

Listening Part 3

1 You are going to listen to an interview. During the interview you will hear the phrases in *italics* in these questions. Discuss the questions in pairs.

1 When could you watch or listen to a *rolling news programme*?
2 Would an *up-market* newspaper be more likely to be read by people who are rich or poor? (What is the opposite of *up-market*?)
3 If you read an *in-depth analysis* of a news story, would you expect a detailed or a superficial study?
4 If people *lap* something *up*, do they enjoy it or not?
5 How do you think *citizen journalism* differs from traditional journalism?

From the <u>NowPublic.com</u> Environment page

2 🎧 **Now listen to the interview, in which the journalist Harry Cameron talks about how news reporting has developed over the last 50 years. For questions 1–6, choose the answer (A, B, C or D) which fits best according to what you hear.**

1 How did Harry Cameron feel when he started work as a journalist?
  A self-important
  B superior
  C privileged
  D respectable

2 Why, according to Harry, has the purpose of newspapers changed?
  A Other news sources are cheaper than newspapers.
  B People don't have time to read newspapers.
  C People prefer to see filmed news reports.
  D There are other more immediate sources of news.

3 How have the more serious newspapers adapted to the new situation?
  A They concentrate on evaluating news stories.
  B They cover stories about the rich and famous.
  C They accompany news stories with photographs.
  D They keep readers up to date with the latest sports news.

4 What is Harry's view of citizen journalism?
  A He feels sorry for the people involved in it.
  B He resents it for professional reasons.
  C He doesn't consider it to be real journalism.
  D He is broadly in favour of it.

5 Harry believes that internet blogs
  A are not as democratic as newspapers.
  B are likely to be politically biased.
  C are as trustworthy as reports written by professionals.
  D are fundamentally unreliable.

6 According to Harry, what is the most attractive option for a journalist today?
  A becoming a citizen journalist and writing about local issues
  B interpreting and writing about current issues
  C writing a regular blog
  D reporting on celebrity lifestyles

3 **Discuss these questions with a partner.**

1 What is the *genie* and what is the *bottle* in this extract from the radio interview?
  Interviewer: So, this [citizen journalism] is not something you think should be controlled in any way?
  Cameron: Absolutely not! Anyway, you couldn't control it even if you wanted to. The *genie's* out of the *bottle*.

2 What other modern situations could this expression be used to describe?

Grammar
Reported speech

❶ The following are reports of what was said during the radio interview. What were the speakers' actual words?

1 Harry said his main memory of those far-off days was the sense of pride he had felt …
  My main memory of those far-off days is …

2 He said he thought they did that very well.

3 The interviewer asked if that [citizen journalism] was a term he was familiar with.

4 Harry replied that it was something he had some sympathy with.

5 The interviewer asked how reliable bloggers and citizen journalists were as sources of information.

6 Harry said that if he were starting out again now, that was the kind of journalism he would get into.

❷ ⟨3⟩ Now listen to parts of the recording again and check your answers.

❸ Work in pairs. What features of reported speech can you find in the sentences in Exercise 1?

❹ What is the difference in meaning between these two reported speech sentences?

a He said he'd written an article which was going to be in the paper the following day.

b He said he'd written an article which is going to be in the paper tomorrow.

▶ Page 156 *Grammar reference: Reported speech*

❺ ⟨4⟩ Work in pairs. You are going to listen to a conversation between Ben and Tom.

Student A: Listen and note down what Tom says about Namibia.

Student B: Listen and note down what Ben finds out from Tom.

❻ Write your notes of what Ben and Tom said, using reported speech. Include some of the verbs in the box. Then compare your sentences with your partner.

> ask   explain   maintain   reply   tell   want to know
> wonder

Example: *Ben asked Tom if he knew anything about Wikipedia.*

Use of English Part 3

❶ Work in pairs. Add prefixes to these adjectives to make them negative.

1 ……*in*..accurate   2 …………important   3 …………legal
4 …………possible   5 …………regular   6 …………tolerant

Now change each negative adjective into a noun.

I *inaccurate – inaccuracy*

❷ Add prefixes to these verbs so that they have the meanings given.

1	appear	become invisible	*disappear*
2	claim	claim back	
3	inform	give the wrong information	
4	judge	in advance	
5	react	react more than is necessary	
6	stabilise	to make something unstable	
7	state	describe something to make it less important	

Now make your answers into nouns.

I *disappear – disappearance*

❸ Add prefixes to these nouns so that they have the meanings given.

1	biography	when a person writes about him/herself	*autobiography*
2	owner	a joint owner	
3	politician	someone who was a politician in the past	
4	trust	feeling of being unable to trust someone	
5	circle	half a circle	

Now make your answers into adjectives. (One noun does not have a related adjective.)

I *autobiography – autobiographical*

AUTOBIOGRAPHIES
WRITE YOUR NAME HERE!
My life

4 **Look back at the Reading text on page 79 and find the following words.**

1 nouns related to these verbs: *consider, contest, direct, employ, entertain, produce* (x 2), *view*
2 adjectives related to these verbs: *accept, cooperate, create, represent, succeed*
3 adjectives related to these nouns: *doctor, ethics*
4 verbs related to these nouns: *height, verb, victim*

5 **Read this letter to a newspaper about media attitudes to the truth, and try to answer these questions. (Don't try to fill the gaps yet.)**

1 Does the letter writer think that television is basically honest or not at the moment?
2 Who does he blame for the current situation?

6 **Read the text again. For questions 1–10 use the word given in capitals at the end of some of the lines to form a word that fits in the gap in the same line. There is an example at the beginning (0).**

Exam advice

Read the whole text quickly first.

When looking at the gaps, decide:

- what type of word you need (noun, adjective, etc.)
- if the word needs a negative prefix (*un-*, *in-*, etc.)
- if it's a noun, should it be plural?
- if it's a verb, is it in the correct form (*-ed*, *-ing*, etc.)?

Broadcasters must find ways to regain public trust

The current problems over the truth and (0) ....honesty.......... of television programmes are symptomatic of a deep (1) .... malaise over how such values are judged. In universities, several generations of students in media, cultural studies and even (2) .... have been taught the theory that there is no such thing as truth or (3) .... in television products. These are all merely a (4) ...., a 'spectacle', produced for audiences who decode and consume them according to their own tastes and pleasures. There is little (5) .... between an episode of a hospital drama and the main evening news bulletin. We have argued against this approach to understanding media. Yet the depth of the problem for the TV companies is (6) .... in that there are now even voices calling for the (7) .... of the traditional principle of (8) .... – because it is thought impossible to give an accurate and fair account of a range of positions in a political (9) .... TV companies should understand that principles such as balance and fairness are crucial to the (10) .... of public trust.

HONEST
INTELLECT

JOURNAL
ACCURATE

CONSTRUCT

DIFFER

APPEAR
ABANDON
PARTIAL

ARGUE

MAINTAIN

Adapted from *The Guardian*

7 **Discuss these questions in pairs.**

1 Do you agree with the view that, from the audience's perspective, there may be *little difference between a hospital drama and a news bulletin*?
2 How far do you trust TV networks in your country to tell you the truth?

Speaking Part 3

1 **Look at the six photographs and discuss these questions briefly.**

1 How much do you think **you** are affected by each of these influences illustrated?
2 Which two would you find it difficult or impossible to live without?
3 Which one could you happily live without? Why?

2 **You are going to hear two people discussing these photos. First, read the examiner's instructions.**

> Here are some pictures showing some of the powerful influences which have an impact on our daily lives. First, talk to each other about how each of these influences affect people today. Then decide which has the most powerful influence on the greatest number of people.

3 🔊 **As you listen to the conversation, think about these questions.**

1 Do the speakers answer both parts of the question equally well?
2 Do they spend too much or too little time talking about any of the photos?
3 Do the two speakers participate equally in the conversation?

4 🔊 **Listen again. Which of these examples of imprecise language do the speakers use? (Imprecise language is used when being accurate is impossible, unnecessary, over-formal or too direct.)**

- *some kind, sort of, stuff, things like that*
- *about, two or three, a bit, several, (quite) a few, (quite) a lot, lots*
- *nearly, fairly, pretty, quite, almost, probably*
- the suffix *-ish*: *-ish* can be added to words to make them less precise, e.g. *green → greenish* (a shade somewhere between blue and green or grey and green), *thirty → thirtyish* (about 30, between 27 and 33).

Exam advice

The opinions and ideas you and your partner express in this part of the Speaking exam are less important than your ability to demonstrate good communication skills. This involves the following:

- Keeping the conversation going. Try to avoid long pauses.
- Effective turn-taking. The examiner will want to see that you allow your partner time to speak, if necessary inviting their opinions.
- Listening and responding to what your partner says, rather than simply saying what you think.

5 **Work in pairs. Answer the question that the two speakers on the recording answered. Remember the following points.**

- Allow enough time to answer both parts of the question fully.
- Make sure each of you speaks for roughly the same length of time.
- Use imprecise words and phrases from the list above where appropriate.

Writing Part 1 A proposal

Exam advice

In Writing Part 1, you may be asked to write a proposal. This is something written for a superior, e.g. a boss or a teacher, or for a peer group, e.g. club members or work colleagues.

You will be expected to make suggestions supported by factual information to persuade a reader of a course of action.

A proposal should be clearly organised and may include headings.

1 Work in pairs. Read this Part 1 writing task. How would you propose using the four 30-minute programmes about your area?

> A national radio station is planning a series of documentaries about aspects of your region and is asking for proposals from interested listeners.
>
> Read the advertisement that appeared in a local newspaper and the notes you made when you read it. Then write your **proposal** for the series of programmes. Write 180–220 words.

WANTED — IDEAS — NOW!

Radio PDX is planning a series of four 30-minute programmes about aspects of your region. We're looking for ideas. Programmes must:

- be up to date and informative.
- be of interest to adults of all ages.
- include the voices of local people.

If you have ideas, send in your proposal as soon as possible. You could win a cash prize.

RADIO PDX

YOUR LOCAL STATION

YOUR NEWS

Everyday life from different points of view e.g.
- *student*
- *family of 4*
- *tourist information officer*

2 Read this sample answer to the task and discuss:

1 Has the writer followed the instructions fully?
2 How could he/she have sounded more persuasive? (Look at the use of modal verbs.)
3 Is the style sufficiently formal?

If you ask me, Radio PDX's plan for a series of programmes on our region will be warmly welcomed by listeners. I suggest that the programmes look at the region today from the points of view of different groups of people.

A family

The first programme might focus on an 'ordinary' family – a couple with children. This would highlight aspects of everyday life with which many listeners would identify: school, getting about, shopping, leisure activities could all be covered.

Students

This programme could provide the perspective of young people who have grown up in our region. Participants would talk about the pros and cons of living here and say whether they intended to stay or move away after their studies.

Tourist information officer

A programme centred on the local tourist information office would inform listeners about historical and cultural features of the region – and events. Anyone listening on the Internet might be persuaded to visit the region.

These programme suggestions would probably be of interest to people in our region and beyond. If successful, they could well mark the beginning of a regular magazine programme.

▶ page 170 *Writing reference: Proposals*

3 Now read this writing task and write your proposal, using some of the ideas from the notes.

> A national TV channel is planning a series of documentaries about unusual hobbies and is looking for people to feature in the programmes. Read the Internet and the notes you made in response to it. Then write your **proposal** for the series. Write 180–220 words.

Do you or does anyone you know have an unusual hobby?

Perhaps you collect chewing gum wrappers or enjoy playing the bagpipes ...

Whatever it is, we want to know about it for a new series of programmes we're making about unusual hobbies.

Why not send us some suggestions for a pilot series of four programmes?

Great idea! Popular with all types of people.

Hobbies need to be visually interesting.

My hobbies?? – Tango dancing / Collecting fossils???

Friends' hobbies – Mushroom growing / Photography

Unit 7 *Vocabulary and grammar review*

Vocabulary

1 Complete these sentences with the correct 'money verbs' from the box.

| ~~afford~~ | buy | cost | earn | hire | make | pay |
| rent | sell | spend | | | | |

1 I'd love to own a sports car, but at the moment I can't ....*afford*............ one.
2 I'll be working in Cairo for two years. Hopefully, we'll .... a flat near the city centre. If we decide to stay longer, maybe we'll .... a house of our own.
3 My brother works in a fast-food restaurant. He only .... £120 a week.
4 I've decided to .... my motorbike and get a car.
5 Last Sunday afternoon we .... bikes and cycled round the lake.
6 Do you know what police officers .... when they finish their training?
7 Those jeans .... a fortune, but it's really the designer label you're .... for.
8 It's amazing how much people .... on birthday presents for their boyfriends or girlfriends.

2 Think of one word which can be used appropriately in all three sentences.

1 My football team was on top .... at the weekend. They won 3-0.
   The application .... was so complicated that it took me over an hour to fill it in.
   As with any .... of exercise, it's important to start slowly and build up gradually.

2 My grandmother took the .... that children should help with the housework.
   There's a fantastic .... of the surrounding countryside from the top of the castle.
   In .... of what she said, I think it would be best to rethink our holiday plans.

3 The eastern part of the country is very .... There are hardly any hills.
   After such an exciting holiday, everyday life seems very .... now.
   Everyone pays the same for driving lessons. We charge a .... rate of £30 per lesson.

3 Find ten different kinds of music in this wordsearch.

O	O	D	K	W	P	O	P	C
U	F	O	L	K	E	R	S	L
T	L	C	H	E	S	O	F	A
B	A	E	Y	E	I	C	O	S
R	T	A	O	B	C	K	P	S
J	I	S	O	U	L	U	E	I
A	N	E	E	C	A	R	R	C
Z	W	O	R	L	D	E	A	A
Z	D	I	S	C	O	M	L	L

Grammar

4 Combine these sets of sentences from film reviews using one of these ways of linking in each case.

- relative clauses
- conjunctions
- participle clauses
- apposition

1 *Libero*
   A boy tries to understand his family. He tries to stop it from breaking apart. At the same time he has to deal with his mother's absence. He finds all this very difficult. The boy is only eleven years old.
   While dealing with his mother's absence, an eleven-year-old boy tries to understand his family ...

2 *Be kind rewind*
   A man unintentionally destroys every tape in a video store. The man's name is Black. His brain becomes magnetised. The store is owned by Black's best friend. Black and his friend feel sorry for the store's most loyal customer. This customer is an elderly woman. She is losing her memory. The two men set out to remake the lost films. These films include *The Lion King* and *Robocop*.

3 *I am Legend*
   A military scientist is left completely alone in New York. The city is deserted. A virus has wiped out the human race. The scientist is played by Will Smith. The film is based on a sci-fi novel by Richard Matheson.

Unit 8 *Vocabulary and grammar review*

Vocabulary

① Complete these words to match the dictionary definitions.

1 ex-*politician*................. (n) someone who used to work in politics.
2 mis.......................... (v) have doubts about someone's honesty
3 il........................... (adj) against the law
4 dis.......................... (v) become invisible
5 auto......................... (n) story of a person's life written by the person him/herself
6 re........................... (n) the act of claiming something back
7 pre.......................... (v) have an opinion before knowing all the facts
8 de........................... (v) make unstable

② Complete the gaps related to these words.

1 ethics (n)   adjective ....*ethical*...........
2 entertain (v)   noun ....
                     adjective ....
3 cooperate (v)   noun ....
                     adjective ....
4 production (n)   verb ....
                     adjective ....
5 consider (v)   noun ....
                     adjective ....
6 creative (adj)   verb ....
                     noun ....

Grammar

③ Rewrite the following quotes in reported speech.

1 'You mustn't tell anyone what you've seen.' (Roland to Joanna)
   Roland told Joanna that she mustn't/wasn't to tell anyone what she'd seen.
2 'It was a real surprise seeing Tom last week. I hadn't seen him since we were at school together.' (Clare)
3 'Shall I do the shopping this week?' (Ben to Jerry)
4 'You should have told me what you were planning to do. I could have helped you.' (Becky to Jamie)
5 'You must stop smoking if you want to get rid of your cough.' (Doctor to me)
6 'If anyone asks for me, I'll be working from home this Friday.' (Nick on the Monday before)
7 'How many languages can you speak?' (Bogdan to me)

④ Rewrite the following as direct quotes.

1 The police officer wanted to know what I was doing out so late.
   'What are you doing out so late?'
2 She asked if I had any plans for the following evening.
3 My doctor advised me to eat regular meals and do more exercise.
4 I said that was the worst programme I'd ever seen.
5 I promised I'd phone her as soon as I got home.
6 Jerry said he hoped he'd be going there the following day.

⑤ Complete each second sentence so that it has a similar meaning to the first sentence, using the word given. Don't change this word. Use between three and six words, including the word given.

1 'I'll never do that again.' (Maria)
   PROMISED
   Maria .*promised never to*. do that again.
2 'I think you should apply for this job.' (Alexei to me)
   ADVISED
   Alexei .... job.
3 'Have you ever thought of starting your own business?' (Simon to me)
   ASKED
   Simon ....
   ever thought of starting my own business.
4 'Let's meet tomorrow.' (Svetlana)
   SUGGESTED
   Svetlana .... day.
5 'Don't drink if you're driving.' (police officer to the motorist)
   WARNED
   The police officer ....
   if he was driving.
6 'We're getting married in May.' (Tom and Alexis)
   ANNOUNCED
   Tom and Alexis .... in May.

Unit 9 At top speed

Starting off

Work in pairs. Discuss these questions.

1   Each of these photos shows a situation where speed is important. Why is speed important in each case?
2   When is it important not to hurry? If you had to choose photos of five situations where it's important not to hurry, which would you choose?
3   Do you enjoy speed? Why (not)?

Listening Part 1

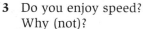 **Work in pairs. You will hear three extracts where people talk about speed. Extract One is about trains in the 19th century. Before you listen: how do you think the invention of trains changed the way people lived?**

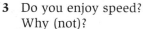 **Now listen to Extract One. For questions 1 and 2 choose the answer (A, B or C) which fits best according to what you hear.**

Exam advice

*   Read both questions carefully, underlining the main ideas before you listen.
*   Listen to the whole piece before choosing your answer.
*   Listen carefully the second time to check your answer.

Extract One

You will hear part of an interview with a historian called Tom Melton.

1   What concerns did people in the early 19th century have about the effects of rail travel?
    A   its impact on the landscape
    B   its effect on the human body
    C   its threat to wildlife

2   How did railway travel affect people's attitude to the natural world?
    A   They believed that they had the power to change it.
    B   They understood their need to be part of it.
    C   They became more interested in painting it.

3 **Work in pairs to discuss the question.**

Tom says 'I doubt if any other invention has had such a profound influence on the human psyche.' Do you agree?

4 **In Extract Two you will hear a man and a woman discussing the limits to human ability in Olympic sports. Before you listen: do you think athletes will continue to break records or is there a limit to their improvement?**

5 **7** **Now listen to Extract Two. For questions 3 and 4 choose the answer (A, B or C) which fits best according to what you hear.**

Extract Two

You will hear two people discussing the future of Olympic sports.

3 What does the man say about Olympic records in the future?
   A They will only represent slight improvements on previous performances.
   B They will become increasingly frequent as athletes improve.
   C They will attract less attention from the news media.

4 What do the two speakers agree about?
   A the effect of professionalism on sporting achievement
   B the need for more specialised sports equipment
   C the prospects for genetic engineering in sports

6 **Work in small groups.**

Do you think people should devote so much effort to breaking world records? Why (not)?

7 **In Extract Three you will hear a scientist talking about travelling in spaceships to other stars. Before you listen:**

- would you like to go on a journey like this?
- what problems do you think this sort of journey would pose for the spaceship's crew?

8 **8** **Now listen to Extract Three. For questions 5 and 6 choose the answer (A, B or C) which fits best according to what you hear.**

Extract Three

You will hear an interview with a space scientist, Dr Ananda Desai, talking about travelling to other stars.

5 What does she say is the main problem of using nuclear propulsion for spaceships?
   A the danger
   B an international agreement
   C the technology

6 How does she feel about the possibility of using a generational spaceship?
   A Few people will want to travel in it.
   B Conflicts may arise amongst the crew.
   C It will be difficult to determine a destination.

9 **Work in pairs. Discuss this question.**

Many people think that money spent on space exploration is money wasted. Do you agree?

Reading Part 2

1 **Work in pairs. You are going to read an article about a very fast car. Before you read:**

1 What things do/would you consider when deciding to buy a car?
2 Some people think manufacturers should limit the speed and power of cars. What do you think?

2 **Six paragraphs have been removed from the article below. Read the article (but not the paragraphs which have been removed) and:**

- note down in a few words what each paragraph in the article is about (see page 19).
- <u>underline</u> any words and phrases that link the text together, which will help you to place the missing paragraphs when you read them. (See Exam advice on page 91).

Bugatti Veyron
by Jeremy Clarkson

Utterly, stunningly, jaw-droppingly brilliant

When you push a car past 300kph, the world actually becomes blurred, like an early Queen pop video. The speed causes a terrifying vibration that rattles your optic nerves, causing double vision. This is not good when you're covering 90 metres a second. Happily, stopping distances become irrelevant because you won't see the obstacle in the first place. By the time you know it was there, you'll have gone through the windscreen.

> **1**

<u>But once you go past 320kph, the biggest problem is the air</u>. At 160kph it's relaxed. At 240kph it's a breeze. But at 320kph it has sufficient power to lift a jumbo jet off the ground. So getting a car to behave itself in conditions like these is tough.

> **2**

You might point out at this juncture that the McLaren Formula One car can top 390kph, but at that speed it is pretty much out of control. And anyway the Bugatti is way, way faster than anything else the roads have seen, but when you look at the history of its development you'll discover it's rather more than just a car.

> **3**

His engineers were horrified. But they set to work anyway, mating two Audi V8s to create an 8-litre W16 engine with four turbochargers. Needless to say, the end result produced about as much power as the Earth's core, which is fine. Then things got tricky because the power had to be harnessed.

> **4**

When this had been done, the Veyron was shipped to Sauber's F1 wind tunnel where it quickly became apparent that while the magic 1000bhp* figure had been achieved, they were miles off the target top speed of 400kph. The body of the car just wasn't aerodynamic enough. The bods at Sauber threw up their hands, saying they only had experience of aerodynamics up to maybe 360kph, which is the effective top speed in Formula One. Beyond this point Bugatti was on its own.

> **5**

After some public failures, fires and accidents, they hit on the idea of a car that automatically changes shape depending on what speed you're going. And that means you can top 400kph. That's 113m a second.

> **6**

I didn't care. On a recent drive across Europe I desperately wanted to reach the top speed but I ran out of road when the needle hit 386kph. Where, astonishingly, it felt totally and utterly rock steady. It felt sublime. From behind the wheel of a Veyron, France is the size of a small coconut. I cannot tell you how good this car is. I just don't have the vocabulary.

From *The Times*

* Brake horsepower – a measure of the power of a vehicle's engine

Exam advice

Pay attention to words and phrases that link the text together, for example:

- pronouns, e.g. *he* – who does *he* refer to?
- adverbs, e.g. *However* – this will introduce a contrast to something in the previous sentence.
- ideas repeated using synonyms, e.g. one sentence says *It created a number of problems.* The following sentence says *The main difficulty was* …

D It all started when Ferdinand Piëch, the former boss of Volkswagen, bought Bugatti and had someone design a concept car. 'This,' he said, 'is what the next Bugatti will look like. And it will have an engine that develops 1000 horsepower and it will be capable of 400kph.'

3 **Choose from the paragraphs A–G the one which fits each gap (1–6). There is one extra paragraph which you do not need to use.**

E Somehow they had to find an extra 30kph, but each extra 1kph increase in speed requires an extra 8bhp from the power plant. An extra 30kph then would need an extra 240bhp. That was not possible.

A At those speeds the front of the car starts to lift. As a result you start to lose your steering, so you can't even steer round whatever it is you can't see because of the vibrations. Make no mistake, 320kph is at the limit of what man can do right now. Which is why the new Bugatti Veyron is special. Because it can do 406kph.

F This car cannot be judged in the same way that we judge other cars. It meets noise and emission regulations and it can be driven by someone whose only qualification is an ability to reverse round corners and do an emergency stop. So technically it is a car. And yet it just isn't.

B For this, Volkswagen went to Ricardo, a British company that makes gearboxes for various Formula One teams. 'It was hard,' said one of the engineers. 'The gearbox in an F1 car only has to last a few hours, but the Veyron's has to last 10 or 20 years.'

G You might want to ponder that for a moment. Covering the length of a football pitch, in a second, in a car. If you stamp on the middle pedal hard, you will pull up from 400kph in just 10 sec. Sounds good, but in those 10 sec you'll have covered a third of a mile. That's five football pitches to stop.

C It has always been thus. When Louis Rigolly broke the 160kph barrier in 1904, the vibration would have been terrifying. And I dare say that driving a Jaguar E-type at 240kph in 1966 must have been a bit sporty as well.

4 **Work in pairs.**

1 Would you like to drive a car like this? Why (not)?
2 Do you enjoy danger and risk? Why (not)?

Grammar
Tenses in time clauses and time adverbials

1 **Work in pairs. Read these sentences from Reading Part 2 and look at the verbs in *italics*. In some sentences, both alternatives are correct but in others only one is correct.**

- Circle the alternatives in each sentence. Where both are correct, is there a difference in meaning?
- Which alternative was used in Reading Part 2?

1 When you (push) / (have pushed) a car past 300kph, the world actually becomes blurred …
   Both are correct, but 'When you push …' says these things happen at the same time whereas 'When you've pushed …' says that the world becomes blurred afterwards.
   The article uses push.

2 The speed causes a terrifying vibration. … This is not good when *you're covering / you cover* 90 metres a second.

3 When you *look / will look* at the history of its development you'll discover it's rather more than just a car.

4 When this *was done / had been done*, the Veyron was shipped to Sauber's F1 wind tunnel …

5 When Louis Rigolly *broke / had broken* the 160kph barrier in 1904, the vibration would have been terrifying.

6 It all started when Ferdinand Piëch, the former boss of Volkswagen, *bought / had bought* Bugatti …

▶ page 157 *Grammar reference: Tenses in time clauses and time adverbials*

2 **Put the verbs in brackets into the correct tense, active or passive.**

1 When Fayed ....retires............ (retire) next year, he'll have been working for this company for forty years.

2 We felt very frustrated because the project was cancelled when we .... (work) on it for almost three years.

3 In many countries it's illegal to answer your mobile phone while you .... (drive).

4 Lots of my friends .... (wait) for me when I got back from my trip.

5 I won't take my driving test until I .... (be) sure I can pass.

6 She offered the book to several publishers before it .... (accept).

3 **⊙ CAE candidates often confuse *when, while, during* and *meanwhile* in time adverbials. Write the correct word in the spaces in the sentences below. (In some cases more than one answer is possible.)**

1 Thanks to this course, I now feel much more confident ....*when*............ I am speaking with our foreign customers.

2 It's a pity to visit the castle for only an hour .... the journey there takes three hours.

3 It's essential that you are involved in the project at every stage: .... negotiations, reaching agreements and signing contracts. You should also be present .... the equipment is delivered and installed.

4 Course participants will be able to get to know each other .... they're being given a guided tour of the town on the first day.

5 It's really hard to drive in a strange city. You have to find your way around in heavy traffic and find somewhere to park. ...., you're struggling with the controls of a rented car which you've never driven before – what a nightmare!

▶ page 158 *Grammar reference: Time adverbials*

4 **⊙ CAE candidates often make mistakes with prepositions in time expressions. Eight of the following sentences contain mistakes. Two of the sentences are correct. Correct the mistakes.**

1 Mariano likes to watch football ~~at~~ Friday night, but he doesn't often get the chance. *on*

2 Could you give us some advice about where to go or what to do at the evening?

3 I was able to visit the United States for the first time of my life.

4 I would recommend going on that tour in the beginning of summer.

5 The other event of May was a swimming gala.

6 There were some problems at the beginning of the strike.

7 They've met in many occasions but they've never become friends.

8 Unfortunately, we are overloaded with printing jobs in busy times of the day, so you cannot count on your order being dealt with immediately.

9 We have some suggestions about what to do if the weather is bad in the day of the boat trip.

10 You'll have to sit an exam at the end of this course.

▶ page 158 *Grammar reference: Prepositions in time expressions*

Vocabulary

Action, activity, event and *programme*

1 ⊙ **CAE candidates often confuse *action, activity, event* and *programme*. Each word has two or three meanings. Match the four words with their definitions (a–k) from *CALD*.**

1 action   2 activity   3 event   4 programme

a   a broadcast on television or radio   *programme*

b   anything that happens, especially something important or unusual

c   the process of doing something, especially when dealing with a problem or difficulty

d   when a lot of things are happening or people are moving around

e   a physical movement

f   a plan of activities to be done or things to be achieved

g   a thin book or piece of paper giving information about a play or musical or sports event, usually bought at the theatre or place where the event happens

h   one of a set of races or competitions

i   something that is done for enjoyment, especially an organised event

j   something that you do

k   the work of a group or organisation to achieve an aim

2 **Complete these sentences from Listening Part 1 with *action, event, programme* or *activity* in the correct form in each gap. Then decide which definition (a–k) from Exercise 1 corresponds with the word in each sentence.**

1 They began to think they could dominate the natural world by their .... (Extract One)
2 Will there ever come a time when athletes at Olympic .... just aren't breaking records any more? (Extract Two)
3 Building such a craft is certainly not on anyone's space .... yet. (Extract Three)
4 What .... would the crew find to do during all this time? (Extract Three)

3 **For questions 1–12, write *action, event, programme* or *activity* in each gap. Most of the sentences are from *CALD*.**

1 After weeks of frenetic .... *activity* .... , the job was finally finished.
2 I looked in the .... to find out the actor's name.
3 It only needs a small wrist .... to start the process.
4 Our special guest on the .... tonight is Robert de Niro.
5 She wrote a strong letter to the paper complaining about the council's .... in closing the town centre to traffic during the festival.
6 Susannah's party was the social .... of the year.

7 Tennis is a very relaxing spare-time ....
8 The school offers an exciting and varied .... of social events.
9 The women's 200-metre .... will be followed by the men's 100 metres.
10 There was a sudden flurry of .... when the director walked in.
11 This problem calls for swift .... from the government.
12 We had expected to arrive an hour late, but in the .... we were early.

4 **Look back at Exercise 3 and note any collocations you can find with *action, event, programme* or *activity*, for example, *frenetic activity*.**

Use of English Part 4

1 Look at the groups of three sentences below. What sort of word is needed to complete each group (noun, verb, adjective or adverb)?

1 This car .... noise and emissions regulations, so it's completely legal.
Our social club .... every Thursday evening at seven o'clock.
Olga .... the bus every afternoon to pick up her children on their way back from school.

2 Few people have such a .... influence on children's characters as their teachers.
You have to have a .... personality to go into politics.
I like my tea .... and with plenty of sugar.

3 People looked at the world in a different .... after the advent of the train.
Could you pick up a loaf of bread on the .... home?
Unfortunately, a lot of people got in the .... so I didn't see the end of the race.

4 Thousands of tourists found themselves trapped in the country when the war .... out.
Bob Beamon .... the record really spectacularly at the 1968 Olympics.
When the president .... his election promises, no one was surprised.

5 The result of the race was very .... although Karen managed to win.
The company has been keeping its plans for the new car a very .... secret.
Marta and Juan have been married for years and have a very .... relationship.

2 Now, for questions 1–5 above, think of one word only which can be used appropriately in all three sentences.

Exam advice

- Read all three sentences and decide what type of word you need (noun, adjective, etc.).
- Decide what meaning might be required for each gap (you're looking for the same word, but with a different meaning or collocation in each sentence).
- Think of possible words which could fit in each sentence. Try these words in the other sentences until you find one which fits in all three.

Speaking Part 2

1 Work in pairs. Look at the pictures below and the examiner's instructions.

1 Which pictures would you choose to talk about?
2 What could you say about each of them?

> Here are your pictures. They show people using different machines or devices. I'd like you to compare two of the pictures and say how the machines or devices help the people to do their work faster.

Set A

- How do the machines and devices help these people to do their work faster?

2 Change partners. Take turns to do the task above.

3 🔊 **Listen to Ana, a student, doing the same speaking task. Which of these does she do?**

1 Although she's not sure, she guesses what the policewoman's device is. *yes*
2 She explains what the device is and what it can be used for.
3 She suggests just one way in which the policewoman could be using the device.
4 She knows exactly what to call the man in the second picture.
5 She corrects herself when she realises she hasn't used the best word for something.
6 She tries to use phrases she's not sure about in order to express herself more clearly.
7 She only answers the first part of the task.

4 🔊 **Complete each of these phrases by writing two words in each space. Then check your answers by listening again.**

1 … using what I think _____*must be*_____ a pda …
2 You know, one _____ hand-held devices which you can use when you want to …
3 The other picture shows, _____ you call the person, a cowboy or a shepherd, I'm not sure …
4 He's moving his herd, _____ his flock of sheep.
5 … because she can do it in, _____ the word, in real time.

5 **In which sentence(s) in Exercise 4 does Ana**

1 correct herself?
2 explain what she's talking about?
3 say she's guessing what something is?
4 say she's not sure what the correct word is?

6 **Work in pairs.**

🔊 **Student A:** Look at the pictures in Set A again, listen to the examiner's instructions and do the speaking task.

🔊 **Student B:** When Student A has finished, look at the pictures in Set B, listen to the examiner's instructions and do the speaking task.

Exam advice

- If you notice you've made a mistake, correct it – don't pretend it hasn't happened!
- Be ready to speculate or guess about what the photos show.
- If you don't know a word, don't avoid the problem. Explain the idea using other words.

Set B

Writing Part 2 An essay

1 **Work in pairs. Read the writing task below and say whether the following statements are true (T) or false (F).**

> During a recent class discussion, one student expressed the following opinion:
>
> *Technological progress makes us live faster, but it also means we have less time for the important things in life, such as relationships.*
>
> Your teacher has asked you to write an **essay** on the subject, saying how far you agree with the statement.

1 An essay is a piece of academic writing done by students. T
2 This essay will be read by the teacher of the class.
3 You can write in an informal style.
4 You should make your opinions on the subject clear.
5 It's not necessary to give reasons for your opinions or include examples.
6 There are at least two ideas you must deal with in the writing task above.

2 Work in small groups. Discuss these questions and note down your opinions and ideas while you are discussing.

1 In what ways does technological progress make us live faster? Think of examples.
2 Do you agree that we have less time for the important things in life, such as relationships? Why (not)?
3 Are there any important things that we have more time for?

3 Work in pairs.

1 Read the essay below without paying attention to the gaps. Which ideas and examples were also mentioned during your discussion?
2 Do you agree with the writer's conclusions? Why (not)?

Technological progress

A Many people worry that we no longer have time for the important things in life, such as relationships and thinking about ourselves and our place in the universe. This may be true (1) ...to some extent... but I think in broad terms that the argument is flawed.

B In my great-grandparents' time technology was slower than it is at present, or non-existent. People travelled to work on foot or by train and may perhaps have had time to think about things while they were travelling. They did not have the distractions of television or all the other technological marvels which compete for our attention today. (2) ...., they probably spent more time together in conversation.

C (3) ...., I doubt if their relationships or the quality of their lives were really better. (4) ...., they had to work much longer hours both in their jobs and in routine household tasks because labour-saving technological devices did not exist. (5) ...., they did not have the financial resources or the technology to enjoy their leisure time like we do now. While they were perhaps not so stressed, (6) ...., they could not learn, travel and relate to people from all over the world with the ease that we do.

D (7) ...., I do not agree that we have less time for the important things in life. (8) ...., I believe we have far greater opportunities to take advantage of the enormous variety of good things life has to offer.

4 Complete the essay by writing a phrase from the box in each of the gaps.

as a result	however	in conclusion	~~to some extent~~
what is more	in contrast	to ourselves	in general
on the contrary			

5 Work in pairs. Which paragraph (A–D):

1 explains in what ways the statement is not true?
2 explains to what extent the statement is true?
3 summarises the writer's argument?
4 tells us what point of view the writer is going to argue?

▶ page 166 *Writing reference: Essays*

6 Work in pairs. Look at the writing task below. How far do you agree with the statement? Note down your ideas and opinions.

During a recent class discussion your teacher made the following statement:

Modern technologies have given us access to vast amounts of information. However, in general we use information for entertainment, not for practical purposes.

Your teacher has now asked you to write an essay on the subject, saying how far you agree with the statement.

Write your **essay** in 220–260 words in an appropriate style.

7 Work in pairs. Write a plan for the essay with a similar structure to the sample essay in Exercise 3 above. Note down the ideas and opinions you will express in each paragraph.

8 Work alone and write your essay.

Exam advice

• When you write an essay, you'll probably have to use quite a formal, academic style.
• Write a clearly structured argument and link your ideas with phrases such as *for example, in conclusion, in contrast*.
• Show that you are aware of counter-arguments, even if you don't agree with them.
• Make sure that your opinion on the subject is clearly expressed.

Unit 10 A lifelong process

Starting off

❶ Work in pairs.

1 Look at the photos of different educational establishments.
How many of these have you attended?
Which did you enjoy most?

2 Tell each other about your education to date.
What do/did you most like and
dislike about the process?

nursery school

primary school

secondary school

❷ How far do you agree or disagree with these opinions about education? Tick the boxes. (1 = strongly agree / 5 = strongly disagree)

		1	2	3	4	5
a	Parents should have the choice of sending children to school or educating them at home.					
b	An education system which does not teach young people how to think for themselves is a failure.					
c	My country's education systems encourage conformity and discourage originality and creativity.					
d	A teacher's main job is to help their pupils or students to pass examinations.					
e	The main purpose of education is to equip young people with the practical skills they need for work.					
f	The purpose of a university education is to produce future generations of leaders.					

university

❸ Compare ideas with your partner and discuss any points of disagreement.

Reading Part 4

1 Work in small groups. Imagine you are about to apply for a university course. Which of these factors would be most important to you in choosing which course to apply for?

- the location of the university
- the quality of teaching
- the reputation of the university
- the cost of tuition
- the number of students in each class/lecture
- the quality of student accommodation
- the help and support provided for applicants
- the atmosphere on the university campus
- the opportunities for socialising
- the facilities, e.g. sports, entertainment, shopping

2 Which of the universities shown in the photos most appeals to you? Why? Compare your answers to this and Exercise 1 with other students.

3 Before you read about the six students, read questions 1–15 below and <u>underline</u> the key ideas in each question.

Which student ...

has had <u>more success</u> than they had anticipated?	**1**
already has a degree and is planning to take a higher degree?	**2**
appreciates being able to work cooperatively with other students?	**3**
came to the university because a family member recommended it?	**4**
came to the university because of where it was?	**5**
chose their university because they had heard people praise it?	**6**
commented on the calmness of life on their campus?	**7**
is not studying at their first-choice university?	**8**
felt at ease after only a short time at their university?	**9**
found communication with the university prior to their arrival very easy?	**10**
found printed information about different universities unhelpful?	**11**
has been too busy to spend time making new friends?	**12**
made a random choice of university?	**13**
would like to repeat the university experience?	**14**
plans to go back home after their course to help improve their country?	**15**

4 For questions 1–15, choose the appropriate students (A–F). The students may be chosen more than once.

5 Work in small groups.

1 Discuss what measures could be taken to improve education in your country. Think about all levels from nursery school to university.
2 Make a list of five suggestions to present to the rest of the class.

What our students say about us

A Francisco (Equatorial Guinea)

The main reason I chose this university is because my brother said how good it was. At the moment I'm taking a foundation course in science for engineering. If I do well enough in my end-of-year exams, I'll be able to get on to a degree course. The best things about my course are the teaching methods and the fact that all the lecturers are so patient. I thoroughly enjoy campus life because it is quiet and safe, and also because everyone has been so kind and considerate. My housemates in particular are good fun to be with. Hopefully, next year I'll be starting a degree in civil engineering here, then, after that I'm planning to return to my country, to play my part in its future development.

B Hiromi (Japan)

At the moment, I'm taking an English language course before I start doing a postgraduate degree course next year. The aim of this course is to improve my academic English with classes covering the skills I'll need in the future. The classes are sufficiently flexible for every individual student's needs and abilities to be taken into consideration. The main reason I chose this university is its location. The fact that you can get to London in just 35 minutes really appealed to me. And there are cinemas, shopping centres, supermarkets, everything you need in the nearest town just a five-minute bus ride away. Another reason I came here is the personal attention I received before I arrived. I always managed to contact the university whenever I needed to – and they always replied quickly and politely to the dozens of questions I asked them.

C Chen (Taiwan)

I chose this course at this university originally because I had heard such good things about it from several friends in my country. And I can honestly say I haven't been disappointed. What has been particularly useful for me is the training in study skills before the main part of the course. I really appreciated the sessions we had on academic writing. They were well structured and took us step-by-step through what can be a daunting process. We had to write an essay every week, which was really hard work, but the practice it gave us has been invaluable – and has stood me in good stead for my main course of study, which is music. The only disappointment for me is that I haven't had the time to mix socially with other students.

D Dasha (Russia)

I knew nothing about the university or the area it's in when I decided to come here. The prospectuses from different universities all claimed they were the best. They all showed good-looking students with happy smiling faces on every page. They didn't look like real students to me. All the courses sounded equally exciting and all the staff seemed equally well qualified. In the end, I simply put the names of five universities into a hat and picked one out. So that's why I'm here. But I needn't have worried, it's been a fantastic experience. I've only been here three weeks, but already I feel at home. I can speak English a hundred per cent better than when I arrived and I've learnt more about this country and its culture than I had in my previous seven years of learning English at school.

E Kulap (Thailand)

I really enjoy studying here now, even though I wasn't so sure at the beginning. This was actually the third university on my top five list – but now I'm really glad to be here. The university has all the facilities a student could possibly need – a large library, computer labs, pleasant classrooms, and a brilliant sports centre. The staff I've had contact with have all been excellent at their subject and very willing to help me and other international students. The class I'm currently in is small enough to allow genuine interaction and dynamic discussion between students. You have to work hard and there's a lot of reading too, but I'm enjoying every minute of it.

F Emma (Germany)

When I came to the university, my main aim was to improve my spoken Chinese because in my home country, Germany, I'm studying Chinese to be a university language teacher. We've had a full schedule of interesting subjects, everything has been well structured, efficiently organised and the teachers have helped us to improve as much as possible during our four-week course. We've had to work very hard, but we've had a lot of fun too. So – as a result I've reached a higher level than I expected, improved my speaking and learned a lot about Chinese culture and customs. All in all I've had a fantastic time and I would love the chance to do it all again some time in the future.

Grammar

Modal verbs expressing ability, possibility and obligation

① Discuss the questions about these extracts from Reading Part 4.

1 Which extracts express ability, which possibility and which obligation?

2 Do the extracts refer to the past, the present, any time or the future?

   a If I do well enough in my end-of-year exams, I'll be able to get on to a degree course.
     ability, future

   b The fact that you can get to London in just 35 minutes really appealed to me.

   c We had to write an essay every week, which was really hard work, …

   d But I needn't have worried, it's been a fantastic experience.

   e I can speak English a hundred per cent better than when I arrived.

   f I always managed to contact the university whenever I needed to.

② Read these pairs of sentences and decide if both in each pair are correct. If both are correct, discuss the difference in meaning between them.

1 a I have to finish this essay, so I can't go out.
   b I must finish this essay. It's really important for me to do well.
   Both are correct. In a, the pressure to finish is from an external source, in b, from the speaker him/herself.

2 a I didn't need to worry about getting home from the airport. My brother said he'd pick me up.
   b I needn't have worried about getting home from the airport. My brother picked me up.

3 a You don't have to go to the lecture this afternoon. It's completely optional.
   b You mustn't go to the lecture this afternoon. It's only for first-year students.

4 a After a lot of effort, I could finally start the car engine.
   b After a lot of effort, I finally managed to start the car engine.

5 a He can stay for up to 90 days with this kind of visa if he wants to.
   b He could stay for up to 90 days with this kind of visa if he wanted to.

6 a In the future, we might not study in classrooms with other students.
   b In the future, we could not study in classrooms with other students.

▶ page 158 *Grammar reference: Expressing ability, possibility and obligation*

③ ⊙ CAE candidates often make mistakes with modal verbs. Find and correct the mistakes in the sentences below.

1 I spent an hour on the Internet, but I couldn't ~~found~~ the information I needed. *find*

2 You needn't to worry about getting here on time – the lesson's cancelled.

3 We need do something to improve the long-term chances of these students.

4 I'm happy to tell you that we could offer you a place on the degree course.

5 If we afford the fees, our daughter will apply to this college.

6 The students at the back of the lecture hall became frustrated because they can't hear very well.

④ Work in pairs. Tell each other about the following.

- Things you can do that you're proud of
- Something you couldn't do for a long time but eventually managed to do
- Something you'd like to be able to do
- Things you have to / don't have to do as part of your job or studies
- Something you needn't have worried about
- Something you really must do in the next few days

100 **Unit 10**

Vocabulary

Chance, occasion, opportunity and *possibility*

1 **Read these definitions and circle the correct alternative in *italics* in the sentences below.**

Occasion – a particular time when something happened or happens *My sister's wedding was a very special **occasion**.*

Collocations

Adjectives	*formal, historic, memorable, rare, solemn, special, unique*
Verbs	**to mark** an occasion, **to rise** to the occasion
Use	**on** one occasion, the occasion **when**

Opportunity – a situation in which it is possible to do something you want to do *I'm going to work in South America for a year. It's a great **opportunity**.*

Collocations

Adjectives	*equal, excellent, golden, perfect, tremendous, welcome*
Verbs	*have, lose, miss, seize, take + the opportunity, opportunity + arise/occur*
Use	*the opportunity **to do** something, the opportunity **for** + noun*

Possibility – a situation where something may or may not happen *There's a definite **possibility** of a strike by refuse collectors next week.*

Collocations

Adjectives	*definite, distinct, real, remote, serious, slight, strong*
Verbs	*face, accept, rule out, recognise, ignore + the possibility*
Use	*the possibility **of doing** something [not **possibility to do**], the possibility **that** + clause*

1 Schools try to ensure that every student has an equal (*opportunity*) / *possibility* to succeed.
2 On several *occasions / opportunities* recently the university has made changes to the syllabus without consulting students.
3 If you study abroad, you should take every *occasion / opportunity* to learn the language.
4 There's a strong *opportunity / possibility* that you will win one of the three available scholarships.
5 Our graduation ceremony next week will be a very special *opportunity / occasion*.
6 According to the weather forecast, there's a distinct *possibility / occasion* of rain tomorrow.

2 **Now read the extract on the right and complete the sentences below it with *chance, occasion, opportunity* or *possibility*. Sometimes two answers are possible.**

Chance can mean *possibility* or *opportunity*, but is generally used less formally than these words.

Chance

1 an occasion which allows something to be done / an opportunity *I'm afraid I didn't get the **chance** to tell him the good news.*

Collocations

Adjectives	*good, ideal, last, second, unexpected*
Verbs	*get, have, deserve, welcome, give someone, take, turn down + the chance*
Use	*the **chance** to do something*

2 likelihood / the level of possibility that something will happen *There's an outside **chance** that I'll have to go to Japan next week.*

Collocations

Adjectives	*fair, outside, realistic, reasonable, slim*
Verbs	*be in with a chance / stand a chance of + -ing*
Use	*the chance **of doing** something, there's a chance **that** + clause, **by any** chance, **on the off** chance, **No** chance!*

1 If you don't do well in your exams, you'll have the ....*chance*........ to retake them again next summer.
2 Our education system is based on the principle of equal ....
3 Have you ever considered the .... of training to be a teacher?
4 If you go on working hard, you stand a good .... of getting to Harvard.
5 Your exams start on Monday, so this weekend is the last .... you'll have to revise.
6 I think there's a real .... that I'll get the grades I need.
7 We're having a party to celebrate the end of our exams – it'll be a great ....
8 Is there any .... that you could help me with my homework?

3 **Complete these sentences with your own words, then compare ideas with a partner.**

1 I hope one day I'll have the opportunity of ...
2 Next year there's a possibility that I'll ...
3 Unfortunately, I have very little chance of ever ...
4 I hope the occasion never arises, when I ...

Listening Part 2

1 **Work in pairs to discuss these questions.**

1 Would you like to study abroad? Why (not)?
2 Which country/countries would you choose? Why?
3 What difficulties might you experience?
4 What difficulties might a foreign student experience in your country?
5 How do you think a period of study abroad would change you?

2 You are going to listen to the experiences of Amy, a British student who is spending a year studying in Egypt. What differences between Britain and Egypt do you think she noticed?

3 🎧 Listen to the recording to find out if any of your ideas are mentioned.

Exam advice

Remember:

- Read the gapped sentences before you listen to get information about the topic of the recording and a clear idea of what you are listening for.
- You will hear the actual words you need to fill the gaps.
- Check that your answer is grammatically correct after you have written it.

4 Now read sentences 1–8. Can you guess which words or phrases are missing from each sentence? The number of missing words is in brackets.

1 The speaker chose to study Arabic because one of the lecturers had a ...*real passion for*... the subject. (3)

2 The .... spoken in Alexandria is commonly understood all across the Arab world. (3)

3 The students were not allowed to stay at the first hotel because they were an .... group. (2)

4 One of the speaker's friends went back home soon after arriving because he was suffering from .... (2)

5 The Alexandria Centre for Languages is located near .... where people sit drinking tea. (3)

6 In the role plays they do with their teacher Ingy, the students learn how to .... taxi drivers. (2)

7 One of the difficulties of learning Arabic for the speaker is that it has two .... – one spoken and the other written. (2)

8 The speaker and her friends spend their weekends at a .... where they can swim and lie by the pool. (2)

5 🎧 Listen to the recording again and complete sentences 1–8 in Exercise 4 with words or phrases you hear.

6 Work in pairs.

1 Imagine you had the chance to study any language in the world:
- which language would you choose?
- where would you choose to learn it?

2 Do you think single-sex groups learn better than mixed-sex groups?

3 How influential do you think teachers are in students' choice of subjects?

Use of English Part 1

1 You are going to read a short article describing the importance of training in the workplace. Before you read, answer the questions in the Exam round-up box.

Exam round-up

How much do you remember about Use of English Part 1? Circle the correct alternative in *italics* in each of these sentences.

1 In Use of English Part 1, there is a text with (*twelve*) / *fifteen* gaps.

2 For each gap you are given a choice of *three* / *four* possible answers.

3 You have about *ten* / *fifteen* minutes for this part of the paper.

4 You should read the text *before* / *after* reading the options.

2 Write your own definitions for these phrases, which appear in the article.

| lifelong learning | retraining | to upgrade (your) skills |

3 Work in pairs. Compare your definitions, then discuss these questions.

1 Why do some adults want to learn something new?

2 How is learning as an adult different from learning as a younger person?

3 Why do you think the idea of *lifelong learning* has become so popular in recent years?

4 Read the article opposite. Does the writer mention any of the ideas you discussed?

5 Read the article again. For questions 1–12, decide which answer (A, B, C or D) best fits each gap. There is an example at the beginning (0).

Why do we need *lifelong learning?*

Incentives play an important (0) .... *C* .... in our decisions to learn. As we get older, the outcomes of (1) .... in learning may not be the same as when we were younger. For example, we are less likely to be (2) .... as a result of training. The type of work-related training or learning we do also changes as we get older. Workers over 45 years old are more likely to participate in learning (3) .... that relate directly to their function. So they may choose to (4) .... those technical skills directly related to their work. By contrast, young workers are more (5) .... to participate in training that is an investment in their future careers.

Organisations also want to continually (6) .... their skills base. Recently, business has (7) .... this largely through a steady inflow of newly-(8) .... young people onto the labour (9) .... Traditionally, we have had a mix of those young people who bring new formal skills to the workplace, and a small proportion of older workers who (10) .... their experience.

What we are seeing now is a decreasing proportion of young people entering the workforce and an increase in the proportion of older people. So, unless we change the (11) .... of our education and learning across life, we will see a (12) .... in formal skills in the working population.

0	A	focus	B	game	C	role	D	feature
1	A	participation	B	contribution	C	attendance	D	activity
2	A	raised	B	promoted	C	advanced	D	upgraded
3	A	actions	B	activities	C	acts	D	modules
4	A	relearn	B	promote	C	restore	D	upgrade
5	A	probable	B	likely	C	possible	D	liable
6	A	restart	B	renovate	C	restore	D	renew
7	A	affected	B	fulfilled	C	achieved	D	succeeded
8	A	educated	B	taught	C	qualified	D	graduated
9	A	workforce	B	employment	C	staff	D	market
10	A	donate	B	supply	C	contribute	D	sell
11	A	way	B	method	C	means	D	nature
12	A	decline	B	cutback	C	fall	D	lessening

Speaking Part 3

❶ Look at the six photographs of different learning situations, and discuss these questions in pairs or small groups.

1 Which of these situations have you personally experienced? What did you like or dislike about the situations?
2 How is the teacher–learner relationship different in the six situations?

❷ You are going to hear two people discussing the photographs. First read what they were asked to talk about.

> Here are some pictures showing different approaches to learning. First, talk about the approaches shown in these pictures, then decide which approach is the most suitable for students learning a foreign language.

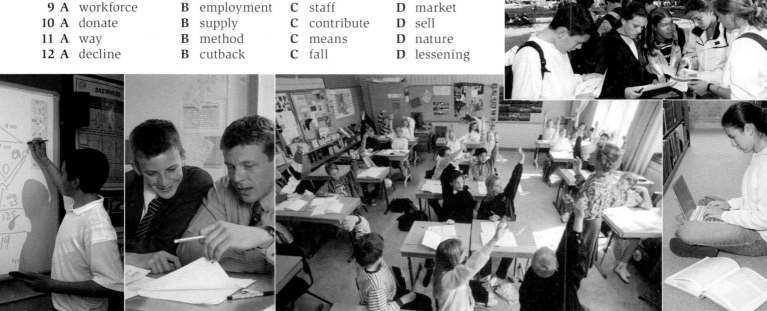

3 🔊(13) **As you listen to the conversation, think about these questions.**

1 How well do the speakers meet these CAE criteria for Speaking Part 3?
 • keeping the conversation flowing
 • exchanging ideas
 • expressing and justifying opinions
 • agreeing and/or disagreeing
 • making suggestions
 • speculating
 • reaching a decision through discussion
2 Do both speakers use 'a range of vocabulary to meet the task requirements'?

4 **The sentences below are quite precise ways of describing the photos. If you don't know the exact words to say something, you can use vaguer, less precise language (see page 84). Replace the words and phrases in *italics* with vaguer alternatives.**

1 ... the next picture is of a student and *instructor* in a sort of one-to-one learning session which would probably be *suitable* for learning *certain skills*.
 ... the next picture is of a student and someone, not sure who, in a ....
2 the next one's *a student* on a computer – probably learning *facts and information* off the net, which again probably wouldn't be *a suitable method of learning* a language ...
3 **M** *Interacting with* people, perhaps.
 W Yes, that'd probably be a good way to learn a language.
 M *Having conversations with them* ...

5 🔊(13) **Listen to the conversation again and check your answers.**

6 **Work in pairs. Answer the same question as the two speakers on the recording. Make sure you:**

 • keep the conversation flowing (it should be continuous)
 • exchange ideas, express and justify opinions
 • agree or disagree
 • make suggestions and speculate
 • use a wide range of vocabulary.

Exam advice

• Although the examiner will ask you to try to reach an agreement with your partner or to make a joint decision, it is more important that you use appropriate language and conversation strategies to negotiate and discuss with each other than that you come to agreement.

• If you do not agree or reach a joint decision, you should express polite disagreement.

Writing Part 1 A report

Exam advice

Read the instructions carefully to identify:
• who will read the report
• the purpose of the report.
You should:
• deal with all the information in the input material
• give factual information and make recommendations
• organise your report clearly into sections with headings.

1 **Work in pairs. Read the writing task below and answer these questions.**

1 What sections would be appropriate for this report? What headings could you give these sections?
2 Are there any points in the notes that could be combined?

You are part of a student committee looking into ways of improving the facilities in your place of study. You have been asked to write a report summarising some of the suggestions made by people you have interviewed as part of your research. You have made a note of comments made by three groups of people.

<u>Students</u>
• more self-study rooms with computers
• more choice in canteen (menu never changes)
• more students than last year, so sports centre always overcrowded

<u>Staff</u>
• more car park spaces for staff (away from visitors' and students' areas)
• each staff member should have own computer – having to share led to inefficiency
• canteen overpriced

<u>Visitors</u>
• clearer signposts to Reception and Department offices
• more car parking for visitors

Write your **report**. Write 180–220 words.

---

2 As you read this sample report, think of suitable headings for the sections.

Report on improving college facilities

(1) .... *Introduction* ....

The purpose of this report is to suggest ways in which college facilities could be improved for students, staff and visitors. The report is based on comments from these three groups.

(2) ....

Both students and staff commented on the need for increased provision of computers. Students would welcome more study areas equipped with computers, while staff felt strongly that they would work more efficiently if they had their own computers.

(3) ....

Staff expressed the view that the cost of food in the canteen was unnecessarily high and recommended a reduction. Students did not mention price, but would appreciate a wider choice of food.

(4) ....

Dissatisfaction with car parking facilities was expressed by staff and visitors. Staff would like reserved spaces away from other parking areas, while visitors would be grateful for extra spaces to be made available to them.

(5) ....

Students suggested that the gym and other sports facilities be enlarged to take account of this year's increase in student numbers.

Visitors would like important places, like the main reception, to be more clearly signposted.

(6) ....

I would recommend implementing all the suggestions listed above with the exception of providing more car parking spaces. It is clear from past experience that demand in this area is never satisfied. I would suggest that drivers should make alternative travel arrangements.

---

3 Read the report again and discuss these questions.

1 What structures are used with the verbs *recommend* and *suggest*?
2 Make a note of the reporting verbs used instead of *said*.
3 What verbs and phrases are used to mean *would like*?

▶ page 171 *Writing reference: Reports*

4 Work in pairs. Read the writing task below.

1 Who will read the report you write?
2 Will you quote directly from the emails? Why (not)?
3 How many sections will you include in your report? What headings will you give these sections?

Your college principal has established a committee of students to write a report recommending how more students can be attracted to the college in the future. Your committee has emailed prospective and current students. Below are extracts from some of the email replies from the two groups.

Prospective students

• 'Why don't you organise an open week when we can sample college activities?'

• 'You need to give new students an incentive that's better for us than the other colleges. Give them a freebie of some kind.'

• 'Get students already there to visit schools to tell us what it's like. We don't know at the moment.'

Current students

• 'You could offer new students a free laptop computer.'

• 'Show how successful the college is – publish our exam results.'

• 'We could make a TV commercial showing what a great place it is.'

Write your **report**. Write 180–220 words.

---

5 Write your report, making use of the following:

• the verbs *suggest* and *recommend*
• a variety of reporting verbs
• a variety of words and phrases meaning the same as *would like*.

Unit 9 *Vocabulary and grammar review*

Vocabulary

❶ Complete the sentences below by writing the correct word, *action, activity, event* **or** *programme,* **in the gaps.**

1 The stadium is a hive of .... *activity* .... with workers hurrying to get it finished before the games.
2 The authorities have asked the police to take .... against anyone caught scrawling graffiti on the town hall.
3 The sporting .... I most enjoy doing is sailing.
4 Can you look on the .... to see when the interval is?
5 For me, one of the most exciting and historic .... of the last century was the fall of the Berlin Wall.
6 The final .... of this weekend's festival of Irish culture will be a traditional folk dance.
7 Thanks to prompt .... by the fire service, the school fire was prevented from spreading to the neighbouring houses.
8 The government plans to unveil its latest .... of tax reform later today.

❷ For questions 1–5, think of one word only which can be used appropriately in all three sentences.

1 By cycling hard we actually managed to .... about 100 kilometres in just under three hours.
   The second volume of the series will .... the period from the French Revolution in 1789 to the Battle of Waterloo in 1815.
   Before placing the fish in the oven, ... it .... with a sheet of aluminium foil.

2 My car broke down yesterday, but then it wasn't very reliable in the first ....
   Igor came in shivering from cold, so we gave him a .... by the fire.
   Tanya lives in rather an old .... behind the paint factory.

3 They admitted the assignment was .... , but they managed to do it nevertheless.
   I think that meat is rather .... so you'd probably do better to buy something more tender.
   Chris must be pretty .... if he wants to pursue a career in the army.

4 Marcia is one of those teachers who enjoys .... out her students' mistakes.
   They clearly think you're the culprit because they're all .... at you!
   Once you've got the gun .... in the right direction, all you have to do is pull the trigger.

5 The fisherman held the boat .... while we all climbed aboard.
   Toni and Paola have had a .... relationship for more than five years.
   Look! My hand is completely .... – it's not shaking at all.

Grammar

❸ Circle the correct alternative in *italics* **in each of the following sentences.**

1 Sonia will call you as soon as she *will finish /* (*has finished*) lunch.
2 I'll do the cooking tonight when everyone else *works / is working.*
3 It wasn't until the match *was / had been* over that he realised he'd strained a muscle.
4 I haven't seen him at all since he *is working / has been working* there.
5 In future, please don't call me while *I have / I'm having* my supper.
6 Rory learnt to speak Arabic perfectly when he *was working / had worked* in Cairo.
7 As soon as the teacher *has arrived / had arrived,* we started work.
8 Tracey and Pierre performed together in perfect harmony and while she *played / was playing* the piano, he sang in a high tenor voice.

Unit 10 *Vocabulary and grammar review*

Vocabulary

❶ Circle the correct words in these sentences.

1 The system aims to give everyone (an equal) / a *same* opportunity at the beginning of their lives.
2 Thursday is the *last* / *late* chance we'll have to enter the competition.
3 The swearing-in of the first woman president was a *historic* / *historical* occasion.
4 There's a *slight* / *little* possibility that I won't be back in time for tomorrow's meeting.
5 Don't *lose* / *miss* this *gold* / *golden* opportunity to win a two-week holiday in the south of France.
6 There seems to be a *factual* / *real* possibility that the party will lose at the next election.
7 The funeral of the firefighters who died in the blaze was a very *depressed* / *solemn* occasion.
8 In my opinion everyone deserves a *next* / *second* chance in life.

❷ Think of one word which can be used appropriately in all three sentences.

1 We tried to wake her, but she was
.... asleep.
Our village is .... becoming a dormitory town for London.
When I was a child I got my head stuck
.... in some railings.

2 Could you .... the cheese, please?
Everyone expects me to .... all my exams, but I'm not so confident.
If you .... a supermarket, could you get me some bread, please?

3 Eventually, we'd like to .... down and have a family of our own.
I've had a letter from my phone company asking me to .... my account immediately.
I'd really like a proper meal, but we're short of time, so I suppose I'll have to ....
for a sandwich.

Grammar

❸ Complete these sentences with the correct form of one of the modal verbs *must*, *need* or *have (to)*. In some cases more than one answer is possible.

1 My new job starts next Monday. Hopefully, I
.....*won't have to*..... work such long hours as I do now.
2 I .... make sure I wake up in time for my first lecture. Yesterday, I didn't have any lectures, so I .... get up at all.
3 Our lecturers have told us that we .... send them our assignments by email, otherwise they won't mark them. This means we .... have our own email.
4 Take it easy! Today's lecture's been cancelled, so you .... hurry.
5 You .... smoke in here. Didn't you see the sign? If you want a cigarette, you .... go outside.
6 I .... get some cash out before the weekend – otherwise I'm going to run out.

❹ Correct any of these sentences with mistakes in the modal verbs.

1 It's a complicated route – I hope I ~~could~~ find my way back. *can*
2 You can find all the information you'll ever need on Wikipedia.
3 We're delighted to inform you that we could offer you the post of manager.
4 At the fourth attempt I could pass my driving test. The first three times, I failed spectacularly.
5 If you were a fast reader, you could be able to finish that novel in one evening.

Unit 11 Being somewhere else

Starting off

1. Work in pairs. The photos here and on page 109 show different types of journey. Choose two of the photos and think of vocabulary, phrases, expressions and topics which are relevant to the photos.

Example:

Picture 1 – hardship, proving themselves, a voyage into the unknown, rapids, waterfalls, mosquitoes, exploration, chilly, remote wilderness, inhospitable countryside.

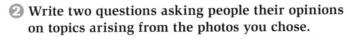

2. Write two questions asking people their opinions on topics arising from the photos you chose.

Example:

Some people think you can learn a lot about yourself from a journey involving hardship. Do you agree?

3. Ask several different people in the class the questions you have written.

4. When you have finished, work with your original partner and compare your answers.

Listening Part 1

❶ **Before you do Listening Part 1, do the exercise in the Exam round-up box.**

❷ **You will hear three different extracts. Before you listen, read the questions and the options for Listening Part 1. Guess which of the words and phrases in the box you would expect to hear with each extract.**

call off	dull	if I were you	miserable
pay up	put off	quite unpleasant otherwise	
walking over rough ground	wrap up		

Extract One

You hear a conversation between a man and a woman who are travelling on a river.

1   How does the man feel about the journey?
A   It's dangerous.
B   It's disappointing.
C   It's unusual.

2   How does the woman react to what the man says?
A   She gives him advice.
B   She agrees with him.
C   She consoles him.

Extract Two

You hear two young men planning a sponsored walk.

3   How would bad weather affect their plans?
A   They'd postpone the journey.
B   They'd cancel the journey.
C   They'd take extra equipment.

4   What will happen if they don't reach their objective?
A   They won't make so much money.
B   Their reputation will suffer.
C   They'll have to try again later.

Extract Three

You hear an interview with a woman who has returned from a journey.

5   What item of clothing does she consider essential?
A   a sweater
B   boots
C   a hat

6   How does she feel about her journey now?
A   relieved that it's over
B   surprised by the conditions she encountered
C   grateful to her travelling companions

❸ **(14) Now listen and check which words/phrases you heard with each extract.**

❹ **(14) Listen again. For questions 1–6, choose the answer (A, B or C) which fits best according to what you hear.**

❺ **Work in pairs. What's the hardest journey you've ever made?**

Grammar
Conditionals

❶ Work in pairs. Look at the ten sentences below from Listening Part 1 and organise them into categories according to what the sentences mean. Sentences can be put into more than one category.

Examples:

– 1 and 9 are both 3rd conditional.
– 1, 3 and 4 all express a complaint.

When you have finished, work with another pair of students and explain your decisions.

1 If I'd known about the mosquitoes, I'd never have come.
2 If I were you, I'd put some insect repellent on right away.
3 If you'd just stop griping for a while, perhaps we'd start enjoying ourselves a bit.
4 If we'd stayed at home, I'd be resting in front of the telly right now instead of paddling up this miserable river.
5 So, what will we do if the weather turns bad?
6 I mean, if things look really bad we can always put things off for a few days and start a bit later.
7 Still, I imagine they'd pay up anyway even if we didn't get there, don't you?
8 I never went out without something to cover my head or I'd have got quite sunburnt.
9 It could all have been quite unpleasant otherwise, you know …
10 You know, they'd make conversation, invite me to coffee and really help me to get to know the country.

⟡ page 159 *Grammar reference: Conditionals*

❷ Put the verbs in brackets into the correct form. You will need to decide on the correct conditional form and whether the verb should be simple or continuous.

1 If you ...*hadn't left*... (not leave) the map at home, we ...*wouldn't be wandering*... (not wander) around this forest right now, looking for somewhere to spend the night.
2 It's a lovely city and if I .... (not rush) to catch a train, I .... (be) happy to show you around a bit.
3 Kamal always thinks he knows best, and if he .... (not be) so obstinate, we .... (probably reach) the hotel by now instead of being stuck in this jam.

4 'What do you do when you fall ill on holiday?'
'Well, it hasn't happened to me yet, but I guess I .... (try) to find a local doctor who spoke some English. If I .... (be) seriously ill, I .... (have) to get help from the consulate.'
5 If I .... (be) you, I .... (carry) my money in a money belt.
6 It was your own fault. The accident .... (not happen) if you .... (concentrate) properly at the time.
7 Karen is an intrepid traveller and I don't imagine she .... (ever abandon) a journey unless she .... (travel) somewhere which turned out to be really unpleasant or dangerous.
8 If you .... (like) to come with me, I .... (show) you to your room.

❸ ⊙ The following sentences all contain mistakes made by candidates in the CAE exam. Correct the mistakes.

1 If you eat your chocolate now, you ~~wouldn't~~ enjoy the delicious cake which your granny made.
   won't
2 I would be grateful if you send me a reply at your earliest convenience.
3 If you will not give me a refund, I am obliged to write to the local council.
4 If you had followed all my instructions, you would now stand in front of the cathedral.
5 In my country few people smoke, so if I were you, I won't smoke at all.
6 I'll join a gym so that early-morning joggers would not have to stare at me if they see me doing my exercises in the park.
7 Although I am reserved in certain situations, I will not describe myself as shy.
8 If I was able to travel back in history and I had the chance to choose where exactly to go, then I would have travelled four centuries into the past.

❹ Work in small groups. If you could travel backwards or forwards in time, where would you choose to go first? Discuss your ideas with your partners.

Speaking Part 1

1 Work in pairs. Which questions below could you answer using conditional verb forms?

1 If you could travel anywhere in the world, where would you choose to go? Why?

2 If some friends from abroad were visiting your region, which places would you take them to see? Why?

3 What things do you most enjoy doing when travelling on holiday? Why?

4 Do you find it's useful that you can speak English when you travel? Why?

5 What's the best time of year for people to visit your country? Why?

6 Would you enjoy going on an adventurous, possibly dangerous journey? Why (not)?

7 Where is the most interesting place you have ever travelled to? Why?

8 If you could choose something completely different from your usual type of holiday, what would you choose? Why?

9 Would you enjoy working with tourists? Why?

10 Would you prefer to spend a year travelling or to spend a year working? Why?

2 🔊 **Listen to three people, Thea, Archie and Nina, answering questions from the list 1–10 above.**

1 Which question is each of them answering?

2 Which people use conditional verb forms in their answers?

3 Do they use conditional verb forms all the time? Why (not)?

4 Who sounds most enthusiastic in their answer? What words does the person use which show enthusiasm? What other ways do they have of showing enthusiasm?

5 Do they repeat the words of the questions, or do they express the ideas using their own vocabulary? Why is this a good idea in the exam?

3 Take turns to ask each other the questions.

Student A: Ask your partner questions 1, 3, 5, 7 and 9.
Student B: Ask your partner questions 2, 4, 6, 8 and 10.

Reading Part 3

1 Before doing Reading Part 3 on pages 112–3, answer the questions in the Exam round-up box.

2 Work in pairs. You will read an extract from a book by Paul Theroux about a journey he made through Africa. Before you read, look at the photos here and on the next page.

1 Which aspects of your daily life and routine would you like to escape from by making a journey?

2 What things do you think a man in his 60s would want to escape from? Why? Do you think they are the same or different from the things young people want to escape from when they travel?

3 Read the text quickly. Why did the writer choose to travel in Africa again?

Disappearing into *Africa*

I wanted the pleasure of being in Africa again. Feeling that the place was so large it contained many untold tales and some hope and comedy and sweetness too, I aimed to reinsert myself in the
5 bundu, as we used to call the bush, and to wander the antique hinterland. There I had lived and worked, happily, almost forty years ago, in the heart of the greenest continent.

In those old undramatic days of my school
10 teaching in the bundu, folks lived their lives on bush paths at the end of unpaved roads of red clay, in villages of grass-roofed huts. They had a new national flag, they had just gotten the vote, some had bikes, many talked about buying their first
15 pair of shoes. They were hopeful, and so was I, a schoolteacher living near a settlement of mud huts among dusty trees and parched fields – children shrieking at play; and women bent double – most with infants slung on their backs – hoeing the corn
20 and beans; and the men sitting in the shade.

The Swahili word *safari* means 'journey', it has nothing to do with animals, someone 'on safari' is just away and unobtainable and out of touch. Out of touch in Africa was where I wanted to be. The wish to
25 disappear sends many travellers away. If you are thoroughly sick of being kept waiting at home or at work, travel is perfect: let other people wait for a change. Travel is a sort of revenge for having been put on hold, or having to leave messages on answering
30 machines, not knowing your party's extension, being kept waiting all your working life – the homebound writer's irritants. But also being kept waiting is the human condition.

Travel in the African bush can also be a sort of
35 revenge on mobile phones and fax machines, on telephones and the daily paper, on the creepier aspects of globalisation that allow anyone who chooses to get their insinuating hands on you. I desired to be unobtainable. I was going to Africa for the best of
40 reasons – in a spirit of discovery; and for the pettiest – simply to disappear, to light out, with a suggestion of I dare you to try to find me.

Home had become a routine, and routines make time pass quickly. I was a sitting duck in this
45 predictable routine: people knew when to call me, they knew when I would be at my desk. I was in such regular touch it was like having a job, a mode of life I hated. I was sick of being called up and importuned, asked for favors, hit up for money. You stick around
50 too long and people begin to impose their own deadlines on you.

Everyone always available at any time in the totally accessible world seemed to me pure horror. It made me want to find a place that was not accessible at
55 all ... no phones, no fax machines, not even mail delivery, the wonderful old world of being out of touch; in short, of being far away.

All I had to do was remove myself. I loved not having to ask permission, and in fact in my domestic life
60 things had begun to get a little predictable, too – Mr Paul at home every evening when Mrs Paul came home from work. 'I made spaghetti sauce ... I seared some tuna ... I'm scrubbing some potatoes ...' The writer in his apron, perspiring over his béchamel
65 sauce, always within earshot of the telephone. You have to pick it up because it is ringing in your ear.

I wanted to drop out. People said, 'Get a mobile phone ... Use FedEx ... Sign up for Hotmail ... Stop in at internet cafés ... Visit my website ...'
70 I said no thanks. The whole point of my leaving was to escape this stuff – to be out of touch. The greatest justification for travel was not self-improvement but rather performing a vanishing act, disappearing without a trace. Africa is one of the last great places
75 on Earth a person can vanish into. I wanted that. Let them wait. I have been kept waiting far too many times for far too long.

I am outta here, I thought. The next website I visit will be that of the poisonous Central African bird
80 eating spider.

From *Dark Star Safari* by Paul Theroux

4 For questions 1–7, choose the answer (A, B, C or D) which you think fits best according to the text.

1 What did Paul expect from his journey?
A to have a variety of enjoyable experiences
B to see how Africa had changed
C to meet some old friends
D to see impressive scenery

2 Forty years ago, how did Paul feel about the future of the country where he lived?
A Little was likely to change.
B People's aspirations were too limited.
C Women would do most of the work.
D Things were likely to improve.

3 One reason Paul wanted to travel to Africa was that
A he wanted people to be unable to contact him.
B he wanted other people to suffer in the same way as he had.
C his health was suffering from staying at home.
D he had been waiting to return to Africa for many years.

4 What aspect of globalisation did Paul wish to escape from?
A people's ability always to manipulate him
B the international media
C communication technologies
D organisations spying on him

5 What does Paul mean by 'I was a sitting duck' in line 44?
A He was bored.
B He was easy to find.
C He had a fixed lifestyle.
D He was not well.

6 Paul mentions his cooking activities
A to show he can look after himself.
B to explain why the phone was within earshot.
C to show how he was a good husband.
D to show why he felt trapped.

7 Paul mentions a spider in the last paragraph to show
A his interest in wildlife.
B his ability to manage modern technology.
C his intention to escape from modern technology.
D how dangerous his journey will be.

5 Work in small groups.

1 Would you be happy to be out of touch on a journey?
2 What aspects of modern life would you like to leave behind when you travel?
3 'The greatest justification for travel was not self-improvement but rather performing a vanishing act, disappearing without a trace.' (lines 71–74) Do you agree?

Vocabulary

At, in and *on* to express location

❶ Complete the sentences below with *at, in* or *on* in each gap. Then check your answers by looking at Reading Part 3 again.

1 I wanted the pleasure of being ....*in*.... Africa again.
2 There I had lived and worked, ... the heart of the greenest continent.
3 ... folks lived their lives .... bush paths .... the end of unpaved roads of red clay, ... villages of grass-roofed huts.
4 If you are thoroughly sick of being kept waiting .... home or .... work, travel is perfect.
5 ... people knew when to call me, they knew when I would be .... my desk.
6 Everyone always available at any time .... the totally accessible world seemed to me pure horror.
7 Africa is one of the last great places .... Earth a person can vanish into.

❷ Work in pairs. Which preposition, *at, in* or *on*, is used to talk about the following? Find examples for each rule in Exercise 1.

a a position which is thought of as a point, not an area   *at, 3 & 5*
b a position in contact with a surface
c a position along a border or boundary (e.g. the coast, the ocean) or along something which connects two places (e.g. a road, a river)
d a position within a larger area or space

▶ page 160 *Grammar reference:* At, in *and* on *to express location*

❸ ⊙ Each of the sentences below contains a mistake with prepositions made by CAE candidates. Correct the mistakes.

1 I come from Mendoza, a town ~~of~~ Argentina. *in*
2 I'd like to introduce you to my boss, whose office is at the 5th floor.
3 Portugal is one of the most beautiful countries of the world.
4 Public phones are available at almost every large square.
5 She spends far too long talking at her mobile phone.
6 There's a garage at the left and I live just two doors along from it.
7 We waited at a queue for more than twenty minutes.
8 You will find a youth hostel in almost every island.
9 You'll find a large shopping centre at the outskirts of the city.
10 She decided to go and live for a year to Italy.

Use of English Part 2

❶ Before doing Use of English Part 2, answer the questions in the Exam round-up box.

Exam round-up

How much do you remember about Use of English Part 2? Complete the following information with the words and phrases in *italics*.

~~15~~ *12   before and after   every question   general idea*
'grammar'   makes sense   spelled   the completed text

• There are (1) ....*15*............ questions in this part and you have about (2) .... minutes to do it.

• The words you need are mainly (3) .... words: articles, pronouns, auxiliary verbs, etc., and parts of expressions, e.g. *take part in*, or phrasal verbs, e.g. *get over*.

• First read the text quickly to get a (4) .... of what it's about.

• Read the words (5) .... the gaps to decide what type of word you need.

• Answer (6) .... with one word only, making sure you have (7) .... it correctly.

• Read (8) .... when you have finished to check that it (9) ....

❷ Work in pairs. Some people suggest that in the future virtual travel using computer and internet technology may replace real travel.

1 What advantages would virtual travel have over real travel?
2 Would you prefer it?

❸ You will read a short article about two people who were searching for an island. Read the article quickly without paying attention to the gaps to find out:

1 how they found the island
2 why the island's owners were willing to let them use it.

❹ For questions 1–15, read the article again and think of the word which best fits each gap. Use only one word in each gap. There is an example at the beginning (0).

❺ Work in pairs.

1 Would you be interested in spending time on a small Pacific island? Why (not)?
2 What do you think is meant by eco-tourism and why is it important?

Island wanted

One year ago Ben Keene and Mark James launched Tribewanted (0) ......*in*........ a torrent of media coverage. It was a simple idea with potentially enormous consequences (1) .... tourism: the creation of an eco-friendly sustainable community existing simultaneously in the virtual world of the Internet and (2) .... an actual desert island.

How do you (3) .... about finding an island? Where (4) .... but the Internet? Just Google it. Ben and Mark looked at islands (5) .... over the world (6) .... typical starting price was one million dollars. They didn't have much luck (7) .... their searches led them to a specialist island broker (8) .... pointed them towards Vorovoro, off the wild north coast of Fiji. With just (9) .... money on Ben's credit card for two return tickets, they decided to go and (10) .... a look. As (11) .... as they saw it, they knew it was right. It was small, just two hundred acres, but it had a beach, blue sea, hills and land for planting. The first hurdle was getting the agreement of the owner of the land, the local chief, Tui Mali. (12) .... of his advisers was his nephew Ulai, who (13) .... a degree in law and was a specialist in aboriginal land rights. The men had seen (14) .... had happened to other idyllic Fijian islands, and did not want to lose their ancestral lands to a large hotel complex or a marina. Finally, however, on the basis of (15) .... handshake and the presentation of a tambua – the tooth of a sperm whale, the historical contractual device of the Fijians – the agreement was made.

From The Guardian

Writing Part 2 A contribution to a longer piece

Exam advice

- You may be asked to contribute to a longer piece of writing, for example, part of a brochure, a guidebook or a piece of research.
- You will have to supply information and opinions.
- Choose a style depending on the purpose of the piece and who your readers are.
- Make sure that you cover all the points outlined in the question.
- Decide what would be a suitable format for the piece and use titles and sections if appropriate, e.g. for a guidebook or brochure.

1 **Work in pairs. Look at this writing task and answer the questions below.**

> Your college is producing a short information booklet for students from other countries. The booklet will include sections on college facilities, study methods, local food and customs, entertainment and sports. You have been asked to write the section headed 'Local places of interest'. You have been asked to cover:
>
> • types of places and what to see there
>
> • things to take with you, e.g. special clothing
>
> • advice about the best time to visit, etc.
>
> You should write about two or three places.
>
> Write your **contribution** to the booklet. Write between 220 and 260 words.

1 Do you have to write the whole booklet?
2 What do you have to write about and what points must you cover?
3 Who is the booklet for?
4 What style would be suitable?

○ page 173 *Writing reference: A contribution to a longer piece*

2 **Work alone. Think of two or three places in the area where you live which would be interesting to visitors from other countries. Make notes about:**

- the types of places and what to see
- things to take with you, e.g. special clothing
- the best time to visit.

3 **Work in small groups. Take turns to present the information in your notes.**

④ Read the contribution below. Which place would you find most interesting?

Local places of interest

You'll find Salisbury itself is steeped in history, but there are two other places just nearby which are well worth a day's visit.

Old Sarum

Old Sarum is where Salisbury used to be situated till about 1,500 years ago when the locals moved from this dry hilltop spot to its present spectacular site by the river. At Old Sarum you can visit the ruins of a prehistoric hill fort, a medieval castle, a cathedral and town. The site is set out with information panels explaining the history of this unusual and atmospheric place. It's best to pick a clear sunny day for your visit, when you'll have a great walk with superb views across many miles of the surrounding area, so it's a good idea to take a pair of binoculars and a warm jacket as it can be quite windy on the hilltop.

Wilton House

No stay in Salisbury would be complete without a visit to splendid Wilton House, the seventeenth-century home of the Earl of Pembroke. You'll see two of the grandest rooms of the period, the Single and Double Cube Rooms, in a house that's full of amazing paintings and furniture. It's set in attractive gardens with fountains and a river. And don't miss the world-famous carpet factory in the same village!

Wilton House is open to the public from April to September and it's a great place to take a picnic. Otherwise you can eat in the excellent restaurant or more reasonably priced cafeteria.

⑤ Work in pairs.

1. Does the contribution cover all the points in the writing task? Where is each point covered?
2. What things to take does the writer include? Would you include any others?
3. What do you notice about the layout?
4. Is it written in an impersonal style, or is the reader addressed?
5. Identify features of an informal style of writing in the contribution.
6. The writer uses a number of adjectives to encourage you to visit the places. <u>Underline</u> the adjectives.

⑥ Now write your own answer to the task with two or three places of interest from the area where you live.

Unit 12 The living world

Starting off

1 Work in pairs. Look at the newspaper headlines and photographs, and discuss these questions.

1 Which headlines do the two photographs illustrate?
2 What environmental issues do the headlines relate to?
3 Which headlines suggest an optimistic view of the future?

A China to Build Wind Power Complex

B U.S. Fish and Wildlife Service to Consider Black-footed Albatross for Protection

C Pollutant linked to bronchitis in toddlers

D Britons top table of carbon emissions from planes

E Is the bio fuel dream over?

F Arctic Melt Opens Northwest Passage

2 Write a headline to draw attention to the environmental issue which you consider to be the most important at the present time – in your country or internationally.

Reading Part 2

1 Before doing Reading Part 2, answer the questions in the Exam round-up box.

Exam round-up

Circle the correct alternative in *italics* for each of the statements below.

In Reading Part 2:
1 the text has *five* / (*six*) gaps
2 there *is one* / *are two* extra paragraph(s) that you do not need to use
3 ideas may be repeated from paragraph to paragraph by the use of *synonyms* / *antonyms*
4 you should start this task by reading the *gapped text* / *missing paragraphs*.

2 You are going to read an article about a speaking parrot. Before you read, discuss these questions.

1 How do you think parrots learn to 'speak'?
2 When a parrot speaks, do you think it understands what it is saying?
3 What other animals could be taught to speak, do you think?

3 Read the main part of the article (but not the missing paragraphs A–G).

1 How does the article answer the three questions you have been discussing?
2 What do the photographs show?

Alex the African Grey

Science's best-known parrot dies, aged 31

THE last time Irene Pepperberg saw Alex, she said goodnight as usual. 'You be good,' said Alex. 'I love you.' 'I love you, too.' 'You'll be in tomorrow?' 'Yes, I'll be in tomorrow.' But Alex died in his cage that night, bringing to an end a life spent learning complex tasks that, it had originally been thought, only primates could master.

| 1 |

Even then, the researchers remained human-centric. Their assumption was that chimpanzees might be able to understand and use human sign language because they are humanity's nearest living relatives. It took a brilliant insight to turn this human-centricity on its head and look at the capabilities of a species only distantly related to humanity, but which can, nevertheless, speak the words people speak: the parrot.

| 2 |

Dr Pepperberg and Alex last shared a common ancestor more than 300 million years ago. But Alex, unlike a chimpanzee, learned to speak words easily. The question was, was Alex merely parroting Dr Pepperberg? Or would that pejorative term have to be redefined? Do parrots actually understand what they are saying?

| 3 |

The reason why primates have evolved intelligence, according to Dr Humphrey, is that they generally live in groups. And, just as group living promotes intelligence, so intelligence allows larger groups to function, providing a spur for the evolution of yet more intelligence. If Dr Humphrey is right, only social animals can be intelligent – and so far this has been borne out.

| 4 |

An additional relevant factor is that, like primates, parrots live long enough to make the time-consuming process of learning worthwhile. Alex lived to the age of 31. Combined with his ability to speak, or at least 'vocalise' words, Alex looked a promising experimental subject.

| 5 |

By the end of this process, Alex had the intelligence of a five-year-old child and had not reached his full potential. He had a vocabulary of 150 words. He knew the names of 50 objects and could describe their colours and shapes. He could answer questions about objects' properties, even when he had not seen that particular combination of properties before. He could ask for things, and would reject a proffered item and ask again if it was not what he wanted. He understood, and could discuss, the concepts of 'bigger', 'smaller', 'same' and 'different'. And he could count up to six, including the number zero. He even knew when and how to apologise if he annoyed Dr Pepperberg or her colleagues.

| 6 |

There are still a few researchers who think Alex's skills were the result of rote learning rather than abstract thought. Alex, though, convinced most in the field that birds as well as mammals can evolve complex and sophisticated cognition, and communicate the results to others.

Adapted from *The Economist*

4 Now choose from the paragraphs A–G the one which fits each gap in the text. There is one extra paragraph which you do not need to use.

A And so it proved. Using a training technique now employed on children with learning difficulties, in which two adults handle and discuss an object, sometimes making deliberate mistakes, Dr Pepperberg and her collaborators at the University of Arizona began teaching Alex how to describe things, how to make his desires known, and even how to ask questions.

B And the fact that there were a lot of collaborators, even strangers, involved in the project was crucial. Researchers in this area live in perpetual fear of the 'Clever Hans' effect. This is named after a horse that seemed to count, but was actually reacting to unconscious cues from his trainer. Alex would talk to and perform for anyone, not just Dr Pepperberg.

C Dr Pepperberg's reason for suspecting that they might – and thus her second reason for picking a parrot – was that in the mid-1970s evolutionary explanations for behaviour were coming back into vogue. A British researcher called Nicholas Humphrey had proposed that intelligence evolves in response to the social environment rather than the natural one. The more complex the society an animal lives in, the more intelligence it needs to prosper.

D Early studies of linguistic ability in apes had concluded it was virtually non-existent. But researchers had made the elementary error of trying to teach their anthropoid subjects to speak. Chimpanzee vocal cords are simply not up to this, and it was not until someone had the idea of teaching chimps sign language that any progress was made.

E However, not all animals which live in groups are social animals. Flocks of, say, starlings or herds of wildebeest do not count as real societies, just protective groupings. But parrots such as Alex live in societies in the wild, in the way that monkeys and apes do, and thus, Dr Pepperberg reasoned, Alex might have evolved advanced cognitive abilities.

F The dictionary definition of to parrot is to repeat exactly what someone says without understanding it. It is used about politicians who simply repeat the party line, or schoolchildren who learn facts by heart. Dr Pepperberg's experiments with Alex have helped to demonstrate the validity of this usage.

G This rather novel approach came to Dr Pepperberg, a theoretical chemist, in 1977. To follow it up, she went to a pet shop and bought an African Grey parrot, which was then just a year old. Thus began one of the best-known double acts in the field of animal-behaviour science.

5 Discuss these questions.

1 Do you think that teaching a parrot to speak has any practical scientific purpose, or is it just an interesting experiment?
2 Do you think experiments involving animals are necessary? Why (not)?

Vocabulary
Word formation

1 What are the noun forms for each of these verbs from the article?

apologise	communicate	conclude	describe
perform	prosper	suspect	

2 What are the verbs related to these nouns from the article?

assumption	behaviour	combination	evolution
explanation	response		

3 Some words, like *progress* and *suspect*, can be nouns or verbs:

- If they are used as verbs, the stress is on the second syllable: *Some researchers sus'pect that Alex's 'abilities' are no more than a circus trick.*
- If they are used as nouns, the stress is on the first syllable: *Investigating the case of the strange phone message, police consider a parrot to be the prime 'suspect.*

Make pairs of sentences using these words as verbs and nouns: *increase, export, progress, rebel.* Then say or read your sentences to a partner, putting the stress in the right place.

Grammar
Nouns and articles

① **Work in pairs. Find the following in the short article below.**

- two singular countable nouns
- three plural countable nouns
- three uncountable nouns
- two of these three uncountable nouns that could be countable in other contexts
- two proper nouns (names), apart from *Baobab*

> Baobab trees, which are found in Africa, are frequently compared with elephants because their bark resembles the skin of an elephant. They consist of the most bulky, twisted tissue of any plant on Earth. The most ancient are believed to be 1,000 years old.

② **Many words have different meanings depending on whether they are countable or uncountable. What is the difference in meaning between these pairs of sentences?**

1. **a** Would you like some *chocolate*?
   b Would you like *a chocolate*?
2. **a** I love *chicken*. **b** I love *chickens*.
3. **a** I like *coffee*. **b** I'd like *a coffee*.
4. **a** I can't see – my *hair* is in my eyes.
   b I've got *a hair* in my eye.
5. **a** Most English *cheese* is hard.
   b There are more than 1,000 British *cheeses*.

⏵ page 160 *Grammar reference: Nouns*

③ **Circle the correct articles in these sentences, without looking at Reading Part 2 (Ø = no article). Then check your answers in the text.**

1. *A* /(*The*) last time Irene Pepperberg saw Alex, she said goodnight as usual.
2. It took *a* / *the* brilliant insight to turn this human-centricity on its head.
3. This rather novel approach came to Dr Pepperberg, *a* / *Ø* 28-year-old theoretical chemist, in 1977.
4. But Alex, unlike *a* / *Ø* chimpanzee, learned to speak words easily.
5. *Ø* / *The* birds as well as *Ø* / *the* mammals can evolve *Ø* / *a* complex and sophisticated cognition.
6. Dr Pepperberg and her collaborators at *a* / *the* University of Arizona began teaching Alex.
7. She went to a pet shop and bought an African Grey parrot, which was then just *a* / *the* year old.
8. ... a species only distantly related to humanity, ... *a* / *the* parrot.

④ **Now match each use of *a/an*, *the* and Ø in Exercise 3 with one of these rules for the use of articles.**

1. Use the definite article, *the*:
   a when there is only one of something/someone
   b with superlative adjectives, including *first*, *last*, *only*, *same*
   c to refer to something/someone that has been mentioned before or that the reader already knows about
   d to refer to all the members of a group or species.
2. Use the indefinite article, *a/an*:
   a to refer to something/someone for the first time
   b in place of the number *one*
   c to refer to something/someone which is not specific (i.e. it doesn't matter which one)
   d to refer to someone's job.
3. Use no article, Ø:
   a with uncountable nouns which refer to something general
   b with plural countable nouns which refer to something general.

⑤ **Complete this text with the correct article: *a/an*, *the* or no article (Ø). For some gaps, more than one answer is possible.**

(1) ....A.... single South China tiger has been caught on camera by (2) .... hunter-turned-farmer, (3) .... first confirmed sighting for 30 years of (4) .... sub-species that (5) .... experts had feared was extinct, (6) .... Xinhua news agency said on Friday. Zhou Zhenglong took over 70 snaps of (7) .... young tiger lying in (8) .... grass near (9) .... cliff in (10) .... mountainous part of China. (11) .... experts confirmed (12) .... images showed one of (13) .... elusive cats.

Curiously, (14) .... villagers from (15) .... farmer's home area had reported (16) .... sightings of (17) .... tigers, and paw-prints, but apparently none had been confirmed for (18) .... decades.

'There has been no record of (19) .... wild South China tiger in more than 30 years, and it was only (20) .... estimate that China still had 20 to 30 such wild tigers,' Xinhua quoted research scientist Lu Xirong.

6 ⊙ **The following sentences contain mistakes with articles made by CAE candidates. There may be more than one mistake in each sentence. Find and correct the mistakes.**

1   Make sure you wear ⋀ suit and tie if it's ⋀ formal occasion.   *a, a*
2   You should get job even though you haven't got the degree in marketing.
3   This report aims to describe advantages and disadvantages of green taxes.
4   Students can access Internet in their classrooms and college library.
5   Society needs to provide affordable accommodation for homeless.
6   A most important thing is to get people talking about the issues.
7   Tokyo is a capital of Japan.
8   Nowadays the technology is everywhere.

▷ page 161 *Grammar reference: Articles*

Listening Part 2

1 **Before doing Listening Part 2, answer the questions in the Exam round-up box.**

Exam round-up

Say if the following statements are true (T) or false (F). If a statement is false, rewrite it to make it true.

In Listening Part 2:

1   you have to complete six sentences F – *you have to complete eight sentences.*
2   no more than two words will be missing from each sentence
3   the sentences are not identical to sentences on the recording
4   you should complete the sentences with words from the recording.

2 **You are going to listen to a radio talk about the effects of climate change on the Inuit people of the Arctic. Before you listen, discuss these questions.**

1   What do you know about the Inuit?
2   What natural resources does the Inuit lifestyle depend on?
3   How do you think climate change is affecting the Inuit?

3 🔊16 **Listen to this brief introduction to the Inuit. Does the speaker confirm any of the things you talked about in answer to Exercise 2?**

4 🔊17 **Now listen to the main recording. Does it include any of the ideas you had in answer to question 3 in Exercise 2 above?**

5 (17) **Listen to the main recording again and complete the sentences with words or phrases you hear.**

Professor Moore believes that the majority of
(1) ..educated adults.. are more likely to be familiar with
the concept of global warming.

The Inuit are aware of an alarming number of
(2) .... to their environment, such as
melting icebergs.

A ring around the moon was one of the
(3) .... which the Inuit people used to rely
on.

Because of global warming, birds such as the
(4) .... have appeared in the Arctic.

The belief of the Inuit people that the Arctic is thawing is
now supported by (5) ....

Warning signs include the erosion of
(6) ...., and the disappearance of lakes.

The Western world used to reject the
(7) .... of the Inuit on the grounds that it
was anecdotal and not reliable.

The elderly Inuit woman believes that her people may be
unable to (8) .... to what is happening to
the environment.

6 **Work in pairs to discuss these questions.**

1 What other examples do you know of groups of people, like the Inuit, who are suffering directly from climate change? Are there any such groups in your country? What can be done to help groups like this?

2 What 'traditional knowledge' is associated with your culture? How do people view this knowledge in the 21st century?

Vocabulary
Prepositions following verbs

1 **Circle the correct prepositions in *italics* in these sentences.**

1 The daily weather markers (on) / *for* which they have relied for thousands of years are becoming less predictable.

2 The Inuit elders and hunters who depend *of* / *on* the land are also disturbed …

3 These feelings are not simply based *on* / *to* Inuit superstition.

4 … scientists have begun paying attention to what the Inuit are reporting, and even incorporating it *into* / *on* their research into climate change.

5 They have adapted *for* / *to* the cold climate …

6 … nor does she try to blame anyone *for* / *on* the change in her environment.

2 ☉ **CAE candidates sometimes use the wrong prepositions after verbs. Correct the mistakes in these sentences.**

1 Many people firmly believe to the traditional wisdom of their ancestors. *in*

2 It is difficult to concentrate in your work if there is loud music playing.

3 I recently participated on a charity event at my college.

4 The company is insisting in the use of low-energy light bulbs in their offices.

5 The government will double the amount it spends in the environment.

6 Every flight you take contributes with global warming.

7 Many TV documentaries are now focusing in environmental issues.

8 The new energy-saving laws apply for all factories and offices.

Speaking Part 3

1 **Before doing Speaking Part 3, answer the questions in the Exam round-up box.**

Exam round-up

Circle the correct alternative in *italics* for each of the statements below.

In Speaking Part 3:

1 you speak to (*your partner*) / *the examiner*

2 you will be given a *picture* / *set of pictures* to talk about

3 you will be expected to talk for *one minute* / *three minutes*

4 communication skills are *more* / *less* important than expressing correct opinions

5 you *must* / *need not* agree with your partner.

2 Look at the six photographs illustrating different environmental problems, and discuss these questions in pairs or small groups.

1 What does each photograph show? Choose a word from List A and another from List B to form a compound noun which describes each problem.

A	B
air	fires
drought	consumption
flood	clearance
forest	conditions
fossil fuel	damage
rainforest	pollution

2 In what way can human activity be said to be responsible for each problem?

3 🎧18 You are going to hear two people answering the Part 3 questions. Read the questions, then listen and discuss the following.

1 Do the two candidates say how the threats in the photographs can affect people's lives?
2 Do they reach a final agreement about which threat will pose the greatest risk to the largest number of people?

• How can each of these threats affect people's lives?

4 Work in pairs. Discuss the same questions (above the photos).

• Try to describe more clearly than the people you have been listening to how the threats can affect people's lives.
• Try to reach agreement about which threat poses the greatest risk.
• Include some of the compound nouns in the list below in your discussions.

Forest fire: *fire risk, fire damage, insurance costs*
Drought conditions: *desert region, water shortage(s), crop failure*
Flood damage: *flood water(s), flood defences, river banks*
Air pollution: *exhaust fumes, vehicle emissions, factory chimneys, breathing difficulties*
Rainforest clearance: *rainforest, farm land, cash crops*
Fossil fuel consumption: *oil rig, fossil fuel, fuel consumption, fuel shortage*

• Which threat will pose the greatest risk to the largest number of people in the future?

Use of English Part 3

1 **Before doing Use of English Part 3, answer the questions in the Exam round-up box.**

Exam round-up

Say if the following statements are true (T) or false (F). If a statement is false, rewrite it to make it true.

In Use of English Part 3:

1 the text has 12 gaps *F – the text has 10 gaps.*

2 this part of the exam mainly tests your knowledge of grammar

3 you may have to add a prefix and a suffix to the words in capitals

4 the spelling of the original word doesn't change whether you add a prefix or a suffix.

2 **Make as many words as you can from the 'root' words in the box. The first word is given as an example.**

| able | help | know | move | nation |

Example: *ability/inability, disability, enable/disable, able/unable, disabled, ably*

3 **Read this text. For questions 1–10 use the word given in capitals at the end of some of the lines to form a word that fits in the gap in the same line. There is an example at the beginning (0).**

# Species loss accelerating >>>	
An international report has shown that human (0) ......*activities*...... are wiping out an average of three animal or plant species every hour. This is equal to 150 species a day, and between 18,000 and 55,000 species a year. The main (1) .... of the report is that we must slow down the worst spate of (2) .... since the (3) .... of the dinosaurs 65 million years ago.	ACT FIND EXTINCT APPEAR
Scientists and (4) .... have identified a range of threats to (5) .... and plants as diverse as right whales, Iberian lynxes, wild potatoes and peanuts. Global warming is adding to existing threats such as land (6) .... for farms or cities, pollution, and rising human populations. In order to deal with these challenges, we need to move more rapidly, and with more (7) .... at all levels – global, (8) .... and local.	ENVIRONMENT CREATE CLEAR DETERMINE NATION
Many experts believe that the world will fail to meet the goal, set by political leaders in 2002, of a major (9) .... in the rate of loss by the year 2015. Rates of species loss are (10) .... rising by more than a thousand times natural rates.	REDUCE CURRENT

4 **Discuss these questions in small groups.**

1 What species of plants or animals are in danger of becoming extinct in your country or region?

2 What can international organisations, national governments and individuals do to slow down the rate at which species are becoming extinct?

Writing Part 2
An information sheet

1 **Work in pairs. Read this Part 2 writing task, then answer the questions below.**

As part of a government environmental awareness campaign, you have been asked by a senior member of staff at your college or place of work to produce an information sheet for your colleagues. You should start by presenting some factual information about the organisation's current waste of resources, and go on to give advice about what individuals can do to reduce this waste.

1 What kind of resources is your organisation currently wasting? Think of materials, such as paper, and less visible resources such as electricity.

2 Make a list of things that individuals can do to reduce this waste. Start with simple things that everyone can do, like print on both sides of a piece of paper; then go on to more radical actions like working from home on one day a week.

2 Read this sample answer to the task above and discuss these points.

1 Has the writer dealt fully with all parts of the task? Is there factual information and advice?
2 Is the information sheet clearly organised?

Information sheet for colleagues: Environment awareness

KEY FACTS	ADVICE
Paper	
Our college currently uses four times as much computer paper as it did two years ago. This is despite the fact that we also store information on our computers and back it up on disks. Unnecessary use of paper affects the environment in two ways: firstly by using up natural resources, and secondly by posing a waste disposal problem.	Only print documents when there is a particular reason for doing so. Students can submit assignments as email attachments. Staff can mark these online and email them back to students. If you print out documents, use both sides of the paper and make sure you use recycled paper.
Electricity	
Lights, heaters and computers are routinely left on in the college when no one is in the building. Televisions and other pieces of electrical equipment are left on stand-by.	Remember to turn off all lights and electrical equipment when they are not in use.
Open windows allow heat to escape, adding to our consumption of electricity.	Close all windows when the heating is on.
Travel	
Some staff and students are making unnecessary journeys to and from the college by car and motorbike. This adds to our total energy consumption.	Do not come to the college unless you need to. When you come, use public transport, cycle or walk. Consider working from home on at least one day a week, using the telephone or email to contact staff or other students.

3 Now discuss these questions.

1 What verb forms does the writer mainly use in the **Key facts** part of the sheet?
2 What verb forms are mainly used in the **Advice** column?

4 What do the words and phrases in *italics* refer to?

1 *This* is despite the fact that ... (line 4)
2 ... we also store information on our computers and back *it* up on disks. (line 6)
3 ... adding to *our* consumption of electricity. (line 18)
4 *This* adds to our total energy consumption. (line 22)
5 Only print documents when there is a particular reason for *doing so*. (line 3)
6 ... turn off all lights and electrical equipment when *they* are not in use. (line 13)

Why are reference words like these used?

page 172 *Writing reference: An information sheet*

5 Now read this writing task and write your information sheet.

Your local council is organising a campaign to make your neighbourhood more 'green'. You have been asked to produce an information sheet for your neighbours. Start by presenting some factual information about the area, pointing out some of the environmental issues, then give advice about practical measures individuals and families can take to make the area more green.

Write your **information sheet** in 220–260 words.

Exam information

In the Writing paper Part 2 you may have the option of writing an 'information sheet'. This is writing which offers help or instruction of some kind. You should:

- produce clear factual information and/or advice on a topic
- organise the information and/or advice clearly.

Unit 11 *Vocabulary and grammar review*

Vocabulary

① Complete each sentence with the correct form of one of the phrasal verbs from the box.

> call off   call up   drop out   pay up   put off
> sign up   stick around   wrap up

1 Helen has a bit of free time and has decided to ....*sign up*.......... for a cookery course.
2 I tried to .... Francesca .... , but she'd got her mobile turned off.
3 If you .... in this job for long enough, you'll eventually get a promotion.
4 The conference has been .... because not enough people are interested in attending.
5 Paul was supposed to come travelling with us but he had to .... at the last minute.
6 Mikhail has had to .... his holiday till next month because he has too much work on at the moment.
7 The forecast says it's going to freeze tonight, so .... well if you're going out!
8 They owe us a lot of money and unless they .... soon, we'll have to take them to court.

② Complete each of the sentences below with a phrase or expression from the box.

> get your hands on   kept waiting   nothing to do with
> out of touch   sick and tired of   the whole point of
> without a trace

1 What I call real travelling has ..*nothing to do with*.. the holiday trips that most tourists tend to go on.
2 With BlackBerries and internet cafés, there's no excuse for being .... when travelling nowadays.
3 I'm a busy man and I hate being .... by people who are late.
4 I am .... people phoning me to sell me things and interrupting my work.
5 If you travel with a group, you miss .... travelling, which is to have completely new experiences and meet completely new people.
6 He disappeared .... somewhere in the Pacific, some weeks after setting off in a small boat to sail round the world.

7 If you can .... a good grammar book, it should help you a lot with your exam preparation.

③ Complete these sentences by writing *at, in* or *on* in each of the gaps.

1 I'll be waiting ....*at*..... the newsstand when you arrive.
2 Did you see Ferenc .... the conference?
3 Samya is .... her third year .... university.
4 Don't interrupt me while I'm .... the phone!
5 We do all our shopping .... that big new shopping centre .... the outskirts of town.
6 I'd love to spend my holidays .... a Pacific island!

Grammar

④ Complete the second sentence so that it has a similar meaning to the first sentence, using the word given. Do not change the word given. You must use between three and six words, including the word given.

1 Dieter missed the plane because he overslept.
WOULD
If Dieter had ..*not overslept, he would not have*.. missed the plane.

2 Nelson didn't get the job because when he came to his job interview, he arrived late.
TIME
If Nelson .... his job interview, he would have got the job.

3 Veronique couldn't apply for the job in IT because she knows that her computer skills aren't yet good enough.
BETTER
Veronique knows that if her computer skills .... for the job in IT.

4 Could you please refund my money as soon as possible?
GRATEFUL
I .... would refund my money as soon as possible.

5 We would have gone swimming if Bruno hadn't advised us not to.
FOR
If it .... , we would have gone swimming.

Unit 12 *Vocabulary and grammar review*

Vocabulary

❶ Use the words in capitals at the end of these sentences to form a word that fits in the gap in the sentence.

1 I don't know why everyone's being so ......*unfriendly*...... towards me. I've done nothing wrong. **FRIEND**

2 Global warming is one of the world's most serious .... problems. **ENVIRONMENT**

3 It can be difficult for people with certain .... to find a job. **ABLE**

4 She has an extensive .... of French history. **KNOW**

5 You can tell from his .... that he spends a lot of money on clothes. **APPEAR**

6 In this job you have to be original and to think .... **CREATE**

7 I hope my solicitor will be able to .... my legal situation. **CLEAR**

8 Yesterday there was a sudden downward .... in share prices. **MOVE**

❷ Most of the prepositions following verbs in these sentences are wrong. Replace them with the correct prepositions.

1 Over a hundred thousand people participated ~~with~~ yesterday's marathon.   *in*

2 Whether we go skiing or not depends to the weather and the state of the snow.

3 Do you have anything useful to contribute in our discussion?

4 This morning's lecture will focus on Picasso's early work.

5 You needn't fill in that section of the form – it doesn't apply for you.

6 If the CD doesn't play properly, I'd take it back to the shop and insist for a refund.

7 Can you turn the TV down? I can't concentrate to what you're saying.

8 Do you believe in supernatural phenomena?

Grammar

❸ Circle the most appropriate articles in *italics* in the first paragraph of this report.

(1) *A* /(*The*) North Polar ice cap is melting at (2) *an* / *Ø* alarming rate due to (3) *the* / *Ø* global warming, NASA scientists said today, with satellite images showing (4) *an* / *the* ice cap continuing to shrink. '(5) *The* / *Ø* part of (6) *the* / *Ø* Arctic Ocean that remains frozen all year round has been shrinking at (7) *the* / *Ø* rate of 10 per cent (8) *a* / *the* decade since 1980,' NASA researcher Josefino Comiso said.

❹ Complete the second paragraph of the same report with the most appropriate article in each gap.

'(1) ......*Ø*...... snow and sea-ice are highly reflective because they are white,' Comiso said. 'Most of (2) .... sun's energy is simply reflected back to (3) .... space. With (4) .... retraction of (5) .... ice cover, that means that less of (6) .... surface is covered by this highly reflective snow and sea-ice, and so more energy has been absorbed and (7) .... climate warms.'
Scientists reported in (8) .... September that (9) .... largest ice shelf in (10) .... Arctic off Canada's coast has broken up due to (11) .... climate change and could endanger (12) .... ships and drilling platforms in (13) .... Beaufort Sea.

Unit 13 Health and lifestyle

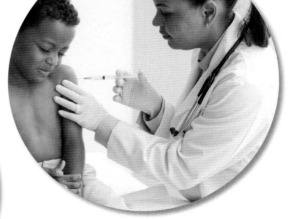

Starting off

Work in pairs. Discuss these questions.

1 What are the health advantages and disadvantages of the following?
   - doing sport or other physical activities
   - having childhood vaccinations
   - living in a rural area
   - living in a city
2 Which do you think has a greater influence on someone's health, their lifestyle or their genes?
3 What do you do to make sure you stay healthy and fit?

Listening Part 3

❶ Before doing Listening Part 3, answer the questions in the Exam round-up box.

Exam round-up

Circle the correct alternative in *italics* for each of the statements below.

In Listening Part 3:

1 you will hear a *talk* / (*conversation*)
2 the recording lasts approximately *two* / *four* minutes
3 you will have to answer *six* / *eight* multiple-choice questions
4 there will be *three* / *four* alternative answers for each question
5 you should listen for the same *ideas* / *words* as are used in the questions.

❷ You are going to hear a radio phone-in programme on the subject of allergies. Before you listen, discuss with a partner what you understand by these words and phrases: *allergen, asthma, immune system, pollen.*

3 **What do you know about allergies? Work in pairs, using the words from Exercise 2.**

1 Do more people suffer from allergies now than in the past?
2 What percentage of the population has an allergy?
3 What aspects of modern life can increase the chance of people suffering from allergies?

4 🎧19 **Listen to the recording and check your answers to the questions in Exercise 3.**

5 **Now read these questions. How many can you already answer?**

1 Which of these possible explanations for the increase in allergies does the programme presenter mention in her introduction?
   A People are exposed to more dangerous substances than in the past.
   B People's resistance to allergens is lower than in the past.
   C More new allergens are being released into the environment.
   D Higher levels of stress have made people more prone to allergies.

2 Which of the questions does the first caller, Tim, want to know the answer to?
   A What is the most likely cause of his allergy?
   B Why is he allergic to grass and pollen?
   C Will he ever be free of the allergy?
   D How can he improve his condition?

3 According to Dr Egerton, allergies
   A affect the very old or the very young.
   B often start between the ages of 30 and 40.
   C can start at any age.
   D are most likely to develop after the age of 60.

4 Arabella, the caller from Amsterdam,
   A thinks she may have passed on her allergy to her children.
   B asks how she can minimise the risk of her children having allergies.
   C wants to know whether her peanut allergy will continue in the future.
   D asks how probable it is that her children will have allergies.

5 If both a child's parents have a particular allergy, that child
   A is more than likely to have the same allergy.
   B has a less than fifty per cent chance of getting the same allergy.
   C will probably develop a different allergy.
   D is at no greater risk of developing the allergy than any other child.

6 According to Dr Bawaldi, some people believe that the increase in asthma among young children may result from
   A living in centrally heated or air-conditioned buildings.
   B being in areas with very high levels of exhaust fumes.
   C spending too much time in hygienic environments.
   D receiving medical treatment for other types of illness.

6 🎧19 **Listen to the recording a second time. For questions 1–6 choose the answer (A, B, C or D) which fits best according to what you hear.**

7 **Work in pairs to discuss these questions.**

1 Would you be prepared to do without air-conditioning and central heating if you were sure that this would lead to a reduction in allergies?
2 Do you agree that our modern culture is obsessive about cleanliness?
3 Some people say that food allergies are more common now than in the past. Why do you think this might be?

Vocabulary
Prepositions after adjectives

1 **Complete these extracts from the recording with the correct prepositions.**

1 These days we're all too familiar _with_ the word 'allergy' …
2 … and phrases like 'I'm allergic .... pollen or eggs or cats.'
3 Are we really becoming less resistant .... allergens?
4 We are getting better .... diagnosing and treating some allergies.
5 Exhaust fumes are widely regarded as being responsible .... the increase in asthma.
6 Some experts blame our modern culture for being obsessed .... cleanliness.

2 ⊙ **CAE candidates often make mistakes with prepositions after adjectives. Five of the following sentences contain preposition mistakes and one of the sentences is correct. Correct the mistakes.**

1 We sincerely apologise and hope this 10% discount will be acceptable ~~by~~ you. *to*
2 Drivers exceeding the speed limit are responsible for 90% of accidents in the city.
3 She has been interested for music since she was about three years old.
4 Living on the outskirts of the city is very convenient to the motorway system.
5 Teachers should try to be sensitive for the needs of their students.
6 That part of the stadium is closed for visitors – it's for athletes only.

Grammar
Ways of contrasting ideas

1 **Look at these extracts from the recording and underline words and phrases used to point out a contrast between two facts or ideas.**

1 Someone who was allergic to eggs would find it fairly easy to avoid eating anything containing eggs, <u>whereas</u> you would find it impossible to avoid all contact with grass and pollen ...
2 I've got to be really careful about foods which contain even small traces of peanuts, but what I'd like to know is ...
3 In your case, this would rise to a 20% risk. However, if the child's father also had an allergy of some kind, this risk would increase to 40%.
4 Even though we are getting better at diagnosing and treating some allergies, there is a year-on-year increase in the number of patients ...
5 Some experts blame our modern culture for being obsessed with cleanliness, while others believe that vaccinations to protect our children from certain diseases may actually weaken their immune system.

2 **Discuss these questions in pairs or groups.**

1 Which underlined words or phrases contrast facts or ideas in a single sentence?
2 Of these, which words or phrases must be placed **between** the two clauses?
3 Which word is an adverb which contrasts facts or ideas in **separate** sentences?
4 What other contrasting words and phrases do you know?
5 Which words or phrases could replace *whereas* and *even though* in extracts 1 and 4 above?

▶ page 161 *Grammar reference: Ways of contrasting ideas*

3 **Complete the following sentences using words from the box.**

~~although~~	but	even though	however	whereas

1 I recognised you as soon as I saw you ...*although*... we'd never met before.
2 Some people seem to enjoy cold, rainy weather, ... I'm not one of them.
3 Adults can be slow to learn new skills, ... children pick things up very quickly.
4 We thought the case was over. .... , new evidence has just come to light.
5 .... I've been here twice before, I'd forgotten where the post office was.

4 **We can also use *despite / in spite of (the fact that)* to express contrast. Which two sentences in Exercise 3 can you change to use one of these, and what other changes would you have to make?**

5 ⊙ **CAE candidates sometimes make mistakes in their use of contrasting link words. Find and correct the mistakes in each of these sentences. (There are often several ways of correcting these sentences.)**

1 ~~Despite~~ you are not a mechanic, you should learn to understand how cars work. *Although / Despite the fact that*
2 There are several kinds of snacks you can have between 9.00 am and 6.00 pm, however hot meals are limited to lunchtime.
3 I would like to point out that however he was usually a very efficient teacher, he wasn't available when I needed this information.
4 I appreciate being asked to give this talk again. Though I would like to suggest ways of improving this year's event.
5 In the past we used to have only a few TV channels, where nowadays we have many more choices.
6 While he left school at the age of 16, he went on to become one of the most famous politicians of his generation.

6 **Complete these sentences with your own endings.**

1 I don't mind going to the dentist, but ...
2 I realise that it's very important to keep fit. However, ...
3 Whereas most people I know go to the gym at least twice a week, I ...
4 Even though many people eat better food than they did a hundred years ago, ...

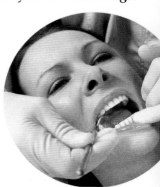

Speaking Part 2

① Before doing Speaking Part 2, answer the questions in the Exam round-up box.

② Work in pairs. Look at the six photographs on this page and discuss these questions.

1   What do all six photographs have in common?
2   Which of these activities are popular with people in your country? How would you explain this?

③ Work in pairs: Student A and Student B. Read this exam task related to Set A of the photos.

> Here are your pictures. They show people involved in physical activities. I'd like you to compare two of the activities, and say how effective they are as a means of keeping fit, and why they are so popular.

Set A

Student A: Prepare to talk for one minute about these photos, then talk about your two photos, with Student B listening.

Student B: You then answer this question: *which groups of people get the most benefit from activities like these?*

④ Now read this exam task related to Set B of the photos.

> Here are your pictures. They show people involved in demanding physical activities. I'd like you to compare two of the activities, and say what qualities a person needs to succeed in them, and why people want to participate in them.

Student B: Prepare to talk for one minute about these photos, then talk about your two photos, with Student A listening.

Student A: You then answer this question: *how are activities like these different from sports like football or basketball?*

⑤ ⟨20⟩ Listen to two people answering the Part 2 tasks that you have been doing. Discuss these questions in pairs.

1   Which candidate do you think does the task more successfully, the woman or the man?
2   What advice would you give each candidate to help them do better next time?

Set B

Reading Part 4

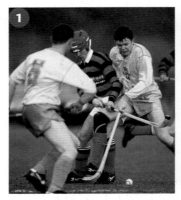

1 Before doing Reading Part 4, answer the questions in the Exam round-up box.

Exam round-up

Circle the correct alternative in *italics* for each of the statements below.

In Reading Part 4:

1 there are *twelve* / *fifteen* questions or statements

2 you *sometimes* / *always* have to match the questions or statements with a number of short texts

3 you have approximately *eight* / *eighteen* minutes for this task

4 you should read the *text(s)* / *questions or statements* first.

2 Look at the photographs of sports and discuss these questions in pairs.

1 Do you know the names of these sports? What similar sports do you know?

2 What kinds of sports are they? Indoor or outdoor? For teams or individuals? For men, women or both? Where are they played?

3 What is the national sport of your country? Who plays it? Is it mainly amateur or professional?

3 Read the questions below and <u>underline</u> the key idea in each one.

Which sport …

allows players to hit a ball with <u>equipment</u> and <u>parts of their body</u>?
1 [ ]

originally involved the use of an animal?
2 [ ]

is based on a traditional native sport?
3 [ ]

allows players to use their bodies to obstruct their opponents?
4 [ ]

makes the wearing of protective equipment optional?
5 [ ]

involves a total of eight players?
6 [ ]

disapproves of players looking at what they are doing?
7 [ ]

often receives funding from business?
8 [ ]

is rapidly increasing in popularity in a particular country?
9 [ ]

is not played all the year round?
10 [ ]

has games that last for approximately three quarters of an hour?
11 [ ]

is played mainly for pleasure and relaxation?
12 [ ]

has a ball which is designed to be picked up easily?
13 [ ]

involves the throwing of flat circular objects?
14 [ ]

involves contestants holding on to part of each other's clothing?
15 [ ]

4 Now read the article about national sports quickly. Are any of the five sports described similar to the sports in the photographs you discussed?

5 Read the article again. For questions 1–15, choose the appropriate sport (A–E). Sports may be chosen more than once.

Unusual national sports

A

Glíma is the oldest form of wrestling in Iceland. The most widespread version of the sport is Byxtagsglíma in which two wrestlers attempt to trip and throw each other by grasping a belt worn around their opponent's waist and thighs. To win, a wrestler must make his opponent touch the ground with a part of his body between the elbow and the knee. Wrestlers have to stand straight and are not allowed to fall on their opponents or to push them down by force. When they are fighting, they should always look over each other's shoulders, because it is considered more gentlemanly to wrestle by touch and feel than by sight. This form of glíma has always been a friendly recreational sport, but there are other, much more violent versions.

B

Hurling is an outdoor sport played mainly in Ireland. Players use an axe-shaped wooden stick, called a hurley, to hit a small ball between the other team's goalposts, either over or under the crossbar. Fewer points are scored if the ball goes over the crossbar. The ball can be caught in the hand and carried for no more than four steps, or hit in the air or on the ground with the stick. It can also be kicked or slapped with an open hand. A player who wants to carry the ball further than three steps has to bounce or balance the ball on the end of the stick. No special clothing or padding is worn by players, but a plastic helmet with a faceguard is recommended.

C

The official national sport of Argentina is **Pato**, a game which is played on horseback and combines elements of polo and basketball. Two four-member teams fight for possession of a ball which has six conveniently sized handles, and score by throwing the ball through vertically positioned rings, located at the top of three-metre-high poles. A closed net, extending downwards, holds the ball after goals are scored. The winner is the team with the most goals scored after six periods of eight minutes. The word *pato* is Spanish for duck, as in the past, instead of the ball, a live duck was used inside a basket.

D

Lacrosse is an outdoor team sport in which players use netted sticks to pass and catch a hard rubber ball. The aim is to score goals by propelling the ball into the opponent's goal. The team which scores more goals wins. Lacrosse is Canada's national summer sport and is one of the fastest-growing sports in the USA. Each team is composed of ten players: three attackers, three midfielders, three defenders and one goaltender. In men's lacrosse, players wear protective equipment on their heads, shoulders, arms and hands, as body-checking is an integral part of the game, and stick-checks to the arms and hands are considered legal.

E

Tejo is a Colombian sport in which players hurl a metallic plate weighing around two kilograms through the air to try to hit a clay-filled box with gunpowder in the middle. When the disc hits this target, there is a loud explosion. Whichever team causes more explosions wins. Turmeque, a more ancient version of the sport, has been played for over 500 years by the indigenous groups living in the different parts of Colombia. Originally, players used a golden disc which evolved into a stone disc and is now a metal disc. Nowadays in Colombia it is very common to find professional tejo teams in the major cities and towns. Most teams are sponsored by local companies.

6 **Work in pairs. Which of the five sports you have read about would you like to try? Are there any you would refuse to play? Give your reasons.**

Grammar
The language of comparison

1 **Read carefully through the article again to find examples of comparison language and note down each example you find.**

Examples:

*Glíma is the oldest form of wrestling in Iceland.
... it is considered more gentlemanly to wrestle by touch and feel than by sight.*

Now group your examples by type. For example:

- Comparative adjectives and adverbs: ***more gentlemanly ... than, ...***
- Superlative adjectives and adverbs: ***the oldest form, ...***
- Comparative/Superlative form + noun: ***the most goals, ...***

2 Answer these questions about comparison language from the examples you found in the article.

1 What kinds of words can follow *more* and *most*?
2 *More* has two opposites: *less* and *fewer*? How are these words used differently? What kinds of words can follow each?
3 Did you find the negative comparison in Text B? Can you think of a way of rephrasing that comparative?

▶ page 162 *Grammar reference: The language of comparison*

3 Rewrite these sentences, using the words in brackets.

1 Many people don't earn as much money as they did five years ago. (*less*)
   Many people earn less money than they did five years ago.
2 Finding a new job was easier than I expected it to be. (*difficult*)
3 There aren't as many unemployed people today as there were ten years ago. (*fewer*)
4 Working conditions are worse than they used to be. (*good*)
5 Increasing numbers of people are going abroad to find work. (*more*)

4 ⊙ CAE candidates sometimes make mistakes in their use of comparative words. Find and correct the mistakes in these sentences.

1 Previous models were much ~~biger~~ than what is available now. *bigger*
2 Actually, eating junk food is even worst for your health than smoking.
3 Doing the exam was much more stressful that I had expected it would be.
4 I noticed that there were less angry people than there had been a year ago.
5 Easily the harder thing about football for me is the training I have to do.
6 Unemployment was lower in some of the countries less industrialised.
7 If you travel at night, you'll find there is fewer traffic on the roads.
8 This will make the problem of obesity difficult even more.

5 Work in pairs. Compare the two most popular sports in your country. Think about the following aspects of the sports: the rules, the players, the spectators and the media interest.

Use of English Part 4

1 Before doing Use of English Part 4, answer the questions in the Exam round-up box.

Exam round-up

How much do you remember about Use of English Part 4? Circle the correct alternative in *italics* in each of these sentences.

In Use of English Part 4:

1 there are *four* / *five* questions
2 there are *three* / *four* gapped sentences in each question
3 the missing word will *always* / *usually* be the same type of word (e.g. a noun)
4 the word *can* / *can't* be in a different form, e.g. singular or plural, in the different sentences.

2 Many words in English have several different meanings. How many meanings can you think of for these words?

Adjectives: bright, fair
Nouns: character, class
Verbs: catch, present

Compare your answers with a partner, then check in a dictionary.

3 Here are three dictionary definitions for the word *plot*. Match each meaning to the use of the word in sentences a–c below.

plot (1) the story of a book, film or play

plot (2) a secret plan made by several people to do something that is wrong, harmful or not legal, especially to do damage to a person or government

plot (3) a small piece of land that has been marked or measured for a particular purpose

a We're going to turn part of our garden into a vegetable *plot*.
b The critics felt that the tortuous *plot* made the story difficult to follow.
c The police have foiled a *plot* to assassinate the president.

4 In Part 4 of the Use of English paper, you have to think of words with three different meanings which will fit into three sentences. For questions 1–5, think of one word only which can be used appropriately in all three sentences.

1 There is growing concern over the .... of our children's health and diet.
He's been governor of the .... of California for just over three years.
After gaining independence in 1957, the nation quickly transformed itself into a modern democratic ....

2 Scientists are going to .... an experiment into the effects of sleep deprivation.
All kinds of metal .... electricity very well.
He's retired now, but he used to .... one of Europe's top orchestras.

3 Did you get the .... I left, asking you to phone me?
I'm rich! I've just found a twenty-pound .... in my pocket.
The pianist played a wrong ...., but nobody noticed.

4 The price of grain is rising as more and more farmers are choosing to .... livestock for food.
Could you all please stand and .... your glasses to the bride and groom.
I'd start my own business if I could .... the money for the equipment I need.

5 You should keep a .... of everything you spend and earn in a month.
The man arrested last night by police has a long criminal ....
She has just set a new world .... for running the 1,000 metres.

Writing Part 1 A letter

1 Answer the questions in the Exam round-up box.

Exam round-up

How much do you remember about Writing Part 1? Complete the following sentences by writing one word or figure from the list below in each space. (There are two words that you do not need to use.)

input no notes persuade reader report review 220 260

1 You have ....*no*........ choice of task.

2 The task may be an article, a letter, a ....
or a proposal.

3 The task is always accompanied by .... material and .... on this.

4 You should write 180– .... words for this part.

5 You should identify the target .... in your writing. You will often have to express opinions, evaluate options and .... the reader.

2 Work in pairs. Read this writing task.

> You belong to a small neighbourhood sports club and have been asked by other members to write a letter of complaint to the club manager, Mandy Dawson, outlining reasons for your dissatisfaction with the club and the way it is currently run.
> Base your letter on the points made in these text messages and emails you have received from other members.
>
> Now write your **letter** in 180–220 words.

> Club's hardly ever busy – if we can't get more people to join, we'll go bust.

> Could make things cheaper for older people and families with kids.

> Some of our people are leaving us and going to cheaper places.

> Really got to resurface tennis courts – incredibly dangerous at the moment.

> ... asked for squash courts and shower rooms 2 years ago ...

③ **Read this sample letter written in answer to the above task. Has the writer answered all parts of the question and included all information provided by the input material?**

Dear Ms Dawson,

I'm writing on behalf of a number of club members who have (1) *been worried* / (*had concerns*) about the club and (2) *the way it's being run / its organisation*.

(3) *For a start, / Firstly*, it has been clear to us for (4) *quite a while / some time* that we have a membership problem. The club, which I visit regularly, has been (5) *noticeably less busy / pretty empty* recently.

In our view, there are two possible explanations for this decline. Firstly, we think that some members are joining other clubs with more up-to-date (6) *facilities / stuff*. Secondly, the cost of membership at our club may be high compared with other clubs (7) *in the area / round here*.

As to what action can be taken, our main suggestion is for the club to (8) *change / rethink* the cost of membership. We could (9) *bring in / introduce* reduced charges for (10) *old people / the elderly*, and also have a family rate to encourage parents to come with their children.

We also believe that we should resurface the tennis courts, which are currently in a dangerous condition. Some time ago, we also asked for squash courts and shower rooms to be provided.

We trust that you will (11) *think about / consider* our ideas and suggestions and we look forward to receiving a response from you (12) *at your earliest convenience / as soon as possible*.

Yours faithfully,

④ **Work in pairs. A letter like this should be written in formal language. Circle the more formal words and phrases (1–12) from the two alternatives given. (You may want to refer back to the list of formal and informal language features on page 33 in Unit 3.)**

⑤ **What is the difference in meaning between these groups of words?**

- *member / membership* (Can you think of other pairs of words like this?)
- *cost / fee / charge / price / fare / rate*

⑥ **What phrases does the writer of the letter use to introduce:**

- explanations for the decline in membership?
- suggestions for solving the problem?

⑦ **Read the following writing task, then before you write your letter, discuss questions 1–3 below.**

> It has recently been announced that your area will receive funding for a range of new sports and fitness facilities for young people. Read the story from a local newspaper and the notes you wrote on the story, then write a letter to the newspaper saying why you think this funding is needed and suggesting ways in which the money could be spent.
>
> Now write your **letter** in 180–220 words.

NEW CASH FOR YOUTH SPORT

The Sports Minister announced yesterday that towns and cities in our area will be eligible for funding for new sports facilities. These will be aimed specifically at increasing fitness levels in children and teenagers. Concerns have been expressed recently that young people all over the country are not as fit as they were twenty years ago. It will be up to local councils to decide exactly how the money should be spent.

Not before time! Desperate need for more up-to-date facilities – and more of them!

schools have cut back on sport

kids would rather do things inside

need sports centres in all towns

youth leagues should be set up for most popular sports

1 What are the implications of the note 'desperate need for more up-to-date facilities – and more of them'?
2 Why do you think schools have 'cut back on sport'?
3 How will setting up 'youth leagues' in the most 'popular sports' help to increase levels of fitness?

⑧ **Write your letter. Remember to use formal language. You may be able to use some of the explanation and suggestion language from the sample.**

⊙ page 173 *Writing reference: Letters*

Unit 14 Moving abroad

Starting off

1 Work in pairs. Why do people migrate? Think of as many reasons as you can.

2 🔊 You are going to hear six people who have migrated talking about their experiences. Listen and match each person with the aspect of migration (A–H) they mention. (There are two aspects you do not need.)

	aspect
Speaker 1	
Speaker 2	
Speaker 3	
Speaker 4	
Speaker 5	
Speaker 6	

A I migrated to fulfil my ambitions.
B I encountered some negative attitudes to start with.
C I've felt homesick since I left.
D I find it difficult to stay in one place for long.
E I moved because of a relationship.
F I wanted a better environment for my children.
G I was fed up with the weather.
H I'm surprised how well my life has turned out.

3 Work in small groups.

1 Do you know anyone whose reasons for emigrating or experiences of emigrating are similar to the ones you've just heard?

2 How can emigration benefit
  • the country people emigrate from?
  • the country people immigrate to?

① The Atlantic Passage

There is a sentence that has stirred the imagination of
Europe as powerfully as any call to arms. I've seen it written
a hundred times, and have always felt a pang of envy for its
lucky author. It is so jaunty, so unreasonably larger than
5 life. It promises to deliver the unexpected – some fantastic
reversal of fortune, some miraculous transfiguration in the
character of the writer. It deserves a paragraph to itself, and
should be printed in ceremonious italics.

Having arrived in Liverpool, I took ship for the New World.

10 Behind the sentence crowd the emigrants themselves – a
crew of people dingy enough to take the shine out of
the words. They stand in line: the long-out-of work, the
illiterate, the hapless optimists, the bankrupt adventurers.
Some are dignified by the involuntary heroism that attaches
15 itself to any persecuted people; but most of the single men
and families on the dock are not – were not – refugees. If
they were on the run, they were more likely to be fleeing
tallymen and creditors than cruel kings and despots. Very
few of them could seriously claim to earn the sentimental
20 welcome which would meet them on the far side of the
ocean as their ship passed the Statue of Liberty on its way
into dock at Ellis Island. Few of them would be able to read
(or understand) the words of Emma Lazarus's poem on
Liberty's plinth, that grandiloquent advance advertising of
25 America as the sanctuary of freedom and democracy. To
most of the immigrants America was simply a tantalising
rumour of easy money – of jobs, clothes, food.

From *Hunting Mister Heartbreak* by Jonathan Raban

Reading Part 1

❶ **Work in pairs. You are going to read three
extracts which are all concerned in some way
with emigration. Before doing Reading Part 1, do
the exercise in the Exam round-up box.**

Exam round-up

How much do you remember about Reading Part 1? Circle the
correct alternative in *italics* in each of these sentences.

In Reading Part 1:

1   there are (three) / *four* texts and (six) / *eight* questions; you
    have to choose the best alternative, A, B, C or D

2   you have about *fifteen* / *eighteen* minutes for this part

3   you should read *the texts quickly before reading the
    questions* / *the questions quickly before reading the texts*

4   you should read the alternatives *before* / *after* reading the
    section of text where a question is answered

5   there *will* / *needn't* be words in the text which support the
    alternative you've chosen.

❷ **Read the texts quite quickly. Where might you
read each of them?**

❸ **For questions 1–6, choose the answer (A, B, C
or D) which you think fits best according to the
text. (Note: there are two questions about each
extract.)**

Extract One

1   How does the writer feel about the person who
    wrote the sentence in line 9?
    A   He wishes he was in the writer's situation.
    B   He worries that the writer will have an
        unpleasant surprise.
    C   He is delighted that the writer will benefit from
        the journey.
    D   He thinks the writer deserves some good luck.

2   According to the writer, why did most migrants
    want to leave their own country?
    A   to escape from oppression
    B   to live in a free society
    C   to escape poverty
    D   to escape family ties

2

When talent goes abroad

In general, when immigrants send money home, this has the greatest impact in country districts, which tend to send the unskilled, not the skilled, abroad. And because the most educated are more likely to emigrate with their families and to integrate quickly into their new homeland, they seem less likely to send money back. One of the few attempts to estimate whether remittances by the skilled offset the loss of intellectual capital to the sending country concluded that they did not.

On the other hand, emigration may bring other benefits to the sending country. The possibility of leaving and the higher income to be earned abroad may encourage more people to go into higher education. As not everyone will leave, the result will be a bigger pool of skills than would otherwise be the case.

What rich countries should do is make migration simple, but temporary. The tougher it is for migrants to enter a country, the more reluctant they will be to risk leaving to go home. However, the longer they stay abroad, the more likely their stay is to become permanent. The old contacts go, and it becomes harder to fit in. Mobility, which fits in comfortably with today's employment patterns, is more likely to benefit both sending and receiving countries than the old idea of migrating for good.

From *The Economist*

3

Getting a Student Visa or Permit

You must provide all the relevant evidence listed on the checklist on the front pages of the **Application to Study in New Zealand** (NZIS 1012). If you do not provide all of the necessary documents, your application may be returned to you. All applicants under Student policy must be bona fide applicants, be of good character and of an acceptable standard of health.

A bona fide applicant is a person who can show they genuinely intend a temporary stay in New Zealand for a lawful purpose. Evidence of genuine intent and lawful purpose may include, but is not limited to, the following:

- any information or submissions showing you have a legitimate need to spend time in New Zealand for a specific period; and

- any documents or submissions showing you meet the Student policy provisions.

Character requirements

If you are aged 17 years or over and intend being in New Zealand *for 24 months or longer*, or are required by a specific policy or a visa or immigration officer to provide evidence of your character, you must provide police certificates from your country of citizenship (unless you can provide satisfactory evidence that you have never lived there) and from any country in which you have lived for five or more years since attaining the age of 17 years. Note: All police certificates must be less than six months old when you make your application.

From *Guide for Studying in New Zealand*

Extract Two

3 What point does the writer make in the first paragraph?
   A People in rural areas benefit from emigration more than urban dwellers.
   B Sending countries do not benefit financially from the emigration of skilled workers.
   C Emigration places an enormous strain on the education systems of sending countries.
   D Skilled workers are more likely to emigrate than unskilled workers.

4 According to the writer, rich countries should ease immigration restrictions in order to
   A help immigrants to integrate.
   B attract skilled immigrants into key industries.
   C give immigrants the chance of permanent jobs.
   D make it easier for immigrants to return to their home country.

Extract Three

5 A bona fide applicant is someone who
   A behaves well and meets health requirements.
   B wishes to make New Zealand their permanent home.
   C intends to stay in New Zealand for a limited period.
   D has never been in trouble with the police.

6 Applicants should provide police certificates if they
   A have never lived in their country of citizenship.
   B are over a certain age and wish to spend long periods in the country.
   C have lived for long periods in countries where they are not citizens.
   D have recently been convicted of a criminal activity.

4 **Work in small groups. Imagine someone your age was thinking of coming to live in your country.**

- What opportunities might there be for them?
- What problems might they face?

Grammar
Comment adverbials

1 Look at these sentences from Starting off. Which word or phrase in each sentence shows the speaker's attitude or opinion about what he says?

You see, unfortunately I'm one of those typical expatriates who spends two years working in this country and three years working in that. I don't think I could ever go back to my home country because quite honestly I just wouldn't fit in.

● page 163 *Grammar reference: Comment adverbials*

2 Rewrite each sentence below, replacing the <u>underlined</u> words with a comment adverbial from the box in each gap.

> apparently ~~Fortunately~~ generally speaking kindly
> obviously personally to be honest undoubtedly

1 <u>It's lucky that</u> she comes from a very supportive family.
......*Fortunately*...... , she comes from a very supportive family.
2 <u>I'm absolutely certain that</u> he's the best player.
He's .... the best player.
3 <u>Most of the time</u> the weather here is pleasant.
.... , the weather here is pleasant.
4 <u>I'm telling you the truth when I say that</u> I found the journey very uncomfortable.
.... , I found the journey very uncomfortable.
5 <u>From what I've heard</u>, Bill is thinking of emigrating to Canada.
.... , Bill is thinking of emigrating to Canada.
6 Anaya's parents have invited me to stay with them, <u>which is very kind of them</u>.
Anaya's parents have .... invited me to stay with them.
7 <u>It's clear that</u> he wasn't happy with the way he was treated.
.... , he wasn't happy with the way he was treated.
8 <u>To give you my opinion</u>, I wouldn't buy that car.
.... , I wouldn't buy that car.

Listening Part 4

1 Work in pairs. You will hear five short extracts in which people are talking about migrants and migration. Before you listen, do the task in the Exam round-up box.

Say if the following statements are true (T) or false (F). If a statement is false, rewrite it to make it true.

In Listening Part 4:

1 you have to do two tasks T
2 you hear five different speakers and you have to choose from seven options
3 you hear the piece twice. You should do the first task the first time you listen and the second task the second time you listen
4 you may hear the answer to the second task before the answer to the first task.

2 (22) **Now listen and complete the two tasks.**

While you listen you must complete both tasks.

Task One

For questions **1–5**, choose from the list **A–H** the aspect of migration that each speaker is referring to.

A loss of local culture

B integration in schools   Speaker 1 [__] **1**

C changing eating habits   Speaker 2 [__] **2**

D finding accommodation   Speaker 3 [__] **3**

E mixed marriages   Speaker 4 [__] **4**

F communication problems

G sending money home   Speaker 5 [__] **5**

H starting a business

Task Two

For questions **6–10**, choose from the list **A–H** the thing which has impressed each speaker the most.

A Employment is created.   Speaker 1 [__] **6**

B Families are divided.

C The quality of life   Speaker 2 [__] **7**
   improves.

D The cost of living rises.

E Standards are raised.   Speaker 3 [__] **8**

F Local people lose their
   jobs.
                                   Speaker 4 [__] **9**
G Local people learn
   something new.

H Attitudes are more diverse.   Speaker 5 [__] **10**

3 **Work in small groups. Take turns to summarise what one of the speakers said. Each student should choose a different speaker.**

- Before you speak, spend a minute or two thinking about what you're going to say.
- Try to use some of the comment adverbials from Grammar Exercise 2 on page 140 when you speak.

Vocabulary

Learn, *find out* and *know*; *provide*, *offer* and *give*

1 **CAE candidates often confuse *learn*, *find out* and *know*. Which verb, *learnt*, *found out* or *knew*, is possible in the sentence below?**

Anyway, I .... that she's working here as a nurse to support her family back home … (Speaker 2)

2 **Match the words with their definitions from *CALD*. (Two of the words have two meanings.)**

1 know   2 find out   3 learn

a to get information about something because you want to know more about it, or to learn a fact or piece of information for the first time

b to get knowledge or skill in a new subject or activity

c to have the information in your mind

d to make yourself remember a piece of writing by reading it or repeating it many times

e to be certain

3 **CAE candidates often confuse *offer*, *give* and *provide**. Complete these extracts from Listening Part 4 by writing *offer*, *give* or *provide* in the correct form in the spaces.**

* *provide somebody with something / provide something for somebody*

1 The other day she was really looking dead tired so I .... to get her a coffee afterwards.
2 Her salary here's enough to .... their schooling, their clothing and all sorts of other things back home.
3 They're already doing so well that they've even been able to .... jobs to a couple of locals as well.

4 **Provide*, *offer* and *give* often have very similar meanings. However, sometimes their meanings are slightly different. When their meanings are different, which word, *provide* or *offer*, means:**

1 to give someone something they need?
2 to ask someone if they would like to have something or if they would like you to do something?

5 ⊙ **Each of the sentences below contains a mistake made by CAE candidates with *learn, find out, know*; *provide, offer* and *give*. Correct the mistakes.**

1 I phoned a taxi company to ~~know~~ the average rate from the airport to the city centre. *find out*
2 You should go to the information desk to know where to pick up your luggage.
3 While studying English, you also know about their customs and traditions.
4 I've checked the timetable to learn the time of the next train to Łódź.
5 Comfy Catering Services aims to give good food for students at low cost.
6 We feel that the authorities should be prepared to give a solution to those parents who wish to take it.
7 Studying at the Ace School in London will offer you the opportunity to make new friends and meet people.
8 I'm writing to complain about the service you offered during our stay in your hotel.

Speaking Part 4

1 **Before doing Speaking Part 4, do the task in the Exam round-up box below.**

Exam round-up

Circle the correct alternative in *italics* in the following sentences.

1 Speaking Part 4 lasts about *two minutes* / *four minutes*.
2 You are asked to give your opinions on *subjects connected with the same theme as Speaking Part 3* / *a new theme*.
3 You and your partner *are asked different questions* / *are expected to discuss your ideas about the same questions*.
4 You should give *a brief answer* / *quite a long answer*.

2 **Work in pairs. Which of the phrases in the box below could you use when answering each of these questions? (You can use some of the phrases with more than one answer.)**

1 What are the benefits of a multicultural society?
2 Should people who go to live in another country adopt the culture of that country? Why (not)?
3 How can governments help immigrants?

cover people's basic needs   create cultural diversity
make society a richer place   open up people's minds
encourage tolerance towards other ways of life
make the transition into a new society
people from different backgrounds, different outlooks
provide housing   help them integrate   to live side by side

3 🎧23 **Now listen to James and Sara answering the questions. Note down their answers to each question.**

4 🎧24 **Complete these extracts from James' and Sara's answers by writing a modal verb (*can, may, should*, etc.) in each gap. Then check your answers by listening to the extracts.**

1 I think it ....*can*........ open up people's minds to other experiences that they .... not be able to have otherwise.
2 I personally think it .... make society itself richer by having diversity within it.
3 I think people .... be allowed to have some of the elements of their own culture as long as they're not detrimental to the good of the majority.
4 What they .... to do is provide lots of information at the beginning so that people .... make the transition into the new society.
5 Housing is something I think they .... be providing.

5 **Work in pairs. Discuss your answers to the three questions in Exercise 2. Try to use some of the phrases from the box in Exercise 2 when you speak.**

6 **Work in pairs to discuss the questions.**

1 Many companies expect their employees to be ready to move to different places and countries to work. Do you think everyone should be ready to move for their job? Why (not)?
2 How has your country changed in recent years as a result of immigration or emigration?
3 Some people suggest that immigrants should be obliged to learn the language of the country they go to. Do you agree?

Use of English Part 5

1 Do the exercise in the Exam round-up box below.

2 Complete the second sentence so that it has a
similar meaning to the first sentence, using the
word given. Do not change the word given. You
must use between three and six words, including
the word given. Work in pairs. For the question
below, which would be the correct answer: a, b, c
or d? Why are the other answers incorrect?

> Boris should have contacted us the moment he
> arrived.
> **TOUCH**
> Boris was supposed ....
> as soon as he arrived.

a Boris was supposed *getting in touch with us* as
 soon as he arrived.

b Boris was supposed *to get in touch with us* as soon
 as he arrived.

c Boris was supposed *to have got in touch with us* as
 soon as he arrived.

d Boris was supposed *to have made contact with us*
 as soon as he arrived.

3 Do questions 1–4, using the clues given to help
you.

1 Could you remind me to phone Charlie on Friday?
 GRATEFUL
 I'd .... me to phone
 Charlie on Friday.
 *Clue: There are two parts to this answer: a request
 and an indirect question.*

2 Mario wasn't given any help completing the
 project.
 ALL
 Mario completed ....
 himself.
 Clue: Use an expression which means 'alone'.

3 You won't get into the national team unless you try
 much harder.
 MAKE
 You'll have ....
 if you're going to get into the national team.
 *Clue: What noun can we use with 'make' to mean
 'try hard'?*

4 Fatima still hasn't decided if she'll study in New
 Zealand next year.
 MIND
 Fatima hasn't ....
 to study in New Zealand next year.
 *Clue: What expression with 'mind' means 'to
 decide'?*

4 Now do these questions without clues (as in the
exam).

1 It's possible that Katya has been delayed by the
 heavy traffic.
 HELD
 Katya may ....
 by the heavy traffic.

2 I wasn't sure who was to blame for the accident.
 FAULT
 I couldn't tell .... was.

3 After Ranjit had discovered the truth, he reported
 the facts to the police.
 OUT
 Having .... ,
 Ranjit reported the facts to the police.

4 Franz said he had tried as hard as he could to
 make Sonia happy.
 BEST
 'I have ....
 make you happy, Sonia,' said Franz.

Grammar
Emphasis

1 Read the Grammar reference on page 163, then look at sentences 1–7 below. Match them with the ways of adding emphasis a–d. (Some of the sentences have more than one way of adding emphasis.)

▶ page 163 *Grammar reference: Emphasis*

a Fronting
b Cleft sentences
c Using adverbs for emphasis
d Using reflexive pronouns

1 Behind the sentence crowd the emigrants themselves. *a, d*
2 To most of the immigrants America was simply a tantalising rumour of easy money …
3 And because the most educated are more likely to emigrate with their families and to integrate quickly into their new homeland, they seem less likely to send money back.
4 What rich countries should do is make migration simple, but temporary.
5 What struck me most was seeing their mums-in-law being taught how to cook new dishes.
6 I thought it was quite remarkable actually because we give the impression of being rather a nationalistic lot but that doesn't seem to be the case at all in fact.
7 I personally think it can make society itself richer by having diversity within it …

2 Express the ideas in the sentences below in a more emphatic way. (There may be several ways of doing this.)

1 I believe that young people benefit from living and working abroad.
   – *I personally believe that young people benefit greatly from living and working abroad.*
   – *I myself believe that by living and working abroad young people benefit greatly.*
2 Many people move overseas because they don't like the climate in their own country.
3 Living in a multicultural society enriches our lives.
4 She feels lonely living away from her family.
5 He finds it impossible to save money although he has a well-paid job.
6 Franz learnt to speak the language perfectly by living in the country.
7 The director of studies taught us when our teacher was ill.
8 A good education teaches people tolerance.

Writing Part 2 An article

1 Work in pairs. Answer question 1 or 2.

1 Have you ever worked abroad? What did you learn from the experience?
2 Would you like to work abroad? What would you expect to gain from the experience?

2 Do the exercise in the Exam round-up box below.

Exam round-up

How much do you remember about how to approach Writing Part 2? Put the following advice in the correct order by writing a number 1–8 by each.

a	Check what you have written looking for specific mistakes you know you make.	
b	Organise your notes into a paragraph-by-paragraph plan including some of the vocabulary you'd like to use.	
c	Read all the questions and choose the one you think you can do best.	1
d	Brainstorm ideas and make rough notes.	
e	Identify who the reader is, decide what would be a suitable style and what effect you want to produce on the reader.	
f	Analyse the question, underlining the things you must deal with in your answer and identifying your objectives in writing.	
g	Write your answer (220–260 words) following your plan.	
h	Take about 45 minutes to do the whole task.	8

3 Look at the writing task below.

1 Who will read the article?
2 What style would be suitable?
3 In what ways would you have to use your imagination to do the task? Work together and invent the details you need.

> You spent last summer doing a temporary job in another country. An international magazine has asked you to write an article describing your experience, saying what you learnt from it and saying whether you would recommend it to other readers.
>
> Write your **article**.

4 Read the answer opposite.

1 Is the style formal or informal?
2 Find examples of each of the following ways of adding emphasis:
   - fronting
   - using adverbs
   - a cleft sentence.
3 Which paragraph deals with each part of the task?
4 <u>Underline</u> words and phrases you might be able to use in other writing tasks.

5 Work in pairs. Look at the writing task below.

1 Who will read the article and what style would be suitable?
2 Make a plan for your article: decide how many paragraphs you need and what you should put in each paragraph.
3 Think of a title for your article.

Last year you decided to spend a few months living in an English-speaking country and staying with an English-speaking family there. An international magazine has asked you to write an article describing your experience, saying what you learnt from it and saying whether you would recommend it to other readers.

Write your **article**.

---

6 Work alone and write your article.

▶ page 166 *Writing reference: Articles*

Two months in an office in Adelaide

Last year, feeling the need for a break in my normal routine, I spent two months working in our Adelaide office as part of the company's exchange programme.

What I discovered from the experience was a completely different office environment. This gave me the opportunity to compare our working methods with those of Australia.

Surprisingly – at least for me at the beginning – relationships in the office both between colleagues and between staff and management were very informal although generally quite friendly. Participants in meetings, I found, were quick to get to the point and ready to express their views directly regardless of hurting other people's feelings.

I came away with a number of extremely positive impressions from my experience. Firstly and very importantly, everyone said what they thought without fear of, for example, upsetting the managers. What this meant was that new ideas were generated and exchanged easily, leading to a far more creative and motivated workplace atmosphere. Also, people were very direct, which made meetings and work discussions highly efficient though not always comfortable. On the other hand, this meant that unfortunately consideration of the human dimension was occasionally missing from relationships and that we were not always treated with great respect.

Despite this minor drawback, I'd strongly recommend working in Australia to anyone who wants a taste of working life on the other side of the world. I found I made a good number of new friends and returned with ideas which I hope will transform my workplace and my professional life.

Unit 13 *Vocabulary and grammar review*

Vocabulary

❶ Complete the puzzle, using these clues.

1 physical reaction to various substances, for example grass, dust
2 powder produced by flowers, trees and grass
3 green or black substance that grows on old food or wet surfaces
4 .... *fumes* come from a car engine and pollute the air
5 *hay* .... is a distinctive type of 1
6 grass and dust are types of this
7 the noun related to clean
8 medical procedure which involves giving someone an injection to make them immune to a particular disease
9 adjective related to 1 and 6

```
                    9
          1 □ _ _ _ _ _
        2 _ _ □ _ _ _
      3 _ _ _ □ _ _
        4 □ _ _ _ _ _
      5 _ _ _ □ _
    6 _ _ _ _ □ _
  7 _ _ _ _ _ □ _ _
    8 _ _ _ □ _ _ _ _ _ _
```

❷ Complete these sentences with the correct prepositions.

1 Be careful what you say to him. He's very sensitive ...*to*.... criticism.
2 As the manager of the department, you are responsible .... recruiting new staff.
3 There are more and more viruses which are resistant .... traditional antibiotics.
4 Are you familiar .... the music of Jan Gabarek?
5 If you want to be better .... playing the guitar, you'll have to practise more.
6 I can't eat omelettes because I'm allergic .... eggs.
7 I like the house itself, but it isn't very convenient .... the supermarket or the station.
8 Please let us know if our offer is acceptable .... you.

Grammar

❸ Rewrite these sentences, correcting any errors in the use of contrasting words or phrases.

1 He thought he had some terrible disease, however it was just a bad case of flu.
He thought he had some terrible disease, <u>but</u> it was just a bad case of flu.
2 My sister seems to catch every cold going although I am rarely ill.
3 Despite he didn't feel well, he went to work as usual.
4 But I exercise every day, I'm still overweight.
5 He refused to see his doctor. Although everyone he knew advised him to.

❹ Complete the second sentence so that it has a similar meaning to the first sentence, using the word given. Don't change this word. Use three to six words including the word given.

1 The public health service is worse than it was ten years ago.
GOOD
The public health service is *not as good as it was* ten years ago.

2 We don't have as many qualified nurses as we need.
FEWER
We .... we need.

3 My new job is not as easy as I expected.
DIFFICULT
My new job .... I expected.

4 I'm really tired. I shall be very glad when we get home.
SOONER
I'm really tired. The .... better.

5 I earned less money than I thought I would last week.
MUCH
I .... as I thought I would last week.

6 Your diet is just as bad as mine.
BETTER
Your diet .... mine.

Unit 14 *Vocabulary and grammar review*

Vocabulary

1 Complete the sentences below by writing *learn, find out, know, provide, offer* or *give* in the correct form in the gaps. You can use any verb more than once.

1 How old were you when you ......*learnt*...... your multiplication tables?
2 I've been trying to .... what I need to do to get a working visa for New Zealand.
3 I think it's the government's duty to .... education for all young people free up to the age of 21.
4 Now where are my keys? I .... they're in my bag somewhere!
5 Rebecca has been .... the chance to improve her Spanish by studying in Argentina for a year.
6 My sister has been .... a job in the company and she's considering it at the moment.
7 I don't think the police will ever manage to .... who stole the money.
8 You'll never .... to drive properly unless you go to a proper driving school.

Grammar

2 Complete the second sentence so that it has a similar meaning to the first sentence, using the word given. Do not change the word given. You must use between three and six words, including the word given.

1 We didn't have as much time as we wanted to understand all this information.
   TAKE
   What we wanted ......*was more time to take*...... in all this information.

2 Everybody agreed that the music at Lenka's presentation was very annoying.
   OBJECTED
   It was the music .... at Lenka's presentation.

3 First, you complete this form and then you post it to the embassy.
   FILL
   What you have .... this form and then send it to the embassy.

4 Audrey is not prepared to leave her current job.
   LAST
   'Getting a new job is .... do!' cried Audrey.

5 Alfredo wanted nothing more than to relax when he got home.
   TAKE
   All Alfredo wanted to .... easy when he got home.

3 Complete the letter below by writing one of the adverbs or adverbial phrases from the box in each of the spaces. Use each adverb/adverbial phrase once only. In some cases more than one answer is possible.

> actually   almost certainly   apparently   hopefully
> obviously   quite surprisingly   ~~thoughtfully~~   to be honest

Dear Odile,

Thank you so much for so (1) ....*thoughtfully*.... inviting me to stay with you and your family for a few months later this year. I will (2) .... take you up on your offer as I've been thinking for some time of doing a gap year before I go to university. (3) .... , I need a break from studying and I think a spell of living abroad would suit me perfectly.

(4) .... , because I'm rather tired of school life, I haven't been working particularly hard this term, but (5) .... , I've managed to pass all my exams with quite good grades. (6) .... , when I go to university (after my gap year), I'll have to work quite a lot harder. I already know several people on the course I want to do and (7) .... it's very demanding. So (8) .... a few months abroad will refresh me enough to really get down to work when I get back.

I'll be in touch when I've got my plans a little clearer.

Very best wishes,

Candice

Grammar reference

Contents

Unit 1

Verb forms to talk about the past

The past simple tense is used to describe:

- something that happened at a specific time in the past: *I first met Greg in 1997. Susie left five minutes ago.*
- a state at a specific time in the past: *Yesterday I felt so tired that I didn't go to work.*
- things which happened over a period of time in the past, but not now: *I studied at the Sorbonne in Paris for four years from 2001 to 2005.*
- actions or events which happened one after the other: *She opened the fridge, took out the milk, gave some to the cat and put some in her coffee.*
- habitual actions or events over specific periods of time in the past: *While he was away on holiday, he telephoned his mother every day to see how she was.*

The past continuous tense is used to describe:

- an activity which started before and continued until an event in the past: *She was driving to work when she was stopped by the police.* (The activity of driving was interrupted by the police stopping her.)
- an activity which started before and continued after an event in the past: *I was cooking lunch when I heard the news.* (And I continued to cook lunch afterwards.)
- situations which were temporary at a time in the past: *I remember the events of that summer well. I was staying with my aunt at the time, just while my flat was being redecorated.*

  Notes:

  Use the past simple if the situation in the past was more permanent: *I lived in Brighton when I was a child.* (not *I was living*)

  Continuous tenses are not normally used with verbs which describe states: ~~Samdi was owning a house in Mayfair.~~

- something that frequently happened with *always* or *forever*, often to express amusement, strangeness or irritation: *My dad was always dressing up in funny hats and making jokes. We moved because we got fed up with the neighbours, who were forever arguing.*

State verbs

We do not usually use the continuous with state verbs. These are commonly:

- verbs which **express opinions**, **feelings** or **knowledge**, e.g. *agree, assume, believe, disagree, hate, hope, know, like, love, prefer, realise, regret*.

- verbs which **describe appearance**, e.g. *appear, look, seem, resemble*.

- verbs which **describe senses** e.g. *feel, smell, taste*.

- these other verbs: *belong, consist, contain, cost, have, own*.

The past perfect simple tense is used:

- to indicate that we are talking about an action which took place, or a state which existed, **before** another activity or situation in the past, which is described in the past simple: *When Maria got home, they had eaten dinner.*

  Compare this with: *When Maria got home, they **ate** dinner.* (This indicates that they ate dinner when she arrived.)

- typically with time expressions like: *when, as soon as, after, before, it was the first time*, etc.: *He went home as soon as he'd finished his work.*

The past perfect continuous tense is used:

- to focus on the length of time: *My eyes were really tired because I'd been reading for two or three hours in bad light.*

- to say how long something happened up to a point in the past: *It was two months before any of the teachers noticed that Mike hadn't been coming to school.*

***Would* + infinitive and *used to* + infinitive** are used to talk about things which happened repeatedly in the past, but don't happen now: *When I was small, my mother would read to me in bed and she'd sing me a song to put me to sleep. While she was reading to me, my father used to wash up the dinner things.*

- Use *used to* not *would* to talk about past states which no longer exist: ~~There would be a grocer's opposite the bus station, but there's a supermarket there now.~~

- *Used to* only exists in the past. It has no other tenses. (**Note:** The negative is *didn't use to: He didn't use to be so short-tempered.* The question form is *Did he (she/you) use to …?: Did you use to enjoy school when you were a kid, because I hated it?*)

- Use the past simple when you say how many times you did something: *Charlie used to be a very successful tennis player. He won the junior championship three times.*

The present perfect tenses:

We use the present perfect with time adverbs that connect the past to present, e.g. *just, already, lately, since, so far, up to now, yet, today* (when it is still the same day), *this morning* (when it is still the same morning): *Have you seen any good films lately? Britain has only won the World Cup once so far. Have you had any interesting phone calls this morning?*

Compare: *Did you have any interesting phone calls this morning?* (It's now the afternoon.)

The present perfect simple and continuous are often interchangeable. However, note the differences in the chart below.

the present perfect simple	the present perfect continuous
emphasises the result: *I've phoned all my friends and they're coming to the party.*	emphasises the activity: *I've been phoning my friends (that's why I haven't done my homework).*
says how much we have done: *I've cooked three pizzas.*	says how long we've been doing something: *I've been cooking all afternoon.*
may give the idea that something is more permanent (and may be accompanied by a time expression which shows this): *He's worked in this shop all his life. I've always lived here.*	may give the idea that something is temporary (and may be accompanied by a time expression which shows this): *I've been working here for the last two months until I go to university. We've been eating dinner in the garden while the weather has been so warm.*
is used when we want to say how many times something has been repeated: *I've invited her two or three times but she always says she's busy.*	is used when we want to emphasise the process of change over a period of time and that these changes are not finished: *Your English has been improving tremendously since you started doing your homework!* The present perfect continuous in this case will often use phrases like *more and more, over the last few days/months*, etc., and comparative adjectives: *My English has been getting better and better over the last few months.*

Unit 2

Expressing purpose, reason and result

Expresses	Phrase(s)	Followed by	Position	Example(s)
purpose	*so (that)*	a clause	between clauses	*He always dresses smartly so (that) people notice him.*
	with the purpose of / with the intention of	verb + *-ing*	after the main clause	*Teresa got up early with the intention of studying before going in to university.*
	so as / in order	infinitive		*Carla came home early so as not to have an argument with her parents.*
		infinitive		*Dieter goes to the gym every day to keep fit.*
reason	*because / since / as*	a clause	at the beginning of the sentence (more emphatic) or between clauses	*We'd better postpone the meeting till after lunch because / since / as Fatima has been delayed.* *Because / As / Since he was feeling ill, he spent the day in bed.*
	in case		after the main clause	*Take your mobile with you in case you need to call me.*
	otherwise			*Candice always writes things down otherwise (= because if she doesn't) she forgets them.*
	because of / due to / owing to	noun / verb + *-ing*	at the beginning of the sentence or after the main clause	*All flights have been cancelled because of / due to / owing to the bad weather.*
	For this reason	a sentence	at the beginning of a sentence and referring to the previous one	*Someone called me unexpectedly. For this reason I was late for the meeting.*
result	*Consequently / as a consequence / as a result*	a sentence	at the beginning of a sentence and referring to the previous one. *As a consequence* and *as a result* can also be used at the end of the sentence.	*Ranjit injured himself in training yesterday. As a consequence, he won't be taking part in the match today.* *Keiko didn't write a very good letter of application. She was rejected as a result.*

using conditional sentences (see page 159)

If children start learning foreign languages when they're young, they learn them effortlessly. (*If children start learning foreign languages when they're young* = possible action; *they learn them effortlessly* = the result.)

Spelling rules for affixes and inflections (-*ed*, -*ing*)

Affixes are either prefixes (syllables added before the word: **dis**pose, **pro**pose) or suffixes (syllables added after the word: expect**ant**, expect**ancy**, expect**ation**). In the CAE exam spellings must be correct for the answer to be considered correct. Below are some spelling rules when adding affixes.

Double the final consonant when you add -*ed*, -*ing*, -*er*, and -*est* to:

- a one-syllable word which ends in consonant-vowel-consonant: *run – runner, clap – clapping* (but *bend – bending, strange – stranger, bad – badly*, etc.). But final *w, x* and *y* are never doubled: *flowed, taxing*.

- verbs of two or more syllables which end in consonant-vowel-consonant and the final syllable is stressed: *occur – occurrence, forget – forgetting, admit – admittance* (but *forgetful, developing*).

- verbs which end in 'l' after one vowel in British English (in American English they may not double): *travel – traveller, cancel – cancellation*.

Don't double the final consonant when:

- there are two final consonants: *correspond – correspondence*.

- there are two vowels before the final consonant: *disappear – disappearance*.

- the verb ends in a vowel: *interfere – interference*.

- the stress is not on the final syllable: *deepen – deepening*.

Change *y* to *i*:

in words which end in *y* after a consonant, the *y* becomes *i* when a suffix is added: *happy – happiness, try – trial / tries, study – studious, family – familiar, rely – reliance*.

But note these exceptions:

- *i* becomes *y* with -*ing*: *lie – lying, die – dying*

- *dry – drier / drily* but *dryness; shy – shyness / shyly; day – daily*

Drop the final -*e*:

- if there is a consonant before it and the suffix begins with a vowel (-*er*, -*ed*, -*ing*, -*ance*, -*ation*, etc.): *nonsense – nonsensical, amaze – amazing, sane – sanity*.

  Note these exceptions: words ending in -*ce*, -*ge* and -*ee*: *noticeable, knowledgeable, disagreeable*.

- the final -*e* is not dropped when the suffix begins with a consonant: *safe – safety, arrange – arrangement, disgrace – disgraceful* (exception: *argue – argument*),

Adding prefixes

When a prefix is added (before the word), the spelling does not change, e.g. with *dis-*, *un-* and *ir-*: *appoint – disappoint, satisfied – dissatisfied, truthful - untruthful, necessary – unnecessary, relevant – irrelevant*.

Note: Use *il-*, *im-* and *ir-* (not *in-*) before words beginning with *l, m, p* or *r*: *illegible, immodest, impractical, irresponsible*.

Unit 3

No, none, not

No

- means *not any* or *not even one* and can be used with countable or uncountable nouns: *I've no idea what you're talking about. There were no cars on the road at that time of the morning.*

- is used with comparative words and *different*: *The traffic is no worse than it was at the same time yesterday. I had to work late every evening last week, and so far this week has been no different.*

None

- is a pronoun and means *not one, not any* or *no part of*. It can be used with countable nouns, uncountable nouns and other pronouns. It is most commonly followed by *of*: *None of my friends know/knows it's my birthday today. None of the milk in the fridge is fresh.*

- can also be used without a noun: *'How much coffee do we have?' 'None (at all). We finished it yesterday.' We need to buy some more bananas – there are none left.*

Note: In formal written English *none* is considered to be a singular word and is followed by a singular verb: *None of my colleagues speaks Japanese.* However, in everyday speech plural verbs are more commonly used: *None of this morning's flights have been delayed.*

Not

- is mainly used to make verbs negative and is often contracted to *n't*: *You have not / haven't answered my question. She told me not to phone her after ten o'clock in the evening.*

- can also make a word or a phrase negative: *Not many people voted in yesterday's election. Not everyone can win the lottery.*

The passive

Form

The passive is formed with the verb *to be* + the past participle of a main verb, e.g. *A large new shopping complex is being built on the outskirts of the city.*

If we want to mention who or what did the action in a passive sentence, we can introduce it with the preposition *by*: *A large new shopping complex is being built by a small local firm.*

Note: Intransitive verbs (e.g. *appear, come, go*) cannot be used in the passive form because they do not have an object.

Uses

We use the passive to focus attention on the person or thing that is affected by the action of the verb:

- when the person or thing that does the action is unknown: *My office was broken into last night.*

- when it is unnecessary to say who or what did the action because it is obvious: *My brother was stopped for dangerous driving.* (Only the police can stop dangerous drivers.)

- when the person or thing that does the action is unimportant or irrelevant: *Tonight's football match has been cancelled due to snow.*

- when the identity of the person or thing that does the action is secret or cannot be revealed, e.g. for legal reasons: *A senior government minister has been seen socialising with known criminals.*

We also use the passive to create a 'flow' in text:

- to put 'known information' at the beginning of a sentence: *The police have started to take a tougher line with* petty criminals. Many of them *are now being given custodial sentences ...*

- to place a subject that would be very long in the active after the verb in the passive: *The player who has won 'footballer of the year' most times addressed the club management.* → *The club management was addressed by the player who has won 'footballer of the year' most times.*

The passive is often also used to describe technical or scientific processes: *Water was added and the mixture was heated to a temperature of 85°C.*

We can use the passive form of verbs like *believe, think, report* + an infinitive to convey information when we are not sure whether it is correct or not. This is often used in reporting: *Bill Gates is thought to be one of the richest people in the world. Twenty people are reported to have been injured in the recent storms.*

Unit 4

Expressing possibility, probability and certainty

Possibility

Modal verbs *may, might, could*

- Use *may, may not, might, might not* or *could* (but not *could not*) to say it's possible that something is true, happens, or will happen, but we don't know: *The photocopier isn't working – there may be some paper stuck inside.*

- Use *could* to emphasise that there are other possibilities in addition to the one you are mentioning: *Bjorn could arrive some time this afternoon.* (or this evening or tomorrow)

- Use *might* to emphasise that the opposite is also possible: *I might go to the party.* (or I might not)

- Use *may, might, could* + *well/easily* to say something is a strong possibility: *The weather may well improve by the weekend. I'd better write it down otherwise I could easily forget.*

- Use *may, might, could* + *possibly/conceivably* or *just might* to say something is a remote possibility: *My boss could conceivably change her mind and decide to give me a pay increase. I just might have time to finish that report this week.*

Other words and phrases to express possibility:

- *It's (just about) possible that* + sentence: *It's just about possible that we'll have finished the project by the end of March.*

- *There's a/some/a slight/little possibility that* + sentence: *There's a slight possibility that the whole project will be abandoned.*

Other words and phrases to express stronger possibility:

- *It's quite/very possible that* + sentence: *It's quite possible that none of our clients will like the new product.*

- *There's a good/strong/serious possibility that* + sentence: *There's a strong possibility that our offices are going to be moved from the city centre to the outskirts.*

Probability

Modal verbs

- Use *should* to say that you expect something is or will be true: *You've got such a good level of English that you should have no difficulty in landing the job.*

Other words and phrases

- *(very/quite/highly) likely* + infinitive: *He's not likely to make the same mistake again.*

- *There's little/some/every/a strong likelihood of* + verb + *-ing*/noun: *I'd say there's a strong likelihood of him getting a first class degree.*

- *There's little/some/every/a strong likelihood that* + sentence: *There's little likelihood that we'll manage to meet our deadline.*

Certainty

Modal verbs

- Use *must* (affirmative) and *can't/couldn't* (negative) to express things you feel certain about because you have evidence: *They must be making a lot of money with so many customers. He didn't know what we were talking about, so he can't have read our letter.*

Note: Don't use *can* or *mustn't* to express possibility, probability or certainty (see Expressing ability on page 158 and Expressing obligation and prohibition on page 159).

Other words and phrases

- *bound* + infinitive: *Their machines are notoriously unreliable and they're bound to break down before long.*

Notes on modal verbs:

- To talk about things happening now, in progress, or arranged for the future use a continuous form, i.e. *may, might, must,* etc. + *be doing*: *You must all be wondering why I have called this meeting.*

- We also use the continuous with modals of possibility (*may, might, could*) in contrast to the simple form to express a weaker possibility. *We might be going out later.* (weaker possibility)

- To talk about things in the past use *may, might, must,* etc.+ *have* + past participle (*done, been, eaten,* etc.): *You must have been very tired after your trip.*

- To talk about actions which took place over a period of time in the past, use *may, might, must,* etc. + *have been doing*: *Ulrike wasn't in when I called – she may have been doing the shopping, I suppose.*

Unit 5

Infinitives and verb + -*ing* forms

1 Verbs followed by *to* + infinitive or the -*ing* form

The infinitive without *to* is used after:

- most modal verbs: *We must hurry or we'll be late. You needn't* worry – there's plenty of time.*

The *to* infinitive is used after:

- some verbs which are modal in meaning: *I have to go to work tomorrow. You ought to get more sleep. You need to think again. / You don't need to* worry.*

* Note: In the affirmative *need* is followed by *to* + infinitive. There are two negative forms: *don't need* + *to* infinitive and *needn't* + infinitive without *to*.

- certain verbs, e.g. *afford, agree, arrange, appear, attempt, choose, decide, expect, hope, intend, learn, manage, offer, pretend, promise, refuse, seem: We can't afford to go on holiday this year.*

- certain verbs + object, e.g. *advise, allow, ask, enable, encourage, forbid, force, get, instruct, invite, order, persuade, recommend, remind, teach, tell, train, want, warn, wish: You can't force people to believe something. My father taught me to swim.*

Note: After the verb *help* the *to* can be omitted before the infinitive: *She helped me revise for my exam. I helped her to complete the job application form.*

The -*ing* form of the verb is used after:

- some verbs which express likes and dislikes, e.g. *dislike, enjoy, loathe, (don't) mind, (can't) stand: She can't stand getting stuck in a traffic jam.* But note the following exceptions:
  - *hate/like/love/prefer* are usually followed by the -*ing* form but are sometimes followed by the *to* infinitive (see below).
  - *would* + *hate/like/love/prefer* is always followed by the *to* infinitive: *I'd hate to get up early every morning.*

- certain verbs, e.g. *admit, appreciate, avoid, can't help, consider, delay, deny, finish, imagine, involve, keep, mind, miss, postpone, prevent, report, resist, risk, suggest: The prime minister has just finished speaking.*

2 Verbs followed by the infinitive and the -*ing* form

A small number of verbs can be followed either by the infinitive or by the -*ing* form.

With no difference in meaning

begin, can't bear, cease, commence, continue, hate, intend, like, love, propose, start: I've just started to learn / learning to ski. He had intended to leave / leaving the party before midnight.

Note: With the verbs *like, love, hate* there can be this slight difference in meaning:

I like to clean my car every week. (= focus on the result of the activity)

I like cleaning my car every week. (= focus on the activity itself, i.e. I enjoy cleaning it)

With different meanings

- *verbs expressing perception (infinitive without to)*
  1. *We saw the plane take off.* (= We saw the whole action or process.)
  2. *We saw the plane taking off.* (= We saw only part of the process.)

- *forget*
  1. *I forgot to phone my brother.* (= I didn't phone him.)
  2. *I'll never forget phoning my sister that night.* (= I phoned her and I recall it well.)

- *remember*
  1. *Tom remembered to close the windows before he left.* (= He did something he had to do; he didn't forget.)
  2. *Tom remembered closing the windows before he left.* (= He recalled doing it.)

- *go on*
  1 *He won his first race when he was seven and went on to break the world record.* (= Breaking the world record was something he did later.)
  2 *He went on walking even though he was exhausted.* (= He didn't stop walking.)
- *mean*
  1 *I'm sorry, I didn't mean to be rude.* (= intend)
  2 *If we want to catch the early train, it'll mean getting up at 5.00.* (= involve)
- *regret*
  1 *I regret to inform you that you have not passed the test this time.* (= be sorry about something you are about to say – often because it is bad news)
  2 *He now regrets taking the day off work.* (= He wishes he hadn't taken the day off work.)
- *stop*
  1 *We'd better stop to look at the map.* (= stop what you are doing in order to do something else)
  2 *There's nothing you can do about it, so stop worrying.* (= finish worrying)
- *try*
  1 *I've been trying to repair my computer all morning.* (= attempt something difficult)
  2 *Have you tried kicking it?* (= do something which might solve a problem)

3 Other uses of the *-ing* form

- as an adjective: *That was a really interesting film.*
- as a noun (the subject or object of a verb): *Driving can be very tiring, especially late at night.*
- as part of a participle clause or phrase (see page 155)
- after a preposition: *Thank you all for being here. What's wrong with lending him my car?*

Unit 6

Avoiding repetition

Using pronouns

Derek Foster worked in advertising after the war. He became a professional painter in the early 60s.

- Use *they/them* for people in the singular when you are talking in general about males and females: *If you ask an artist how they started painting, they'll frequently say their grandfather or grandmother taught them.*
- Use *himself, herself, themselves*, etc. when the object is the same as the subject: *He poured himself a glass of water.* (Compare with: *He poured him a glass of water,* where *him* refers to a different person).

- Use *it, this, that, these, those* to refer to the things last mentioned: *Artists now have a vast range of materials at their disposal. This means that they can be much more versatile than in the past.*
- *That* is often used when giving reasons: *The artist's my cousin and that's why I'm here.*

One, another, the ones, the other, the others, both, neither, all, none:

- Use *one* to refer to singular countable nouns from a group. Use *A(n) … one* with an adjective: *There are several excellent exhibitions on in London at the moment. I strongly recommend the one at the National Gallery. I've bought a lot of new shirts recently, but for gardening I prefer to wear an old one.*
- Use *another* to refer to the second, third, etc. singular countable noun from a group: *One picture showed a girl combing her hair. Another was of the same girl dancing.*
- Use *ones* to avoid repeating a plural noun: *I enjoy romantic films, especially sad ones.*
- Use *the other* when referring to the second of two things/people already mentioned: *Pablo has two houses. One is in São Paulo and the other is in Singapore.*
- Use *the others* when referring to the rest of a number of things/people already mentioned: *Most of the actors went to a party. The others went home to bed.*
- Use *both* and *neither* to refer to two things/people: *He's written two novels. Both became bestsellers almost immediately. Neither is autobiographical.*
- Use *all* and *none* to refer to more than two things/people: *He's written twenty-three novels and I've read all of them. Mariella invited all her friends to a party but none of them came.*

Who, which, whose – see Relative clauses below.

Using auxiliary/modal verbs

- We can avoid repeating words by using an auxiliary verb: *A year ago I couldn't speak any Turkish, but now I can. Not many people have read 'The Dungeon' and I'm one of the few that have.*
- Use a form of *do* to replace a verb in the present or past simple: *I really enjoy good comedy films, but then I think everyone does. In contrast, not everyone likes science fiction films, although I have to admit that I do.*

Using *so*

- Use *so* to avoid repeating a sentence: *Do you think Real Madrid will win the championship again? – I guess so.* (= I guess they will win the championship again.)
- Use *do so* to avoid repeating a verb + the words which follow: *I told my students to hand in the writing task on Monday and nearly all of them did so.* (= handed in the writing task on Monday)

Omitting words

- It's sometimes possible to use *to* instead of a phrase with an infinitive beginning with *to* and to omit the rest: *Katie suggested going to the ballet, but I didn't want to. Do call me if you're able to. I'd like to be able to solve your problems but I just don't know how to.*

Unit 7

Ways of linking ideas

Relative clauses

Relative clauses contain a main verb and begin with a relative pronoun (*that, which, who/whom, whose*) or a relative adverb (*when, where, why*).

- Use *that, who, whom, whose* to refer to people: *Max is the boy whose father is a firefighter. A firefighter is someone who puts out fires and rescues people. The firefighter that rescued me was only 19 years old.*

  Note: *Whom* is formal and is used mainly with prepositions: *The person to whom this letter is addressed lives in Madrid.*

- Use *that* and *which* to refer to things: *The tree that was blown down in the storm was over a hundred years old. The book which won the prize was written by an 18-year-old girl.*

- Use *when* to refer to times: *The weekend is a time when many people relax.*

- Use *where* to refer to places: *The place where they live is in the middle of nowhere.*

- Use *why* to refer to reasons: *The reason why I'm late is that my flight was cancelled.*

Relative clauses can be at the end of a sentence or can be embedded in another clause: *Madrid is the city where I grew up. Madrid, where I grew up, is the capital of Spain.*

There are two main types of relative clause: **identifying** (or **defining**) and **non-identifying** (or **non-defining**).

- The relative pronoun in an **identifying** relative clause defines the noun which immediately precedes it, and is therefore essential to the meaning of a sentence: *The couple who brought me up were not my real parents.* (The relative clause tells us which couple.)

- **Non-identifying** relative clauses add additional information, but are not essential to the meaning of a sentence: *The hotel, which has a hundred bedrooms, is on the outskirts of the city.*

- Another type of non-identifying clause is a **comment clause**. In these, we use *which* to introduce a comment on a previous clause or phrase: *It had been raining non-stop for the 24 hours, which is why I didn't go out. We were stuck in the traffic jam for three hours, which I found really frustrating.*

Notes:

- In writing, non-identifying relative clauses are separated from the main clause by commas: *My car, which is seven years old, has already done 200,000 kilometres.* In speech, slight pauses are used to show that a relative clause is non-identifying.

- The pronoun *that* cannot be used instead of *who* or *which* to introduce a non-identifying relative clause.

Relative pronouns can be the subject or the object of the relative clause.

- Subject: *The people who know me best are my family and close friends.*

- Object: *The people who I know best are my family and close friends.*

- Object relative pronouns can be left out of an identifying relative clause: *The people (who) I know best are my family and close friends. The CD (that) you gave me for my birthday is fantastic.*

- *When* and *why* can also be left out of identifying relative clauses: *1997 was the year (when) I left university. That's the reason (why) I'm so disappointed.*

- If *where* is left out of an identifying relative clause, other changes need to be made: *That's the house where I grew up. That's the house I grew up in.*

Participle clauses

Participle clauses can begin with a present participle (*Concentrating on what I was doing, I didn't realise how late it was.*), with a past participle (*Seen from a distance, the Pyramids look quite small.*) or a perfect participle (*Having finished his speech, he left the room.*):

- In each case the subject of the participle clause is the same as the subject of the main part of the sentence.

- Participle clauses which precede the main part of a sentence are followed by a comma.

- Participle clauses are most frequently used in formal written English, and only rarely in speech.

Use participle clauses for the following reasons:

- to link two events in time: *Opening the door, I saw someone I hadn't seen for over ten years.* (= when I opened the door, I saw …)

- to provide a reason: *Having left our map at home, we couldn't find our way back to the motorway.* (= because we had left our map at home, we couldn't …)

- instead of a conditional construction: *Eaten in small quantities, chocolate is good for you.* (= If it is eaten in small quantities, chocolate …)

Note: *having* + past participle is the equivalent in meaning to a past perfect verb: *Having worked hard all day, we spent the evening relaxing.* = *Because we had worked hard all day, we spent the evening relaxing.*

Participle clauses often follow conjunctions and prepositions: *After seeing that film, I'm too scared to go to bed.*

Note: In sentences like these, the participle clause can follow the main clause, but is not normally preceded by a comma: *I'm too scared to go to bed after seeing that film.*

Participle clauses can also be used instead of identifying relative clauses: *Anyone (who is) caught shoplifting will be prosecuted. Who are those people (who are) climbing over the wall?* These clauses are sometimes called reduced relative clauses.

Noun phrases occurring together (apposition)

A common, economical way, of linking two or more facts about the same person, thing or place, is to put them next to each other in a sentence: *Her friend Klaus is a computer engineer. I'm going to see my tutor, Bev Jackson.*

Note: As with relative clauses, the second noun or noun phrase in sentences like these can be identifying or non-identifying.

- If it tells us who or what no commas are used: *Her friend Klaus is a computer engineer.*
- If it provides additional descriptive information, commas are used: *I'm going to see my tutor, Bev Jackson.*

Unit 8

Reported speech

Verb tense changes

If the reporting verb is in the past, e.g. *said*, the tense of the verb that follows is often 'further back' in time than the direct speech verb:

- 'I'm feeling exhausted.' → *He said he was feeling exhausted.*
- 'We drove for six hours non-stop.' → *They said they had driven for six hours non-stop.*
- We'll see you tomorrow.' → *They said they'd see us the following day.*

The verb tense does not need to change:

- if we want to make it clear that what the speaker said is still true now or remains relevant: 'I love black coffee.' → *He said he loves black coffee.*
- if the reporting verb is in the present: 'I'm looking forward to my holiday.' → *She says she is looking forward to her holiday.*
- with the following verbs and verb forms:

Direct speech	Reported speech
Past perfect: 'I'd never spoken to her before.'	*He said he'd never spoken to her before.*
Past perfect continuous: 'I'd been thinking of changing jobs for several months'	*She said she'd been thinking of changing jobs for several months.*
Modal verbs *would, could, should*: 'I wouldn't go skiing again.' 'I could drive you to the station.' 'You should have warned us about the traffic.'	*He said he wouldn't go skiing again. She said she could drive me to the station. They said we should have warned them about the traffic.*
Unreal past expressions 'If I were starting out again now, I'd choose a different career.'	*He said if he were starting out again now, he'd choose a different career.*

Pronoun and adverb changes

- Pronouns change when the reporter is different from the original speaker: 'I love you,' Dan said. → *Dan said he loved/loves me.* But the pronoun does not change if the reporter is the original speaker: 'I've lost my phone' → *I said I'd lost my phone.*
- Time and place adverbs change if the time or place is different from in the direct speech: 'I'll see you tomorrow.' → *Jackie said she'd see me the next/following day.* 'We've lived here for six years.' → *They said they'd lived there for six years.* But the adverb does not change if the time/place remains the same: 'I came here yesterday.' → (reported the same day) *He says he came here yesterday.*

- These are some of the time reference changes:

Direct speech	Reported speech
(ten minutes) ago	*(ten minutes) before/ earlier*
last week/month/year	*the previous week/month/ year; the week/month/year before*
next week/month/year	*the following week/month/ year; the week/month/year after*
now	*at that time/immediately/ then*
this week	*last/that week*
today	*that day / yesterday / on Monday, Tuesday, etc.*
tomorrow	*the next day / the day after / the following day*
yesterday	*the day before / the previous day*

Reporting questions

- We also change the original question into a statement and do not use auxiliary *do, does, did* in the present and past simple: 'Where do you live?' → *She asked me where I lived/live.*
- When we report *Yes/No* questions, we add *if* or *whether*: 'Do you speak Italian?' → *He asked me if/whether I spoke/speak Italian.*

Reporting commands and other functions

- Command/order: 'Phone me later!' → *He told her to phone him later.*
- Request: 'Could you answer the phone please?' → *She asked him to answer the phone.*
- Advice: 'You really should get more sleep.' → *He advised her to get more sleep.*
- Warning: 'If you do that again, I'll …' → *He warned her not to do that again.*
- Suggestion: 'Let's try the new Japanese restaurant.' → *He suggested (that) we (should) try the new Japanese restaurant / He suggested trying the new Japanese restaurant.*

Unit 9

Tenses in time clauses and time adverbials

Time adverbials are words or phrases which say when something happens/happened: *I went jogging after I'd finished lunch. Terry is playing hockey tomorrow afternoon. Marisa gets up at six o'clock every morning to go to work.*

Time clauses are often introduced by words and phrases like *when, as soon as, until, after,* etc.: *I'll give you a call as soon as I arrive. Chen didn't learn to drive until he was thirty.*

Tenses in time clauses

In present and past time clauses, use:

- a present tense to talk about the present: *Martina can't bear people interrupting while she's talking.*
- a past tense to talk about the past: *Fydor refused to respond when he was interrogated by the police.*
- either simple or perfect tenses to talk about an action which is finished before another action in the main clause: *Passengers are always eager to leave the plane as soon as it stops / has stopped. When he finished / had finished the race, he was given a medal.* However, use the simple in the time clause when you want to emphasise both actions equally and use the perfect when you want to put more emphasis on the action in the main clause.
- a perfect tense in the time adverbial to talk about an action happening for some time before the time in the main clause: *He sat down to write the report when he'd collected enough data.* (Compare: *He sat down to write the report when his secretary arrived.* Collecting the data took some time; his secretary arrived in a moment.)
- a simple tense (not a perfect tense) if the actions take place at the same time: *I did my homework while I waited for the train.*
- a continuous tense when you want to describe something which is/was in progress when something happens/happened: *I twisted my ankle while I was jogging last Saturday.*

(See also Participle clauses on page 155.)

In time clauses which refer to future time, use:

- a present tense (not a future tense): *I'll call you when I get home.* (when I will get home)
- the present simple in time adverbials for things which will happen at a particular moment in the future, e.g. *As soon as I get to Milan, I'll book into a hotel.*
- the present simple for things which will happen in the same time period as something else mentioned in the future, e.g. *I'll do the shopping while Marina cleans the house.*
- the present continuous to talk about something which will be in progress at a time in the future, e.g. *I'll call you when my train is arriving at the station.*
- the present perfect for things which have finished before a time in the future, e.g. *I'll call you when I've finished my homework.* Compare this with *I'll call you when I finish my homework.* (i.e. immediately after finishing my homework)

Time adverbials: *when, while, during* or *meanwhile*?

- **Use *when*, not *while*:**
  - if the action in the main clause happens over a longer time: *I was studying at university when I met my wife.* (But: *I met my wife when/while I was studying at university* – here the action in the main clause happens over the shorter time, so *while* is also possible.)
  - when you talk about one thing which happens immediately after another, often as a result, but not at the same time: *When he scored the winning goal, the crowd went wild.*
  - to describe what happened at a period of time in the past: *No one worried about global warming when I was a child.*
- **Use *while*, not *when*,** to talk about two longer actions which happen at the same time: *While Katya slept, I cooked lunch.*
- **Use *during*:**
  - before a noun/noun phrase (but not before a verb + -*ing* when there is an alternative, e.g. not *During walking, we…* but *During our walk, we…*).
  - (or *in*) to talk about something which happened within part of the time mentioned: *I'm hoping to visit Prague during/in the summer.*
  - not *in*, to talk about something which happened within part of an activity or event: *Three players were given a red card during the match.*
- **Use *meanwhile*** to talk about something which happens/ happened when another event/activity takes or took place. This activity is mentioned in the previous sentence. *Meanwhile* starts a new sentence: *Paz spent several hours yesterday afternoon surfing the Internet. Meanwhile, the rest of the family went for a long walk.*

Prepositions in time expressions

Use *at*:

- with points of time: *at four o'clock, at dawn, at midday.*
- with short periods which we think of as points: *I'm always short of money at the end of the month.*
- with mealtimes: *We can discuss it at lunch tomorrow.* (**Note:** We can also say: *We can discuss it over/during lunch tomorrow.*)
- with *the weekend, Christmas* and *Easter*: *What are you doing at the weekend?* (**Note:** in American English: *What are you doing on the weekend?* is also possible.)
- with *night* when talking about nights in general, not a particular night: *The traffic noise makes it difficult for me to sleep at night.* (See *in the night* below, under 'parts of the day'.)

Use *in:*

- for periods of time: *in 2006, in March, in the autumn.*
- for parts of the day: *Sam always goes shopping in the morning.* (but *Sam always goes shopping on Saturday morning.* See below.)

  Note: we use *at night* when talking about nights in general (see above) and *in the night* to mean *during a particular night*: *The pavement was wet this morning because it had rained in/during the night.*

- to say the period of time before something happens or how long something takes: *I'll call you back in 20 minutes. In six months' time I'll have finished university. Clara managed to do all her homework in just 20 minutes.*

Use *on:*

- for particular dates, days or parts of days: *I'm going on holiday on July 22nd. We're having a party on Saturday if you'd like to come. We always go bowling on Friday nights.*
- With *occasion*: *Tatiana has visited us on several occasions in the past.*

Unit 10

Expressing ability, possibility and obligation

Ability

Use *can* and *could* to refer to skills and abilities: *Cats can see in the dark. My sister could walk when she was nine months old.*

- Use *can/can't* for general or specific present abilities: *I can/can't drive.*
- Use *could* to refer to general past abilities but not specific past abilities: *When I was younger, I could run very fast.* For specific past abilities use *be able to, manage to* or *succeed in* + -*ing* form: *We couldn't open the door using the key. Eventually we managed to get in / succeeded in getting in / were able to get in by breaking a window.*
- Use *couldn't* for a general ability or a specific failed attempt: *I couldn't walk until I was nearly two years old. When I tried to walk, I fell down and couldn't get up again.*
- *Can* and *could* are often used with verbs describing mental states: *I can quite believe that you're thinking of moving out of the city. I can't imagine living on an island.*
- To refer to conditional ability use *could/would be able to* or *could have* + past participle / *would have been able to*: *If we hadn't broken the window, we couldn't have got / wouldn't have been able to get into the house.*
- *Be able/unable to* is often used instead of *can/could* to express the future and other forms where there is no option with *can* or where *can/could* would be incorrect: *I'd like to be able to see better.*

  Unable to is often used in formal writing: *Unfortunately, I will be unable to attend the committee meeting next Friday.*

Possibility

- Use *can/could* to refer to present and past possibilities: *You can drive to London in less than an hour. Where we used to live, you could get there by train in just over an hour.*

- Use *could* to refer to future possibilities: *According to the weather forecast, it could be very windy this evening. But we do not use couldn't for future possibilities; use may not or might not instead: It may not rain this weekend.*

- Use *can't* + infinitive for logical impossibility in the present, and *couldn't have* + past participle for past impossibility: *It can't be Paul at the door. He's in Japan. He can't have finished his work already. He's only been doing it for half an hour.*

- *May* or *might* can also be used to refer to future possibilities: *We may go to Spain for our holidays. I might see Becky next week.*

- Use *could have / may have / might have* to refer to past possibilities: *Paul should be here by now, but I suppose he could/may/might have been held up on the motorway.*

Obligation and prohibition

- Personal obligation, i.e. obligation you agree with: *I must phone my sister today. I mustn't forget.*

- Duty/obligation from an external source: *I have to be at a meeting at 8.30 tomorrow morning.*

  Note: There is a subtle difference in meaning between *must* and *have to*:
  I must finish this report by tomorrow. (The speaker believes this.)
  You must drive carefully in future. (This is a law the speaker accepts.)
  I have to finish this report by tomorrow. (This is something someone else is insisting on.)
  I have to drive more carefully in future. (This is what the police officer said.)

- Prohibition: *You mustn't smoke in public buildings.*

  Note: The negative forms *mustn't* and *don't have to* have different meanings: *You mustn't smoke in public buildings.* (It's against the law.) *You don't have to go to the party if you don't want to. It's your choice.* (Lack of obligation or necessity.)

- *Must/mustn't* is rarely used in speech when talking to other people. We are more likely to use *should/shouldn't, ought to* or other expressions such as *You'd better (not), I wouldn't (do that) if I were you. / I don't think It's a good idea to …*

  However, *must / mustn't* is often used when we are talking about or to ourselves: *I mustn't forget to phone the dentist. I must get some coffee when I go out.*

Necessity

- Use *need* or *have to*: *To get to the airport in time, we need to catch the 4.30 train.*

- There are two negative forms of *need*: *We have plenty of time, so we needn't hurry / don't need to hurry.*

- In the past these two forms have different meanings: *We didn't need to hurry.* (We didn't hurry because there was no need.) *We needn't have hurried.* (We hurried but it wasn't necessary.)

Unit 11

Conditionals

1st conditional

Form

If/unless + present simple/continuous tense - *will/may/must*, etc. + infinitive

Use

To talk about very possible or probable situations in the present or future: *If you miss the last train home, you can always stay at my place.*

2nd conditional

Form

If/unless + past simple/continuous tense - *would/could/might* + infinitive

Use

- To talk about less possible or improbable situations in the present or future: *If I got the job, I'd have to move to Bristol.*

- To talk about imaginary situations or events in the present: *If I had more money, I'd travel first class on the train. (I'm imagining having more money, contrary to the facts: I don't have much money. I don't travel first class on the train.)*

3rd conditional

Form

If/unless + past perfect simple or continuous tense – *would have / could have / might have* + past participle (*been, done, eaten, etc.*)

Use

To talk about imaginary situations or events in the past: *If you had been born in the 19th century, you would have travelled to work by horse.* (Imaginary, contrary to the facts: you weren't born in the 19th century; you're imagining a journey to work in the 19th century.)

In all types of conditional sentence the conditional clause (starting with *if/unless*) is understood and therefore often omitted: *How would you communicate with someone whose language you couldn't speak? – I'd use sign language.*

If one part of the sentence speaks about the present/future and the other part about the past, 2nd and 3rd conditionals can be 'mixed':

If I hadn't met Julia when I was travelling in Bulgaria last year (3rd conditional) *we wouldn't be married now* (2nd conditional).

Anastasia would never have bought such an expensive book (3rd conditional), *if she wasn't studying the subject for her PhD* (2nd conditional).

Other conditional structures

- If it weren't / wasn't / hadn't been for + noun: *If it weren't for Karol's sense of adventure, we wouldn't have mounted this expedition.*
- If + noun/pronoun + were to + infinitive (formal): *If the company were to lower the fares, we'd have more money for other things.*

Using *otherwise*, *or* and *even if*

- *Otherwise* can be used to introduce a conditional idea: *Arsenal were really lucky. Otherwise they would have lost the match.* (i.e. If Arsenal hadn't been lucky …)
- In spoken English *or* can be used instead of *otherwise*, but it joins the two sentences: *Arsenal were really lucky, or they wouldn't have won the match.*
- Use *even if* to emphasise the conditional clause: *With the traffic like it is today Ferran would still have been late even if he'd left half an hour earlier.*

Other uses of conditionals

You can:

- give advice using *if I were you + I would + infinitive: If I were you, I'd take that laptop as hand luggage.*
- make criticisms or strong requests using:
  If you would + infinitive – would + infinitive
  If you'd stop making so much noise, perhaps we'd all be able to enjoy the programme.
- make polite formal requests using the following (listed from quite formal to very formal):
  - *I'd appreciate it if you would/could: I'd appreciate it if you could hand in the report by Thursday.* (**Note:** this form can also be used for making polite complaints or criticisms: *I'd appreciate it if you'd make less noise!*)
  - *if you'd be so kind as to + infinitive (– will + infinitive): If you'd be so kind as to close the window.*

At, *in* and *on* to express location

Use *at*:

- when a place is thought of as a point, not an area (including *at home, at school, at work, at university*): *I'll meet you at the airport when you arrive.*
- to talk about an event involving a number of people: *Tina met Joe at Charlie's wedding.*
- for addresses: *She lives at Number 11, Abbey Road.*

Use *in*:

- when a place is thought of as somewhere with an area or space: *Gary lives in a small flat at the top of a tower block.*
- for cars and taxis: *Let's talk in the car.*
- normally with *in class, in hospital, in prison, in court: He studied for a law degree while he was in prison.*
- with people or things which form lines: *Wait in the queue!*
- for the world: *It's the tallest building in the world.*

Use *on*:

- to talk about a position in contact with a surface: *We've hung that picture you gave us on the wall above the fireplace. She lay on the beach soaking up the warm spring sunshine.*
- to talk about a position on something thought of as a line, e.g. a coast, a road, the outskirts, the edge, etc: *Keyhaven is a small village on the south coast. There were huge traffic jams on the motorway yesterday evening.*
- with means of transport apart from cars and taxis (see above): *Hi Karen – I'm on a train and I'll be getting to you about six. OK?*
- for technology: *I've seen him on television. I'm afraid she's on the phone at the moment.*
- with *left* and *right: You'll find the post office on your left just past the supermarket.*
- with lists: *I'll put 'sausages' on the shopping list.*
- with *premises, farm, floor* and *island: It's on the fifth floor.*

Unit 12

Nouns

Countable and uncountable nouns

Countable nouns:

- can be singular or plural and are used for individual things which we can count. *In our family we have a cat and two dogs.*
- in the singular form can be preceded by the indefinite article *a/an, one, this/that, each, every*, etc.: *A human being has two hands. Each hand has a thumb and four fingers.*
- in the plural form can be preceded by numbers or determiners such as *any, many, (a) few, some, no, these/those: Last night there were no children in the audience and only a few teenagers.*

Uncountable nouns:

- are neither singular nor plural and are used for things that are not normally divided into separate items: *In our apartment we use gas for cooking and electricity for heating.*

- are used with singular verbs and can be preceded by determiners such as *some, no, much, any, a little, this/that*: *'Is there any water left?' 'No, but there's some apple juice.'*

   Note: *a/an*, *one*, *each* and *every* cannot be used with uncountable nouns.

- To refer to particular quantities of an uncountable noun, use a phrase which includes a countable noun and *of*: *a jug of water, two cups of tea, a loaf of bread, three slices of toast, twenty litres of oil.*

Many nouns can be countable or uncountable:

Type	Examples
mass noun	*'Do you like chocolate?'* (= the substance chocolate)
individual	*'Yes, I love a chocolate or two in the evening.'* (= individual chocolates)
substance	*French people love wine and cheese.* (= these substances in general)
types	*France has so many different wines and cheeses.* (= types of wine and cheese)
substance individual	*I can't stand lamb or chicken.* (= meat) *I love lambs and chickens.* (= animals)
drinks	*Tea and coffee is expensive in Iceland.* (= the substances) *Can I have two teas and three coffees, please.* (= cups of tea and coffee)
general action or idea	*I'm not very good at painting.* (general action) *People are crazy about sport.* (general idea)
specific example	*This is one of my paintings.* (specific) *Football is a sport* (specific).

Note: Some nouns which are uncountable in English may be countable in other languages, e.g. *advice, applause, bread, damage, equipment, fruit, furniture, homework, housework, information, knowledge, luggage, money, news, rubbish, shopping, traffic, travel.*

Nouns formed from adjectives

Nouns for groups of people can be formed from adjectives. They are usually preceded by the definite article and followed by a plural verb: *There is a growing divide between the rich and the poor.* Other adjectives that can be used like this: *the living, the dead, the blind, the deaf, the unemployed.*

Proper nouns

Proper nouns are the names of people, places, things, ideas which are unique in some way. They are written with capital initials: *The Beatles, Robert Redford, Cairo, the New York Times, Everest, the Pacific Ocean, Harvard University, the Amazon.* (Some proper nouns are preceded by the definite article; other are used with no article – see below.)

Articles

The indefinite article *a/an*

A/an is used for something general or non-specific, or when we refer to something for the first time: *Have you got a bicycle?* (= any kind of bicycle) *He's a good gymnast.* (= one of many) *There's a tennis club in our town.*

Other uses:

- to refer to someone's job or function: *She used to be a hotel receptionist.*

- to mean *one*: *I have a sister and two brothers. My grandfather lived to a hundred.*

The definite article *the*

The is used when we know what is being discussed, e.g. it may be something specific, it may have been mentioned before, or there may be only one of it: *When is the furniture arriving?* (= the furniture we ordered last week) *There's a tennis club in our town. It's the club where I learnt to play. She's at the college.* (= the local college, the only one)

We also use *the* with plural countable nouns to refer to something known, to something specific or to something that has been mentioned before: *Grades are given according to accuracy and creativity. The grades range from A–F.*

No article

- with plural countable nouns and uncountable nouns with a general meaning: *Cats chase mice. Pollution is ruining our towns and cities.*

- in certain phrases which relate to places, institutions or situations: *Did you go to university.* (= Were you a student?) *What did you do in class today?* (= What did you learn?)

   Other similar phrases: *be in / go to church, court, hospital, prison; be at / go to sea, school, university, work; be at / go home.*

Unit 13

Ways of contrasting ideas

Conjunctions

- *But* can contrast words, phrases and clauses: *The work was tiring but worthwhile. But* is not used at the beginning of a sentence in formal writing. However, it may be used to start a sentence in informal writing: *The work was tiring. But at least it was well paid.*

- *Whereas* and *while* are used to contrast different, but not contradictory, ideas: *He can eat anything he likes without putting on weight whereas most people have to be more careful. While I accept the fact that she's not perfect, I am actually very fond of her.*

  Note: The *while* clause usually comes before the main clause.

- *Though / although / even though* introduce an idea that contradicts the one in the main clause: *He failed his driving test although / even though he had practised every day for the previous two weeks.*

  Note: *even though* is more emphatic than *though/ although*.

- *Even if* is similar to *even though*, but adds a conditional meaning: *I'm going to New Zealand for my holiday next year even if I have to save all year.*

Note: *But* must come between the two clauses it joins. Unlike the other words and phrases in this section, it cannot start a sentence: *I felt perfectly OK but I didn't go to work.* We cannot say: *~~But~~ I felt perfectly OK, I didn't go to work.*

Prepositions

Despite and *in spite of* are prepositions that express contrast, and therefore they are followed by a noun or an *-ing* form: *The journey was very quick despite / in spite of the heavy traffic. Despite / In spite of feeling ill / the fact that I felt ill, I thoroughly enjoyed the party.*

Adverbs

We can use the following adverbs and adverb phrases to contrast ideas between sentences.

- *However: This is one possible solution to the problem. However, there are others. / There are others, however. / There are, however, others.*

  Note: *However* cannot be used between two clauses in the same sentence.

- *Nevertheless: This is a really difficult decision. Nevertheless, it's one that we have to make.*

  Note: *Nevertheless* is only used in formal speech or writing.

The use of commas

- If a sentence starts with a clause introduced by *whereas, while, though, although, even though, even if , despite,* etc. a comma is used to separate the first clause from the rest of the sentence: *Even though I felt ill, I thoroughly enjoyed the party.*

- No comma is used if these clauses come after the main clause: *I thoroughly enjoyed the party even though I felt ill.*

- *However* and *nevertheless* are followed by and sometimes also preceded by commas: *I enjoy going to the gym. However, I can't stand running. I enjoy going to the gym. John, however, can't stand it.*

The language of comparison

Adjectives and adverbs

- To compare two things or actions we use comparative adjectives or adverbs: *Glíma is less violent than other forms of Icelandic wrestling. She works more efficiently than most of her colleagues.*

- To compare more than two things or actions we use superlative adjectives or adverbs: *Glíma is the oldest form of wrestling in Iceland. That was the least interesting film I've ever seen. She works the most efficiently of all our staff.*

- *No + comparative adjective: Running is no better for you than walking fast.*

- *the + superlative + of + plural noun: It was the simplest of ideas. He was the kindest of teachers.*

- *the + superlative + noun + imaginable/possible: We had the worst weather imaginable.*

- *as/so … as* point out similarities or differences between things or people: *My little brother is nearly as tall as me. I'm not as/so hard-working as my sister.*

- *the + comparative word/phrase + the: The longer you work, the more you get paid. The faster we walk the sooner we'll get there.*

- comparative adjective + comparative adjective: *He walked faster and faster until he was almost running.*

- in some expressions with *better* no verb is needed: *'What time shall I ring you' 'The sooner the better.'*

Nouns

Use *more/most* to express a greater number/amount:

- *More/Most + plural countable noun: There were more people at the concert than there were last year. Most (of the) people were in their twenties.*

- *More + uncountable noun: I wish I could spend more time with my friends.*

- *Most of the + uncountable noun: After the accident, most of the oil leaked out of the tanker into the sea.*

Use *less/fewer* to express a smaller number/amount:

- *Less + uncountable noun: I'm getting less money now than in my last job.*

- *Fewer + plural countable noun: There were fewer people at tonight's match – probably because of the cold weather.*

Qualifying comparative language

Use *a lot / slightly / (quite) a bit / a great deal / even / still / yet / by far* to qualify comparative language: *My sister's a lot / a great deal more intelligent than me, but my younger brother is even cleverer than her.*

Unit 14

Comment adverbials

- express how certain the speaker is about something.

  Some common adverbs: *certainly, definitely, possibly, probably, undoubtedly: She's definitely happier now than she was when she first arrived in the country.*

  Some common adverbial phrases: *without a doubt, in theory, in all likelihood: In all likelihood, there are more advantages to relaxing controls on immigration than disadvantages.*

- express the speaker's attitude or opinion about what they say.

  Some common adverbs: *frankly, personally, unfortunately, surprisingly: I, personally, would only emigrate if I was sure it would improve my standard of living.*

  Some common adverbial phrases: *in my opinion, quite honestly, generally speaking, to my surprise: Quite honestly, I don't think you should have given him so much money.*

- express the speaker's opinion of their or someone else's actions: *cleverly, kindly, mistakenly, strangely, foolishly,* etc. (These adverbs depend on the action taken and therefore it is not possible to provide a list of the most common ones.): *The government has mistakenly, I think, put restrictions on immigration from certain countries.* (i.e. I think the government's action is a mistake); *Strangely, I haven't heard anything from her since she moved house.* (i.e. I think her failure to communicate is strange.)

Comment adverbials are often placed at the beginning of the sentence: *Frankly, if I could choose, I'd leave Manchester and migrate back to the country.*

However, they can also be placed:

- in the middle position in the sentence (between the subject and the verb): *She was unfortunately extremely late for the appointment.*
- or at the end of the sentence: *Dimetrio is thinking of emigrating to Australia, apparently.*

Note: In writing, comment adverbials are usually separated from the rest of the sentence by a comma when used at the beginning or end of a sentence.

Emphasis

Emphasis is showing or stating that something is particularly important or worth giving attention to. Some common ways of adding emphasis are:

Fronting

Fronting involves placing information at or near the beginning of a sentence.

- Placing the complement or direct object of a verb before the subject: *I met Sasha and Natalia five years ago. **Olga** I didn't meet till last month.*

- Placing the subordinate clause before the main clause: ***Because he was feeling depressed**, Pierre stayed in bed all day.*

- Placing preposition and adverb phrases that are not part of another phrase before the subject of the sentence: ***Despite its high cost of living**, Switzerland attracts a lot of foreign visitors.*

- The verb can come before the subject of the sentence if it comes after a linking word for sequence (e.g. *first, then, next, later*): ***First came the wind** and **then came the rain**.*

Cleft sentences

- *What* + subject + auxiliary verb + *is/was* + infinitive with/without *to: They advertised on television.* → *What they did was (to) advertise on television.*

- *What* + subject + main verb + *is/was* + *to* infinitive: *I really want to find a job in New Zealand.* → *What I really want is to find a job in New Zealand.*

- *It* + *is/was* + *(that): I like visiting other countries, but I don't enjoy flying.* → *I like visiting other countries, but it's flying (that) I don't enjoy.*

- *All / The last thing* + subject + verb + *is/was: My house needs a swimming pool to make it perfect.* → *All my house needs is a swimming pool to make it perfect. Carrie definitely doesn't want to have to leave the town where she grew up.* → *The last thing Carrie wants is to leave the town where she grew up.*

Using adverbs

A large number of adverbs can be used to add emphasis. Note how the adverbs in **bold** in the sentences below add emphasis:

*I **personally** always fly on scheduled airlines.*

*When I first arrived in the country couldn't speak the language. I couldn't **even** say 'good morning' and 'thank you'.*

Reflexive pronouns

We can use reflexive pronouns (*myself, himself, itself, themselves,* etc.) to emphasise nouns or pronouns: *I phoned my bank and the phone was answered by the manager himself.* (I was expecting someone less senior to answer the phone.)

Note: We often use reflexive pronouns to emphasise that someone did something alone and without help: *He's sailing round the world in a boat he built himself.* We emphasise the surprising ability to also build boats – compare this with: *He's sailing round the world in a boat he built.*

Writing reference

What to expect in the exam

The writing paper is Paper 2. It lasts 1 hour 30 minutes.

You do two tasks:

- In Part 1, there is one task which you **must** do.
- In Part 2, you choose **one** of four tasks.

Part 1

You are asked to write an article, a proposal, a report or a letter based on material that you given to read. This may be, e.g. an advert, part of a letter or email, an article, notes, diaries. In this part you must follow the instructions exactly.

Length: 180–220 words

Time: approximately 45 minutes (the Writing Paper lasts 1 hour 30 minutes, so if you spend more time on this part, you will have less time for the other part).

This part tests your ability to:

- identify who will read what you are writing and the reason(s) for writing
- write in a style appropriate for your reader(s)
- inform, describe, evaluate, recommend, express opinions, discuss possibilities and persuade
- organise your answer in a logical way
- write accurate English.

This part will always expect you to persuade the reader to a point of view or a course of action.

How to do Part 1

1 Read the instructions and the material, notes, etc. that you're given carefully. (2–3 minutes)

2 Find and underline the points which explain why you're writing and the information which tells you what you must write about. Remember: if it's not clear why you are writing and you don't include all the key information asked for in the task, you'll lose marks. (2–3 minutes)

3 Identify who will read what you write and decide what would be a suitable style.

4 Make notes on what you'll put in your answer and organise your notes into a plan. When writing your plan, decide how many paragraphs you need and what you'll say in each paragraph. (5 minutes)

5 Check that you have included all the information necessary.

6 Write your answer, following your plan. (25–30 minutes)

Part 2

In Part 2 you must choose to do one of four writing tasks.

Note: The last task is a choice of questions on the set texts. If you wish to read a set text, you can visit the Cambridge ESOL website at www.cambridgeesol.org/exams/ general-english/cae.html to find which are the set texts for this year. This book doesn't deal with set texts because they change every year. If you haven't read a set text, you choose from three tasks.

The tasks may be an article, an essay, a competition entry, a review, a proposal, a report, an information sheet, a contribution to a longer piece or a letter.

For each of these tasks, the instructions and reading material are much shorter than in Part 1 (a maximum of 80 words). You answer the task with your own ideas.

Length: 220–260 words

Time: approximately 45 minutes (remember: the Writing Paper lasts 1 hour 30 minutes, so if you spend more time on this part, you will have less time for the other part).

This part tests your ability to:

- organise and structure your writing
- use an appropriate range of vocabulary and grammatical structures
- use an appropriate style
- compare, give advice, express opinions, justify your point of view, persuade, etc. depending on the task.

How to do Part 2

1 Read the questions and choose the task you think is easiest for you. (1–2 minutes)

2 Read the task you choose carefully and underline:
   - the points you **must** deal with
   - who will read what you write
   - anything else you think is important. (2–3 minutes)

3 Decide what style is appropriate.

4 Think of ideas you can use to deal with the question and write a plan. When writing it, decide how many paragraphs you need and what to say in each one. (5–7 minutes)

5 Think of useful vocabulary you can include in your answer and note it down in your plan. (2–3 minutes)

6 Write your answer, following your plan. (25–30 minutes)

7 When you've finished, check your answer for mistakes. (5 minutes)

Preparing for the writing paper

Before you do a writing task as homework or exam preparation:

Set aside the time you need

In the exam you'll have about 45 minutes to do the task. At the beginning of your course, spend longer doing the task and working on the writing skills needed to produce a good answer. Nearer the exam, practise answering the question within the time allowed.

Before writing

1 Brainstorm your ideas, make notes and write a plan. Your plan should have a clear structure, divided into paragraphs or sections.

2 Study the model answers in the units and in this Writing reference. Pay attention to the structure and layout of the answers, underline language you can use and read the suggestions and advice accompanying the answers.

3 Compare your plan with the model(s). If your plan is different, do you have good reasons for answering the question in a different way?

4 Use the resources at your disposal:

- Try to use some of the words/phrases you have underlined in the unit, or copied into your notebook or from your photocopiable word lists. Take the opportunity to use new language in your answers: if you use it correctly, then you've learnt something and made progress; if you make a mistake, your teacher will give you feedback so that you use it correctly next time.
- Use a good learner's dictionary to check spellings, meanings and usage.
- Try to include grammatical structures you've studied recently. This will reinforce your learning.

5 Include vocabulary and grammatical structures you want to use in your plan.

6 Read and incorporate your teacher's advice and suggestions on other pieces of writing you've done.

When writing

1 Follow your plan so that when you write, you concentrate on producing language to express ideas you've already generated.

2 Avoid repeating the same words too often – use synonyms where possible (a good learner's dictionary will help you).

3 If you need to correct something, cross out the mistake and continue writing – you won't lose marks as long as your corrections are clear. In the exam you won't have time to copy out your answer again.

After writing

1 Check what you've written: ask yourself, 'Have I expressed myself clearly?'

2 Check for mistakes, particularly mistakes you've made in previous writing tasks, and correct them (see below).

When your teacher hands back your written work

1 Go through it carefully, checking your mistakes and your teacher's suggestions. Keep a section of your notebook for noting down your mistakes and the corrections. Look at this extract from a student's work and the section in her notebook where she notes her mistakes:

cancellation
The cancelling of our opening speech because our actor
the first bad impression made on our guests
couldn't come was the first bad impression our guests had.

I think it would be a good idea during our next activity day to
invite
host Colin Briggs, the famous footballer. This would please
children
the kids and many of their parents as well.

Mistake	Details	Correction
cancelling	Should use the noun when it exists, not verb +-ing.	cancellation
the first bad impression our guests had	The collocation is 'make a bad impression on sb'.	the first bad impression made on our guests
to host	'Host' means 'to introduce guests or performers on a radio or television show or programme'.	invite
kids	'Kids' is informal.	children

2 Update your list after every writing task. When a mistake disappears from your writing, remove it from the list. When you do the writing paper in the CAE exam itself, check for the mistakes you know are on your list: in the exam you're more likely to repeat mistakes you've made before than make new ones.

Articles and essays

Articles are written for a newspaper or magazine, while essays are usually written for a teacher. However, in both you have to develop an idea or point of view, comment and express your personal opinions.

Article

You may be asked to write an article for an English-language magazine or newspaper. You must try to capture the reader's interest, so you should express your opinions or comment as well, perhaps, as including descriptions and anecdotes.

You studied how to write articles in Units 3 (Writing Part 1) and 14 (Writing Part 2).

Exercise 1

Read the task below and <u>underline</u> the areas you must deal with.

> You have seen the following announcement in an international magazine.
>
> *We invite readers to send in articles on the following subject.*
>
> **The Internet and language learning**
> * *Has the Internet made learning another language more or less necessary?*
> * *How has the Internet changed the way you learn languages?*
> * *How do you think it will affect language learning in the future?*
>
> Write your **article**.

Exercise 2

1   Read the sample answer below. Has the writer dealt with all parts of the task? In which paragraph is each part dealt with?

2   Find two anecdotes that the writer tells. What point does each anecdote make?

The Internet and language-learning: creating the need and supplying a solution

Just recently I wanted to book a flight. I could have done it the old-fashioned way by ringing my travel agent. However, I wanted to compare prices and check times myself, so I found myself surfing the net in search of the best deal. Needless to say, while some sites were available in my native Italian, the majority were in English. Clearly, if we're going to live and work using the Internet for so many things from shopping to research, English will be a great help.

Before the Internet's arrival, a qualification in English was a desirable addition to our CVs. We attended classes, we read books and we occasionally watched television in English. Now, however, it's something that has invaded almost all areas of our lives so that we pick up lots of the language by immersion. In fact, the Internet has meant that we are so surrounded by the language that going to class, though necessary, is only one of the many ways we learn.

Some people suggest that the future of learning is online courses. In fact, a couple of years ago I tried using one to learn Portuguese. The problem was that I found myself a bit isolated because I was studying alone. Languages are for communicating with each other and for this reason classes are vital.

In the future, I believe the Internet will become better at delivering language-learning materials. While I don't believe it will entirely replace the classroom, it will supplement our learning experience and allow us to learn the language more quickly and thoroughly.

> Start with a heading which catches attention.

> Make the readers feel involved by using *you* and *your*, or *we* and *our*.

> You want to relate to the reader, so use a more informal and conversational style.

> Use adverbials such as *clearly*, *in fact*, etc. to help readers follow your argument.

Essay

An essay is usually a piece of academic writing in which you discuss issues connected with a topic. You may previously have discussed this topic in class. You should express your opinions on the topic and the reasons for them. The reader is normally your teacher.

You studied how to write essays in Unit 9.

Exercise 1

Look at the writing task below.

1 Do you agree with the statement? Why (not)?

2 What arguments for and against the statement can you think of? Make a list.

3 Who will read your essay? What style would be suitable?

> Following a class discussion your teacher has asked you to write an essay giving your views on this topic:
>
> *Most students go into higher education too soon. They would do better to work for a few years beforehand. Then they would make better use of higher education when they come to it.*
>
> Write your **essay**.

Exercise 2

Read the sample answer below.

1 How many arguments for the statement does the writer use?

2 And how many against?

3 Where does the writer express his/her opinion? Does he/she give reasons?

> Write a short introductory paragraph.

> Give reasons for and against to provide a balanced discussion and show you are aware of both sides of the argument.

> Use words and phrases like *firstly, secondly, the other (reason)* to help the reader follow the argument.

> Make sure that you express your opinion clearly and give reasons for it.

The majority of students in my country go into higher education as soon as they have finished school and this can give rise to a number of problems.

For students themselves there are often two problems. Firstly, many start courses without being sure whether it is really what they want to do. This lack of commitment means many of them are unmotivated and likely to change courses or drop out of full-time education altogether. Secondly, many are not sufficiently mature to make best use of university life.

These problems cause corresponding difficulties for educational institutions. Firstly, universities often struggle to teach unmotivated or immature students. Secondly, considerable economic resources are wasted when students abandon or change courses. It is therefore sometimes argued that school leavers should first work for a few years. When they decide to study again, they will have the experience and maturity to take advantage of their courses. Moreover, they will know what they want to study and how this will help them to achieve their ambitions.

In my opinion, although these arguments sound attractive, they are generally impractical for two reasons. The first is that people who have been working often lose their study habits and are unable to learn as quickly or efficiently as before. The other reason is that their lives often change after they leave education. If they settle down and have children, their family responsibilities may prevent them from returning to full-time study. For these reasons, despite the problems involved, I believe that it is best to attend university soon after leaving school.

Sentences which introduce paragraphs

It often helps the reader if you start a paragraph with a short introductory sentence which states what you are going to deal with in the paragraph. Here are some examples:

For individual students, there are two problems. Firstly, …

In my opinion, although these arguments sound attractive, they are generally impractical for two reasons.

There are three reasons why students delay going into higher education.

There are a number of arguments against this point of view.

Introducing your opinions

(Personally,) I believe/think/feel that …

In my point of view …

In my opinion …

Introducing other people's opinions

It is often a good idea to show the reader how your own ideas contrast from the opinions of other people (e.g. **Some people say** the Internet has ruined our lives **but in my opinion**, the Internet has transformed the world for the better.) .

Some people suggest/believe/say that …

It is often/sometimes said/argued/ suggested that …

It can be argued that …

According to many/some people …

Adverbs to say something is obvious

Sometimes you need to express an obvious point as part of an argument and you need to point out to readers that you're not saying anything unusual:

*obviously   clearly   undoubtedly
of course   needless to say
it goes without saying that
without a doubt*

Competition entries and reviews

In a competition entry you will have to nominate someone for a prize or award and support your nomination by explaining your reasons or giving a description. A review will also require some description leading to a recommendation.

Competition entry

When you write a competition entry, your readers will be a judge or panel of judges. You will usually have to nominate somebody for something or propose yourself for selection for something (e.g. a grant to study). You will have to try to persuade the judges and give reason(s) why your choice is best.

You studied how to write a competition entry in Unit 5.

Exercise 1

Read the writing task below. There are four areas you must cover. What could you say about each of these to persuade the judges?

> You have seen the following announcement on your college notice board:
>
> **Cambridge Study Competition**
>
> We are offering a prize to students of a two-week English course in Cambridge next summer. Entrants should explain why they should be chosen and say:
>
> • what they find most enjoyable about studying English
>
> • what things they do outside class to improve their English and
>
> • how they expect to use English in the future.
>
> Write your **competition entry**.

Exercise 2

1 Find where the writer has dealt with each of the points in the task.

2 What impression does the writer give of his personality?

3 How do the writer's answers to the points compare with yours?

4 What aspects of the competition entry convey the writer's enthusiasm?

Studying English is challenging and occasionally frustrating. Its complex grammar and enormous vocabulary make learning it a daunting and possibly unending task. But I take pleasure in words and the power of words. I have always enjoyed being able to choose words to express certain feelings or convey particular meanings in my own language and now I would like the opportunity to be able to do this in English, my second language. This is why I would like to put myself forward for this competition.

After class, I spend forty minutes or more going over my notes, looking up words in the dictionary and checking my grammar notes against what my grammar says. Apart from this, I read extensively in English – I've just finished a novel by the recent Nobel Prize winner Doris Lessing – and whenever possible I go to the cinema to watch films in English. Books and films in their original language are infinitely better than in translation.

This brings me to my reason for wishing to study in Britain. My great ambition is to join the diplomatic service, for which an advanced knowledge of other languages is really essential. If I achieve this with English, it will help my chances of pursuing a career as a diplomat.

All in all, I believe I should be chosen for the reasons expressed above: I am a conscientious, hard-working and enthusiastic student both in class and in my free time. Moreover, the better my English, the more success I am likely to enjoy in my future career.

> Avoid repeating the same vocabulary – look at the other ways the writer has used of expressing the idea 'enjoy.'

> To win a competition, you must always sound enthusiastic and have good reasons for persuading the judges.

Review

In a review, usually for an international magazine or newspaper, you're expected to express your opinion about something which readers may be thinking of seeing, doing or buying, e.g. a film, a concert or an exhibition. You can assume that the readers are people with similar interests to yours. You usually have to make a recommendation about the thing you are reviewing.

You studied how to write a review in Unit 6.

Exercise 1

Read the writing task below.

1 What things should you deal with in your review?

2 Who will read it and what style would be suitable?

> You have seen this announcement in an international magazine:
>
> **Where to buy clothes**
>
> Our readers are interested in clothes shops to visit when on holiday or travelling. Can you write a review for visitors to your town comparing two clothes shops, saying what sort of clothes they sell, commenting on the quality of the service, value for money, how fashionable they are and giving recommendations?
>
> Write your **review**.

Exercise 2

Read the sample answer below.

1 Does the writer cover all the points mentioned in the Writing task?

2 How does the writer start the review?

3 What adjectives does the writer use to describe:
  a the clothes?
  b the staff?

4 Does the writer use a formal or an informal style?

5 What do you notice about the layout?

6 Explain the writer's recommendations in your own words.

Shopping in Linz

Buying clothes might not be the first thing you think of when visiting Linz, but in fact there are some attractive boutiques in the old town and you can come away looking fashionable and stylish. Here are my favourites.

Melanie's

Melanie's sells clothes for women and while it is quite a small shop it has a wide range of the latest styles. If you want to look really fashionable, it's certainly worth a visit. The shop has a selection of formal and casual clothes from some of the world's top designers, so they're not cheap. However, you can occasionally pick up a bargain. The staff are attentive and can speak English and they'll help you to combine clothes and accessories so that you'll leave the shop looking like a million dollars, even though it will cost you quite a lot in the process!

The Parallel

If you don't feel like spending so much, The Parallel is a good alternative. This shop belongs to some local designers and sells their unique range of clothes and shoes for women at quite competitive prices. The clothes tend to be in distinctive bright colours, but the quality is generally good, so the shop represents good value for money. You'll have to look after yourself as, apart from the security guard, the only staff you'll find are on the cash desk. While they're polite and friendly, they don't have time to give much help.

My recommendations

To sum up, for something really special, go to Melanie's, but be careful or your credit card will suffer. For bright clothes at a reasonable price The Parallel is a better bet.

> Make your review sound as authentic as possible: address the reader, give an introduction and mention the town.

> Think about the details the reader will want to know and include them.

> You can use a little humour to maintain your reader's interest.

> You can divide the review into sections as here, but it's not always necessary.

Summarising

To summarise, …   All in all, …   To sum up, …   In summary, …

Proposals and reports

In both proposals and reports, you're expected to write in clearly organised sections and include factual information leading to a suggestion, recommendation or conclusion.

Proposal

When you write a proposal you're trying to persuade readers to follow a course of action. Your readers may be a boss or teacher (in which case you will need quite a formal style), or colleagues or members of your club (in which case the style will be a little less formal – you can address your readers more personally, perhaps use contractions). In both cases the format should be the same. You'll have to make a suggestion or suggestions based on some factual information.

You studied how to write a proposal in Unit 8.

Exercise 1

Look at the Part 1 task on the right.

1 Underline the things you must deal with in your answer.

2 Who is going to read the proposal? So, what would be a suitable style?

> Answer using your own vocabulary, not the vocabulary of the question where possible. Planning before you write will help with this.

> If you have to write a proposal, use the format of a proposal, i.e. a title, sections, headings, an introduction and a conclusion.

> Don't spend a long time counting words, but keep within the word limit:
> * if you write too little, you are probably missing important points.
> * if you write too much, you risk being irrelevant.

You are a member of the Students' Council at the college where you study. The principal of your college wants to make it easier for new foreign students to integrate into college life and has written you an email asking for your suggestions. Read the email from the Principal and the notes you made. Then write a proposal with your suggestions and the reasons for them.

> I know you're friendly with a lot of students from other countries. What problems do they have? Here are some ideas for making their lives easier – could you say what you think of them?
>
> Improved student guidebook – *needs new section on academic system here*
> Social club – hardly anybody uses it – *needs publicising*
> Weekend activities – *maybe, what do other students think?*
> Student advisors – *good idea! For each new student, an experienced student who gives help and advice*

Write your **proposal**.

Exercise 2

Read the sample answer below.

1 Has the writer dealt with all parts of the task?

2 Find examples of where the writer has avoided repeating vocabulary from the question by using synonyms (e.g. *improved – revised*). Why is this a good approach?

3 Underline phrases used to introduce suggestions and recommendations, e.g. *I would suggest …* .

Proposal for integrating new students

Introduction
The purpose of this proposal is to suggest ways of facilitating overseas students' integration into this college.

Overseas students' problems
There are two difficulties which newly-arrived students have. Firstly, they are unfamiliar with our academic system. Secondly, they often find it hard to integrate on a social level with people here.

Revised student guidebook
The existing guidebook is extremely helpful. However, I would suggest including a section on how our academic system works as this is often confusing for students from other educational backgrounds.

Social activities
Judging by attendance figures, the college social club could hardly be described as thriving and its activities should be advertised more widely. Furthermore, I would recommend asking students for their ideas on how to involve new overseas students in weekend activities.

Student advisors
It would also be a good idea to instigate a mentoring system. This, more than anything, would overcome students' problems with both the academic system and their social life. A more experienced mentor would be responsible for helping them understand the system by giving them guidance and advice while also introducing them to other students and helping them to make friends.

Conclusion
I suggest that we ask for volunteers to help with all the areas mentioned above.

Report

When you write a report your readers may be, e.g. your boss or a teacher (in which case you will need a more formal style) or your colleagues or members of your club (in which case the style will be a little less formal – you can address your readers more personally, perhaps use contractions). In both cases the format should be the same. You will have to give some factual information and make suggestions or recommendations. You must organise your report carefully and it's a good idea to use sections with headings.

You studied how to write reports in Units 2, 4 and 10.

Exercise 1

1 Read the task below. Underline:
   - the points you must cover in your report and
   - who will read it.
2 How formal should this report be?
3 When you write about what you like and dislike, do you think you should refer mainly to educational matters, to personal experiences, or both?

> You have been studying in an English-speaking country for some time as part of an educational exchange. The director of the exchange programme is interested in improving the experience for future students. He has asked you to write a report outlining why you have been doing the exchange, what you like and dislike about it and making recommendations for how it could be improved.
>
> Write your **report**.

Exercise 2

1 Read the sample report on the right. What things did the writer like and dislike about the programme?
2 Find examples of a formal style in the sample report.

Pegasus educational exchange programme

Introduction
The purpose of this report is to outline my reasons for doing the exchange, the positive and negative aspects of the experience and to make recommendations for improvements.

Reasons for doing the exchange
I have been in New Zealand as part of the Pegasus programme for the last nine months. I participated in the exchange in order to do an MA in Environmental Science at the University of Auckland. At the same time I had the opportunity to improve my English.

Positive and negative aspects
The benefits of doing this exchange far outweigh the disadvantages. The main professional advantage is the opportunity to exchange ideas with teachers and students from a completely different part of the world (I come from Portugal) and with an entirely different outlook on environmental problems. This allows us to see such problems from a variety of angles. I believe as a result I will return to my country with innovative solutions to local problems. In addition, I have acquired improved language skills and increased cultural awareness.

The negative aspect from my point of view is that the programme does not receive enough financial support and I have found it very expensive as a result. This is a problem which is likely to discourage prospective exchange students from participating in the programme.

Recommendations
I strongly recommend that the programme organisers should make interest-free loans available to people wishing to take part in an exchange. This would allow considerable numbers of talented students to benefit from something which they would otherwise be unable to do.

Give your report a title. Organise it in sections with section headings including an Introduction and Recommendations.

Outline the purpose of the report.

Avoid just repeating the words in the question.

Use vocabulary and collocations appropriate to formal writing.

Explain the reasons for recommendations you make and the consequences of problems you mention.

Making suggestions and recommendations

Formal

- *I would suggest* + verb + *-ing*: *I would suggest including a section on our academic system.*
- *I suggest that …*: *I suggest that we ask for volunteers.*
- *should*: *Its activities should be advertised more widely.*
- *I would recommend* + verb + *-ing*: *I would recommend canvassing students' ideas.*
- *I recommend that …*: *I recommend that we start a social club.*
- *It would be a good idea* + *to* infinitive: *It would be a good idea to instigate a mentoring system.*

Less formal

- *Why not* + infinitive without *to*: *Why not phone one of your friends?*
- *Why don't we / you* + infinitive without *to*: *Why don't we just send them an email?*
- *How about* + verb + *-ing*: *How about meeting up after work tomorrow?*
- *Let's* + infinitive without *to*: *Let's have a party.*

Information sheets and contributions to a longer piece

Information sheets and contributions to a longer piece require you to give an amount of factual information, together with your opinion and some advice.

Information sheet

In an information sheet you have to give people instructions and/or advice. You must write clear factual information and/or advice and organise it clearly.

You studied how to write an information sheet in Unit 12.

Exercise 1

Read the Writing task below.

1 What things would you mention for the four points you must deal with?

2 Who will read the information sheet? So what style would be suitable?

A number of students from other countries are coming to study for a month in your town. They will be staying as guests with local families. You have been asked to produce an information sheet for them giving information and advice on the following areas:

- climate and clothes
- family customs and guests
- meals
- getting around

Write your **information sheet**.

Exercise 2

Read the sample answer below.

1 What do you notice about the layout? How is it different from the sample information sheet on page 125?

2 This information sheet is written in an informal style. Find features of an informal style in the answer.

An information sheet like this should have a short, friendly introduction.

Use a clear, uncomplicated organisation.

Concentrate on giving clear, simple information and advice which is easily understood. Your aim is to help your readers.

Information sheet for visiting students

We're looking forward to welcoming you to Exmouth next month. We hope you have a thoroughly enjoyable and productive stay here. To make sure your visit goes as smoothly as possible, here are the answers to some FAQs.

What will the weather be like and what clothes should I bring?
The weather in November can be quite variable and you can expect at least some days of cold and rain though it's unlikely to snow. You should bring warm clothes, including at least two jerseys and a waterproof jacket. It's also a good idea to bring a scarf and gloves.

How should I behave with my host family and should I bring them a present?
Your host family are inviting you because they're interested in getting to know someone from your country, so spend time with them, join in with any excursions they organise and be ready to help them a bit with housework. Try to integrate into their family life and you'll have a great experience! It's customary to bring them a small present, such as a box of chocolates or a souvenir from your country.

What should I do if I have a special diet?
If you have a special diet, please let the organisers know and they'll inform your host family.

What's the best way to get around in Exmouth?
Exmouth is a small town and most places are within a short walking distance. If you want to go further afield, there are bus and train services.

Contribution to a longer piece

When you write a contribution to a longer piece, you are writing part of something such as a brochure, a guidebook or a piece of research. (It is assumed that other people will be writing other parts.) You will have to supply information and opinions. The style you choose will depend on the purpose of the longer piece and who its readers are.

You studied how to write a contribution to a longer piece in Unit 11.

Exercise 1

Read the writing task below.

1 Which dishes would you describe?

2 Should you list all the ingredients and give the recipes?

3 Which restaurant would you mention?

4 What other information should your contribution contain?

5 Who will read the contribution? What style would be suitable?

You have received this email from a friend:

Hi,

I'm preparing an article called 'Tasting the world' for an international magazine. Can you contribute a piece about food in your region? The piece is really for people thinking of visiting your country and we need:

• a general introduction to the area

• a description of a couple of dishes which give a taste of your region

• a typical place to eat and why visitors will enjoy it.

Write your **contribution**.

Exercise 2

Read the sample answer below and say whether these statements are true (T) or false (F).

1 The contribution has an introduction and a conclusion.

2 It gives an overview of the area, two dishes and a restaurant.

3 The reader would feel interested in visiting the area and trying the food.

Tasting 'El Delta'

The Ebro Delta is a corner of Spain unlike any other on the Mediterranean coast. It has escaped the building and tourist boom of recent years and its rich agricultural region specialises in the cultivation of rice. It's surrounded by long golden beaches, sea-water lagoons, salt marshes and rich fishing grounds. These features have all made their contribution to its very individual gastronomy.

Sarsuela de peix

This is a dish which every visitor should experience. It's a sort of rich fish and seafood stew cooked in an enormous flat pan, with a tasty sauce. It looks spectacular when brought to your table and tastes wonderful. Normally, because this dish is so large there should be at least two people in your party who wish to try it.

Duck paella

The Delta is a stopping point for millions of sea birds which migrate between northern Europe and Africa every year. If you happen to visit the area in autumn, you shouldn't miss one of the distinctive tastes of the Delta: duck cooked with yellow rice, which is again an unforgettable experience.

Where to eat

One of the best places to sample these dishes is the Estany restaurant, surrounded by rice fields on the edge of a nature reserve. The owner works hard at preserving the traditional foods of the region and he's keen on introducing them to visitors. If you go there at weekends, you'll probably also experience some traditional music and dancing.

> Always think what effect you want to have on your readers – do you want to encourage or discourage them from visiting the area and trying the food?

> Vary the vocabulary you use.

> When appropriate, write in sections with headings.

> Use collocations you know which are specific to the topic, e.g. *tasty sauce, distinctive taste, unforgettable experience, sample dishes* – they'll produce a positive effect on the reader.

Letters

You may be asked to write a letter responding to a situation described in the question. You must use a style which is suitable for the person you are writing to, for example the editor of a newspaper or magazine, the director of a company or college. In your letter, you may have to recount some personal experience or give factual information.

The types of letter you may have to write include:

• a letter to the editor of a newspaper or magazine

• a letter of application, or giving a reference for someone applying for a job

• a letter to the director(s) of an organisation, or to a college principal

• an informal letter to a friend.

You studied how to write letters in Units 1, 7 and 13.

Exercise 1

1 Read the Part 1 writing task below, <u>underlining</u> the points you must deal with in your answer.

2 What would be a suitable style for readers of a music magazine?

3 Write a paragraph-by-paragraph plan for the letter. When you have finished writing your plan, check that you have included all the points that you have underlined.

You and your friends recently attended a pop festival near your town, which you enjoyed very much. However, you have been disappointed by a bad review published in an international music magazine. You have decided to write a letter to the editor to explain how much you and your friends enjoyed the festival and how you feel about the review. Read the extracts from the review and the comments which you and your friends noted down.

- fans had to walk for more than a mile to get from the car park to the stage - *but beautiful venue!*

- most of the acts were only on stage for a few minutes - *but great choice of groups and great atmosphere*

- poor selection of places to buy food - *most fans brought their own!*

- not enough washing facilities - *true - needed more showers. Definitely coming back next year*

Got something to say? Then write to letters editor Charlie Moon at cm@worldmusicmag.com

Write your **letter**.

Exercise 2

1 Read the sample answer below. Has the writer included all the points you underlined?

2 How would you describe the style of the letter?

3 Has the writer included anything which is not in the instructions? Why (not)?

Dear Charlie,

We read your review of the Middleton Music Festival last month and we're unhappy with some of your comments because we all had a really fantastic time. You criticised the distance from the car parks to the stage but you didn't mention that the location chosen for the festival was superb – a lovely meadow beside a river – so we didn't mind the walk. Admittedly, the acts were very short and we'd have liked everything to go on for much longer, but on the other hand, the programme featured some top bands and singers and their performances were absolutely brilliant. Also, the atmosphere was just unbelievable.

You also complained that there weren't enough food stalls and cafés. However, we brought our own food with us and noticed that most other people did too, so that wasn't really a great problem.

We do agree with you about one thing, however, and that was that there weren't enough showers. When the rain (predictably) started coming down, we all got hopelessly muddy and needed a wash – especially before we went to our tents for the night!

Still, that's a minor complaint and really all part of the fun. We just can't wait for next year's festival.

Yours,

> When you write a letter, get straight to the point.

> When you're doing an exam-style writing task, you're really doing a role play – here of someone who has had a wonderful experience.

> You'll need to add substance to the notes in the writing task by using your own ideas.

> Think of a natural way to finish the letter.

Starting and finishing letters

If you know the person's name:

- Start with: *Dear Susana* (if you would use their first name when you speak to them), *Dear Mrs Emmett* (if you don't feel comfortable using their first name).
- Finish with:
  - *Best wishes, Regards, Kind regards* (if you're writing to a friend)
  - *Love* or *With love* (if you're writing to a very close friend or a member of your family)
  - *Yours sincerely* or *Yours* (if you're writing to someone you don't know well).

If you don't know the person's name:

- Start with: *Dear Sir* or *Madam*
- Finish with: *Yours faithfully*.

Adding extra points

Formal	Informal
Firstly, secondly, finally, etc.	*Besides,*
In addition, moreover,	*Also,*
furthermore, what is more	*One thing / Another thing (was that …)*
	Apart from this/that …

Speaking reference

What to expect in the exam

The Speaking paper is Paper 5.

- It lasts 15 minutes and has four parts.
- You do the Speaking paper in pairs.
- There are two examiners in the room; one gives you instructions and asks you questions, the other listens but does not join in the conversation.

Part 1 (Interview)

Part 1 lasts three minutes and is a conversation between the examiner and each candidate individually. You will be asked questions about yourself, your family, sports and other leisure activities, your likes and dislikes, your education and where you live. Questions may also be about your past experiences and your future plans.

You studied and practised Part 1 in Units 1 and 11.

How to do Part 1

1. Listen to the questions carefully and give clear, direct answers. If appropriate, include a few extra details, or a reason for an answer you give.
2. Try to relax. Look confidently at the examiner and smile a little when you answer the questions.
3. Take the opportunity to show how fluently you can speak.
4. **Don't** prepare answers before you do the exam, but **do** make sure that you know the vocabulary you will need to talk about the topics that are likely to come up.

Exercise

Here are some typical questions that you may be asked in Part 1 of the Speaking exam. Work through some of the questions with a partner, taking turns to be the examiner and the student. Try to use relevant vocabulary from the Useful language boxes.

Questions	Useful language
Introductory questions Where are you from? What do you do here/there? How long have you been studying English? What do you most enjoy about learning English?	*born in*; *grow up in/near*; *be brought up in* (place) *by* (people) *small / quite a large / extended family* *I've been working/studying at … since* (+ point in time) *for* (+ length of time) *Actually,* (+ unexpected/surprising information) *I've only been learning English for two years.* *What I really love about (-ing) is …* *The thing I like most of all is …*
Leisure time What are your main interests and leisure time activities? How important are sport and exercise in your life? What types of TV programmes do you think are worth watching? What kinds of music do you enjoy listening to?	*I'm fanatical about …* *I … whenever I can / get the chance.* *quite / not terribly important (to me)* *I'm really keen on …* *I never miss …* *I love …* *I can't stand …*
Learning What is your happiest memory of school? What were the most useful things you learned at school? What do you enjoy learning? If you had the opportunity to learn something new, what would you choose?	*I can remember* (event) *very well/clearly.* *Probably … / I suppose things like …* *I really like (… / -ing).* *That's an easy / a difficult question to answer.* *Let me think, …*

Future plans	
What do you hope to be doing this time next year? How might you use your English in the future? Would you consider living abroad permanently? Are you someone who likes to plan for the future, or do you prefer to let things happen?	*I hope to be (+ -ing) at (place).* *I expect I'll be … (+ -ing)* *I'd certainly consider … (+ -ing) / I'd have to think carefully about … / It's not something I'd rush into.* *I'm someone who … / I'm (not) the kind of person who …*
Travel and holidays	
What kinds of holiday appeal to you most? Why? Which countries would you most like to visit? Why? Which part/s of your country would you recommend to tourists? Why? Would you like to work in the travel industry? Why (not)?	*I (tend to) prefer … (mainly) because …* *My main reason is that …* *I've always wanted to … I don't know / can't explain why.* *I'd recommend / suggest …* *Firstly, because … and secondly, because …* *I've never thought about it. / I'm not sure …* *I'd have to think about that …*
Daily life	
Which part of the day do you enjoy most? Why? What do you like to do at weekends? What do you do to relax? Do you prefer to follow a routine or do you like to do something different every day?	*I'm not very good / I'm best at/in (time of day).* *I'm a night / early morning person.* *I try to catch up on (activity); I spend time …-ing.* *Mainly / Most of the time I …* *My problem is I …* *The thing about me is, I …* *I'd always rather (verb) than (verb).*

Part 2 (Long turn)

Part 2 lasts about three minutes altogether.

The examiner will give you and your partner a set of three pictures to talk about. You then take turns to speak individually for a minute about two of the three pictures, describing and comparing them, and speculating or expressing opinions about them. After your partner has spoken for a minute, the examiner will ask you to give a brief response to questions about your partner's pictures.

You studied and practised Part 2 in Units 2, 5, 7, 9 and 13.

How to do Part 2

1 The three pictures will always have a common theme, so talk about the general ideas they illustrate. Don't describe them in detail.

2 You'll need to choose two of the three pictures and then compare them with each other. If you are not sure what they show, speculate.

3 It is important to answer the question the examiner asks you. This will be printed on the same sheet as the pictures.

4 Whenever possible, give reasons or explanations for the answers you give.

5 Speak for the whole minute. Don't stop until the examiner says 'Thank you'.

6 When it's your partner's turn to talk about the photos, listen but don't interrupt. The examiner will ask you a question about your partner's pictures at the end. You should answer this question quite briefly.

Useful language

Comparing (See also Grammar reference Unit 13)

Here / In this photo, I can see / someone is / there are … / … whereas in this photo …

On the other hand, this picture shows …

Giving reasons/explanations (See also Grammar reference Unit 2)

The (main) reason for this is that …

I think / I'd say this is because …

This can be explained quite easily – …

Speculating (See also Grammar reference Units 4 and 11)

This person looks as if she's/he's …

He seems to be …

Perhaps/Maybe they're …

They're probably …

He could be / might be …

Exercise

Work through the sample question with a partner. Take turns to speak for one minute. You should each compare a different pair of pictures.

Examiner's instructions

In this part of the test, I'm going to give each of you three pictures. I'd like you to talk about them on your own for about a minute, and also to answer a question briefly about your partner's picture.

(*To Candidate A*) It's your turn first. Here are your pictures. They show people shopping.

I'd like you to compare two of the pictures and say what different methods of shopping they show, and why people might choose one method rather than another.

(*After A has spoken for a minute*) Thank you.

(*To Candidate B*) Which picture do you think shows the least stressful method of shopping? Why?

- What different methods of shopping do they show?
- Why might people choose one method rather than another?

Part 3 (Collaborative task)

Part 3 lasts four minutes.

This part involves a discussion between you and your partner. The key skills being tested are fluency and the ability to participate in and maintain a conversation. The examiner tells you what to do and gives you a set of pictures to discuss. Your task will be to reach a decision by negotiation. During your discussion, you will be expected to exchange ideas, express and justify opinions, agree and/or disagree, suggest, speculate and evaluate.

You studied and practised Part 3 in Units 3, 6, 8, 10 and 12.

How to do Part 3

1 Listen carefully to the instructions and questions you are given by the examiner. The key questions are also printed on the page you are given.

2 The first question will ask you to discuss what the pictures show. This will be followed by an instruction to make a decision related to the subject of the pictures.

3 If you start the conversation, make sure you don't speak for too long. Give a brief opinion, then ask your partner for their thoughts on the subject.

4 When your partner is speaking, show that you're listening. React and respond appropriately. This can include nodding and smiling, as well as speaking.

5 Try to make what you say sound like normal conversation.

6 Spend roughly the same length of time on each question, but above all, make sure you leave plenty of time to discuss the second question and reach your decision.

7 Try not to reach your decision too quickly. If you do, you'll still have to keep the discussion going until the examiner tells you to stop by saying 'Thank you'.

Useful language

Bringing your partner into the conversation

What do you think? / Do you have any thoughts on this?

Do you agree (with me)?   I'd say … / What about you?

Keeping the discussion moving

Let's move on to the next picture.   So, how about this picture?   Shall we go on to second question?

Agreeing and disagreeing

I (completely) agree.   Yes, and (another thing) …

I (totally) disagree.   I can't agree (with you there).

You've got a point (there), but (the way I see it) …

Reaching a decision

Now we have to decide …   OK, let's make our decision.

So, is that agreed? / do we agree on that?

Exercise

Work through this sample task with a partner. Make sure you each speak for approximately the same length of time.

Examiner's instructions

Now I'd like you to talk about something together for about four minutes.

Here are some pictures showing people paying for things in different ways. First, talk to each other about the importance of money in today's society. Then decide which picture shows the safest way of paying for something.

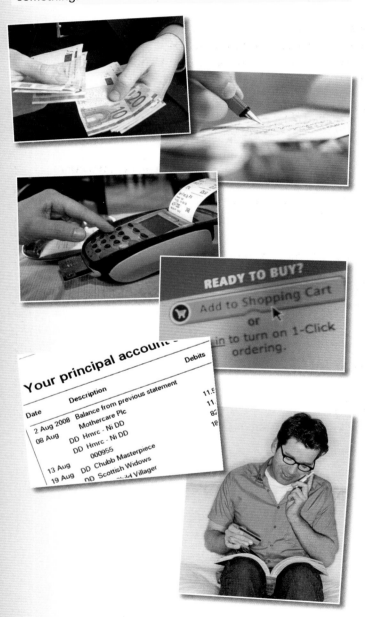

- How important is money in today's society?
- Which photo shows the safest way of paying for something?

Part 4 (Discussion)

Part 4 lasts four minutes.

This is a discussion between you, your partner and the examiner. The examiner will ask you and your partner questions related to the topic you discussed in Part 3. You are expected to express and justify opinions and to agree or disagree.

You studied and practised Part 4 in Units 4 and 14.

How to do Part 4

1 Listen carefully to the question. The question itself may be preceded by a statement, which you are then asked to agree or disagree with or to express an opinion about. If you don't understand the statement or the question, ask the examiner to repeat it.

2 Answer the question with opinions and reasons. Follow the same guidelines as for Part 3 with regard to including your partner in the discussion and to keeping the conversation moving.

Useful language

Introducing an opinion and giving a reason

Well, in my opinion… …because…

I think / feel … I'm not sure. I think …

Introducing an explanation

I mean … You see…

Giving an example

For example … For instance … … such as …

Exercise

Work through one or more of these typical questions (related to the topic of Part 3 above) with a partner. Make sure you each speak for approximately the same length of time.

- Some people say that, in the future, traditional forms of money, coins banknotes, and even cheques will completely disappear within the next few years and be entirely replaced by credit cards and other mechanical or digital methods of paying. What's your opinion?
- What are the advantages and disadvantages of relying solely on credit or debit cards as your method of paying for goods and services?
- How far do you agree that people who regularly pay for things online risk becoming the victims of fraud or identity theft?
- What can be done to protect people's bank accounts at a time when computer crime is on the increase?

PAPER 1: READING Part 1

Part 1

You are going to read three extracts which are all concerned in some way with books. For questions **1–6**, choose the answer (**A**, **B**, **C** or **D**) which you think fits best according to the text.

Mark your answers **on the separate answer sheet**.

Literary Prizes

The panels which judge literary prizes are notoriously hard to second guess, and that game is not a fruitful one anyway, unless you set store by an ability to predict the unpredictable. But as the book market becomes increasingly uncertain, with serious resources only directed towards sure-fire sellers, so the literary prizes bestowed on books become a key element in their successful marketing.

Unsurprisingly, those who express doubt at the 'glitzification' of literary prizes are routinely ignored. Don't we want people to buy more books? We do. Does the popularity of a book rule out its artistic or intellectual merit? It doesn't. But do we wonder if the pressures of promotion compromise the already shaky integrity of the literary prizes? Possibly.

Mediocre writers are often spoken of as 'promotable', which roughly translates as physically attractive or possessed of an interesting personal life, but which can easily become confused with ability. There are several examples of such contrived reputations currently walking around, while writers of real innovation, quality and depth battle to stay on their publishers' lists.

1   What do we learn about literary competitions in the first paragraph?

   A   You cannot be sure which way the voting will go.
   B   They do not generate much public interest.
   C   It is difficult to know who the judges will be.
   D   The outcomes are frequently unpopular.

2   According to the text, becoming successful as a writer

   A   always requires a great deal of determination.
   B   is sometimes unrelated to literary skill.
   C   is often easier for people with original ideas.
   D   usually depends on getting a leading publisher.

Adapting Literary Classics

The present vogue for filmed adaptations of the most celebrated English novels poses intriguing problems for those, like myself, who combine a professional commitment to the study and teaching of such works, with a practical interest in the business of adapting them for the screen. In recent years the rush of film and TV executives to plunder the library shelves for bankable literary classics has become something of a stampede. Jane Austen is the market leader. She offers, or seems to offer, what film-makers like best, a formula; her novels define an identifiable territory and her style, visually translated into production values as a world of lace bonnets, flowing gowns, English gardens and stately homes, has the readily marketable appeal of a nostalgic cult. Even that distinctive ironic voice, however edited into one-liners, diffused among different characters, or used to cue in some comic cameo, seems to nourish a hunger for wholemeal dialogue among screen audiences jaded with junk-food slang.

3   The writer has written the piece from the standpoint of someone

    A   assessing the range of novels available for adaptation.
    B   whose interest is focused on the literary merit of adaptations.
    C   whose main purpose is to question the relevance of Jane Austen's message.
    D   who has more than an academic involvement in the subject.

4   According to the writer, what is the attraction of Jane Austen for the film industry?

    A   The books she wrote appeal to all ages.
    B   The films based on her work require little advertising.
    C   The potential audience knows what to expect from her.
    D   The language she used requires no modification.

Extract from a novel

Mary the critic

In no profession but journalism is it possible to ascend with the rapidity Mary now achieved. With Ivo's patronage and a lively turn of phrase her success was almost guaranteed, but what made her notorious was her reviews. Every critic has his or her own private agenda, which ripples through the surface of their writing while remaining invisible to the ordinary newspaper reader. For some, it is the simple wish to make their by-line better known. For others, it is the opportunity to put over a particular aesthetic, religious or moral perspective. Others still wish to alert publishers that they have an uncommissioned book on the same subject in them, or to pay back scores of an entirely professional nature.

Mary's novelty was not that she was prepared to be rude, or witty, at the author's expense, for both of these were commonplace enough. Nor was it even that she was so well-read. She had suddenly discovered that she had a voice. It was not the voice she used when talking to people, any more than the voice columnists use reflects their conversation. On paper, it roared and railed and spat and hissed all the things she had kept silent about; and when a writer discovers such a voice it is usually heard even if what it is saying is mistaken.

5   What is said about critics in the first paragraph?

    A   They all have personal motives for what they say in reviews.
    B   They all resent being forced to do that kind of work.
    C   They all express opinions that they do not genuinely hold.
    D   They all feel obliged to make negative comments in reviews.

6   Mary differed from other critics in that

    A   she was better educated than they were.
    B   she was not concerned about the effect of her reviews on others.
    C   her reviews consisted mainly of negative comments.
    D   there was a very distinctive style to what she wrote.

Part 2

You are going to read a newspaper article about climbing. Six paragraphs have been removed from the article. Choose from the paragraphs **A–G** the one which fits each gap (**7–12**). There is one extra paragraph which you do not need to use.

Mark your answers **on the separate answer sheet**.

Sea, Ice & Rock

*Mountaineer Chris Bonnington is best known for scaling the summit of Everest in 1985. Robin Knox-Johnston began his sea career in the Merchant Navy. In 1968-9 he was the first to circumnavigate the world single-handed, in his yacht **Sunhaili**. The two teamed up to sail and climb in Greenland, recording the trip in their new book: **Sea, Ice and Rock**.*

In 1979 I was working on *Quest for Adventure*, a study of post-war adventure. I called Robin to ask for an interview and he said would I like to join him for a sail. I could show him some climbing techniques and he could show me the rudiments of sailing.

7

The route was quite difficult and I was impressed at how steady Robin was in tricky conditions. He just padded quietly along. After a bit we arrived at this huge drop. I asked Robin if he had ever climbed before. He hadn't, so I showed him. When I had finished, Robin very politely asked if he could go down the way he climbed down ropes on his boat.

8

His proposal that we should combine our skills on a joint trip to Greenland was just an extension, on a rather grand scale, of our voyage to Skye. Robin impressed me immensely as a leader. Traditionally, the skipper makes all the decisions. But Robin made a point of consulting everyone first.

To be frank, I found the sailing very boring. The moments of crisis which we had on the way back were easy to deal with: the adrenaline pumps and you get all worked up. The bit I found difficult was spending day after day in the middle of the sea.

9

I therefore felt a bit useless at times; I found that very trying. The crew was also packed very close together: six people on a 10-metre yacht, designed to sleep four. At least when you're on a mountain expedition you have a chance to get away from each other.

10

Robin isn't a natural climber, which made his efforts even more impressive. The first time we tried to reach the pinnacle, we were on the go for 24 hours. On the way down we were dropping asleep on 50 degree slopes, 500 metres above the ground. Robin went to hell and back, but he totally put his confidence in me.

11

Yet he was all in favour of us having another go at climbing the mountain. The only time there was a near-crisis in our relationship was on the yacht on the way home. We were taking it in turns to be on watch. I was supposed to get up at 4 am for my shift, but Robin decided not to wake me. He felt he could do it himself.

12

While we enjoyed the Skye trip, we didn't really know each other until the end of the Greenland expedition. I found that underneath his bluff exterior, Robin was a kind-hearted, sensitive person.

A The previous night I'd almost dropped asleep. I felt that he didn't trust me – I felt insecure, and I said so. Robin immediately reassured me that I'd jumped to the wrong conclusion.

B The winds were tricky and once again it was my turn to be on watch. I was aware that if I made a mistake I could take the mast out, which is horribly expensive and a real nuisance.

C It was the first time I'd been on a yacht. We sailed for a while and then anchored. Robin's wife and daughter stayed on the boat and we paddled to the shore to exercise Robin's skills at climbing.

D When we reached Greenland and it was my turn to 'lead' the expedition, I found it difficult taking responsibility for Robin's life. There were many instances climbing together when if Robin had fallen, he could have pulled me off with him. I had to watch for that constantly. I underestimated how difficult the Cathedral – Greenland's highest mountain – would be.

E He just followed. When it got too difficult and I realised we'd have to turn back, he accepted it. I also knew that Robin was worried about the boat: whether we'd be able to get it through the ice, whether it was in one piece.

F He was used to using his arms, I wanted him to use his legs. I wasn't too happy about it, but he lowered himself down quite safely. It was during that trip to Skye that Robin and I built the foundation of a very real friendship.

G I am a land-lover and not really a do-it-yourself type of person. Robin, in contrast, is a natural sailor and seemed to enjoy tinkering with the engine or mending the lavatory. I was aware that Robin didn't really need me.

Part 3

You are going to read an extract from a book. For questions **13–19**, choose the answer (**A**, **B**, **C** or **D**) which you think fits best according to the text.

Mark your answers **on the separate answer sheet**.

Revolution in Time

Clocks and the making of the modern world

'I know what time is,' said Augustine in the sixth century, 'but if someone asks me, I cannot tell him.' Things have not changed very much since then. The learned man, physicist or philosopher, is not so sure he knows, but is ready to write volumes on the subject of his conjectures. The ordinary man couldn't care less. What matters to him is that he can measure time. If, like the vast majority of the world's people, he lives in a rural society, his time is measured for him by natural events: sunrise, high noon, sunset. He needs no more accurate division, for these are the events that demarcate his round of waking, working, sleeping. City dwellers measure time by the clock. Animals do not wake them; an alarm does. Their activities are punctuated by points on an abstract continuum, points designated as hours and minutes. If they have a job or class that starts, say, at nine o'clock, they try to get there *on time*. They have *appointments*, and these are fixed by points on the time scale.

Picture an immensely complicated and unevenly but often densely tracked railway marshalling yard, with components shifting and shunting about in all directions; only instead of trains directed from without, we have people, sometimes directed but more often self-steering. That is the world of social and personal interaction which works only because the member units have learnt a common language of time measurement. Without this language and without general access to instruments accurate enough to provide uniform indications of location in time, urban life and civilisation, as we know it, would be impossible. Just about everything we do depends in some way on going and coming, meeting and parting.

Indications, of course, are not enough. Knowledge of the time must be combined with obedience – what social scientists like to call 'time discipline'. The indications are in effect commands, for responsiveness to these cues is imprinted on us and we ignore them at our peril. Punctuality is a virtue, lateness a sin, and repeated lateness may be grounds for dismissal. The sense of punctuality is inculcated very early, indeed from infancy. Parents may feed their babies on demand, but their own schedules inevitably impinge on the consciousness of their children. As soon as children understand language, they pick up such notions as mealtime and bedtime. A child whose parents live and work by the clock soon learns that time is the most inexorable of disciplinarians. It passes slowly for children; but it waits for no one. It compels the laggard to hurry, for what one member of the family does with time affects the others. One of the most powerful notions to shape a child's consciousness is that of being late or of missing – missing a party or missing a plane.

Most people operate within a margin of plus or minus several minutes. If they have a train to catch, they arrive a few minutes early; likewise for appointments. For this range of tolerance, it is sufficient to check one's timepiece by radio and television announcements given to the nearest minute. Only the most precise people will want to know the time to the nearest ten-second interval as given by the telephone or Internet. For some, however, hours and minutes are not enough. Astronomers were the first to want to measure time in seconds and fractions of a second, well before instruments existed that could do so. It was not until the 1970s that timers calibrated in hundredths of seconds were used by officials at the Olympic Games. But the demands of sport are as nothing compared to those of some branches of science. When one enters the world of the physicist assigning times to subatomic events, one leaves hundredths and thousandths of seconds far behind. This is the world of microseconds and nanoseconds – units invented for scientific analysis.

The invention of the mechanical clock in medieval Europe was one of the great inventions in the history of humankind – not in the same class as fire and the wheel, but comparable to the advent of typesetting in its revolutionary implications for cultural values, technological change, social and political organisation, and personality. Why so important? After all, man had long known and used other kinds of timekeepers – sundials, water clocks, sand clocks – some of which were at least as accurate as the early mechanical clocks. Wherein lay the novelty, and why was this device so much more influential than its predecessors?

The answer, briefly put, lay in its enormous technological potential. The mechanical clock was self-contained, and once horologists learned to drive it by means of a coiled spring, it could be miniaturised so as to be portable, whether in the household or on the person. It was this possibility of widespread private use that laid the basis for *time discipline*, as against *time obedience*. One can use public clocks to summon people for one purpose or another, but that is not punctuality. Punctuality comes from within, not from without. It is the mechanical clock that has made possible, for better or worse, a civilisation attentive to the passage of time, hence to productivity and performance.

---

13 What does the writer say about attempts to define the meaning of time?

    A   They have led to a strong sense of conviction in many people.
    B   It would require an educated person to do this successfully.
    C   There has been considerable progress made in this area.
    D   It is a matter of speculation with little relevance to most people.

14 The writer uses the example of the railway marshalling yard to show that

    A   the number of external forces controlling people's lives has risen.
    B   it is essential in today's world that transport systems operate efficiently.
    C   the functioning of the modern world relies on the ability to measure time.
    D   city dwellers have a greater understanding of time than people in rural areas.

15 In the third paragraph, the writer says that people respond to time pressures because

    A   it enables them to lead less complicated lives.
    B   failure to do so can have severe consequences.
    C   they enjoy the sense they get of being organised.
    D   it is part of human nature to obey commands.

16 The writer believes it is inevitable that young people

    A   resent the consequences of being late.
    B   try to alter the schedules forced on them.
    C   become conditioned in their attitude towards time.
    D   have a different approach to timekeeping from adults.

17 What overall point does the writer make about time measurement in the fourth paragraph?

    A   The majority of people trust the accuracy of their watches.
    B   The purpose of the measurement determines the scale used.
    C   Some instruments that measure time are of no practical use.
    D   Constantly checking the time is a compulsive form of behaviour.

18 What does the writer say about the invention of the mechanical clock?

    A   It was of equal significance to that of the printing press.
    B   It had an immediate and extensive impact on other inventions.
    C   It provided people with their first reliable means of telling the time.
    D   It led to greater technological change than the creation of the wheel.

19 According to the writer, the most important effect of the invention of the mechanical clock was that

    A   it could be mass-produced at an affordable price.
    B   it eliminated the need for cities to build public clocks.
    C   it allowed people to choose the time when they performed certain tasks.
    D   it resulted in a population whose individuals accepted responsibility for timekeeping.

Part 4

You are going to read an article about women in sport. For questions **20–34**, choose from the sportswomen (**A–F**). The sports may be chosen more than once.

Mark your answers **on the separate answer sheet**.

Which sportswoman says:

she takes part in her sport on equal terms with men? **20** ☐

her concentration at work is affected by her sporting activities? **21** ☐

she was surprised to discover her talent for her sport? **22** ☐

she invests her earnings in her sport? **23** ☐

it is considered strange for women to take part in her sport? **24** ☐

she spends less time on other activities than she used to? **25** ☐

the age at which women start her particular sport is significant? **26** ☐

she was once under pressure to achieve her target by a certain date? **27** ☐

she has a good income from her sport? **28** ☐

she has endured physical suffering? **29** ☐

it is difficult for women to get good training in her sport? **30** ☐

she is sometimes afraid when taking part in her sport? **31** ☐

she doesn't want her appearance to affect her sporting reputation? **32** ☐

her personality has changed since she started doing her sport? **33** ☐

women's achievements in her sport receive less publicity than men's? **34** ☐

Women in Sport

A Jill, 27, skier

'It's a great feeling to fly through the air and land cleanly, but it can be scary. Sometimes you don't feel well or it's windy and you can't see, but you just get on with it. It's not easy to have a career outside skiing because we train for ten months of the year. You give up a lot of your social life and friends. But it was my choice. There are six men and three women in the British team. We all compete on the same courses at the same competitions and get treated the same – it's a young sport.'

B Caroline, 22, cyclist

'Two years ago I borrowed a bike to take part in a charity race. I won overall just because I cycled faster than everyone else, which was amazing because I'd never cycled before! I'm well paid as a pro, and cycling has lots of potential in terms of endorsements. However, I know I'm not ugly and it worries me that people may think I've got where I am because of how I look, not because I'm the best cyclist. So I tend to concentrate on the cycling at the moment, rather than earning money. I do at least four hours' training every day on the bike, plus some stretching exercises, swimming and running. My boyfriend's a cyclist as well, so he knows the time you have to put into it – it would be impossible otherwise.'

C Annabel, 26, rower

'Rowing is hard for girls to get into because very few girls' schools do it. So most don't start till they're 19 or 20 which makes it harder to succeed at an international level. Also, you usually have coaches who only stay a year or so. There's no continuity, so the women's squad is basically a shambles. But it's great fun and I love being fit, plus there's a good social life.'

D Ffyona, 24, long distance walker

'At 13 I dreamed of walking around the world – I didn't know just how big it was then! But Britain was too claustrophobic, too safe. I was very headstrong; I hated anyone having control over me. Now I am more tactful. Each walk has been different. The walk across Australia was the worst experience I've ever had as far as pain is concerned. I was doing 80 kilometres and 21 hours each day with three hours' sleep in high temperatures and walking with 15 blisters on each foot. But I got the record! I had to, because my sponsorship money was going to run out after 95 days. Men think that women are more likely to fail, so sponsoring them is always seen as a higher risk.'

E Lisa, 26, saloon car racer

'Some men have huge egos when they're driving – you see it on motorways. When I'm doing well, they don't talk to me. Being a woman has its disadvantages. When I get to a corner, the men think "I've got to beat her", so I've had a lot of knocks! You have to be naturally competitive and aggressive. It's very difficult to earn any money, and what I do make goes back into the sport. Women have been racing since the twenties and have always been classed as eccentrics. It's great that there are now more and more women taking up racing every year. For me, the appeal of saloon car racing is aiming for perfection – always trying to get round with a perfect lap.'

F Alison, 28, triathlete

'I get up at 5.30 three morning a week to swim. I need Tuesday and Thursday mornings to catch up on my sleep. In the evening I just cycle or run. Yes, I do fall asleep at my desk sometimes! There is a lot of nervous build-up beforehand and when you're racing you really push yourself – you don't feel good if you don't. Several times I've asked myself why I do it. The answer is a) I'm happier when I keep fit, b) I'm a slob at heart and if I didn't make myself do this I'd really be one, c) racing is very social. Men and women usually compete together but when an event is given coverage in the press, 90 per cent of the article will explain the men's event and 10 per cent will say, "Oh, by the way, so-and-so won the women's event". The prize money isn't as good either, of course. But now we've formed an International Triathlon Women's Commission, so we're working on it.'

PAPER 2: WRITING Part 1

You **must** answer this question. Write your answer in **180–220** words in an appropriate style on the opposite page.

---

1   You are studying at a college in Australia, which is improving its website. The college principal has asked you to write a proposal suggesting which would be the two best college facilities to promote on the website.

Read the extract from the principal's email below and the notes you have made. Then, **using the information appropriately**, write a proposal for the principal suggesting which two aspects of the college should feature on the website and justifying your choices.

---

email

From: principal@ffe.ac.uk
Sent: 15th March 2009
Subject: Website

We're putting more information on the college website, and I'd like you to write me a proposal about this. It's very important we feature two aspects of the college which are very different in order to show the variety we offer. Some ideas are below. Remember the aim is to attract new students to the college.

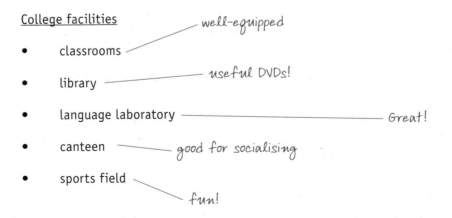

College facilities

•   classrooms   *well-equipped*

•   library   *useful DVDs!*

•   language laboratory   *Great!*

•   canteen   *good for socialising*

•   sports field   *fun!*

Now write your **proposal** for the principal, as outlined above. You should use your own words as far as possible.

PAPER 2: WRITING Part 2

Part 2

Write an answer to **one** of the questions **2–5** in this part. Write your answer in **220–260** words in an appropriate style.

---

2   A guidebook is being produced for visitors to your country. You have been asked to write an entry on the wild animals in your country. You should include specific information on **at least two** animals and give details about where visitors can see these animals in their natural surroundings. If appropriate, you should include safety advice.

Write your **contribution** for the guidebook.

3   You have seen this advertisement in an international magazine.

> **Attention All Readers!**
>
> We are looking for people to write articles about what is going on in your local area that would interest our international readership. Do you have:
>
> • a good knowledge of your local area
> • an awareness of issues which are important to your local community
> • some experience of writing?
>
> If so, we want to hear from you! Send us a letter of application, telling us why you are suitable and describing two or three important issues for your local community.

Write your **letter of application**.

4   You see this notice in an in-flight magazine.

> **Does your home match your lifestyle?**
>
> We are hoping to publish a series of articles on how satisfied people are with their homes.
>
> Write us an article:
>
> • describing your house or flat
> • outlining at least **two** changes you would like to make to it
> • explaining how these changes would improve your way of life.

Write your **article**.

5   Answer **one** of the following two questions based on **one** of the titles below.

(a) Kingsley Amis: *Lucky Jim*

You have been asked to write a review of *Lucky Jim* for your college magazine. In your review, explain which character you find most unpleasant and why, and say whether you would recommend *Lucky Jim* to other students.

Write your **review**.

(b) John Grisham: *The Pelican Brief*

As part of your course, your teacher has asked you for suggestions for a story to study in class. You decide to write about *The Pelican Brief*. In your report, briefly outline the plot, say whether the story is likely to interest students in your class and whether it will help them with their language learning.

Write your **report**.

PAPER 3: USE OF ENGLISH Part 1

Part 1

For questions **1–12**, read the text below and decide which answer (**A**, **B**, **C** or **D**) best fits each gap.

There is an example at the beginning **(0)**.

Mark your answers **on the separate answer sheet**.

Example:

0   **A**   arranged   **B**   sorted   **C**   managed   **D**   formed

0	A	B	C	D

Picture Imperfect

A couple who **(0)** .... a second wedding ceremony after photographs of the **(1)** .... ceremony were ruined are claiming compensation from the photographer who captured their special day on film. The bride, Sophie Wright, **(2)** .... into tears when she was given the initial **(3)** .... of her 'big day'. Most of the photographs were out of focus and in some her face was actually obscured.

She and her husband David are currently in dispute with the company that took the wedding photographs. Two days after the ceremony, the Wrights had to **(4)** .... the ceremony again with a different photographer. The final **(5)** .... was perfect, but they **(6)** .... that the distress ruined their honeymoon. They have already **(7)** .... the offer of a refund of three hundred pounds. The new Mrs Wright said, 'I was absolutely **(8)** .... I couldn't believe that it had happened to us after we had saved up for so long. It was supposed to be a perfect day, but the photographs were more like holiday snaps that had been taken by a real **(9)** .... '. Her husband added, 'The second **(10)** .... of pictures is excellent but the company gave the false **(11)** .... that everything went well the first time around. Now all those magic moments from the first ceremony have vanished. They are something you can never **(12)** .... '

1   **A** genuine   **B** original   **C** valid   **D** authentic

2   **A** broke   **B** burst   **C** flooded   **D** fell

3   **A** record   **B** model   **C** document   **D** description

4   **A** go through   **B** pass through   **C** go over   **D** pass over

5   **A** effect   **B** product   **C** output   **D** work

6   **A** persist   **B** resist   **C** insist   **D** assist

7   **A** dismissed   **B** denied   **C** removed   **D** rejected

8   **A** devastated   **B** demolished   **C** overpowered   **D** overwhelmed

9   **A** newcomer   **B** apprentice   **C** amateur   **D** trainee

10 **A** collection   **B** pile   **C** set   **D** bunch

11 **A** view   **B** interpretation   **C** impression   **D** opinion

12 **A** take back   **B** bring back   **C** take in   **D** bring in

Part 2

For questions **13–27**, read the text below and think of the word which best fits each gap. Use only one word in each gap. There is an example at the beginning **(0)**.

Write your answers **IN CAPITAL LETTERS on the separate answer sheet**.

Example: | **0** | B | E | E | N | | | | | |

Mars

People have always **(0)** .... fascinated by the planet Mars. It has been the subject of countless science-fiction films **(13)** .... many years and now, with recent advances **(14)** .... technology, has come a better understanding of this planet. It now seems that **(15)** .... the atmosphere on Mars is thinner than on Earth, **(16)** .... therefore unable to support life as we know **(17)** .... , the planet does share many characteristics with our own. Its surface is rocky **(18)** .... ours, days are almost **(19)** .... same length, and it has four distinct seasons. It also has winds, clouds and high mountains with volcanoes, one of **(20)** .... is three times as high as Everest. Huge cracks on the planet's surface suggest there **(21)** .... once channels, hundreds of miles wide and hundreds of feet deep, and water **(22)** .... thought to lie under the planet's crust.

However, there are some notable differences in **(23)** .... Mars is smaller than Earth, much further from the Sun, and as a consequence, has far lower temperatures. Also, years are twice as long, and it has two moons. Probably the most significant difference is that **(24)** .... spacesuits it is impossible to breathe, but scientists are now developing schemes **(25)** .... give the planet a breathable atmosphere.

Scientists believe that Mars was **(26)** .... always like it is today. It is thought that several thousand million years ago it was warm and lush, probably with a thick atmosphere. Today, Mars appears to be a lifeless desert with nothing **(27)** .... red sand, rock and rubble. However, its crust contains the six elements essential to life: hydrogen, oxygen, carbon, nitrogen, phosphorous and sulphur.

Part 3

For questions **28–37**, read the text below. Use the word given in capitals at the end of some of the lines to form a word that fits in the gap in the same line. There is an example at the beginning **(0)**. Write your answers **IN CAPITAL LETTERS on the separate answer sheet.**

Example: | 0 | E | C | O | N | O | M | I | C | | |

Are you a responsible tourist?

Responsible tourism is travel that brings **(0)** .... benefits for the host country **ECONOMY**

and minimises negative cultural and **(28)** .... impacts. There are many **ENVIRONMENT**

ways in which you can make a difference. Eat in locally owned restaurants

and buy local products, but not souvenirs made from **(29)** .... animals **DANGER**

or plants. Finding out about your destination beforehand will **(30)** .... **ABLE**

you to make informed decisions about where to go and what to see, while

learning even a few words of the language shows **(31)** .... to communicate **WILL**

with local people. Always ask **(32)** .... before taking photographs and **PERMIT**

don't cause **(33)** .... by wearing clothes that might be considered **OFFEND**

(34) .... **APPROPRIATE**

Rather than hiring a car for shorter journeys, it's **(35)** .... to walk or use **PREFER**

public transport. If you are trekking, keep to the paths to avoid causing

(36) .... to fields and hillsides and if you're camping, only use designated **ERODE**

sites. Finally, bear in mind that you don't have to fly to an exotic location; there

is probably somewhere equally interesting in your own country. Don't forget

that air travel is the most polluting form of transport and the fastest growing

contributor to the **(37)** .... of the earth's environment. **DESTROY**

PAPER 3: USE OF ENGLISH Part 4

Part 4

For questions **38–42**, think of **one** word only which can be used appropriately in all three sentences. Here is an example **(0)**.

Example:

0   The company which owns the car park has the .... to issue fines if you don't display your ticket.

The school was plunged into darkness when a storm brought some overhead .... cables down nearby.

Harry's songs are so full of emotional .... that they move me in ways that other people's songs simply do not.

Example: | 0 | P | O | W | E | R | | | |

Write **only** the missing words **IN CAPITAL LETTERS on the separate answer sheet**.

---

38   Zack makes a .... of never eating food that contains additives.

They were now so wet that there was little .... in opening their umbrellas.

The trouble with Roger's anecdotes is that it takes him ages to get to the ....

39   Most of the movie is being .... on location in the Alps.

As soon as the door opened, the dog .... out and ran off across the fields.

The first arrow he .... missed the target completely.

40   Carla told her son to .... so as not to be late for school.

The Manchester train always used to .... on time, but recently it has often been late.

My father has always wanted to .... his own business.

41 It is quite .... to get to know new people when you move to a new city.

Let the liquid toffee cool and only eat it when it is quite .... to the touch.

Pamela thought the teacher had been quite .... on her when marking her homework.

42 A number of diseases are .... by insects such as mosquitoes and flies.

In the seventeenth-century, cargoes of spices and perfumes were .... to Europe from India and Indonesia in sailing ships.

The instructor told the trainees that all the information had to be .... in their heads, because there wouldn't be time to write anything down.

PAPER 3: USE OF ENGLISH Part 5

Part 5

For questions **43–50**, complete the second sentence so that it has a similar meaning to the first sentence, using the word given. **Do not change the word given**. You must use between **three** and **six** words, including the word given. Here is an example **(0)**.

Example:

0 Chris has been late for work so often that there's a risk he will lose his job.

DANGER

Chris is .... his job because he's been late for work so often.

The gap can be filled with the words 'in danger of losing', so you write:

Example: | **0** | IN DANGER OF LOSING

Write the missing words **IN CAPITAL LETTERS on the separate answer sheet**.

---

43 Making a good documentary film requires a lot of work.

DEAL

A .... required to make a good documentary film.

44 'This problem must be solved immediately!' said the Managing Director.

FIND

'Please take immediate .... to this problem!' said the Managing Director.

45 There are worries regarding the poor quality of the water.

EXPRESSED

Concerns are .... regard to the poor quality of the water.

46 Students with an ID card won't have to pay to get in.

ADMITTED

Students with an ID card .... of charge.

47   Thank you very much for the information you sent me about voluntary jobs abroad.

GRATEFUL

I am really .... sending me the information about voluntary jobs abroad.

48   I don't think you'll find it difficult to learn to drive an automatic car.

MUCH

I don't think .... learning to drive an automatic car.

49   The lift hasn't been working for a week.

ORDER

The lift has .... for a week.

50   Paul wasn't surprised to hear that Fatima had got married.

CAME

Fatima's marriage .... to Paul.

PAPER 4: LISTENING Part 1

Part 1

You will hear three different extracts. For questions **1–6**, choose the answer (**A**, **B** or **C**) which fits best according to what you hear. There are two questions for each extract.

Extract One

You hear part of a radio programme in which a recent prize-winning book is being discussed.

1   The woman suggests that the book won the prize because

    A   its subject matter was unusual.

    B   it brought the subject to life.

    C   it was well researched.

2   The man mentions jellyfish in order to underline

    A   how committed scientists are to their subject.

    B   how an unlikely subject can be made interesting.

    C   how time-consuming some research can be.

Extract Two

You hear a man called Ian telling a friend about learning to play the piano.

3   What makes learning to play the piano enjoyable for Ian?

    A   the satisfaction of acquiring a new skill

    B   the opportunity to play with other musicians

    C   the fact that it is an escape from the stress of his work

4   How does Ian feel about his music teacher?

    A   He respects her theoretical knowledge.

    B   He is impressed by her musical ability.

    C   He is grateful for her patience.

Extract Three

You hear part of a radio discussion about the work of the nineteenth-century writer, Charles Dickens.

5   What does Alan appreciate about the way Dickens wrote?

    A   the precise way he planned his long novels

    B   the courage with which he tried out new ideas

    C   the uniform style that characterises his work

6   Because of his own experience, Alan can understand Dickens'

    A   wish to keep his options open.

    B   desire to win parental support.

    C   need to find financial security.

Part 2

You will hear the food historian Nina Travis talking about the tradition of smoking fish in the Scottish town of Arbroath. For questions **7–14**, complete the sentences.

SMOKED FISH

Traditionally, haddock was smoked on the [_____ **7**] coast of Scotland, especially in the town of Arbroath.

An old story says that smoked haddock was first discovered under some [_____ **8**] in a ruined house.

When fishermen arrived in Arbroath with fresh haddock, a man used a [_____ **9**] to inform possible buyers.

The fresh haddock were sold in the [_____ **10**] area of Arbroath.

People preferred to use a hard wood like [_____ **11**] when smoking the fish.

Haddock is now being smoked in a modern [_____ **12**] in Arbroath.

Nina suggests baking smoked haddock with mushrooms, [_____ **13**] and onions.

Nina says she uses the word [_____ **14**] to describe some modern foods.

Part 3

You will hear a radio interview in which a composer, Sam Tilbrook, is talking about his life and work. For questions **15–20**, choose the answer (**A**, **B**, **C** or **D**) which fits best according to what you hear.

---

15 What first made Sam start composing music?

    A   His mother suggested he should take it up.
    B   He studied composition as part of his college course.
    C   It was a natural progression after learning to read music.
    D   Playing the clarinet gave him the idea of writing music for it.

16 How does Sam describe his approach to composing?

    A   He only writes what his inner voice tells him.
    B   He bases his work on classical music forms.
    C   He waits for a sudden moment of inspiration.
    D   He builds up musical sounds by analysing them.

17 According to Sam, how was he influenced by the French composer Messiaen?

    A   He was encouraged by Messiaen's pioneering work.
    B   Messiaen's composing techniques fascinated him.
    C   Messiaen explained the importance of tradition to him.
    D   He borrowed one of Messiaen's musical ideas.

18 What effect did Sam's experience of theatre have on him?

    A   Having to learn a speaking part improved his memory.
    B   He understood what kind of music works best in a play.
    C   He was thrilled by stage performances at an early age.
    D   Performing in a team gave him a sense of responsibility.

19 Sam says that when he is having difficulty composing a piece of music, he feels

    A   determined to complete the work in a given timescale.
    B   happy to be involved in a creative process.
    C   confident that he will be able to finish it.
    D   reluctant to adopt an obvious solution.

20 According to Sam, painting a picture is different from composing music because

    A   artists are more reflective than musicians.
    B   music involves more technical details than art.
    C   first impressions are more important in music than art.
    D   painters find expressing their ideas harder than musicians.

Part 4

You will hear five short extracts in which people are talking about education.

TASK ONE

For questions **21–25**, choose from the list **A–H** each person's occupation.

TASK TWO

For questions **26–30**, choose from the list **A–H** what each person is doing when they speak.

While you listen you must complete both tasks.

A politician		**A** asking someone for advice	
B employer	Speaker 1 [ ] **21**	**B** complaining about something	Speaker 1 [ ] **26**
C primary-school teacher	Speaker 2 [ ] **22**	**C** ordering something	Speaker 2 [ ] **27**
D parent	Speaker 3 [ ] **23**	**D** offering to do something	Speaker 3 [ ] **28**
E sports coach	Speaker 4 [ ] **24**	**E** apologising to somebody	Speaker 4 [ ] **29**
F university professor	Speaker 5 [ ] **25**	**F** describing part of a job	Speaker 5 [ ] **30**
G museum guide		**G** explaining a procedure	
H student		**H** outlining a plan	

PAPER 5: SPEAKING Part 1

Part 1

3 minutes (5 minutes for groups of three)

Interlocutor

Good morning/afternoon/evening. My name is .... and this is my colleague ....

And your names are?

Can I have your mark sheets, please?

Thank you.

First of all, we'd like to know something about you.

Select one or two questions and ask candidates in turn, as appropriate.

- Where are you from?
- What do you do here/there?
- How long have you been studying English?
- What do you enjoy most about learning English?

Select one or more questions from either of the following categories, as appropriate.

Personal experience

- **In what ways do you hope to use your English in the future?**
- **Looking back in your life, what has been a memorable event for you?**
- **Can you tell me about a person who has been really important in your life?**

The media

- **Do you prefer watching films at home or in the cinema?** .... **(Why?)**
- **How important are newspapers for you?** .... **(Why do you say that?)**
- **Do you ever go to the theatre?** .... **(What kind of plays do you enjoy?)**

1 A visit 2 Approaches to learning	Part 2 4 minutes (6 minutes for groups of three)

Interlocutor	In this part of the test, I'm going to give each of you three pictures. I'd like you to talk about them on your own for about a minute, and also to answer a question briefly about your partner's pictures.
	(*Candidate A*), it's your turn first. Here are your pictures. **They show people making different kinds of visits.**
	I'd like you to compare two of the pictures, and say **why the people might be making these visits, and how important the visits might be for the people involved.**
	All right?
Candidate A	....
⏱ *1 minute*	
Interlocutor	Thank you.
	(*Candidate B*), **which visit do you think would be the most memorable?**
Candidate B	....
⏱ *approximately 30 seconds*	
Interlocutor	Thank you. (Can I have the booklet, please?)
	Now, (*Candidate B*), here are your pictures. They show **people learning in different situations.**
	I'd like you to compare two of the pictures, and say **how the atmosphere is different in each situation, and what the benefits of each method of learning might be.**
	All right?
Candidate B	....
⏱ *1 minute*	
Interlocutor	Thank you.
	(*Candidate A*), **which method of learning do you think is the most effective?**
Candidate A	....
⏱ *approximately 30 seconds*	
Interlocutor	Thank you. (Can I have the booklet, please?)

PAPER 5: SPEAKING Part 2

How different is the atmosphere in each situation?

What might the benefits of each method of learning be?

Why might the people be making these visits?

How important might the visits be for the people involved?

PAPER 5: SPEAKING Parts 3 and 4

3 Contributions to society	Parts 3 and 4
	8 minutes (12 minutes for groups of three)

Part 3

Interlocutor   Now, I'd like you to talk about something together for about three minutes.
(5 minutes for groups of three)

Here are some pictures showing people who are important to society for different reasons.

First, talk to each other about **why these people are important to society**. Then decide **which two people make the most valuable contributions to society as a whole**.

All right?

Candidates
🕐 *3 minutes*
(5 minutes for groups of three)

....

Interlocutor   Thank you. (Can I have the booklet, please?)

Part 4

Interlocutor   *Select any of the following questions as appropriate:*

- **Do you think that people like these will be as important in the future as they are today? ...... (Why? / Why not?)**

> *Select any of the following prompts as appropriate:*
> - **What do you think?**
> - **Do you agree?**
> - **How about you?**

- **What makes some people more successful in life than others?**

- **Do you believe that success often changes people? (Why do you say that?)**

- **Do you think it's true that too much emphasis is placed on making money nowadays? ...... (Why? / Why not?)**

- **Some people say that the most important thing in life is to enjoy ourselves. What's your opinion?**

Thank you. That is the end of the test.

Why are these people important to society?

Which two people make the most valuable contribution to society as a whole?

Answer key

Note: You can use contractions to answer the questions, e.g. 'I am working' ⟶ 'I'm working', 'she has done' ⟶ 'she's done', etc.

1 Our people

Listening Part 4

① 1 A 7 B 1 C 6 D 4 E 5 F 8 G 3 H 2   **2** *Students' own answers*   **3** *Students' own answers*

② *Suggested answers:*   **A** his/her underwater adventures, out in all weathers   **B** out in all weathers   **C** complete dedication to his/her craft   **D** perform a new trick, complete dedication to his/her craft   **E** a few of his/her recordings   **F** what it would be like tomorrow   **G** digging at some excavation or other, out in all weathers, the first person to set foot in a place   **H** the first person to set foot in a place, out in all weathers, his/her underwater adventures

④ 1 B   2 G   3 D   4 A   5 E   6 E   7 F   8 D   9 G   10 A

Recording script   CD1 Track 2

Speaker 1:   You know, it's funny because when I was a kid I was never really aware of just what an extraordinary woman my Aunt Patty is. I mean, she's always lived in the same town as us, but she was always away working so I didn't really see too much of her, to tell the truth. Not till much later, that is, when she invited me to come out on one of her trips – I guess I must have been fourteen or fifteen by then probably – and it was a real eye-opener to see her at work. I mean, she was doing what many

Q1 people think is a man's job. <u>She'd be out in all weathers, even in these really mountainous</u>

Q6 <u>seas</u>, but you know <u>she never used to panic – she just got on with the job whatever the danger. She seemed to know just what to do even when things got really rough</u>. She was just totally in her element and she impressed me no end.

Speaker 2:   For my dad nothing was too much trouble, especially when people showed a bit of interest in what he was up to. You know, when he was working – he's retired now, well more

Q2 or less anyway – <u>he'd be digging away at some excavation or other</u> and members of the public, visitors, would just come up to him and

Q7 start talking to him and <u>he'd drop whatever he was doing and, you know, even if he was tired because he'd been working all day, he'd probably give them a tour of the site and a free lecture on top of that</u>. Personally, I wouldn't have that sort of patience. I'm more like my mum in that way.

Speaker 3:   Yeah, yeah, my brother's a real perfectionist too. You know, he's been getting this new

Q3 show ready recently and <u>he's been going to incredible lengths to get this new trick right</u>. Yeah, right, yeah, like he's been practising and practising in front of this video camera he's got for weeks, it seems – it's been driving the rest

Q8 of us mad! Yeah. <u>You see, he plays it back afterwards, the camera I mean, to check you can't see how it's done from any angle</u>. He just wants to hoodwink absolutely everyone in the audience even though they're usually only just kids, so he goes on and on till he's got everything absolutely perfect.

Speaker 4:   Ivan was really one of my dad's mates, but as he was single and a really good friend of Dad's,

Q9 we counted him as one of the family. <u>And he was incredibly generous with us kids</u> – always came back with some unusual gift or other from his trips. And then he'd sit down with us and help us do our schoolwork and so on. We

Q4 loved him and we loved his <u>stories of his underwater adventures and the strange creatures he'd seen</u>. He made it sound as if he'd been doing something extremely dangerous and he'd been incredibly brave. All tremendously exaggerated, no doubt, but we lapped it all up.

Speaker 5: Margo was one of my mother's cousins, actually. Personally, I never got to know her well because she was always travelling here and there – she had so many engagements.

Q5 I have got a few of her recordings from her younger days, though. The sound quality is not too good now because we've listened to them so many times, but I think her playing really

Q10 does reflect her optimism and joy. You just wouldn't suspect that she was going blind at the time. What courage in the face of such an affliction, don't you think?

Grammar
Verb forms to talk about the past

① 2 b 3 a 4 e 5 h 6 g 7 d 8 f

② 2 *would* + infinitive, *used to* + infinitive 3 past continuous 4 past perfect simple 5 past perfect continuous 6 present perfect continuous 7 present perfect simple

③ 1 left 2 has been studying, has not gone/been 3 came, started, was making, continued 4 had, had been working / had worked, had not been wearing / was not wearing 5 grew, belonged / had belonged, have sold

④ 2 never used to bring 3 would always ask 4 used to be 5 built 6 used to know 7 have come 8 have gradually been changing 9 used to go 10 were 11 would look

⑤ 2 were 3 was 4 hadn't organised 5 didn't take 6 have been invited 7 have only been living, has lived 8 haven't noticed

Reading Part 1

② Text 1: **b** Text 2: **a** Text 3: **c**

③ *Suggested answers*: **1** That the bookseller could tell her as much about the country's history as she could learn from reading a book. **2** People in the family were more relaxed and talked and joked more openly than the people the author had eaten with in the mountains. **3** Mel used the remote control, thereby breaking a rule in their relationship. **4** He likes watching television, he likes clear rules in his relationships, he's a little frightened by his girlfriend. **5** They would have preferred her to have become a lawyer although they said she should do what she liked; they never

dreamt that she would become a fisherman.
6 By working on the boat for longer than any of the other crew members.

④ 1 D 2 A 3 D 4 C 5 C 6 C

Vocabulary
Collocations with *give*, *do* and *make*

① B

② 2 ~~gives~~ does 3 ~~did not show~~ did not give 4 ~~give~~ make 5 *correct* 6 ~~made~~ given 7 ~~give~~ make 8 *correct* 9 ~~made~~ given 10 ~~give~~ make

③ 2 give 3 make 4 give 5 give 6 do 7 make 8 make 9 give

Use of English Part 4

① d

② 1 a 2 c 3 b

③ 1 adjective 2 noun 3 noun 4 noun

④ 1 warm 2 job 3 force 4 life

⑤ 1 position 2 running 3 take 4 strict 5 switched

Speaking Part 1

① **a** 1, 3, 4 **b** 2, 5, 6, 7, 8

② Nagwa: 2 Carlos: 6

Recording script CD1 Track 3

1

Nagwa: Yes, I was able to give a friend a room once when she had to move out of her house quite quickly – she'd been having problems with one of her flatmates, so she came to stay with us

Q2 for a while, just for a few months, and I think that helped her quite a lot in her situation.

2

Carlos: **Q6** One of the best is really from the summer vacation which we always used to spend together as a family at the seaside and going out fishing with my dad in a small boat. Yes, that's a very good one, because I loved being close to my dad and doing things with him, you know, things I wouldn't have done with my mum.

---

3 1 F   2 T   3 T   4 T

Writing   Part 1 A letter

1 1 your friend Elena   2 informal   3 *Students should underline*: letter saying whether you think she should study at the college … and giving your reasons, Should come because …, worried about feeling lonely, friend I made the first day, want to have time off, our free-time activities, are the teachers good? Our teacher is great because …
4 *Suggested answers*: she'll learn a lot of English, expensive but good value for money, interesting people, chance to visit the region, good social life, excellent teacher(s), etc.

2 1 Yes   2 informal   3 you'll learn so much English, you'll make plenty of friends, plenty of free time, visited quite a few places, playing tennis, having a really good time, teacher is excellent, she's experienced and interesting, Do come if you can – you won't regret it!

3 2 actually met   3 were sitting   4 had been
5 we've been doing   6 I've already visited
7 joined   8 we've played   9 I've been having
10 She's taught   11 was   12 actually used to teach

2   Mastering languages

Starting off

1 2 switch   3 fashionable loanwords
4 mother tongue   5 a bit rusty   6 pick up
7 an excellent command   8 highly articulate
9 accurately   10 fluency   11 persuasion

Woman 4:	We live in a highly competitive world. Countries compete with each other, employers compete with each other and people compete. Consequently, we should be teaching young people to use language for <u>persuasion</u> rather than self-expression. It's all very well being able to say what you think and feel, but you've got to be able to sell yourself, sell your product, achieve your aims.
Q11	

Reading Part 2

2 talk to a native speaker; start with parts of the body, then common objects; after learning the nouns you can start to make sentences and get attuned to the sounds

3 *Para 2*: How Ken learnt languages   *Para 3*: The biological basis of language   *Para 4*: Ken's origins
Para 5: A language Ken helped save
Para 6: Ken's involvement in language theory
Para 7: Reasons for protecting languages under threat

4 1 B   2 G   3 F   4 A   5 E   6 D

Vocabulary

Collocations with *make*, *get* and *do*

1 2 make   3 get   4 made   5 done

2

make	get	do
a comment, a decision, a mistake, an effort, a point, a proposal, a suggestion, an apology, complaints, changes, friends, the right choice, use of something, an improvement	a job, a qualification, business, further information, money back	a job, a course, activities, business, exercise, harm, one's best, some shopping, sport, household chores, the cooking

3 2 ~~receive~~ get   3 ~~give~~ make   4 ~~turn~~ make
5 ~~make~~ do   6 ~~achieve~~ do   7 ~~make~~ do
8 ~~practising~~ doing

Listening Part 1

2 1 C   2 B   3 C   4 A   5 C   6 A

Recording script   CD1 Track 6

Extract One

Woman:	It's actually a remarkable book, Colin, and particularly because, unlike other travel writers, you've managed to get behind the scenes, talk to ordinary Mongolians in their own language and on their own terms. How in fact did you go about learning Khalkha? Did you go to classes?
Colin: *Q1*	Not exactly. I'd done that for Russian and Chinese, both of which I now speak fluently, but for Khalkha, well, <u>I thought I should pick it up while I was there</u>, you know, learn it on my own and in my own way, so as soon as I arrived I settled into a flat and immersed myself in the neighbourhood and just started talking to people and getting to know them.
Woman:	And now you speak it fluently?
Colin:	Well, I reckon I can more or less hold my own in a conversation.
Woman:	And what do you think is the key to good language learning? Do you have to be naturally gifted?
Colin: *Q2*	Well, obviously for an adult it helps to have some sort of gift, and that's not something we've all got. Being fairly outgoing and uninhibited helps too. I mean, you won't get very far if you're scared of making a fool of yourself, but <u>basically it's application. It's really getting down to it, whatever the circumstances, and getting stuck into it</u> because, you know, any language you learn is going to be more complicated than maths, and you don't learn maths just by being uninhibited!
Woman:	Eventually, while you were there you had the amazing experience of being invited to live with a Mongolian family, didn't you? Tell us a little about that …

Extract Two

Rajiv:	I mean I remember the trauma as a small child of …
Susan:	Come off it, don't exaggerate! Trauma!

Rajiv: I'm not! Let me finish! The trauma of learning how to spell – you know, they used to give us dictations in class to make sure we knew things like putting a double 'p' in 'approve' and spelling 'right' with 'GHT'. It's frankly absurd.

Susan: But it's part of the character and beauty of the language – not everything has to be reduced to something functional.

Rajiv: Maybe not, but as a language teacher it would make my life a lot easier …

Susan: I wonder if that's true – after all, it's not you but your students that get into trouble with bad spelling. Anyway, nowadays with spellcheckers that's hardly their biggest handicap.

Rajiv: But they just don't know how to say new words correctly!

Susan: Then perhaps it's your teaching methods that need reforming!

Rajiv: *Q3* You've really got it in for me today, haven't you? Anyway, <u>I got to thinking about all this some time ago when I came across something in a magazine quite by chance</u>. One thing it mentioned was that spelling reform would cut the space it takes to write something by about fifteen percent. Imagine: newspapers, libraries and bookshops with fifteen percent more room!

Susan: *Q4* And think about having to reprint every book and replace every road sign. I think you're being unrealistic, quite honestly. <u>Mind you, I've read a lot about dyslexia amongst English kids and apparently our complicated spelling system is a major factor there …</u>

Rajiv: If you can call it a system.

Susan: So you might have something there.

Extract Three

Simon: Doing a job interview in English is becoming a common experience for many people from overseas, Peggy, but what can they do to avoid coming a cropper?

Peggy: *Q5* Well, Simon, the problem is that <u>the candidate often lacks the sort of cultural background that would stand them in good stead in these situations, with the result that while their English is up to scratch, their responses take the interviewer by surprise</u>. You know, a question like 'What do you most enjoy about your present job?', where the interviewer is expecting something about the challenge or working with friendly colleagues or such like, and the interviewee is completely thrown because in some cultures people don't necessarily equate work with pleasure at all.

Simon: It's more for making ends meet.

Peggy: Exactly. And at the same time, because they're nervous, they may be less expressive than normal anyway and this may also show up in their gestures and so on as well. In fact, for many jobs, especially jobs where language skills are not absolutely essential, interviewing isn't necessarily the best way of selecting the right employee anyway. And this goes for native speakers just as much as for people from overseas. *Q6* <u>A better approach might be to set up a simulation of the job in question so as to see whether the candidate has the skills and attitude they're looking for</u>. Anyway, interviewers need to realise that they can't always expect people who've recently arrived from abroad to deal with interviews in a way that they, the interviewers, would find natural.

Simon: So the fault is often more with the interviewer, not the interviewee?

Peggy: Yes.

Use of English Part 3

❶ *Suggested answers:* *care*: carer, caring, uncaring, careful, carefully, careless, carelessly, carefree; *critic*: criticise, criticism, critical, critically, uncritical, uncritically; *child*: children, childhood, childlike, childish, childishly, childishness, childless; *break*: broken, unbroken, breakable, unbreakable, unbreakably, outbreak, breakdown; *occasion*: occasional, occasionally; *force*: forceful, forcefully, forcible, forcibly, enforce, reinforce; *deep*: deepen, depth, deeply, deepening; *fragile*: fragility; *friend*: friendly, friendliness, unfriendly, unfriendliness, friendship, befriend, friendless

❷ **1** -ise, -en **2** -ion, -ment, -hood, -ity, -ship **3** -less, -able, -ly, -ful **4** -ally, -ly

3 *Suggested answers*: *verbs*: -ify (intense – intensify); *nouns*: -age (bag – baggage), -al (arrive – arrival), -ant (participate – participant), -ance/-ence (interfere – interference), -dom (free – freedom), -ee (employ – employee), -er/-or (instruct – instructor), -ism (liberal – liberalism), -ist (motor – motorist); *adjectives*: -al (logic – logical), -ial (face – facial), -ed (embarrass – embarrassed), -en (wood – wooden), -ese (Japan – Japanese), -ic (base – basic), -ing (embarrass – embarrassing), -ish (child – childish), -ive (act – active), -ian (Mars – Martian), -like (business – businesslike), -ly (friend – friendly), -ous (mountain – mountainous), -y (snow – snowy); *adverbs*: -wards (back – backwards), -wise (clock – anticlockwise)

4 *Incorrectly spelled words*: happening, development, reference, really, beautifully, truthful, dissatisfied, irregularity, undeniable, usable, refusing, basically, argument

5 2 beginning   3 successful   4 government
5 environment   6 really

7 1 They investigate thousands of possible names, they run competitions amongst their employees, they check possible names for legal and linguistic problems.   2 The names are not legally available in all countries, the name is not pronounceable, the name may be irrelevant or taboo.

8 1 savings   2 reality   3 actually   4 development
5 acceptable   6 unsuccessfully   7 competition
8 submitted   9 unusable   10 irrelevant

Grammar
Expressing reason, purpose and result

1 2 g   3 f   4 h   5 b   6 a   7 e   8 d

2 1 **a** 1, 2, 4, 6   **b** 5, 7, 8   **c** 3
2 **a** so as   **b** with the intention of, due to
c so, with the result that, in case, otherwise

3 2 For   3 because of   4 so that   5 in order not to

Speaking Part 2

2 1 Yes   2 chef demonstrating to a group how to prepare a dish, coach telling team how to win match, tactics, both tough explanations, but the coach has the toughest explanation because it's a large group of people, match might be crucial, has to use words, not screen.

3 actually, obviously, perhaps, probably, really

Recording script CD1 Track 7

Bethia: OK, there's one picture of a man, he's a chef and he's talking to a group of people, could be giving them a demonstration of how to cook a meal? And there's a video screen, erm, and a mirror above showing the meal being cooked so people can see everything clearly. Yeah, <u>perhaps</u> he's mixing the food and putting it into pans and describing how to prepare this dish. And another picture is of a coach talking to his team, <u>perhaps</u> telling them how to win the match, giving them some tactics and things like that. So both of them are <u>probably</u> quite <u>tough</u> explanations to give because <u>obviously</u> they're talking to large groups of people. Well, the coach is talking to a large group of people, not the cookery teacher, and he has to explain everything with words and the match might be a crucial one while the cookery teacher can <u>actually</u> show people in the mirror, so <u>really</u> I'd say the coach has got the <u>hardest</u> job, yeah.

---

4 tough, hard(-est)

Writing Part 2 A report

1 1 people in an international media company
2 formal   3 how popular, why, the effect on local culture, recommended changes   4 *Suggested answer*: probably the same order as in the question

2 2 accounted for   3 means   4 the result   5 meant
6 As a consequence   7 resulted   8 due to   9 so as
10 the effect

3 1 It has a title and sections with section headings.
2 Yes   3 Yes

4 1 the languages people learn, who learns them and where, recommendations for improving language-learning   2 people at an educational publishing company   3 formal   4 *Students' own answers*

Vocabulary and grammar review Unit 1

Vocabulary

① **2** making **3** doing **4** made, giving **5** give **6** gave **7** give **8** making

② **1** stand **2** dropped **3** natural **4** free **5** wearing

Grammar

③ **2** We'd been standing, were feeling **3** I've driven **4** she's been studying **5** had been eating **6** used to work **7** had been coming, were repairing **8** went

Vocabulary and grammar review Unit 2

Vocabulary

①

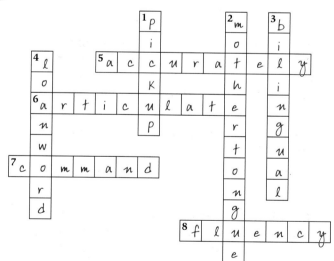

② **2** making **3** doing **4** made **5** make **6** do

③ **1** opening **2** successful **3** arguments, development **4** beginning **5** studying, knowledgeable **6** disappointed, cancellation

Grammar

④ **2** so as **3** in case **4** otherwise **5** due to **6** so that

3 All in the mind

Listening Part 2

③ face-blindness

> ### Recording script CD1 Track 8
>
> **Presenter:** This week's *All in the Mind* examines an unusual condition you may never have heard of before: prosopagnosia. Here's Professor Alexander Scharma to explain.
>
> **Professor Scharma:** Hello. Well, let's start with an image some of you may be familiar with: a painting called *The Son of Man*, by the surrealist artist René Magritte. In the picture, an apple floats in front of a man's face, covering the features that would normally allow him to be recognised. The painting perfectly illustrates the concept of prosopagnosia, or face-blindness.

④ **1** F He compares face-blindness to tone-deafness: that is, the inability to distinguish between different musical notes **2** T **3** F They could not distinguish between the faces, but they could distinguish between the pictures of other things.

⑥ **2** leaves **3** severely affected **4** (human) evolution **5** private brain mechanism **6** face-blind volunteers **7** other objects **8** face recognition skills

> ### Recording script CD1 Track 9
>
> **Presenter:** This week's *All in the Mind* examines an unusual condition you may never have heard of before: prosopagnosia. Here's Professor Alexander Scharma to explain.
>
> **Professor Scharma:** Hello. Well, let's start with an image some of you may be familiar with: a painting called *The Son of Man*, by the surrealist artist René Magritte. In the picture, an apple floats in front of a man's face, covering the features that would normally allow
> *Q6.1* him to be recognised. The painting perfectly underline>illustrates the concept of prosopagnosia, or face-blindness. To people with this condition,
> *Q6.2* as soon as someone leaves their sight the memory of that person's face is blank – or,

	at best, a set of jumbled features.
Q4.1	<u>Face-blindness is a little like tone-deafness</u>: the tone can be heard, or the face seen, but distinguishing between different tones or faces is nearly impossible. The effects of prosopagnosia can be so bad that people
Q6.3	<u>severely affected</u> cannot recognise their own
Q4.2	parents or children. <u>If we understood how the normal brain recalls faces</u>, we would be well on the way to understanding this strange disorder.
Q6.4	It might also help us to understand <u>human evolution</u>, since the ability to recognise faces is more or less equal to the ability to recognise individuals. This ability helps to hold societies together and has enabled humanity to develop a complex culture which is unique in the animal kingdom. The question scientists need to answer is whether this basic ability has its
Q6.5	own <u>private brain mechanism</u>, or whether it is simply one aspect of a general ability to recognise individual members of a particular class of objects. Researchers have used
Q6.6	<u>face-blind volunteers</u> to explore this question. The subjects were shown images of cars, tools, guns, houses and landscapes, and also black-and-white pictures of faces with no hair on their heads. Ten of these images were repeated. The subjects were asked to indicate, as quickly as possible, whether each image they saw was new or repeated. The results
Q4.3	were surprising. <u>None of the face-blind subjects could recognise the faces in the series well, but they could distinguish between the other repeated pictures</u> as easily as people without prosopagnosia could. That confirms the idea that faces are handled differently
Q6.7	by the brain from <u>other objects</u>. It has been shown in experiments that people with face-blindness can be taught to improve their <u>face</u>
Q6.8	<u>recognition skills</u>, but it is still not known what prosopagnosia sufferers are missing when they recall a blur instead of a face. This is not to say that prosopagnosia has no advantages. As one person with the condition writes on her website, 'You can wake up in the morning and pretend you don't know your own kids. Then you don't have to give them any pocket money.'

Grammar
No, none, not

1 1 no 2 None 3 not 4 not, no

2 2 ~~no~~ not 3 ~~no~~ any 4 *correct* 5 ~~nothing~~ anything 6 ~~not~~ no 7 ~~All the students did not hand~~ None of the students handed / No student handed / Not all the students handed (i.e. some handed in ...) 8 ~~none~~ no

Grammar
The passive

1 b were asked, (was) repeated c are handled d has been shown, can be taught

2 1 an academic essay, the description of a scientific process, a job application, a report for a committee 2 a and b

3 1 c (the brain) 2 *Suggested answers:* **a–b** scientists, psychologists, researchers **d** scientists, psychologists, researchers, special trainers 3 Because the agent is unknown, obvious, or relatively unimportant in the particular context.

4 *Suggested answers:* 1 It is commonly believed that *intelligence can be measured.* 2 It has been reported in the last few days that *the price of oil is going up again.* 3 It has been proved beyond doubt that *smoking can damage your health.*

5 2 Galton was known 3 Darwin's *The Origin of Species* was published 4 most of Galton's time was spent 5 It was thought 6 Galton was not satisfied by this idea 7 mental characteristics were determined by physical factors

Reading Part 3

3 1 C 2 A 3 B 4 C 5 D 6 C 7 C

Vocabulary
Formal or informal?

1 *asap*: informal (an informal abbreviation for *as soon as possible*); *They've / they're*: informal (contracted verb forms); *What on earth are you doing?*: informal (colloquial language); *We will / the fog has*: formal (full, uncontracted verb forms); *contemplated residing / neighbourhood*: formal (formal choice of vocabulary – longer words); *put up with*: informal (phrasal verb – more colloquial);

with whom: formal (preposition placed before relative pronoun in relative clause); *is believed*: formal (passive construction); *Grub's up*: informal (slang); *(the girl I go to school) with*: informal (omission of relative pronoun and preposition at the end of sentence)

2 1 *Contractions*: <u>I'm</u> connected, <u>I'll</u> browse, etc. *Colloquial language*: <u>I don't know where I'd be</u> without it. *Full verb forms*: <u>we are</u> running, how <u>they will</u> be affected. *Formal vocabulary*: <u>evolution</u>, <u>transforming</u> our brains, <u>discriminate</u>, what <u>determines</u> the things that interest them?, skills, <u>values</u> and <u>limits are instilled</u>. *Phrasal verb*: We're <u>bringing up</u> a whole generation
2 A combination   3 The chatty, personal parts of the article, those designed to interest and engage readers, tend to use spoken language which is more informal. The parts which provide authoritative factual information are written in more formal language.

Use of English Part 2

1 1 *Students' own answers*   2 The article concludes that a combination of nature and nurture is responsible for our personalities. (See the last two sentences.)

3 1 for   2 your   3 by   4 less   5 and   6 has   7 do   8 of   9 play   10 as   11 is   12 Other   13 because   14 of   15 with

Speaking Part 3

2 1 Stress can cause insomnia / not sleeping, loss of appetite, eating more than you want to, bad-temperedness, being snappy, headaches, tiredness.
2 *Students' own answers*

Recording script   CD1 Track 10

Woman 1: Well, stress can affect people in many ways: <u>insomnia</u> …

Woman 2: Sally would know about that one.

Woman 1: <u>Not sleeping, losing your appetite or eating more than you want to, bad-temperedness, being snappy</u>.

Woman 2: How about the pictures?

Woman 1: OK – the first one looks like an exam situation …

Woman 2: Very, very stressful.

Woman 1: Yes.

Woman 2: Time pressure, trying to get everything down that you know, worrying about questions and that sort of thing.

Woman 1: And the second one, someone in hospital – could be a relative that's ill and you're particularly worried about them.

Woman 2: Or it's yourself and you're particularly worried about yourself with the doctor in there and you're waiting for the diagnosis, having to have blood tests – that would be horrible.

Woman 1: And the third one is an airport.

Woman 2: That is, like, super-stressful in my family – I'm not sure that would be quite so stressful for anyone else.

Woman 1: I've never found airports stressful.

Woman 2: I once spent, like, three days in an airport with my family.

Woman 1: Flights can get delayed a lot, can't they?

Woman 2: Yeah, if you're trying to get home for something important, it can be quite stressful as well and not speaking the language if you're somewhere abroad.

Woman 1: Mmm – the fourth picture: I'm really not entirely sure what's happening.

Woman 2: No, I'm not. It looks like they can't communicate very well with each other.

Woman 1: Yes, he's trying to think of what to say.

Woman 2: The fifth one looks like work stress.

Woman 1: It does – <u>headaches</u>, probably from looking at a computer screen or reading.

Woman 2: Headaches from having to listen to your boss talk too much.

Woman 1: <u>Tiredness</u> from having missed lunch because you're so dedicated to your work.

Woman 2: Long hours, too many deadlines …

Woman 1: Incompetent staff around you …

Woman 2: Hmm – relying on other people, not knowing what to do.

Woman 1: Not being told what to do properly …

Woman 2: Yeah – being given the wrong information.

Woman 1: And the last one looks like a traffic jam …

Woman 2: A major traffic jam.

Woman 1: Of stationary cars.

Woman 2: If it's hot, it's usually more stressful …

Woman 1: Or if you're trying to get somewhere important.

Woman 2:	Hmm.
Woman 1:	To the airport perhaps – that's one stressful situation after another.
Woman 2:	Anyway – which is the most stressful situation, do you reckon?
Woman 1:	Erm, traffic jams because they're so commonplace, whereas perhaps personal illness or something doesn't happen so often.
Woman 2:	Yes, I think I'd agree. They just seem to happen so often these days, and it's nearly always when you're in a hurry to get somewhere.

③ 1 c 2 b 3 d 4 a

Writing Part 1 An article

① 1 an eye-catching title, a first paragraph that arouses your interest, interesting content, the writer's opinions or ideas (You would expect the other features in the following kinds of writing: *informative sub-headings*: a report; *a formal language style*: a report / a proposal / an essay / a formal letter, etc.; *factually accurate detailed information*: a report; *content aimed at a specialist readership*: a report.)
2 *Students' own answers* 3 *Students' own answers*

② 1 people preparing for exams 2 to advise on preparing for exams and dealing with stress

③ 1 *Suggested answer*: Don't let nerves ruin your chances of exam success or Revision without stress
2 *Students' own answers*

④ 1 parts that need to interest and engage the reader
2 parts that include important factual information

4   Office space

Starting off

① a 1 b 5 c 3 d 2 e 4
② *Students' own answers*

Reading Part 4

② *Suggested answers*: **a** 2, 8, 10, 14, 15 **b** 1, 5, 7, 13
c 4, 6, 9 **d** 3, 11, 12

③ 1 D 2 F 3 D 4 B 5 D 6 E 7 F 8 A 9 B
10 C 11 E 12 E 13 F 14 C 15 A

Vocabulary
Adjective/noun collocations (1)

① 1 long, wide 2 deep
② 2 ~~extreme~~ 3 ~~big~~ 4 ~~high~~ 5 ~~big~~ 6 ~~high~~ 7 ~~great~~
8 ~~strong~~ 9 ~~high~~ 10 ~~strong~~

Listening Part 2

① a 2 b 5 c 1 d 4 e 3 f 6
② *Suggested answers*: attract and retain: a, b, c, d   unattractive: e, f
③ *Suggested answers*: 2 a type of industry or an area of the world 3 another type of economy
4 a type of worker 5 A plural noun is needed, but it's hard to predict further. 6 a type of subject
7 a type of skill 8 a type of action or activity
④ 1 with talent 2 technology and financial
3 emerging (economies) 4 software engineers
5 university populations 6 wrong subjects
7 management 8 raising salaries

Recording script   CD1 Track 11

Expert:	As I've been saying, there are a lot of things that have been changing in the world of work over the last few years. Businesses nowadays are having to work harder to recruit people
Q1	with talent. You see, what people have realised (and this in fact has become a sort of management tenet) is that what really gives a company an edge is its staff. In other words, to get ahead of your competitors you've got to have better staff. This seems to be right across the board and in almost all fields, but the fiercest rivalry has been amongst firms
Q2	in the technology and financial sectors. And better staff means better managers, better computer programmers, better receptionists and better drivers. Everyone. Interestingly, you know, this phenomenon started off in the West, but that's been changing and now it's
Q3	characteristic of emerging economies as well, where shortages of skilled personnel are becoming more acute. Just take the south Indian town of Bangalore, which for years has been a place where a lot of computer-based work has been outsourced for companies around the world. In a sense it's become a victim of its own success and it's thought that

Q4 soon there may well be vacancies for <u>software engineers</u>. By some estimates as many as 200,000. Amazing, isn't it, but why is it happening? Well, in Bangalore the answer is its booming IT industry that attracts customers from all over the world. In Europe, on the other hand, the birth rate has been falling and so

Q5 <u>university populations</u> have shrunk. There are fewer skilled people to go round – more and more of the skilled workforce is made up of people in their 40s, 50s and 60s. In fact, many of us could easily find ourselves working on well into our 70s.

Another cause of the situation is bad planning. What I mean by that is that an excessive number of students are actually doing what

Q6 I'd call the <u>wrong subjects</u> at university – for example history, philosophy and literature, things which interest them, not vocational courses which lead to the sorts of jobs which are in demand nowadays. Also, workforces are becoming more diverse. That's one of the by-products of globalisation. Increasingly, organisations employ people in different countries to work together on the same project, and so multinational companies have difficulty finding people with the necessary

Q7 <u>management</u> skills to coordinate such diverse teams and workforces. How to deal with the problem? Well, it's not easy to attract good people when there's such a choice of people

Q8 and places to work. <u>Raising salaries</u> could be an option for some employers, but the trouble with that is that the company's costs rise and they risk pricing themselves out of the market. However, to deal with this situation many organisations are …

Grammar
Expressing possibility, probability and certainty

① 1 a   2 a   3 b

③ 2 ~~you bound to~~ you are bound to   3 ~~most likely~~ more likely   4 ~~posible~~ possible   5 ~~as one of the possibly best schools~~ as possibly one of the best schools   6 ~~Probably you will want to go~~ You will probably want to go   7 ~~the worst trip I probably have~~ probably the worst trip I have / the worst trip I have probably   8 ~~That may be the possible reason~~ That may possibly be the reason

Use of English Part 1

② *Ideas reflected in the text*: 1, 3, 4

③ 1 A   2 D   3 C   4 B   5 D   6 A   7 B   8 C   9 B   10 D   11 B   12 D

Speaking Part 4

① *Questions asked*: 2, 4, 6 (in Exercise 5)

② 2 T   3 F   4 T   5 F

③ 2 quite, just sort of   3 actually   4 horrifically, obviously, generally   5 completely, fairly

Recording script   CD1 Track 12

1

Frances: Advantages? Advantages are that you don't have to commute, and that you don't <u>necessarily</u> have to deal with in-line work colleagues and issues such as the tea run and things like that. The disadvantages are that it might be <u>quite</u> difficult to separate work and home life, because you can <u>just sort of</u> see your office as you walk past and think, oh, I'll just check my emails again.

Sally: You might need more self-motivation …

Frances: Yes.

Sally: … to <u>actually</u> do things and not just go to the kitchen every five minutes and get something.

Frances: And watch soaps like *Neighbours*.

Sally: If you've got a family it can be very useful for child care as well. People in my office have children and so they kind of balance it that way.

2

Sally: I think some things, yes, because some very basic manual work is going to be <u>horrifically</u> boring for whoever has to do it, so having it done electronically would be a lot better for them – but then <u>obviously</u> you're losing lots of your workforce and creating more unemployment, but <u>generally</u> it would be great.

Frances: A robot would be better than my boss. At least it would be consistent.

3

Frances: I'd look for <u>completely</u> the opposite of my boss now. I'd look for somebody who's a good communicator, that tells you what's going on, that doesn't yell at you, that doesn't smell, that has, sets, like, boundaries, that helps you prioritise your workload and doesn't give you half their workload without giving you any support. That's all <u>fairly</u> negative.

4 **2** *quite*: fairly, i.e. it reduces the force of *difficult*; *just sort of*: you see it by chance, by accident **3** *actually*: adds emphasis – you do things in fact and not just partly **4** *horrifically*: adds a lot of emphasis; *obviously*: I'm saying something you probably know and will agree with; *generally*: in most cases **5** *completely*: adds emphasis; *fairly*: quite, i.e. it reduces the force of *negative*

Writing Part 1 A report

1 **1** Formal – it's at work, for your manager. **2** Generally not, as you will want to express the ideas in a more formal style. The examiners will give extra marks where you use your own vocabulary rather than just repeating the vocabulary in the question. **3** *Students' own answers* **4** *Changes*: more space for relaxation and exchange of ideas, less extreme heating and air conditioning, checking the lighting *Possible reasons*: improvements to staff morale and comfort, increases in productivity, protecting the environment **5** *Students' own answers*

3 **2** make recommendations **3** mentioned **4** contribute towards **5** consult **6** ensure **7** satisfactory **8** improved **9** create **10** exchanges **11** beneficial **12** implementing

4 **1** The reader will not be persuaded if you address them in an inappropriate style, i.e. too formal or too informal for the subject or for your relationship with them. **2** *Students should underline*: contribute towards protecting the environment, ensure that every employee works with comfortable, healthy lighting, might well be beneficial to the company, I would recommend … help to retain staff and improve their productivity

5 **1** the human resources manager **2** formal **3 & 4** *Students' own answers*

Vocabulary and grammar review   Unit 3

Vocabulary

1 **2** f **3** a **4** g **5** b **6** e **7** c **8** d

2 **2** expressing (my) ideas, win an argument **3** exert control **4** running an experiment

Grammar

3 **2** ~~no~~ not / ~~no my sister~~ my sister doesn't **3** ~~none~~ any / ~~didn't get none~~ got none **4** *correct* **5** ~~no~~ none **6** *correct* (*None of Patrick's friends* is also possible.) **7** ~~no~~ not **8** ~~none~~ no

4 *Suggested answers*: **1** (Amnesia can) be caused by specific medical conditions. **2** It is very well known that our memory is formed from/by our real experiences. But could a false memory be put into our heads? Could we be persuaded (to believe) that we had experienced something that never actually took place? **3** Our semantic memory is used to store our knowledge of the world … normally it can be accessed quickly and easily. The meanings of words and the names of people and places are included in our semantic memory.
4 It can be thought of as the ability to remember and use a limited amount of information for a short amount of time … If you are distracted, the information can be lost and the task has to be started again.
5 Forgetting is now being studied (by researchers) and is thought of, not as a failure of memory, but as a more active process. It is even believed that it may be driven by a specific biological mechanism.

5 *Students' own answers*

Vocabulary and grammar review   Unit 4

Vocabulary

1 **2** huge/powerful **3** constant/huge **4** excellent **5** fierce **6** huge/vast **7** extensive/vast **8** specialist

2 **1** A **2** C **3** A **4** A **5** B **6** B **7** D **8** C

Grammar and vocabulary

3 **2** might not **3** couldn't have **4** possible **5** highly **6** can't **7** bound to **8** slight **9** conceivably

5   Dramatic events

Listening Part 1

2 *Suggested answers*: **1** I was scared to death, a strange whirring noise, it all happened so quickly, it didn't stop for nearly six hours, the engine was flooded **2** I was scared to death, I felt as if I wasn't alone, I've always been very cynical about the supernatural **3** a strange whirring noise, it all happened so quickly, there was an explosion and all the lights went out

3 *Suggested answers*: **1** To the gym; He's been involved in an accident / been injured; His own / the gym company's. **2** He had some kind of accident while driving, perhaps he hit some trees; The man had been driving dangerously / a crime had been committed / someone was injured. **3** Because of damage due to a flood/fire/gale/explosion, etc; Because her home is badly damaged.

4 **1** B **2** C **3** C **4** A **5** B **6** A

Recording script   CD1 Track 13

Extract One

Jasmine:	Are you all right now?
Harry: *Q1*	Hmm, so so – some days are better than others. <u>I'm still having occasional flashbacks</u>.
Jasmine:	What happened?
Harry:	Well, I was doing my normal Thursday workout on the treadmill. I started with a gentle jog for ten minutes or so, then I decided to run fast for ten minutes. So I pressed the increase button.
Jasmine:	Had you been on that machine before?
Harry:	Not that one, but one very like it, so I was quite familiar with the controls, I mean, I knew how it worked.
Jasmine:	So, then what happened?
Harry:	Well, nothing happened for a few seconds, then the belt suddenly speeded up. I tried to slow it down, but nothing happened. When I tried pressing the automatic slow-down button, it was like I was putting my foot on a car accelerator.

Jasmine:	That must have been terrifying. What did you do?
Harry:	I looked round for help, thought maybe someone could switch the electricity off. It would have been a very sudden jolt, but better than not stopping at all. But there was no one else in the room. In the end, all I could do was jump off and keep my fingers crossed.
Jasmine:	And that's how you broke your leg? Are you going to do anything about it?
Harry: *Q2*	I'm not sure yet. I'm considering taking the company that runs the gym to court – that's what my solicitor suggests, but <u>I'm in two minds about it</u>.

Extract Two

Police officer:	OK, just tell me in your own words what happened, Mr Philips.
Driver: *Q3*	I'll do my best, but <u>it's all a bit of a blur</u>.
Police officer:	Tell me as much as you can. It was about midnight, wasn't it?
Driver:	I'd say it was nearer one o'clock. We were coming home from a holiday in Germany. We'd spent all day travelling, so I suppose we were pretty tired.
Police officer:	How far were you from home?
Driver:	About half an hour. We were travelling fairly fast – the roads were empty and we were just looking forward to going to bed.
Police officer:	What's the first thing that happened?
Driver: *Q4*	We were driving under a bridge when there was a crash of breaking glass and something hit my left arm. I managed to keep my right hand on the steering wheel but I didn't have much control over the car. Before I knew what was happening, we'd left the road and were heading for a clump of trees. <u>I was sure we'd had it</u>.
Police officer:	What's the next thing you remember?
Driver:	Well, everything happened so quickly. I remember waking up on the grass verge with people looking down at me.
Police officer:	And when did you realise what had actually happened?
Driver:	When one of the paramedics showed me the stone that had come through the windscreen.

Extract Three

Reporter: So, what is your situation at the moment?

Resident: We're sleeping in the main hall of the local secondary school, with many of our neighbours.

Q5 We're all in the same situation – just doing our best to look on the bright side.

Reporter: Do you know when you can move back?

Resident: No, at the moment all our houses are still under a metre of water – and apparently it's still rising. It hasn't stopped raining since Sunday.

Reporter: What happened exactly?

Resident: Well, there's a river at the bottom of our garden – more of a sluggish stream most of the time, actually. Last weekend, with all the rain we'd had, it burst its banks and washed over our garden. It was very quick once it started. I was frantically trying to stop it by digging ditches to take the water away – but there was too much of it, and in the end I just gave up digging and got out as quickly as possible.

Reporter: And what's the damage?

Resident: Well, everything downstairs is ruined. We'll need new furniture and carpets, and we'll probably need to have the walls replastered.

Q6 I keep thinking how disastrous it could have been. At one stage I imagined seeing the whole building collapse. Some of our neighbours are …

⑤ **1** *Flashbacks* can be either pleasant or unpleasant; they are often caused by traumatic events.
2 They walk or run on a treadmill. A treadmill is an exercise machine with a moving strip on which you walk or run without moving forward. Hard, boring and repetitive.   **3** If you *put your foot on the accelerator,* a car goes faster; *brakes, clutch, gear stick*   **4** For example, if something happened really fast and the events aren't clear.   **5** He thought he and his passengers were going to die.

Vocabulary
Idiomatic language

1 hope for good luck   **2** try hard to persuade me (but without force)   **3** makes me angry   **4** betray you or be disloyal to you when you are not expecting it
5 pretend not to notice something   **6** joking/teasing

Grammar
Verbs followed by *to* + infinitive or the *-ing* form

① **2** taking   **3** thinking   **4** to stop   **5** digging

②

verbs followed by *to* + infinitive	verbs followed by *-ing*
afford, agree, choose, expect, hope, offer, pretend, promise, refuse	admit, avoid, can't help, deny, enjoy, finish, involve, keep on, mind, put off, resent, risk, suggest

③ **1** **a** I have a memory of doing this.   **b** Don't forget to do it.
2 **a** This was an experiment – to see what would happen.   **b** I attempted to do this but failed.
3 **a** We saw part of the taking-off process. **b** We saw the entire landing process.
4 **a** I wish I hadn't said anything.   **b** I'm sorry to tell you that …
5 **a** This involves doing something.   **b** I didn't intend to offend you.

④ **2** help maintaining help maintain / help to maintain   **3** to sail sailing   **4** phoning to phone, to worry worry   **5** to do doing   **6** work working

Use of English   Part 5

① **1** Yes   **2** Yes   **3** No – it doesn't use the key word (*until*) and it uses more than six words to complete the sentence.   **4** It *was not until we were* on dry land again that we felt safe.

② (*Answers to the clues are in brackets at the end of the sentences.*) **1** Adventure holidays *don't / do not appeal to me* in the least. (*to*)   **2** They had offered him a .38 gun so *that he could protect* himself. (*that*)   **3** It *is against the law to* have an unlicensed gun in your possession. (*against the law*)
4 Tennis *is generally considered (to be)* a safe sport. (It becomes passive.)   **5** The further we travelled *inland, the more primitive* our surroundings became. (*the* + comparative adjective, *the* + comparative adjective)   **6** You *should avoid climbing* mountains after a heavy snowfall. (*should*)   **7** You can't control the weather; the only thing to do *is (to) hope for* the best. (*for*)   **8** At the last minute she *lost her nerve* and pulled out of the competition. (*lose*)

❸ 2 h **3** f **4** b **5** g **6** a **7** d **8** c

❹ *Suggested answers*: **1** The football World Cup *takes place* every four years. **2** We couldn't take our car away until *we had settled up* with the garage. **3** Considering how foggy it was, *it's a wonder* that the plane was able to take off. **4** *I can't wait* for the end of next week – that's when my holidays start. **5** Could you *keep an eye on* the children for me while I go shopping? **6** Sorry I didn't phone you back – I've been *tied up* all day. **7** I've had a cold for the last two weeks, but at last I'm *on the mend*. **8** I don't know why he was so rude to me – I think he was trying to *pick a fight*.

Reading Part 1

❶ a 3 **b** 1 **c** 2

❷ 1 B **2** D **3** A **4** B **5** C **6** D

❸ *Suggested answers*: **1** Cal and his father may be part of a criminal gang / involved in a feud / involved in terrorism. **2** He may have been worried that he would die if he allowed himself to sleep. **3** *jumpy* means *nervy, anxious, apprehensive*, so could be used to describe any situation where someone is afraid of the unknown, e.g. someone breaking down on a lonely road.

Speaking Part 2

❷ 1 The two photos being compared are the fireman and the diver. **2** The words and phrases express varying degrees of doubt or certainty.

Recording script   CD1 Track 14

Student: OK, well, in this photo there's a firefighter putting out a fire with a hosepipe and he's almost certainly doing it to save people's lives and property. It's a pretty dangerous job because obviously he could die in a fire or get seriously burnt. And he's doing it, I don't know, because someone's got to do it. It must be a worthwhile occupation – you know, very rewarding when you save someone's life. And in this photo there's a diver - he could be a police diver - he seems to be in a lake, or it could be a river. This is probably quite dangerous because the water could be deep

or there could be strong currents. There could be glass or other dangerous things in the water, and divers can get their equipment tangled up somehow. I suppose police divers find their work quite exciting – I'm sure it's never boring, and it's very worthwhile - though they must never know quite what they're going to find in the water.

Teacher: What kind of qualities do you think are most important for someone doing occupations like this?

Student: I'd say you've got to be brave, you know, not frightened easily – perhaps enjoy excitement that comes from doing dangerous things.

Writing Part 2 A competition entry

❹ I am writing **c**   an ordinary working mother **a**   Helen was driving home **c**   looking forward to **b**   a relaxing weekend **a**   Without thinking **d**   flames were coming **c**   succeeded in dragging **d**   reason for nominating **d**   person going about her daily life **e**   leaving the emergency services **b**   stopped and helped, saving a man's life **b**   reason for choosing Helen **d**   training is needed **f**

❺ 2 ~~keep up~~ keeping up **3** *correct* **4** ~~hardwork~~ hardworking, ~~interest~~ interesting, ~~improve~~ improving, ~~be~~ being **5** ~~To bring in~~ Bringing in **6** ~~to leave~~ leaving

6 Picture yourself

Starting off

2 *Suggested answers*: Speaker A: 1 Speaker B: 5
Speaker C: 4

Recording script CD1 Track 15

A

Magda: This portrait is one which I started from a photo of myself actually, but after a time I came to the conclusion that photos aren't that good when you're trying to be creative. You know, I found myself sort of imitating the photo and that wasn't very satisfying. So I switched to drawing in front of a mirror instead. Anyway, I like this self-portrait because I think it says a few things about me, like that I'm quite neat for example, perhaps a little unadventurous in the way I dress – not like most artists – but I think I've captured quite a sincere and thoughtful expression on my face. Also, I think I look quite sort of approachable, not at all threatening, someone it's nice to be around. At least I hope so.

B

Evelyn: You know, I've done quite a few portraits of friends and classmates and so on, normally from photographs, and people are usually quite complimentary about them, but you should have heard some of the things my friends said about this one! 'You're so serious!' 'We never see you concentrating like that!' 'You're not like that at all – you're normally always joking and laughing!' You see, I did the drawing in front of a mirror as a sort of experiment to see if I could do a self-portrait from life like Rembrandt or someone, and I found I kept having to move my head, so my hair kept getting in the way and I got quite frustrated. It took me hours! Still, I'm quite proud of the way my eyes turned out, sort of thoughful and sincere.

C

Lindsay: I've looked at quite a few self-portraits because I was interested how this one turned out, which was not at all how I expected. Most artists look like they're really concentrating hard and you don't catch them smiling much. In this one I look like sort of uptight, moody, even a bit aggressive or angry. I'd just come back from holiday and my face was pretty tanned. I found it pretty difficult to capture that tanned look and my fair hair in a black-and-white portrait. I'd like to look more relaxed, though.

Reading Part 3

1 *Suggested answers*: (ruthless honesty, ways of deceiving,) pretty-faced teenager, soft-focus fashion model, alone and misunderstood, sheer exuberance, toothy grins, grimacing teenage angst, young people doing anything from brushing their teeth to donning funny hats to listening to iPods, less self-consciously presented, caught unprepared, mapped out the spots on their faces, advertisements for L'Oréal, bad-hair days, cloned clumps, engaged, enthusiastic and eager

3 **1** C **2** D **3** A **4** B **5** D **6** A **7** B

Grammar
Avoiding repetition

1 **2** themselves, another, they **3** those, they **4** this **5** whose **6** that

2 **2** it one **3** it so/this **4** it one **5** these this **6** all everything / it all **7** it one **8** it that/this **9** yourself you

3 *Suggested answers*: **2** Fewer and fewer people listen to classical music. This means / , which means that less is being recorded. **3** I have to read lots of books for my Business Studies course. The ones / Those I enjoy most are the ones on management theory. **4** I'm hoping to be given a pay rise. This / That / , which / It will mean I can buy a better car. **5** I want Karl, Pau, Ludmila and Mar to come to the meeting. I've told Karl. Can you tell the others? **6** Marina doesn't like spending a lot of money on books, so she tends to buy second-hand ones. **7** My mother asked you to help her and she'd have been so happy if you'd done so / if you had. **8** When Raul feels strongly about something, he says so. **9** She didn't do the shopping because no one asked her to. / no one asked her to do so/it. **10** Someone left a message on the answering machine but they didn't leave their name.

Listening Part 3

❸ 1 B   2 A   3 C   4 A   5 D   6 D

Recording script   CD1 Track 16

Interviewer: Good evening. I have in the studio with me today the distinguished still-life and portrait artist, Liam Carolan. Liam, when did you first realise you had artistic talent?

Liam Carolan: Well, it was always impressed upon me when I was young, because both my parents were artistic, the family shall we say. <u>My father taught in an art school and was also a very good portrait painter, though he did them really just out of interest – not to earn a living that way</u>. He had a fair number of exhibitions in London before the war, but with abstract paintings, and so he was quite avant-garde for the time. He even had one with Picasso.

Q1

Interviewer: So did you always have it in mind to be a professional artist?

Liam Carolan: Well, no, I wouldn't say … I think my experience in art college made me sceptical of that idea and I was rather disillusioned for quite a long time and I didn't do very much in the way of art after leaving college. The training that I had wasn't really directed towards the sort of things I'm doing now. In those days students were encouraged towards more cerebral attitudes to art and <u>what I do is, some people would say, obsolete or even perhaps naïve</u>, but I'm still painting figurative paintings today.

Q2

Interviewer: Why would people prefer a painted portrait to a photograph of themselves?

Liam Carolan: I think generally most people feel that <u>if you have something made by hand rather than by a machine and if it's a design feature in the house, then a portrait hanging on the wall is much better to live with</u>, although people who like living in very modern environments might prefer to have a photograph hanging on the wall. But whether it's a portrait or a landscape, I think most people if you asked, 'Do you prefer a photograph or a painting?', I think most people would say a painting.

Q3

Interviewer: Do you tend to paint your subjects from life or from photos?

Liam Carolan: Well, I used to paint from photos but now I tell people I'd prefer not to. But interestingly, when I have done so the reaction has been, 'I thought that was a photograph!' In other words the painting looks like the photo, so <u>I think a painting from life gives life to the painting</u> and why that's the case is for many reasons to do with your contact with the person that's in front of you, the tension that's created when you're dealing with an individual one to one. There's a nervousness and an adrenalin that goes into that painting which is sparked off by that interaction. It's not something you think about when you're in the process of doing it, but the technique is completely different when you're painting someone as a three-dimensional object.

Q4

Interviewer: Mmm. How do you go about capturing the personality of your sitters?

Liam Carolan: I think just to try and paint what you see in front of you, which is a difficult enough task, is sufficient. And I think that if you do that, then something about the person will come through without you forcing it. And often <u>I think perceptions of the qualities of a sitter or a subject are things that are noticed by the observer of a portrait rather than things produced by the painter</u>. I think there's something about a painted portrait as opposed to a photograph which draws the viewer in and then they see things about the subject that they'd never noticed before.

Q5

Interviewer: You've done a number of self-portraits, haven't you? Why did you do those?

Liam Carolan: Really just for practice. If I haven't got a model around, then I'm left with myself. Actually, I've usually been dissatisfied with the results. It's not necessarily more difficult than doing other people, but <u>there is a problem of getting the scale. I always stand almost next to the sitter when I'm doing an oil painting to get it life size and if you're looking in a mirror, the image that you see is always smaller</u>. I've got one self-portrait that I like and I think that most people think that I look rather ferocious. But from a technical point of view I think that it's good. It isn't, I think, a particularly flattering one in fact.

Q6

Vocabulary
Adjective/noun collocations (2)

1 big

2 *Common collocations include*: **2** amazing/huge/wide **3** loud/terrible/tremendous **4** considerable/great/huge/tremendous **5** heavy/terrible/tremendous **6** amazing/good/great/tremendous/valuable **7** high/large **8** amazing/considerable/good/great/huge/satisfactory/tremendous **9** considerable/huge/tremendous/wide **10** amazing/considerable/endless/great/huge/tremendous/wide

3 *Suggested answers*: Words like *huge* and *tremendous* have a more extreme meaning than *great*, *considerable* or *large*. They also tend to be used in more colloquial situations. *Amazing* conveys surprise at how much; *terrible* conveys a negative attitude towards how much; *good*, *valuable*, *satisfactory* and *great* (in most contexts) convey a positive attitude.

Speaking Part 3

2 **1** Pair A **2** Pair B **3** Pair A **4** Both pairs **5** Both pairs **6** Pair A **7** Pair B **8** Pair B

Recording script CD1 Track 17

Pair A

Teacher: Here are some pictures showing some of the roles books play in our lives. First, talk to each other about the different roles which books play in our lives. Then decide which activity is the most demanding.

Martyna: Do you read books, Hans?

Hans: Not much, to tell you the truth.

Martyna: Well, I do. I'm studying literature at university, so I read a huge number of books – not for pleasure, though I do read some books for pleasure as well.

Hans: Well, the photos. This one here looks quite demanding – there's a librarian putting books back on the shelves, she's having to be very methodical, she's probably having to work quite quietly, not make a loud noise, so as not to disturb people in the library …

Martyna: Yes, I think if I was doing that, I'd probably feel a bit frustrated, because I like to chat and talk quite a lot and I'm not too organised so I'd find that quite demanding.

Hans: And there's this one with someone just relaxing and reading a novel probably …

Martyna: Yes, not very demanding, but quite enjoyable. And this one here of the teacher helping the child to learn to read …

Hans: Yes, that could be quite demanding because as a child it's probably quite hard to grasp the concept of reading.

Martyna: And for the teacher too to have the patience. I think if I was the teacher, I'd find it very satisfying to actually teach kids how to read for the first time.

Hans: But again, you'd have to be very methodical, which you say you aren't, so I imagine for you that would be pretty demanding. And here's another one with a boy studying, taking notes, which could be quite demanding. It depends what it is, though. He could be studying …

Pair B

Teacher: Here are some pictures showing some of the roles books play in our lives. First, talk to each other about the different roles which books play in our lives. Then decide which activity is the most demanding.

Carlos: Well, the first picture shows someone writing in their diary. I think this shows how books can be used to keep a record of what we do and our lives …

Antonia: Yes, and also our thoughts and our feelings. Then in the second one there's a teacher using a textbook – I think it is to teach something and this shows how books can be a store of knowledge …

Carlos: Yes, all the things we can't carry in our heads can be kept in books …

Antonia: Or on computers nowadays …

Carlos: Yes, and the third one shows a librarian, someone working with books … So let's move on to the next part. Which do you think is the most demanding, Antonia?

Antonia: Well, although I like the idea of keeping a diary with all the things I've done each day and the people I've seen, I think this one with the diary would probably be the one I'd find the hardest because I'm just too tired at the end of the day. What about you?

Carlos: Yes, I'm the same, but also perhaps the one of the student taking notes, because he might have to grasp some quite difficult concepts …

3 1 *Suggested answer*: Both pairs deal with the task well, although the first pair doesn't immediately deal with the task. The second pair is more methodical. **2** hardest, difficult, challenging

4 **2** was doing that **3** this one **4** which **5** that would be **6** the one **7** which others

Use of English Part 2

2 1 It reduces stress, raises productivity and creative thinking, stimulates and inspires, makes employees feel cared for. **2** Previously it was aimed at visitors and customers, now it's also aimed at employees.

3 1 what **2** done **3** cuts **4** will **5** one **6** those/these **7** likely **8** some **9** their/the **10** who **11** in **12** longer **13** throughout/through/around **14** it/this **15** so

Writing Part 2 A review

1 1 *Suggested answers*: **a** No – a general overview of the plot without giving away the ending **b** No – brief summaries of main characters **c** No – this is not asked for in the task. **d** Yes **e** Maybe – this is not asked for but you can include some criticism. **f** Yes **g** Maybe – if it is connected with why you enjoyed it. **h** Yes **2** *Students' own answers* **3** what other readers may find interesting about it

2 descriptions of the main characters (h), a general recommendation (d), what was most enjoyable about the book (f), a synopsis of the plot (h)

3 **a** paragraphs 1 and 2 **b** paragraphs 1, 2 and 3 **c** paragraphs 1, 2 and 4 **d** paragraph 4

4 I was fascinated; I was spellbound … horrified and caught up in the suspense

5 *Characters*: *Inman*: army deserter, thoughtful, observant hero, desperate to escape, motivated by love, capable of extreme violence; *Ada*: the heroine, well-off, sheltered background, incapable of surviving, becomes self-sufficient and decisive; *Ruby*: brash but lovable country girl
Places: war-torn, wild, isolated, harsh conditions, rural backwater

Vocabulary and grammar review   Unit 5

Vocabulary

1

B	L	O	O	D	M	F	L	U
U	F	I	N	G	E	R	S	D
T	K	C	H	E	S	T	F	N
B	N	E	Y	E	I	I	O	L
R	E	A	O	B	C	P	O	E
E	E	S	W	A	A	U	T	G
X	A	E	E	C	A	R	M	A
R	I	N	F	K	H	E	A	D

2 1 fingers, d **2** eye, e **3** leg, f **4** blood, a **5** arm, b **6** back, c

3 *Students' own answers*

Grammar

4 1 to help, to train, to be **2** to climb, to leave, to be rescued **3** waiting, phoning, to put out, realising, putting **4** to take, getting, snowing / to snow, climbing, to admit, telephoning, to ask, contact, regretting, to ignore

5 **2** We *were lucky to avoid / have avoided* the floods. **3** I *regret having made* that phone call to my sister. **4** We *can't afford to buy* a new car. **5** He *denies (ever) seeing / having seen* her before.

Vocabulary and grammar review Unit 6

Vocabulary

1 2 wide   3 large   4 deep   5 high   6 heavy   7 big
8 high

Grammar

2 *Suggested answers*: 2 When a child feels unhappy,
they will ask for their mother more often than for
their father.   3 Gustav bought a large house by the
sea about ten years ago, which / This / It turned
out to be a good investment.   4 Leonardo lived in
Canada as a child, which is / That's why he speaks
such fluent English.   5 Svetlana spent several
months trying to decide which car to buy and she
finally bought one last week.   6 Three runners
entered the race, but only one (of them) finished
because one twisted her ankle and another stopped
to talk to her friends among the spectators.
7 Matthew likes reading novels, especially romantic
ones.   8 Violeta bought some apples in the market.
She put some (of them) in the fruit bowl and used
the others to make an apple pie.   9 Narayan has
had two jobs. Both were in a bank but unfortunately
neither was well paid.   10 There are five official
languages in Spain and Manolo speaks all of
them.   11 Pete had never spoken to Ann although
he'd often wanted to.   12 Maria often invites me
to go with her on business trips to New York, but I
never have / I've never done so.

3 2 The judges *tended to be keener* on portraits
painted from life than portraits painted from
photos.   3 This painting *does not look as if/though
/ like it* is finished.   4 Several of the applicants
were passed over due/owing to their age.
5 Appearance is *what matters (the) most to* many
teenagers.

7 Leisure and entertainment

Listening Part 4

1 **CD1 Track 18**   1 folk   2 opera   3 disco   4 Latin
5 pop   6 classical   7 soul   8 jazz   9 rock   10 world

2 1 E   2 A   3 H   4 possibly B   5 D
3 1 D   2 H   3 E   4 A   5 B   6 H   7 G   8 A   9 C
10 E

Recording script   CD1 Track 19

Speaker 1:
Q1 I've been involved in traditional music since I
was a kid. My father was well known round
here as a singer of the old songs. He sang
at family gatherings, and he also played
the accordion in a band that performed at
weddings and other local functions. My
grandfather was a genuine traditional singer
who had a whole repertoire of family songs
that had been passed down from generation to
generation. All the songs were handwritten in
a big book. As he got older he relied more and
more on the book, but his voice was strong
until he died. **Q6** I'm proud to say I continue to
sing some of the family songs – but not just in
our village. I've travelled all over the world and
played in front of audiences of thousands. It
would have made my grandfather smile.

Speaker 2: Until a few years ago I'd thought of tango as
something that only older people did, but then
we went to a concert by the Gotan Project
when they were playing in London, and I
Q7 couldn't believe how exciting tango could be.
For a start the music was amazing. As well
as having normal tango instruments – the
violin and guitar and bandoneon – they also
used electronic music – you know, samples
and beats. The rhythm was so infectious that
some people got up and bopped in front of the
stage, whether they could actually tango or
Q2 not. Since then, I've joined a class and learned
some of the basic moves.

Speaker 3:
Q8 & Q3 I love my iPod and quite frankly I'd be lost
without it. I listen to it nearly all the time,
whether I'm commuting, exercising or trying to
drown out some noise and relax. I mainly listen
to rock music, but I quite like jazz and I even
listen to classical stuff if I'm feeling stressed – it
can be very relaxing listening to composers
like Mozart if you're in a crowded train or
sitting in a traffic jam somewhere. It's a brilliant
invention. I've got over seven thousand songs
on mine – that's nearly my whole CD collection
and of course I download stuff from time to
time – usually single tracks rather than whole
albums.

Speaker 4: I'm trying to start a jazz band with a friend – I play percussion and Ed plays trombone, but **Q4** our main interest is composing. The band we have in mind would have seventeen players – obviously we wouldn't be professional, at least not until we'd built up a reputation. Most of the musicians we're approaching play in various different outfits – rock, jazz, folk and classical – so they wouldn't be available all the time. **Q9** We're hoping to make a CD but the logistics are a nightmare. Rehearsals would be tricky – getting so many people into a studio at once, and there'd be the expense. So at the moment it's just a dream.

Speaker 5: I've just come back from Womad in Singapore – it was awesome. I went with a few friends and we got in for free because we were in the hospitality crew. We had to carry loads of stuff from one place to the next, but we still had plenty of time to get into the music – dance around like mad. We got to talk to quite a lot of the acts – we got signatures and photos. **Q10** It was a great experience, especially when the artists thank you for doing such a good job. There was a really great line-up of artists. Most of them I'd never heard of before, but I'll be listening to them from now on – until next **Q5** year's festival.

④ **1 a** occasions when whole families get together, for example for a birthday party, wedding etc. – usually private   **b** social gatherings or ceremonies, for example parties, weddings etc. – usually public   **c** I couldn't manage / function properly if I didn't have it.   **d** it isn't likely to happen / it's a fantasy   **2** *Students' own answers*

Vocabulary
Prepositional phrases

② **2** means   **3** keeping   **4** addition   **5** start

Reading Part 2

② **1** listening to music (music festival) / going to nightclubs   **2** They are put in 'prison': a cornfield, where they are made to watch black-and-white public service television announcements from the 1950s in a continuous loop.

③ *Suggested answers*: *Para B*: to point out a political

aspect of *Second Life*   *Para C*: to show how *Second Life* can be used for commercial purposes   *Para D*: to show how *Second Life* can be used for publicity/ advertising purposes   *Para E*: to give an example of how the virtual world and the real world interact   *Para F*: to illustrate the range of activities that users of *Second Life* are involved in   *Para G*: to point out that *Second Life* is not an original concept

④ **1** E   **2** F   **3** G   **4** A   **5** D   **6** C

⑤ **1** *gatecrashing*: going to a party (etc.) that you have not been invited to. *subcultures*: groups of people who have their own shared values, traditions, etc. within a larger society.   **2** *user-generated*: produced by users.   **3** *killer*: (informal) exceptionally powerful/exciting, having a great impact on people.

Grammar
Ways of linking ideas

① **2** c   **3** b   **4** a   **5** d

② **a** a relative clause   **b** a participle clause   **c** a descriptive noun phrase   **d** a descriptive noun phrase   **e** a conjunction

④ *Suggested answers*: **1** The novel *Snow Crash*, (which was) written in 1992, foresaw a futuristic virtual world called the metaverse in which characters controlled digital representations of themselves, known as avatars.   **2** Players can convert their 'play money' into US dollars, using their credit card at online currency exchanges.   **3** Because a player's real-world personal reputation may be affected by their virtual representation in the virtual social world, they are even more likely to spend real money on their avatars.   **4** *Second Life* participants pay 'Linden dollars', (which are) the game's currency (and) which they use to rent or buy apartments from Chung, (who is) the property developer, so that they have a place to build and show off their creations.

Use of English Part 1

③ **1** B   **2** C   **3** B   **4** B   **5** D   **6** B   **7** A   **8** B   **9** D   **10** B   **11** C   **12** A

Vocabulary
Money verbs

1 2 hired   3 earn, buying, selling   4 selling
5 spend

2 2 make   3 buy   4 pay   5 afford, costs

3 2 ~~afford~~ cover, ~~spend~~ pay   3 ~~pay~~ buy   4 ~~buy~~
shop   5 ~~rent~~ borrow   6 ~~buy~~ spend   7 ~~earned~~
raised

Speaking Part 2

2 2 a the game of chess and the people cooking
b The second speaker is better because she answers
all parts of the question.   c The first speaker
doesn't say what skills and abilities are needed or
why participants enjoy doing the activities. Most of
the time is spent talking about his own reactions
to / feelings about the activity – in this part of the
exam, this is irrelevant.

3 *See underlining in script below*

4 *Suggested answers*: **1** active, agile, analytical,
clear, creative, inventive, methodical, sharp
2 boundless, enormous, great, incredible
3 basic, human, natural; basic, expert, great,
manual, special, technical   **4** awkward, formidable,
fundamental, major, practical, pressing, recurrent,
serious, severe, underlying, unexpected

Writing Part 2 An informal letter

2 *Formal–informal*: **5** B   **4** E   **3** C   **2** D   **1** A
1 A Friend asking to be put up for a few days
B Holiday company confirming payment and
reminding holiday-maker of conditions of stay
C Invitation to staff and students to end-of-term
party   **D** Thank-you note to musicians who played
at party   **E** Apology from company for breakage
of CD in transit   **2 A** Someone writing to a friend/
acquaintance   **B** Holiday company finance office
writing to holidaymaker customer   **C** Tutor or
student writing to (other) students doing their
course   **D** Party organiser/host writing to
musicians who provided entertainment   **E** CD
company writing to customer who complained
3 A am looking (leaving out *I*), put me up, didn't,
meet up, I'd, I'll be around, Don't worry, it's,
loads of other people, it'd be good   **B** *no informal
features*   **C** to get everyone together, we're asking,
ask someone over, It's, hopefully, shouldn't   **D** Just
a short note (leaving out *This is*), as well, set the
evening up   **E** *no informal features*

3 *Suggested answers*: **1** (This is) Just to let you know
(that) …   **2** the holiday you're about to go on /
you're going on soon / you've got coming up
3 will be taken from your credit card   **4** the week
after you leave   **5** I'm very sorry about this.
6 We try very/really hard

5 *Suggested answers*: *Nearer the beginning*: comment
on the fact that your friend is planning to learn
your language, ask about the language course your
friend is attending, give some general information
about your town *Nearer the end*: say you're looking
forward to seeing your penfriend, suggest meeting
during the friend's stay

8 Don't blame the media

Reading Part 3

② 1 The writer interviewed people he knew. / He had worked in TV.   2 Entertainment is the priority – more important than ethical considerations.
3 American spellings of e.g. *program, behavior, verbalize.*

③ 1 C   2 D   3 B   4 A   5 B   6 D   7 C

Vocabulary
'Talking' verbs

① 2 spoke/talked   3 told   4 spoke/talked   5 said
6 comments

② 2 saying, speak   3 mention   4 expressed   5 says
6 comment   7 told, mention   8 speak

Grammar
Transitive verbs

① 1 told me, had never given them ethical direction
2 informed me

② 2 tell *me*   3 gave *it* to me   4 will allow *us* to
5 introduced *me* to   6 called *me* a liar
7 wish *you* the best of luck   8 give *me* more money

Listening Part 3

① 1 At any time of the day or night. It is non-stop news.   2 *Up-market newspapers* are usually aimed at the interests of readers who are wealthy. (The opposite is *down-market.*)   3 a detailed study
4 enjoy it greatly   5 *Citizen journalism* is written by ordinary people, rather than traditionally trained journalists.

② 1 C   2 D   3 A   4 D   5 C   6 B

Recording script   CD2 Track 2

Interviewer: In today's *On Message* I'm joined by Harry Cameron, the veteran journalist who has witnessed many changes in his profession over the last nearly sixty years as a reporter. Harry, welcome.

Cameron: Thank you – it's a pleasure to be here.

Interviewer: Harry, I'd like to start if I may by asking you what being a journalist was like when you started your first job as a junior reporter on the *Daily Journal.*

Cameron:
Q1
My main memory of those far-off days is the sense of pride I felt at writing for a respected national newspaper. <u>It was a real honour.</u> What you have to remember is that in those days people got most of their information about what was going on in the world from their daily newspapers. And almost everyone read a paper every day. Television was in its infancy – something only the rich could afford. The radio broadcast regular news bulletins, but newspapers gave people the pictures to go with the stories. Journalists like me travelled the world and filed reports which kept people up to date with everything important that was going on. I remember once in the early 1950s reporting from a war zone in East Asia. I wrote my report sitting on the bed in my hotel bedroom. I could hear gunfire and see plumes of smoke. I wrote my story, then phoned it through to my editor for publication a day or two later. I was telling people about something thousands of miles from home – and more importantly, something they didn't already know.

Interviewer: But people still read newspapers today, don't they?

Cameron:
Q2
Yes, of course, but their function has changed. If you want to know what's going on in the world at any particular time, <u>you don't read a newspaper, do you? You turn on the telly</u>. And you'll probably have an extensive choice of news programmes to watch – some of them, like CNN or News 24, rolling news programmes which are broadcast 24 hours a day. And then, whatever channel you're watching, there'll be regular news updates. And, on top of all that, <u>there's the Internet.</u>

Interviewer: So, what can newspapers provide if not current news?

Cameron:
Q3
Well, I suppose different newspapers provide different things, don't they? <u>The more up-market ones give us background to the news stories and an in-depth analysis of the issues involved.</u> *I think they do this very well.* At the more popular end of the market, papers these days focus more and more on stories involving celebrities from the world of sport, TV, cinema, etc. And sport itself, of course. There's sport everywhere, always accompanied by photographs – action shots. People lap all this up, and I suppose it is news of a kind, but to my mind it's a somewhat distorted definition of news.

Interviewer: And what about 'citizen journalism'? *Is this a term you're familiar with?*

Cameron:
Q4
Yes, it is, and <u>*it's something I have some sympathy with,*</u> even though it may put some of my own colleagues out of work in the long run.

Interviewer: So how would you explain its sudden appearance as a source of information?

Cameron: It's quite simple – the fact is that the Internet has given everyone access to a wealth of information and to a worldwide audience. So a citizen journalist in a war zone, like me fifty years ago, doesn't have to write a story and send it to an editor who can decide whether or not to run the story in their newspaper – they can simply add information to a news website like NowPublic or write their own blog. Bloggers are the new journalists. And of course they can take photos with their mobile phones and send them straight to an internet site or blog.

Interviewer: And *how reliable are bloggers and citizen journalists as sources of information?*

Cameron:
Q5
<u>At least as reliable as the traditional news providers,</u> whose stories are usually revised and cut by editors who may be under political pressure from a newspaper owner or even their government. And of course some news websites allow other members of the public to add to, update or correct stories that are already there. I'd say it's a very democratic editorial process.

Interviewer: So, this is not something you think should be controlled in any way?

Cameron: Absolutely not! Anyway, you couldn't control it even if you wanted to. The genie's out of the bottle.

Interviewer: And you have no regrets about the effect of this form of journalism on the profession you were so proud to be part of when you first became a reporter?

Cameron:
Q6
I suppose I'm a little sad, but the important thing is that people have reliable sources of up-to-date information. Of course there will always be a role, in newspapers and elsewhere, <u>for intelligent comment and analysis of the news, and *if I were starting out now, that's the kind of journalism I'd get into*</u>.

Interviewer: And you'd do it extremely well, I have no doubt. Harry Cameron, thanks for being my guest on today's *On Message*.

Cameron: It's been my pleasure.

3 1 The *genie* is citizen journalism. The *bottle* is the system which restricted access to news media in the past. 2 *Students' own answers*

Grammar
Reported speech

1 1 the sense of pride I felt 2 I think they do this very well. 3 Is this a term you're familiar with? 4 It's something I have some sympathy with. 5 How reliable are bloggers and citizen journalists as sources of information? 6 If I were starting out again now, that's the kind of journalism I'd get into.

2 **CD2 Track 3** See sections in italics in the Recording script for Listening Part 3.

3 Change of tense, e.g. *is – was, felt – had felt* (1); change of pronoun, e.g. *I – he* (2); change of *this* to *that* (3); word order in reported questions (3, 5)

4 In **a** the article has (probably) already been published. In **b** the article has not been published yet.

5

Recording script CD2 Track 4

Ben: Do you know anything about Wikipedia?

Tom: Yes, I often use it.

Ben: So how do you look for information?

Tom:	It's like any search engine – you simply type in a keyword, press Return and the information you want appears.
Ben:	What do you use it for?
Tom:	All kinds of things. Yesterday, for example, I needed to find out about wildlife conservation in Namibia. It took me about a minute to find the information I wanted on Wikipedia.
Ben:	Have you any idea how accurate that information is?
Tom:	No, but that's no different from any other source of information. The article on Namibia had been revised the day before yesterday, so it was up to date.
Ben:	So, would you recommend using Wikipedia?
Tom:	Yes, definitely. It's free, as well as being quick and easy to use.

6 *Suggested answers*:

- Tom told Ben / replied that he often uses/used it.
- Ben asked Tom how he looks/looked for information. / Ben wanted to know how Tom looks/looked for information.
- Tom said (that) it is/was like any search engine. He said that you simply type/typed in a keyword, press/pressed Return and the information you want/wanted appears/appeared / will/would appear.
- Ben asked Tom what he uses/used it for. / Ben wondered what Tom uses/used it for.
- Tom explained that he uses/used it for all kinds of things. The day before / The previous day, for example, he had needed to find out about wildlife conservation in Namibia. He maintained (that) it had taken him about a minute to find the information he (had) wanted on Wikipedia.
- Ben asked if/whether Tom has/had any idea how accurate the information is/was.
- Tom said (that) he doesn't/didn't, but that it is/was no different from any other source of information. He said that the article on Namibia had been revised two days earlier/previously/before, so he thought (that) it is/was up to date.
- Ben asked Tom if he would recommend using Wikipedia.
- Tom said that he would, definitely. He added that it is/was free, as well as being quick and easy to use.

Use of English Part 3

1 **2** *un*important   **3** *il*legal   **4** *im*possible
5 *ir*regular   **6** *in*tolerant
Nouns: **2** unimport*ance*   **3** illega*lity*
4 impossi*bility*   **5** irregula*rity*   **6** intoler*ance*

2 **2** *re*claim   **3** *mis*inform   **4** *pre*judge   **5** *over*react
6 *de*stabilise   **7** *under*state
Nouns: **2** recla*mation*   **3** misinform*ation*
4 prejudge*ment*   **5** overreac*tion*   **6** destabilis*ation*
7 understate*ment*

3 **2** *co*-owner   **3** *ex*-politician   **4** *mis*trust
5 *semi*-circle
Adjectives: **2** co-own*ed*   **3** *no adjective*
4 mistrust*ful*   **5** semi-circ*ular*

4 **1** consider – consider*ation*, contest – contest*ant*, direct – direct*ive*, employ – employ*ee*, entertain – entertain*ment*, produce – produc*tion*, produc*er*, view – view*er*
2 accept – accept*able*, cooperate – cooperat*ive*, create – creat*ive*, represent – representat*ive*, succeed – success*ful*
3 doctor – doctor*al*, ethics – ethic*al*
4 height – height*en*, verb – verb*alize* (UK verb*alise*), victim – victim*ize* (UK victim*ise*)

5 **1** basically dishonest   **2** universities

6 **1** intellectual   **2** journalism   **3** accuracy
4 construction   **5** difference   **6** apparent
7 abandonment   **8** impartiality   **9** argument
10 maintenance

Speaking Part 3

3 *Suggested answers*: **1** No – they spend more time discussing the individual influences and do not decide together which has the most powerful influence.   **2** They spend very little time on newspapers or advertising and too much time on radio.   **3** Yes, but Woman 2 says a bit more than Woman 1.

4 *See underlining in script below.*

Recording script   CD2 Track 5

Woman 1:   Well, I'd say that <u>nearly</u> everyone watches the news on TV – if they're above a certain age. I have to say when I was younger I never watched the news.

Woman 2:   No, I used to hate the news. I used to get really bored when my parents put it on.

Woman 1:	But now I'm <u>quite</u> interested to hear what's going on.
Woman 2:	I don't actually watch the news – I prefer to listen to it on the radio, but I think that's <u>fairly</u> unusual.
Woman 1:	Mmm. Yeah, I think I'd rather watch it on TV.
Woman 2:	I think it gets <u>pretty</u> depressing if you watch it – there's so much bad news. I think they cover much more bad news than good news – and I don't want to watch about wars and famines <u>and things like that</u>.
Woman 1:	OK – now we've got newspapers. I would say <u>quite a few</u> people read these, but I think people tend to read the newspapers that agree with their political opinions.
Woman 2:	Or if they just want amusement, they read one of the tabloids.
Woman 1:	Erm – advertising, erm, is in everything.
Woman 2:	There's so much brand management now – it's all <u>sort of</u> half subconscious. People sponsoring things and …
Woman 1:	Too much money spent on advertising.
Woman 2:	Yeah … Radio, which we've already mentioned.
Woman 1:	Yeah, with me it sort of goes through phases. I like listening to the radio when I get up because I like to know what's going on.
Woman 2:	Apparently we seem to be in a visual age – I don't know, but over time I would imagine radio listening has <u>probably</u> gone down.
Woman 1:	I think actually it's just changed – I mean people listen to the radio on their mobile phone now …
Woman 2:	Yeah, or the Internet – there are lots of radio stations and programmes you can listen to on the Internet …
Woman 1:	Yeah – live or often you can listen again.
Woman 2:	Or on your iPod. There are <u>about</u> eight million people listen to the breakfast show, so …
Woman 1:	Hmm – that's <u>quite a lot</u> of people.
Woman 2:	Yeah – very much a background thing, though, these days. I mean, every café you go into's going to have a radio programme on, aren't they?
Woman 1:	OK – we're on to the Internet and the World Wide Web. I think this is massive – it's fantastic – in western countries the most influential of all of these things.

Woman 2:	You can just find out anything.
Woman 1:	Yeah, absolutely anything – Wikipedia, and all the social networking sites and <u>stuff</u>.
Woman 2:	And at least with the Internet people have a huge choice.
Woman 1:	But don't forget the banner ads.
Woman 2:	You see, you can never get away from advertising of <u>some kind</u>.
Woman 1:	I know – even Google mail, when you sign up – they advertise certain things that you like, they look for your keywords.
Woman 2:	Big business is, I guess, <u>a lot</u> more influential than we realise – because their wealth gives them power.
Woman 1:	Yeah – but it's less direct power, isn't it?
Woman 2:	I wouldn't say it's less direct. It may be less obvious, but there's no doubt that large sections of the media are owned and controlled by the business interests of a few powerful individuals. This allows them to influence people's political views and control advertising. This in turn means that they have an influence on how we spend our money.
Woman 1:	It's all <u>a bit</u> sinister, don't you think?
Woman 2:	Yeah, <u>a bit</u> Big Brother-<u>ish</u> – being told what to think.

Writing Part 1 A proposal

2 *Suggested answers:* **1** No – only three programme ideas are suggested instead of the four asked for in the question. **2** The use of *will* instead of *might*, *could* and *would* would make the ideas seem more concrete and real in the writer's mind. **3** The style is appropriately formal except for *If you ask me*, which is too informal and should be more formal, e.g. *In my opinion*

Vocabulary and grammar review   Unit 7

Vocabulary

1 **2** rent, buy   **3** makes/earns   **4** sell   **5** hired
6 earn / make   **7** cost, paying   **8** spend

2 **1** form   **2** view   **3** flat

3

O	O	D	K	W	P	O	P	C
U	F	O	L	K	E	R	S	L
T	L	C	H	E	S	O	F	A
B	A	E	Y	E	I	C	O	S
R	T	A	O	B	C	K	P	S
J	I	S	O	U	L	U	E	I
A	N	E	E	C	A	R	R	C
Z	W	O	R	L	D	E	A	A
Z	D	I	S	C	O	M	L	L

Grammar

4 *Suggested answers:* **1** ... and stop it from breaking apart, (all of) which he finds very difficult. / An eleven-year-old boy tries to understand his family and stop it from breaking apart while dealing with his mother's absence, (all of) which he finds very difficult. **2** A man called Black, whose brain becomes magnetised, destroys every tape in a video store, (which is) owned by his best friend. Feeling sorry for the store's most loyal customer, an elderly woman who is losing her memory, Black and his friend set out to remake the lost films, which include / including *The Lion King* and *Robocop*. **3** In this film, (which is) based on a sci-fi novel by Richard Matheson, a military scientist, played by Will Smith, is left completely alone in New York, which is deserted after a virus has wiped out the human race.

Vocabulary and grammar review   Unit 8

Vocabulary

1 **2** mistrust   **3** illegal   **4** disappear
5 autobiography   **6** reclamation   **7** prejudge
8 destabilise

2 **2** entertainment/entertainer, entertaining
3 cooperation, cooperative   **4** produce, productive
5 consideration, considerate/considerable
6 create, creation/creator

Grammar

3 *Suggested answers*: **2** Clare said it was a real surprise seeing Tom last week / had been a real surprise seeing Tom the previous week. She said she hadn't seen him since they were / they'd been at school together. **3** Ben asked Jerry if he should do / if he wanted him to do the shopping that week. **4** Becky said to Jamie that he should have told her what he'd been planning to do. She said she could have helped him. **5** The doctor told me that I had to stop smoking if I wanted to get rid of my cough. **6** Nick said that if anyone asked for him, he'd be working at home on the following Friday. **7** Bogdan asked me how many languages I could/can speak.

4 **2** 'Do you have / Have you got any plans for tomorrow evening?' **3** 'You should / ought to eat regular meals and do more exercise.' **4** 'This is the worst programme I've ever seen.' **5** 'I'll phone you as soon as I get home.' **6** 'I hope I'm going / I'll be going there tomorrow.'

5 **1** *Alternative answer*: Maria *promised (that) she would never* do that again.
2 Alexei *advised me to apply for that* job.
3 Simon *asked me if I'd / I had* ever thought of starting my own business. **4** Svetlana *suggested meeting the following / suggested (that) we (should) meet the following* day. **5** The police officer *warned the motorist not to drink* if he was driving. **6** Tom and Alexis *announced that they were getting married* in May.

9 At top speed

Listening Part 1

② 1 B   2 A

Recording script   CD2 Track 6

Extract One

Interviewer: The advent of the steam train made an enormous difference to nineteenth-century society in all sorts of ways, didn't it, Tom?

Tom: Yes, the change was tremendous. People's entire conception of the world, the way they related to it and the way they lived underwent a profound transformation. It wasn't all immediate, of course, but eventually, and to a very great extent it fashioned the way we live today. It started with things which we find laughable today such as *people's terror that the trains' vibrations would shatter their skeletons*. When they got onto trains, they found everything going past in a blur of speed, and that blur is something which was eventually reflected in the work of pre-impressionist and impressionist painters later in the century. And over the next hundred years railways had profound effects on the countryside, making it possible for people to live there and travel in to work in the cities. Outlying villages became suburbs and dormitory towns. And also quite suddenly human beings went from being comparatively slow and clumsy to being faster than any other living thing and I think this had a subtle but strong effect on the way people regarded the natural world. *They began to think they could dominate it by their actions.* I doubt if any other invention has had such a profound influence on the human psyche. Nineteenth-century literature and art is full of it.

Q1

Q2

Interviewer: The early steam trains also suffered some quite horrific accidents, didn't they?

⑤ 3 A   4 C

Recording script   CD2 Track 7

Extract Two

Woman: Do you think there are any limits to the speed people can run at? I mean, will there ever come a time when athletes at Olympic events just aren't breaking records any more?

Man: Well, we're already quite close to that stage, aren't we? When athletes broke Olympic records in the past, some of their feats were mind-blowing. For example, when Bob Beamon broke the long jump record in 1968, his jump was 55 centimetres longer than the previous record and it wasn't until 1991 that someone managed to better it. *I can't imagine anyone making such a difference nowadays.*

Q3

Woman: Although there'll always be those exceptional individuals who grab the headlines with their exploits.

Man: Though I suspect that they'll be relatively few and far between. Still, newspapers and TV have to live off something and they'll hype a relatively small achievement into something far bigger than it really is.

Woman: Small achievement! Breaking a record even by a millisecond is always going to be pretty incredible, something enormous for the individual who does it.

Man: But when all is said and done, we're pretty close to the limits of human potential now.

Woman: Maybe. In the past what made a difference was when sport stopped being for amateurs and people could devote themselves to it full time, not to mention new technologies which affected shoe or track design. *Perhaps the next big step forward will be altering genes to produce better athletes.*

Q4

Man: *Yeah, that used to smack of science fiction, didn't it, but now it really is looking more and more likely, isn't it?*

Woman: Yes, and not just better athletes, better everyone!

8 5 B 6 B

Recording script CD2 Track 8

Extract Three

Interviewer: Dr Desai, the difficulties of interstellar travel are enormous, aren't they?

Desai: Vast. When you think that the nearest star is 4.2 light years away, a spaceship using current technology would take seventy-two thousand years to get there. Much more than the entire known history of this planet.

Interviewer: What are the possibilities of building a spaceship that travels much, much faster?

Desai: Well, I'd say that with research and development it could be technically feasible, but it would probably need to be powered by a nuclear explosion to get it travelling at close to the speed of light. Building such a craft is certainly not on anyone's space programme yet. The explosion would of course have to be set off at a good safe distance from the Earth, *Q5* but you have to remember that current treaties prohibit nuclear explosions in space, so at present it's a non-starter.

Interviewer: In your book you mention non-nuclear technology and in particular a generational spaceship. Can you explain for listeners exactly what this is?

Desai: Yes, indeed. Given the vast distances and the time involved, even a very fast spaceship using non-nuclear technology would take several thousand years to reach another star. And there are quite a lot of good candidates not too far away where we have identified planets. This means that the people volunteering to go on this journey, assuming that there are volunteers, won't live long enough to reach their destination, nor will their grandchildren or their great grandchildren, but many generations later on. These people, probably a hundred and fifty or two hundred of them, will have to live together in a confined space for thousands of years, travelling through the emptiness of space to we know not what they will encounter when they get there. What activities could we find for the crew to do during all this time? What would be the point

Q6 of their lives? And there's always the risk that they could degenerate into barbarism and fighting amongst themselves like some small isolated societies here on Earth.

Interviewer: So, are there any realistic prospects for interstellar space travel in the near future?

Reading Part 2

2 *Suggested answers*: *Para 1*: the effects of driving very fast *Para 2*: the problems of driving at high speed *Para 3*: comparison with a Formula One car *Para 4*: how the engineer produced enough power *Para 5*: the problem of aerodynamics *Para 6*: the solution to the aerodynamics *Para 7*: how it feels to drive this car.

Suggested words to underline: at this juncture, when you look at the history of its development, His engineers were horrified, Then things got tricky, When this had been done, they hit on the idea, I didn't care

3 1 C 2 A 3 D 4 B 5 E 6 G

Grammar
Tenses in time clauses and time adverbials

1 2 you're covering 3 look 4 was done / had been done (*both are correct and have the same meaning, i.e. one thing happened after the other*) 5 broke 6 bought

2 2 had been working / had worked 3 are driving 4 were waiting 5 am 6 was accepted

3 2 when 3 during, when/while 4 while/when 5 Meanwhile

4 2 ~~at~~ in 3 ~~of~~ in 4 ~~in~~ at 5 ~~of~~ in 6 *correct* 7 ~~in~~ on 8 ~~in~~ at 9 ~~in~~ on 10 *correct*

Vocabulary
Action, activity, event and *programme*

1 1 c, e, j 2 d, i, k 3 b, h 4 f, g

2 1 actions, j 2 events, h 3 programme, f 4 activities, i

3 2 programme 3 action 4 programme 5 action 6 event 7 activity 8 programme 9 event 10 activity 11 action 12 event

4 *Collocations*: frenetic activity, social event, spare-time activity, programme of (social) events, flurry of activity, call for swift action

Use of English Part 4

1 **1** verb **2** adjective **3** noun **4** verb **5** adjective

2 **1** meets **2** strong **3** way **4** broke **5** close

Speaking Part 2

3 **2** Yes **3** No **4** No **5** Yes **6** Yes **7** No

4 **2** of those **3** what do **4** I mean **5** what's

5 **1** 4 **2** 2 **3** 1 and 3 **4** 3 and 5

Writing Part 2 An essay

1 **2** T **3** F **4** T **5** F **6** T

4 **2** As a result **3** However **4** In contrast to ourselves **5** What is more **6** in general **7** In conclusion **8** On the contrary

5 **1** paragraph C **2** paragraph B **3** paragraph D **4** paragraph A

10   A lifelong process

Reading Part 4

3 *Students should underline:* **2** take a higher degree **3** work with other students **4** family member **5** where it was **6** people praise it **7** calmness **8** not / first choice **9** at ease / short time **10** communication easy **11** printed information / unhelpful **12** too busy **13** random choice **14** repeat **15** go back home

4 **1** F **2** B **3** E **4** A **5** B **6** C **7** A **8** E **9** D **10** B **11** D **12** C **13** D **14** F **15** A

Grammar

Modal verbs expressing ability, possibility and obligation

1 1&2 **b** possibility, any time **c** obligation, past **d** obligation, past **e** ability, present **f** ability, past

2 2 **a** I didn't worry. **b** I worried but it wasn't necessary. 3 **a** It isn't necessary for you to go to the lecture. **b** You are prohibited from going to the lecture. 4 **a** *incorrect* (We cannot use the affirmative *could* [ability] to refer to a single occasion in the past.) **b** *correct* (We use *managed to / succeeded in + -ing* or *was able to* to refer to single occasions.) 5 **a** It is possible for him to stay, and it is certain or quite likely that he will stay. **b** It would be possible, but it is not certain that he will stay. 6 **a** *correct* **b** *incorrect* (We do not use *could not* to refer to a future possibility.)

3 2 ~~needn't to~~ needn't **3** ~~need do~~ need to do **4** ~~could~~ can (this is a definite offer – *could* would suggest that the offer was conditional) **5** ~~we afford~~ we can afford **6** ~~can't~~ couldn't

Vocabulary

Chance, occasion, opportunity and possibility

1 2 occasions **3** opportunity **4** possibility **5** occasion **6** possibility

2 1 *Alternative answer*: opportunity **2** opportunity **3** possibility **4** chance **5** opportunity / chance **6** possibility / chance **7** occasion **8** chance / possibility

Listening Part 2

The alternatives in brackets are possible but they do not conform to the suggested number of words.

5 2 colloquial Egyptian dialect (Arabic) **3** unmarried mixed **4** culture shock **5** shops and cafés (cafés) **6** bargain with **7** dissimilar forms **8** country club

---

Recording script CD2 Track 12

Presenter: In today's programme, we're going to hear about the experiences of a British student who is spending a year studying in Egypt. Amy, could you tell us what your life is like in Egypt?

Amy: Well, I wake up at about 3 am when a man wearing a grey, floor-length galabiyya marches down the street, banging a small drum and calling to people to wake up for the meal they eat before they start fasting at dawn. It's Ramadan at the moment. Four hours later, my electronic alarm goes off and I roll out of bed. I dress carefully, ensuring that my legs, stomach and shoulders are covered despite the heat. Three friends and I have travelled to the Alexandria Centre for Languages for an Arabic course as part of our degree course at Bristol University. In our first year at Bristol we were offered the choice of several modern languages. Persian, Turkish and Arabic were available, but I was charmed by the Arabic

Q1 lecturer who had a huge smile and a <u>real passion for</u> his subject. As the course developed, so did my fascination with Arabic, its different alphabet – and the culture. I researched the possibility of studying in a Middle Eastern country. In the end we settled on Alexandria: the city has a lively cultural

Q2 scene, and its <u>colloquial Egyptian dialect</u> is the most widely understood throughout the Arab World. We arrived in September and got to our hotel at about 10 pm. Unfortunately, the staff were nervous about letting us stay, as we were

Q3 an <u>unmarried, mixed</u> group. We eventually found another hotel, where we bartered for the price of rooms. We spent the next few days settling in and getting to know the city. Then our course leader arranged flats for us to look around. We chose a light, spacious flat, with a friendly and helpful landlady. It's much better than I was used to in Bristol. It was a

Q4 fascinating time for us, but the <u>culture shock</u> was so great that within the first week one of our group returned home. The area around the

Q5 language centre is crowded with <u>shops and cafés</u>, where people sit and drink tea. We usually have lunch at the centre: small flatbreads stuffed with falafel or beans; or large circular pieces of bread, filled with strips of beef and pieces of cheese. We have two teachers. Rania is a young woman who wears a hijab that always matches her jeans. In her lessons we learn how to greet, congratulate and explain why we are in Alexandria. Ingy is more liberally dressed: jeans, short sleeves, no hijab. With her, we do role plays where

Q6 we bargain with taxi drivers, buy groceries or haggle for gold at the jeweller's. The teachers seem unaffected by the pressures of Ramadan. They teach for 4½ hours a day, Sunday to Thursday, with no food or water from sunrise until sunset. One of the most difficult challenges in learning Arabic is that it has

Q7 two dissimilar forms. Alongside 'amiyya, the colloquial dialect, is fusha, which dominates the media and written forms of Arabic, including the Qur'an. Although they share some vocabulary, it's like learning two languages alongside each other.

Q8 At weekends we relax at the Acacia Country Club, where membership costs £10 a month, and lie by the pool, where dress rules are more relaxed. In the evenings we sit in cafés by the sea and smoke apple sheesha. I'm writing my dissertation at the Bibliotheca Alexandrina. Its exterior is covered with characters from every alphabet in the world, symbolic of the array of knowledge that was once contained in the old library and of what will be contained in the new one. Soon the crescent moon will signal the end of Ramadan, and Egypt will show us another face.

Use of English Part 1

1 **2** four **3** ten **4** before

2 *Suggested answers*: *lifelong learning*: learning that can take place at any time during a person's life, learning not limited to years of formal/compulsory education; *retraining*: learning how to do a different job; *to upgrade (your) skills*: to improve how good you are at doing something, to learn new, higher-level, more up-to-date skills

5 **1** A **2** B **3** B **4** D **5** B **6** D **7** C **8** C **9** D **10** C **11** D **12** A

Speaking Part 3

3 **1** In general, both speakers meet the criteria listed, but the woman is better at keeping the conversation flowing and expressing opinions. The man tends either to react to what the woman has said or simply to describe a new photo. There is not much scope for students to make suggestions or speculate in relation to this particular task. **2** Their range of vocabulary meets the task requirements.

Recording script   CD2 Track 13

Woman:	OK, the first picture is obviously a classroom – someone working on an interactive whiteboard. Do you think that's a good way to learn?
Man:	It's probably quite a good way to learn, yeah. And the next picture's of a student and of someone, not sure who, in a sort of one-to-one learning session which would probably be quite good for learning some things.
Woman:	Yeah, it's not really a group environment, though, not like the …
Man:	Probably not good for learning a language …
Woman:	The next one is kids all sat in a classroom. I suppose it'd be quite interactive – you could learn together, but …
Man:	Yeah, the next one's someone on a computer – probably learning stuff off the net, which again probably wouldn't be a good way to learn a language – wouldn't be able to, you know, talk much.
Woman:	No … The next one I think is a group of girls just talking and writing on clipboards.
Man:	Talking to people, perhaps, …
Woman:	Yes, that'd probably be a good way to learn a language.
Man:	Conversation.
Woman:	And being outdoors and seeing things.
Man:	And finally there's a lecture theatre with a big screen at the front and a guy giving a talk on a podium by the looks of it.
Woman:	So, which one do you reckon would be the best?
Man:	Probably the first one or …
Woman:	I don't know, though, because you wouldn't get much one-to-one, would you?

Man:	Mmm.
Woman:	I think it would be the one outside just walking around talking to people ... Which one shall we go for?
Man:	Well, I'll go for that one as well, then.
Woman:	OK – the field trip.

4 & **5** **1** which would probably be *quite good* for learning *some things*. **2** the next one's *someone* on a computer – probably learning *stuff* off the net, which again probably wouldn't be *a good way to learn* a language. **3** M: *Talking to* people, perhaps. / W: Yes, that'd probably be a good way to learn a language. / M: *Conversation*.

Writing Part 1 A report

1 *Suggested answers*: **1** Introduction, Computers, Accommodation and other facilities, Car parking, Conclusions and recommendations **2** Both students and staff commented on access to computers and problems with the canteen. Both staff and visitors commented on parking facilities.

2 *Suggested answers*: **2** The provision of computers / Access to computers **3** The canteen **4** Car parking facilities / Car parks **5** Other suggestions **6** Conclusions and recommendations

3 **1** *recommend* + noun phrase (Staff ... recommended a reduction); *(would) recommend* + *-ing* (I would recommend implementing all the suggestions); *suggest* + noun phrase (to suggest ways in which ...); *suggest that* + clause with subjunctive verb (Students suggested that the gym ... be enlarged); *(would) suggest that* + clause with *should* (I would suggest that drivers should make alternative arrangements) **2** commented on, felt strongly that, expressed the view that, did not mention, suggested that **3** would welcome, would appreciate, would be grateful for

4 *Suggested answers*: **1** The college principal and perhaps other senior managers **2** No – comments in emails will be regarded as speech, so in the report will be turned into quite formal reported speech. **3** Four: Introduction / The issue, Information and publicity, Incentives, Conclusions and recommendations

Vocabulary and grammar review   Unit 9

Vocabulary

1 **2** action **3** activity **4** programme **5** events **6** event **7** action **8** programme

2 **1** cover **2** place **3** tough **4** pointing **5** steady

Grammar

3 **2** is working **3** was **4** has been working **5** I'm having **6** was working **7** had arrived **8** played

Vocabulary and grammar review   Unit 10

Vocabulary

1 **2** last **3** historic **4** slight **5** miss, golden **6** real **7** solemn **8** second

2 **1** fast **2** pass **3** settle

Grammar

3 **2** must, didn't have to / didn't need to **3** must, have to / need to **4** needn't / don't need to / don't have to **5** mustn't, have to **6** need to / must / have to

4 **2** *correct* **3** ~~could~~ can **4** ~~could~~ managed to pass/ ~~could pass~~ succeeded in passing **5** ~~be able to~~ / ~~could~~ would

11 Being somewhere else

Listening Part 1

1 2 different themes   3 A, B, or C, twice
4 read the questions and underline the key ideas
5 listen to the whole extract before making your choices

3 **Extract One** dull, if I were you, miserable
Extract Two call off, put off, pay up
Extract Three wrap up, walking over rough ground, quite unpleasant otherwise

4 1 B   2 A   3 A   4 B   5 C   6 C

Recording script   CD2 Track 14

Extract One

Woman: It'll be getting dark soon, won't it? What about over there? That looks quite a good place to stop and camp for the night, doesn't it?

Man: Maybe.

Woman: Very peaceful.

Man:
Q1 I doubt if it'll be that. If I'd known about the mosquitoes, I'd never have come. <u>I was expecting excitement and rapids and spectacular landscapes and all we're getting is bitten on a flat river surrounded by dull little trees – and the mountains are miles away!</u> It's not as if we had to come here. There were lots of other places we could have gone.

Woman:
Q2 Come on, Don. It's not so bad. <u>If I were you, I'd put some insect repellent on right away, just like I've done,</u> and then they won't bite you. And if you'd just stop griping for a while, perhaps we'd start enjoying ourselves a bit. Just think about how quiet and peaceful it all is and what a lovely rest from city life!

Man: Rest! If we'd stayed at home, I'd be resting in front of the telly right now, instead of paddling up this miserable river.

Woman: Don!

Extract Two

Man 1: So, what will we do if the weather turns bad? Just carry on, or do you think we'd have to call things off?

Man 2: Call things off? No way! Not after all the preparations we've made. Look, we're taking wet-weather gear and we've got good warm waterproof sleeping bags. <u>I mean, if things look really bad, we can always put things off for a few days and start a bit later</u>.
Q3

Man 1: OK, but we're not really going at the best time of year, you know. North-west Spain in winter can be pretty icy.

Man 2: Of course, but that's all part of it, isn't it? I mean, we've committed ourselves to this thing, so <u>we've got to get there or else we'll never live it down. I'm sure we'll make it, I mean, our names will be dirt with all our sponsors if we don't.</u> And a little hardship never hurt anyone. It's good for you!
Q4

Man 1: Still, I imagine they'd pay up anyway even if we didn't get there, don't you?

Extract Three

Interviewer: So, Kate, in your book *Lesser Known Egypt* you recommend all sorts of exciting and interesting places off the beaten tourist track.

Kate: Yes, and for the really intrepid tourist none of them is at all difficult to get to.

Interviewer: Right.

Kate: All you need is a little bit of planning in advance and even that's easy if you use my book.

Interviewer: You suggest people should go in the winter when the heat is not so overwhelming, don't you?

Kate: Exactly, and it can even get quite chilly at night, so you might need something warm to wrap up in. Mind you, in the daytime you'll find it's almost always sunny. You have to do quite a lot of walking over rough ground in the desert, and of course there's no shade, so <u>I never went out without something to cover my head</u> or I'd have got quite sunburnt. I'd strongly advise other people to do the same.
Q5

Interviewer: And what was the most enjoyable thing you found about travelling around Egypt on your own?

Kate:	*Q6*	<u>Without a doubt the people I travelled with. It could all have been quite unpleasant otherwise</u>, you know, waiting for buses in dusty villages and so on, but I found everyone so kind. You know, they'd make conversation, invite me to coffee and really help me to get to know the country. Otherwise I wouldn't have enjoyed things nearly so much. As it was, I felt that I wanted the journey to go on forever.
Interviewer:		Fantastic.
Kate:		Yes, indeed.

Grammar
Conditionals

❶ *Suggested answers*: **5** and **6** are both 1st conditional, **4** and **7** are both 2nd conditional, **2** and **3** are both 2nd conditional, used to try to persuade the listener to do something (in **2** by giving advice, in **3** by complaining about the listener's behaviour). **4** is a mixed 2nd and 3rd conditional, **3** and **4** refer to things which are not happening in the present but which the speaker would like to be happening, **1**, **4**, **8** and **9** all talk about the past or make a reference to it, **5**, **6** and **7** all refer to future possibilities and what might happen if they occur, **5** and **7** both ask for an opinion about a future possibility. **10** is not conditional – it uses *would* to talk about past habit.

❷ **2** wasn't / weren't rushing, would be   **3** wasn't/ weren't, would probably have reached / probably would have reached   **4** would try, was/were, would have   **5** were, would carry   **6** wouldn't have happened, had been concentrating / had concentrated   **7** would ever abandon, was/were travelling   **8** would like, will show

❸ **2** ~~send~~ would send   **3** (possibly) ~~will not~~ do not, ~~am~~ will be   **4** ~~stand~~ be standing   **5** ~~won't~~ wouldn't **6** ~~would~~ will   **7** ~~will~~ would   **8** ~~have travelled~~ travel

Speaking Part 1

❶ *Suggested answer*: All except 3 and 7.

❷ **1** *Thea*: 6 *Archie*: 4 *Nina*: 1 or 8   **2** Thea and Nina **3** No, because sometimes they're describing reality rather than an imagined situation or event. **4** Nina – wonderful, such a lovely area, fabulous, great, I'd really love that, the chance of a lifetime. She also shows enthusiasm through her intonation. **5** They use their own vocabulary – this shows range of vocabulary, knowledge of synonyms, understanding of the question, confidence with English.

Recording script   CD2 Track 15

Thea:	Well, it depends where to. I'm certainly not afraid of taking risks for a bit of excitement and I get a real buzz from a bit of danger. But it would have to be a journey to somewhere interesting, somewhere that was worth visiting. I wouldn't want to do it just for the excitement.
Archie:	Well, it certainly helps with the day-to-day problems like buying tickets, getting information and so on. But I'd say it's generally better to try to speak the local language if you can, because then you can get to know people, talk to them on their own terms and that's when real communication starts happening. On the other hand, you can't learn the language of every country you want to visit, and in those cases English is definitely better than nothing.
Nina:	Normally I go to the Scottish Highlands for a couple of weeks in the summer, which is wonderful, it's such a lovely area, but the chance to go further afield and have some completely different experiences, well, for example to spend two or three months travelling round Africa, would be fabulous. It'd be great to see some of those places you only normally see on television, for example the Ngorongoro Crater or the Kruger National Park. I'd really love that. It'd be the chance of a lifetime!

Reading Part 3

❶ **2** F – you have about 18 minutes.   **3** T   **4** T **5** F – there must be evidence in the text to support your choice.

❸ *Any or all of these reasons*: to disappear, to break out of his predictable routine, to be inaccessible / unobtainable / out of touch; also for pleasure, for untold tales, hope, comedy and sweetness, to wander the hinterland, for revenge for being kept waiting, to get away from domestic life and modern technology, in the spirit of discovery

❹ **1** A   **2** D   **3** A   **4** C   **5** B   **6** D   **7** C

Vocabulary
At, in and on to express location

1 **2** in   **3** on, at, in   **4** at, at   **5** at   **6** in   **7** on

2 **b** on (7)   **c** on (3)   **d** in (1, 2, 6)

3 **2** at on   **3** of in   **4** at in   **5** at on   **6** at on
7 at in   **8** in on   **9** at on   **10** to in

Use of English Part 2

1 **2** 12   **3** 'grammar'   **4** general idea   **5** before
and after   **6** every question   **7** spelled   **8** the
completed text   **9** makes sense

3 **1** They tried *Googling* it on the Internet, but they
finally found it through an island broker.
2 To avoid what had happened to other Fijian
islands, i.e. hotel complexes and marinas.

4 **1** for   **2** on   **3** go/set   **4** else   **5** all   **6** whose
7 until   **8** who   **9** enough   **10** have/take   **11** soon
12 One   **13** had   **14** what   **15** a

Writing Part 2 A contribution to a longer piece

1 **1** No   **2** local places of interest for a college
information booklet – types of places and what
to see there, things to take with you (e.g. special
clothing), advice about the best time to visit,
etc.   **3** students from other countries
4 informal, personal

5 **1** Yes   **2** *Old Sarum*: binoculars and a warm
jacket; *Wilton House*: a picnic   **3** It's divided into
sections with a short introduction.   **4** The reader is
addressed as *you*.   **5** *Suggested answers*: use of *you*,
contractions, choice of vocabulary, e.g. *spot* instead
of *location*, *pick* instead of *choose*, use of informal
punctuation such as exclamation marks
6 *Students should underline*: well worth,
spectacular, unusual, atmospheric, great, superb,
splendid, grandest, amazing, attractive, world-
famous, excellent, reasonably priced

12 The living world

Starting off

1 **1** A and F
2 *Suggested answers*: **A** green energy / alternative
sources of energy / greenhouse gases **B** animal
conservation / protection of endangered species
C effects of pollution on human health **D** pollution
/ greenhouse gases / global warming **E** energy
conservation **F** climate change / global warming
3 A and B

Reading Part 2

1 **2** is one   **3** synonyms   **4** gapped text

3 **1**   1 The article does not explain exactly how
parrots learn, but does give these suggestions
for why parrots have the ability to speak: their
intelligence has evolved, they can 'vocalise' words,
they live a long time so have time to learn.
2 Yes – see paragraph 6.   3 No others are
mentioned (primates, e.g. chimpanzees, can
communicate but can't speak).   **2** The photos show
the parrot choosing letters / communicating with
Dr Pepperberg.

4 **1** D   **2** G   **3** C   **4** E   **5** A   **6** B

Vocabulary
Word formation

1 apology; communication, communicator;
conclusion; description; performance, performer;
prosperity; suspect, suspicion

2 assume, behave, combine, evolve, explain, respond

3 *Suggested answers*: They say the price of oil is going
to in'crease. / There was a significant 'increase in
annual rainfall last year. Many countries ex'port
goods to other countries. / There was a fall in the
value of our 'exports last year. If students do well
in the test, they can pro'gress to the next level. /
I think I'm making good 'progress. The chief of
police expects people to re'bel against the recent
rise in taxes. / He's always been a bit of a 'rebel,
even when he was a small child.

Grammar
Nouns and articles

1 *singular countable nouns*: elephant, plant
plural countable nouns: trees, elephants, years
uncountable nouns: bark, skin, tissue *uncountable nouns that could be countable in other contexts*:
skin, tissue (*a skin* = the whole covering of an animal (also known as *a pelt*), especially when it is used for something when the animal is dead; *a tissue* = a paper handkerchief) *proper nouns (names)*: Africa, Earth

2 1 **a** part of a bar of chocolate, **b** a small individual chocolate – probably from a box   2 **a** meat from a chicken, **b** the birds themselves   3 **a** the taste or the drink in general, **b** a cup of coffee
4 **a** mass of hair, **b** a single strand of hair
5 **a** the substance, **b** different types of cheese

3 2 a   3 a   4 a   5 ø, ø, ø   6 the   7 a   8 the

4 (*The numbers 1–8 refer to the sentences in Exercise 3.*)   1 1b   2 2a   3 2d   4 2c   5 3b, 3b, 3a   6 1a
7 2b   8 1d

5 2 a   3 the   4 a   5 ø   6 the   7 the   8 ø (grass in general) *or* the (particular grass which was near a cliff)   9 a   10 a   11 The (the particular experts already referred to) *or* ø (experts in general)
12 the   13 the   14 ø   15 the   16 ø   17 ø (any tigers / tigers in general) *or* the (the particular tigers that this article is about)   18 ø   19 the (the species) *or* a (a single specimen of the species)
20 an

6 2 You should get *the / a* job even though you haven't got ~~the~~ *a* degree in marketing.   3 This report aims to describe *the* advantages and *(the)* disadvantages of green taxes.   4 Students can access *the* Internet in their classrooms and *the* college library.   5 Society needs to provide affordable accommodation for *the* homeless.
6 ~~A~~ *The* most important thing is to get people talking about the issues.   7 Tokyo is ~~a~~ *the* capital of Japan.   8 Nowadays ~~the~~ technology is everywhere.

Listening Part 2

1 2 F – no more than three words will be missing from each sentence.   3 T   4 T

3 1 *Students' own answers*   2 *Resources for food*: aquatic mammals such as seals, walruses, and whales *Other resources*: stone (for houses), wood, animal skins, snow   3 *Student's own answers*

5 2 (physical) changes   3 (daily) weather markers / messages / signs   4 robin   5 (strong) scientific evidence   6 coastlines   7 traditional knowledge
8 adapt

Q2 phenomena in our daily lives? The Inuit, however, are being affected in a very real way, on a daily basis by a frightening array of physical <u>changes</u> they see and feel around them. They see icebergs melting, tides changing, and notice the thinning of the

Q3 polar bear population. They see how the daily <u>weather markers</u> on which they have relied for thousands of years are becoming less predictable as their fragile climate changes. In the past, if there was a ring around the moon, it meant a change of weather in the next few days – it was one of nature's messages to the Inuit hunters. Now such signs mean nothing. But these are just the most immediately visible signs of the changes taking place. Talk to the Inuit elders and hunters who depend on the land and you will hear disturbing accounts of deformed fish, diseased caribou, and baby seals left by their mothers to starve. In the last

Q4 year or so, <u>robins</u> have appeared where robins have never been seen before. Interestingly, there is no word for 'robin' in the Inuit language.

These feelings are not simply based on Inuit superstition; there is increasingly strong

Q5 <u>scientific evidence</u> that the Arctic, this desert of snow, ice and killing cold wind, is thawing.

Q6 Glaciers are receding; <u>coastlines</u> are eroding; lakes are disappearing. Autumn freezes are coming later and the winters are not as cold. For years, what the Inuit elders and hunters understood about the Arctic climate, known

Q7 as '<u>traditional knowledge</u>', was largely disregarded by the Western world. It was often dismissed as anecdotal and unreliable by scientists who visited the area with their recording devices, and their theories. Some even viewed the Inuit as ignorant about a land which they have inhabited for thousands of years. But more recently, scientists have begun paying attention to what the Inuit are reporting. According to geophysicist George Hobson, traditional Inuit knowledge was just waiting to be passed down. He says this deep knowledge and understanding of the land and its wildlife have enabled the Inuit people to survive in the harsh Arctic environment. For thousands of years, the Inuit have lived by rules that require them to respect animals and the land. They have adapted to the cold climate as they hunted seals, walruses and whales. Siloah

Atagoojuk, an elderly Inuit woman who lives in the city of Iqaluit, does not want to pretend she knows more than anyone else – nor does she try to blame anyone for the change in her environment. She is simply worried. Her world is not as it used to be and her people may not

Q8 be able to <u>adapt</u> to it. She says that the Inuit have known all along that there would be a time when the Earth would be destroyed or would destroy itself. She believes that this process has begun.

I believe that it is now up to our governments to show Siloah and her people that we can slow or even reverse this process.

Vocabulary
Prepositions following verbs

① 2 on   3 on   4 into   5 to   6 for

② 2 ~~in~~ on   3 ~~on~~ in   4 ~~in~~ on   5 ~~in~~ on   6 ~~with~~ to
7 ~~in~~ on   8 ~~for~~ to

Speaking Part 3

① 2 set of pictures   3 three minutes   4 more
5 need not

② 1 *photo 1*: forest fires *photo 2*: drought conditions
photo 3: flood damage *photo 4*: air pollution
photo 5: rainforest clearance *photo 6*: fossil fuel consumption
2 *Suggested answers*: *forest fires*: arson, carelessness, discarded cigarettes; *drought conditions*: global warming, burning of fossil fuels; *flood damage*: climate change, global warming; *air pollution*: vehicle exhaust fumes, heavy industry, factory emissions; *rainforest clearance*: wood used for timber, land used for grazing animals; *fossil fuel consumption*: population growth, increase in number of vehicles

③ 1 They mention some effects of forest fires, drought, air pollution and fossil fuel consumption, but not of floods or rainforest clearance. (Rainforest clearance is not mentioned at all.)   2 They do not decide which threat poses the greatest risk. The male speaker mentions drought and air pollution; the woman mentions drought, flood and finding an alternative to fossil fuel.

Recording script   CD2 Track 18

Woman: Well, this one's quite relevant because it's been in the news recently – it's forest fires over in the States, and I think it shows the threat of global warming – which is going to be a big problem. What do you think?

Man: You've also got flood damage which is something that we're seeing now, in different parts of the world.

Woman: That's true.

Man: And the opposite, of course – drought conditions as well.

Woman: Well, that used to just be in Africa but I think these days we're more worried about it in Europe – I mean, do you remember that thing a few years ago when all those people died in the heatwave?

Man: That's very true, yeah. What about air pollution as well, which is obviously on the minds of many politicians at the moment, but that's going to affect us perhaps more in the long term than now.

Woman: Well it already does, doesn't it? Think about how many more people there are now with allergies and skin problems.

Man: Very true – and fossil fuel consumption, erm …

Woman: The price of oil these days …

Man: And the global tension that that's causing as well.

Woman: True – that's very worrying. So, which one do you think is going to be the biggest threat?

Man: I think it's going to be drought conditions in the short term and air pollution perhaps in the longer term.

Woman: Do you think so? You could be right. Maybe either drought or floods – one of the two related to climate change. And I think we really do need to find an alternative to oil – that's going to be a real problem.

Use of English Part 3

① **2** F – it tests knowledge of vocabulary and word-building. **3** T **4** F – adding a prefix does not change the spelling, but adding a suffix often does.

② *Suggested answers*: **help** *nouns*: help, helper, helpfulness, helplessness; *verb*: help; *adjectives*: helpful, unhelpful, helpless; *adverbs*: helpfully, unhelpfully, helplessly **know** *noun*: knowledge; *verb*: know; *adjectives*: knowledgeable, knowing, unknowing, unknown, unknowable; *adverbs*: knowledgeably, knowingly, unknowingly **move** *nouns*: move, movement, removal, *verbs*: move, remove; *adjectives*: moving, unmoved, movable, immovable; *adverbs*: movingly, movably, immovably **nation** *nouns*: nation, nationality, nationalist, nationhood; *verbs*: nationalise, denationalise, renationalise; *adjectives*: national, international, multinational; *adverbs*: nationally, internationally

③ **1** finding **2** extinctions **3** disappearance **4** environmentalists **5** creatures **6** clearance(s) **7** determination **8** national **9** reduction **10** currently

④ *Suggested answers*: **1** *Students' own answers* **2** Set up conservation areas to protect natural habitats, breeding areas and sources of food; prevent further destruction of natural habitat; give legal protection to animal species by outlawing hunting; keep breeding pairs in zoos.

Writing Part 2 An information sheet

② **1** Yes, yes **2** Yes

③ **1** present simple **2** imperatives

④ **1** the fact that the college uses four times as much computer paper as it did two years ago **2** information **3** the college we work at **4** the fact that some students and staff are making unnecessary journeys by car and motorbike **5** printing out documents **6** lights and electrical equipment
Words like this are used to avoid repetition of nouns/verbs, etc. and to link sentences / parts of sentences.

Vocabulary and grammar review   Unit 11

Vocabulary

1 2 call … up   3 stick around   4 called off
5 drop out   6 put off   7 wrap up   8 pay up

2 2 out of touch   3 kept waiting   4 sick and tired of
5 the whole point of   6 without a trace   7 get your
hands on

3 2 at   3 in, at   4 on   5 at/in, on   6 on

Grammar

4 2 If Nelson *had arrived on/in time for* his job
interview, he would have got the job.
3 Veronique knows that if her computer skills *were
better, she could have applied* for the job in IT.
4 I *would be (most/very/extremely/sincerely)
grateful if you* would refund my money as soon
as possible.
5 If it *had not been for Bruno's advice*, we would
have gone swimming.

Vocabulary and grammar review   Unit 12

Vocabulary

1 2 environmental   3 disabilities   4 knowledge
5 appearance   6 creatively   7 clarify
8 movement

2 2 ~~to~~ on   3 ~~in~~ to   4 *correct*   5 ~~for~~ to   6 ~~for~~ on
7 ~~to~~ on   8 *correct*

Grammar

3 2 an   3 ø   4 the   5 The   6 the   7 the   8 a

4 2 the   3 ø   4 the   5 the   6 the   7 the   8 ø
9 the   10 the   11 ø   12 the / ø   13 the

13   Health and lifestyle

Starting off

Suggested answers: **1 Sport, etc.** *Advantages*: keeps
you physically fit, helps keep heart and lungs healthy,
helps prevent obesity *Disadvantages*: time-consuming,
not everyone enjoys sport   **Vaccination** *Advantage*:
prevents childhood diseases *Disadvantage*: some
vaccinations may cause illness in a minority   **Rural
area** *Advantages*: clean air and environment, less
stressful life, less traffic *Disadvantages*: too quiet,
fewer facilities, less entertainment   **City life**
Advantages: many facilities, more work, plenty
of entertainment *Disadvantages*: pollution, poor
environment, often stressful **2 & 3** *Students' own
answers*

Listening   Part 3

1 2 four   3 six   4 four   5 ideas

4 1 Yes – there is a year-on-year increase in the
number of patients visiting their doctor with
asthma and various food allergies.   2 20%–30%
of the population of Britain and the USA   3 air-
conditioning and central heating, more and more
people work in offices, dust and mould, vehicle
exhaust, modern obsession with cleanliness,
childhood vaccinations

5 1 B   2 C   3 C   4 D   5 A   6 B

Recording script   CD2 Track 19

Presenter: These days we're all too familiar with the word
allergy and phrases like 'I'm allergic to pollen
or eggs or cats'. There's a general perception
too that more people have allergies than in the
past. Is this because the subject is getting

Q1 more exposure in the media, or <u>are we really
becoming less resistant to allergens</u>? These
are just some of the questions we'll be tackling
in today's phone-in programme. In the studio
with me today are Dr Mary Egerton, a family
doctor, and allergy specialist Dr Mohamed
Bawadi to answer your questions. Our first
caller today is Tim from Edinburgh. Tim, what's
your question?

Tim: Hi, right, well, I suffer from hay fever, you know – I'm very allergic to grass and the pollen from certain trees – especially in the spring. The really peculiar thing is that my allergy didn't begin until I was in my mid-thirties. What I **Q2** want to know is, why did I start so late, and <u>do you think my allergy could disappear again just as suddenly, or am I stuck with it now?</u>

Presenter: Dr Egerton, would you like to answer Tim first?

Mary Egerton: Hello, Tim. Your story is a very common one. The fact is that allergies do not discriminate – they're just as likely to affect the old as they are the young. I'm afraid <u>they **Q3** can develop at any time of life from one day to 60 years and beyond</u>. As to whether you're stuck with your allergy, that depends. The best way to treat any allergy is to avoid contact with whatever causes the allergic reaction. Someone who was allergic to eggs would find it fairly easy to avoid eating anything containing eggs, whereas you would find it impossible to avoid all contact with grass and pollen unless you lived in a desert area or high in a mountain range.

Mohamed Bawadi: Can I just add to what Mary has said? There is now evidence from research around the world that the most common age to develop an allergy is in your late teens, so you've not done too badly, Tim.

Presenter: Our next caller is Arabella from Amsterdam in the Netherlands. What's your question, Arabella?

Arabella: Hello. I'm allergic to peanuts – so of course I've got to be really careful about foods which **Q4** contain even small traces of peanuts, but <u>what I'd like to know is whether I'm likely to pass these allergies on to any children I may have in the future.</u>

Presenter: Thank you. Dr Bawadi?

Mohamed Bawadi: Hello, Arabella. This is an interesting question. In developed countries all children have a twelve per cent risk of developing an allergy. In your case this would rise to a twenty per cent risk. However, if the child's father also had an allergy of some kind, this risk would increase to forty per cent.

Arabella: <u>So, what about if the father and the **Q5** mother have the same allergy?</u>

Mohamed Bawadi: <u>Then, I'm afraid there's a seventy per cent chance that the child will develop that allergy.</u>

Presenter: Thank you, Arabella. I hope that answers your question. Just before we move on to the next caller, can I ask you both whether we are in fact seeing a higher incidence of allergies in the population than in the past?

Mary Egerton: We most certainly are. Even though we're getting better at diagnosing and treating some allergies, there is a year-on-year increase in the number of patients visiting their doctor with asthma and various food allergies. Recent research has shown that in Britain and the USA, between twenty and thirty per cent of the population suffer from some kind of allergy.

Presenter: Why is this happening, Dr Bawadi?

Mohamed Bawadi: Well, it's a complex problem. There are many theories about why more people are affected by allergies. Certain aspects of modern living are blamed by some experts. For example, the widespread use of air-conditioning and central heating, combined with the fact that more and more people now work in offices, is thought to have led to an increase in allergic reactions to dust and **Q6** mould. <u>Vehicle exhaust fumes are widely regarded as being responsible for the increase in asthma in young children</u>. You only have to walk through the streets of a large modern city to understand the strength of that argument. Some experts blame our modern culture for being obsessed with cleanliness, while others believe that vaccinations to protect our children from certain diseases may actually weaken their immune system and make them less resistant to allergens.

Presenter: Thank you, that's very interesting. Let's move on, we have several people waiting on the phone-in line. Let's speak to …

Vocabulary
Prepositions after adjectives

① **2** to   **3** to   **4** at   **5** for   **6** with

② **2** *correct*   **3** ~~for~~ in   **4** ~~to~~ for   **5** ~~for~~ to
6 ~~for~~ to (visitors)

Grammar
Ways of contrasting ideas

1 2 but   3 However   4 Even though   5 while

2 1 but, Even though, while   2 but   3 However
4 *Suggested answers*: although, though, despite /
in spite of (the fact that), (and) yet, Nevertheless,
Even so, All the same, Still, On the other hand
5 *Instead of 'whereas' in 1*: but; *Instead of 'Even
though' in 4*: Although

3 2 but   3 whereas/but   4 However   5 Although /
Even though

4 *Sentences 1 and 5*:   1 I recognised you as soon as I
saw you *in spite of / despite* the fact we'd never met
before. / I recognised you as soon as I saw you *in
spite of / despite* (my) never having met you before.
5 *In spite of / Despite* the fact that I've been here
twice before, I'd forgotten where the post office
was. / *In spite of / Despite* having been here twice
before, I'd forgotten where the post office was.

5 2 ~~however~~, but / However,   3 ~~however~~ even
though / although / despite the fact that
4 ~~Though~~ However,   5 ~~where~~ whereas
6 ~~While~~ Although / Even though / Despite the fact
that

Speaking Part 2

1 2 T   3 F – Correct a mistake if you make one.   4 T

2 1 They are all physical activities which people do
to keep fit.   2 *Students' own answers*

5 *Suggested answers*: 1 The woman fulfils the
requirements of the given task better than the man,
but although she talks coherently about why the
activities are popular, she doesn't say how effective
they are. She talks about her own personal
preferences, which are irrelevant here as they are
not part of the task. The man talks about all three
activities instead of selecting two. He doesn't fulfil
the requirements of either part of the task he is set,
although he does say a little about the qualities
needed for rock-climbing. Like the woman, he
talks about his own personal preferences instead of
saying why people participate in the activities.
2 *Advice to the woman*: Listen carefully to what you
are asked to do. Don't be sidetracked into talking
about yourself. *Advice to the man*: Select two of the
photos to talk about. Listen carefully to what you
are asked to do. Think for a few seconds before you
start to talk. Once you have started talking, try not
to pause too often.

Reading Part 4

1 2 sometimes   3 eighteen   4 questions or
statements

2 1 1 hurling   2 tossing the caber   3 polo   4 judo
2 1 outdoor / team / for men (there is a similar
game for women called *camogie*) / Ireland
2 outdoor / individual / for men / Scotland
3 outdoor / team / for men and women /
international   4 indoor / individual / for men
and women / international

3 Students' own answers

❸ Students should underline: **2** use of an animal
3 traditional native sport **4** use their bodies to
obstruct **5** protective equipment optional
6 eight players **7** disapproves of players
looking **8** funding from business **9** increasing in
popularity **10** not played all the year **11** three
quarters of an hour **12** pleasure and relaxation
13 ball / picked up easily **14** flat circular objects
15 holding / clothing

❺ **1** B **2** C **3** E **4** D **5** B **6** C **7** A **8** E **9** D
10 D **11** C **12** A **13** C **14** E **15** A

Grammar
The language of comparison

❶ *Comparative adjectives and adverbs*: more violent
versions, further than three steps, a more ancient
version; *Superlative adjectives*: the most widespread
version, the fastest-growing sports; *Comparative/
Superlative form + noun*: Fewer points, no more
than four steps, the most goals, more goals, more
explosions, Most teams

❷ **1** nouns, long adjectives, adverbs **2** *Less* can be
an adverb (e.g. *People smoke less than they used
to.*) and may be followed by an adjective or another
adverb (e.g. *He's less practical than his brother. She
works less efficiently than her sister.*). *Less* can also
be a determiner followed by an uncountable noun
(e.g. *We have less money than we thought.*). *Fewer* is
a determiner and is followed by a plural noun (e.g.
These days fewer people smoke than in the past.).
3 carried for no more than four steps = ... up to
four steps

❸ **2** Finding a new job was less difficult than / not as
difficult as I expected it to be. **3** There are fewer
unemployed people now than there were ten years
ago. / Fewer people are unemployed now than ten
years ago. **4** Working conditions are not as/so
good as they used to be. **5** More people are going
abroad to find work.

❹ **2** ~~worst~~ worse **3** ~~that~~ than **4** ~~less~~ fewer
5 ~~harder~~ hardest **6** ~~countries less industrialised~~
less industrialised countries **7** ~~fewer~~ less
8 ~~difficult even more~~ even more difficult

Use of English Part 4

❶ **2** three **3** always **4** can't

❷ *Suggested answers*: **Adjectives** – *bright*: strong
(light/colour), intelligent, happy; *fair*: just (honest/
right), pale (opposite of dark), average (not good,
not bad), quite large, probable (e.g. a fair idea),
pleasant (weather)
Nouns – *character*: letter of the alphabet,
personality, person in a novel, film or play; *class*:
school group, lesson, social group, type, refinement
(style)
Verbs – *catch*: contract (a disease), hold on to (a
ball), not miss (a train), trap (an animal), capture
(a person, e.g. a criminal), surprise (someone in
the process of doing something wrong), manage
to hear (something that is said); *present*: give (an
award, a gift, etc.), offer (apologies, compliments),
show or display, put (something) forward
for official consideration, formally introduce
(someone), bring (a play or film, etc.) to the public

❸ **a** 3 **b** 1 **c** 2

❹ **1** state **2** conduct **3** note **4** raise **5** record

Writing Part 1 A letter

❶ **2** report **3** input, notes **4** 220
5 reader, persuade

❸ The writer has answered all parts of the question
and included the information provided by the input
material.

❹ **2** its organisation **3** Firstly, **4** some time
5 noticeably less busy **6** facilities **7** in the
area **8** rethink **9** introduce **10** the elderly
11 consider **12** at your earliest convenience

❺ *member*: an individual who belongs to a group
or organisation *membership*: the whole group of
individuals who belong to a group; the condition
of belonging to a group or organisation *Similar
pairs of words*: partner/partnership, friend/
friendship, relation/relationship, *cost*: the amount
of money needed to pay for something (cost of
living, cut costs) *fee(s)*: money paid to or charged
by a professional individual or organisation (e.g.
legal fees, school fees) *charge(s)*: amount of money
needed to pay for a service (electricity charges,
admission charge) *price*: amount of money needed
to buy something (high price, house prices, price
rise) *fare*: cost of a journey by bus, train, etc. (rail
fares, a bus fare) *rate*: usual cost of a particular

service for a particular person or group (hourly rate of pay, fixed rate of interest, special rates for children)

6 *Explanations*: In our view, there are two possible explanations … Firstly, we think … Secondly, … *Suggestions*: As to what action can be taken, our main suggestion is … We could … We also believe that we should …

7 *Suggested answers*: **1** At present, the facilities are out of date, run down and inadequate for the demand. **2** sport not considered as important as other subjects; lack of funding/facilities; insufficient numbers of trained teachers **3** It will provide structured opportunities for more children to do sport and encourage competition between teams.

14 **Moving abroad**

Starting off

2 1 C 2 F 3 B 4 G 5 D 6 A

Recording script CD2 Track 21

Speaker 1: I've been here now for about fifteen years. It's a good life, though I work hard, but frankly <u>I miss my country and the town where I grew up</u> and dream of going back. I feel special ties to the place and when I retire I hope to return there to be among my friends and my family.

Speaker 2: <u>We were just fed up with the crime and feeling of insecurity that surrounded us</u> and it was precisely for that reason that we moved away. <u>What really worried us was the effect it might have on the kids</u> going to the local school. We felt it just wasn't worth the risk. On the other hand, it hasn't been easy coping with the language barrier, I have to admit. At least not for us parents. The kids integrated straight away, of course.

Speaker 3: I haven't changed countries, but I've moved from the country to the city because it has better services and more opportunities. <u>To my surprise, many people looked down on me when I first arrived</u>, which didn't exactly make things easy. I suppose they thought: here's some country bumpkin come to the city to make good, and I guess they were right because I have!

Speaker 4: I love lots of things about my country: the food, the sense of humour, the newspapers, lots of things. Actually, I have to admit <u>it was the climate I couldn't stand any longer</u>. The short grey days and the continual rain. Mind you, the heat is sometimes a problem here and then I dream of going home. But that's only the odd day here and there. Mostly it's fine.

Speaker 5: I guess you could call me a rolling stone, if people still use that expression – I mean, I've been abroad for so long I don't know all the latest slang. You see, unfortunately <u>I'm one of those typical expatriates who spends two years working in this country and three years working in that</u>. I don't think I could ever go back to my home country because quite honestly I just wouldn't fit in. I'd feel like a fish out of water.

Speaker 6: As a professional ballet dancer there's just no way I could have stayed in my home town. Obviously, <u>you have to be prepared to move abroad if you want to get to the top</u> and there's no point in being in this business unless that's your aim.

Reading Part 1

1 2 eighteen 3 the texts quickly before reading the questions 4 after 5 will

2 Text 1 is from a travel book. Text 2 is from a magazine article. Text 3 is from a website information page for potential students.

3 1 A 2 C 3 A 4 D 5 C 6 B

Grammar
Comment adverbials

1 unfortunately, quite honestly

2 2 undoubtedly 3 Generally speaking 4 To be honest 5 Apparently 6 kindly 7 Obviously 8 Personally

Listening Part 4

1 2 F – You have to choose from eight options. 3 Maybe - you should decide whether this way suits you best or whether you perform better when you deal with both tasks both times you listen 4 T

2 1 E 2 G 3 H 4 F 5 B 6 G 7 B 8 A 9 H
10 E

Recording script CD2 Track 22

Speaker 1:
Q1
I was watching this really interesting programme the other day about people who'd come over here to work and had originally meant to stay just a couple of years, but then ended up meeting someone and settling down and things. I thought it was quite remarkable actually because we give the impression of being rather a nationalistic lot but that doesn't seem to be the case at all in fact. They went into people's houses and showed us how they'd been accepted by their in-laws who were adopting all sorts of new customs and behaviours you wouldn't expect.

Q6
What struck me most was seeing their mums-in-law being taught how to cook new dishes. It was fascinating, a real eye-opener.

Speaker 2:
I go to dancing classes every Thursday evening. Anyway, there's a student there, quite a young woman, who has only just recently come to this country and the other day she was really looking dead tired so I offered to get her a coffee afterwards and we got talking.

Q2
Anyway, I found out that she's working here as a nurse to support her family back home; they've stayed behind, you see. Apparently, there are lots of other people in the same situation as her. Her salary here's enough to provide their schooling, their clothing and all sorts of other things back home. But she's doing incredibly long hours.

Q7
Actually, the worst thing must be being away from your children and family for years on end! I think I'd find that unbearable.

Speaker 3:
My daughter goes to school with this girl, Mariska. Her family has just arrived here. They sit together in class, they're friends, and we've got to know the parents a bit. Anyway, they've only been here what seems like a couple of

Q3
months or so, but they've already set up a travel agency for people thinking of visiting their region. They've got all these local contacts which is a bit of an advantage I suppose, but they're already doing so well that

Q8
they've even been able to give jobs to a couple of locals as well. I think that's pretty amazing, don't you?

Speaker 4:
Don't get me wrong, as far as I'm concerned immigration is fine. In fact I think it's really necessary considering the skills shortage we've got here. But it does mean that we've ended up with quite a cultural mix in our office

Q4
and sometimes it's quite hard for people to get their ideas across and, you know, sort of marry

Q9
up their different approaches to work. I'm continually surprised by the sheer variety of different takes on a situation and the different expectations people have. Personally, I think this sort of intercultural mix is one of the biggest challenges at work today.

Speaker 5:
When I started, everyone was born here and spoke the same language. Now it's a real melting pot and that gives rise to no end of problems, not least with the parents. But you have to be flexible and turn these things

Q5
to your advantage and having kids of five or ten different ethnic backgrounds learning together is a culturally enriching experience for everyone, including me! Many of the children who have come from abroad are so

Q10
hardworking that it's actually pressuring our local kids to put in more of an effort too. They're getting better results now, which is just the opposite of what I'd have expected and quite a challenge to my preconceptions!

Vocabulary

Learn, find out and *know*; *provide, offer* and *give*

1 Only *found out* is possible.

2 1 c and e   2 a   3 b and d

3 1 offered   2 provide   3 give

4 1 provide   2 offer

5 2 ~~know~~ find out   3 ~~know~~ learn *or* find out
4 ~~learn~~ find out   5 ~~give~~ provide   6 ~~give~~ offer   7 ~~offer~~ give   8 ~~offered~~ provided

Speaking Part 4

1 2 subjects connected with the same theme as Speaking Part 3 3 are expected to discuss your ideas about the same questions 4 quite a long answer

2 1 create cultural diversity, make society a richer place, open up people's minds, encourage tolerance towards other ways of life, people from different backgrounds, different outlooks, to live side by side   2 open up people's minds, encourage tolerance towards other ways of life, people from different backgrounds, different outlooks, to live side by side   3 cover people's basic needs, make the transition into a new society, provide housing, help them integrate

3

Recording script   CD2 Track 23

Teacher:	What are the benefits of a multicultural society?
Sara:	I think it encourages tolerance towards other cultures, other ways of life, other religions perhaps, and that can be very educational. I think it can open up people's minds to other experiences that they might not be able to have otherwise.
James:	I personally think it can make society itself richer by having diversity within it and lots of people from different backgrounds, different outlooks, different ways of doing things and different cultural experiences.
Teacher:	Should people who go to live in another country adopt the culture of the country where they go to live?
Sara:	That's a contentious issue! Not necessarily. I think it's possible for different cultures to live side by side and I think with most cultures there's a certain overlap of similarity and I think people should be allowed to have some of the elements of their own culture as long as they're not detrimental to the good of the majority.
James:	Yes, I'd go along with that.
Teacher:	How can governments help immigrants?
James:	What they need to do is provide lots of information at the beginning so that people can make the transition into the new society. Housing is something I think they should be providing, so they're covering people's basic needs to help them integrate as quickly as possible. Also, I think there should be offers of tuition in the new language, tuition about the new culture, possibly. I don't know if that should be compulsory, but at least it should be on offer.

---

4 1 might   2 can   3 should   4 need, can   5 should

Recording script   CD2 Track 24

1   I think it <u>can</u> open up people's minds to other experiences that they <u>might</u> not be able to have otherwise.

2   I personally think it <u>can</u> make society itself richer by having diversity within it …

3   I think people <u>should</u> be allowed to have some of the elements of their own culture as long as they're not detrimental to the good of the majority.

4   What they <u>need</u> to do is provide lots of information at the beginning so that people <u>can</u> make the transition into the new society.

5   Housing is something I think they <u>should</u> be providing.

Use of English Part 5

1 2 six   3 word   4 Contractions   5 change   6 same   7 number   8 given

2 *Correct answer*: **b** (Answer **a** is incorrect grammatically; **c** exceeds the six-word limit; **d** doesn't use the word given)

3 1 I'd *be grateful if you could/would remind* me to phone Charlie on Friday.   2 Mario completed *the project all by* himself.   3 You'll have *to make much more / a much greater / a lot more effort* if you're going to get into the national team.   4 Fatima hasn't *(yet) made up her mind whether* to study in New Zealand next year.

4 1 Katya may *(well) have been held up* by the heavy traffic.   2 I couldn't tell *whose fault the accident* was.   3 Having *found out the truth*, Ranjit reported the facts to the police.   4 'I have *done/tried my best to* make you happy, Sonia,' said Franz.

Grammar
Adding emphasis

1 2 a, c   3 a   4 b   5 b   6 c   7 c, d

2 *Suggested answers*: **2** It's because they don't like the climate in their own country that many people move overseas. / Because they really don't like the climate in their own country, many people move overseas. **3** What enriches our lives enormously is living in a multicultural society. **4** She feels extremely lonely living away from her family. **5** Even though he has an extremely well-paid job, he finds it absolutely impossible to save money. **6** It was by living in the country that Franz learnt to speak the language perfectly. **7** The director of studies himself taught us when our teacher was ill. **8** What a good education teaches people is tolerance.

Writing Part 2 An article

2 **2** f **3** e **4** d **5** b **6** g **7** a

3 **1** readers of the magazine, people who are interested in travel or working abroad **2** quite an informal style **3** *Students' own answers*

4 **1** fairly formal **2** *Fronting*: feeling the need …, Despite this minor drawback; *Using adverbs*: completely, very importantly, highly, strongly; *Cleft sentences*: What I discovered from the experience was …, What this meant was …
3 *Paragraph 1*: temporary job in another country; *Paragraph 2*: your experience and what you learnt; *Paragraph 3*: your experience and what you learnt (positive and negative); *Paragraph 4*: whether you would recommend it to others

5 **1** readers of the magazine, informal style **2** & **3** *Students' own answers*

Vocabulary and grammar review Unit 13

Vocabulary

1 **1** allergy **2** pollen **3** mould **4** exhaust **5** fever **6** allergen **7** cleanliness **8** vaccination **9** allergic

2 **2** for **3** to **4** with **5** at **6** to **7** for **8** to

Grammar

3 **1** *Alternative answer*: ~~disease, however~~ disease. However, **2** ~~although~~ whereas **3** ~~Despite~~ Despite the fact that / ~~Despite he didn't feel~~ Despite not feeling **4** ~~But~~ Although / Even though **5** ~~doctor. Although~~ doctor, although

4 **2** We *have fewer qualified nurses than* we need. **3** My new job *is more difficult than* I expected. **4** The *sooner we get home the* better. **5** I *didn't earn as much money* as I thought I would last week. **6** Your diet *is no better than* mine.

Vocabulary and grammar review Unit 14

Vocabulary

1 **2** find out **3** provide **4** know **5** given **6** offered **7** find out **8** learn

Grammar

2 **2** It was the music *that everyone/everybody objected to* at Lenka's presentation. **3** What you have *to do is fill in/out* this form and then send it to the embassy. **4** 'Getting a new job is *the last thing I want to / will* do!' cried Audrey. **5** All Alfredo wanted to *do was (to) take things/it* easy when he got home.

3 *Suggested answers*: **2** almost certainly **3** To be honest/Actually **4** Actually/To be honest **5** quite surprisingly **6** Obviously **7** apparently **8** hopefully

Writing reference

Article

Exercise 1

Students should underline: more or less necessary, changed the way you learn languages, affect language learning in the future

Exercise 2

1 Yes – *more or less necessary*: paragraph 1; *changed the way you learn languages*: paragraph 2; *affect language learning in the future*: paragraph 3

2 first anecdote about booking a flight: you may get a better deal by checking the Internet; second anecdote about trying to learn Portuguese: the writer found himself/herself isolated studying an online course.

Essay

Exercise 1

1 *Students' own answers*

2 *Students' own answers*

3 my teacher; a formal style

Exercise 2

1 four (many embark on courses without being sure, many are not sufficiently mature, universities struggle, resources are wasted)

2 two (people lose study habits, acquire obligations)

3 in the last paragraph; yes

Competition entry

Exercise 1

Students' own answers

Exercise 2

1 *why they should be chosen*: paragraph 4; *what they find most enjoyable about studying English*: paragraph 1; *what things they do outside class to improve their English*: paragraph 2; *how they expect use English in the future*: paragraph 3

2 *Suggested answers*: enthusiastic, hardworking, determined, constant, thorough, methodical, conscientious, ambitious

3 *Students' own answers*

4 phases such as *I love, I take pleasure in, I have always enjoyed*; the activities the writer describes; the adjectives he uses to describe himself

Review

Exercise 1

1 You should compare two clothes shops, say what sort of clothes they sell, comment on the quality of the service, value for money, how fashionable they are and give recommendations.

2 readers of the magazine; informal

Exercise 2

1 Yes

2 with an introduction to shopping in Linz

3 **a** fashionable, formal, casual, not cheap, unique, competitive prices, in distinctive bright colours, generally good   **b** attentive, polite, friendly

4 informal

5 It has a heading, and is divided into sections with section headings. (However, this is not essential for a review.)

6 *Suggested answer*: You can buy special clothes in Melanie's but be careful because they're expensive. If you want brightly-coloured clothes which are less expensive, The Parallel is a better choice.

Proposal

Exercise 1

1 *Students should underline*: make it easier for new foreign students to integrate, problems, say what you think, improved guidebook, social club, weekend activities, student advisors

2 The college Principal; formal

Exercise 2

1 Yes

2 *Suggested answers*: make easier – facilitate; have problems – have difficulties, find it hard; foreign – overseas; new – newly-arrived; from other countries – from other educational backgrounds; advisor – mentor

3 I would suggest, I would recommend, It would be a good idea to, I suggest

Report

Exercise 1

1 *Students should underline*: why you did the exchange, what you liked and disliked, recommendations for how it could be improved, director of the exchange programme

2 very formal

3 You must refer to educational matters and you can refer to personal experiences as well.

Exercise 2

1 *Things the writer liked*: opportunity to exchange ideas with teachers and students from another part of the world and with a different outlook, innovative solutions to local problems, improved language skills, increased cultural awareness
Things the writer didn't like: insufficient financial support, considerable expense

2 choice of formal vocabulary, e.g. *positive and negative aspects, recommendations for improvements, participated in the exchange, The benefits far outweigh the disadvantages*, etc.

Information sheet

Exercise 1

1 *Students' own answers*

2 students from other countries; quite informal

Exercise 2

1 It has a heading, an introduction, then questions (*FAQs = frequently asked questions*) and answers to the questions. The information sheet in Unit 12 was arranged as a table, with a column of information and a column of advice.

2 contractions, addressing the reader personally, use of imperative

Contribution to a longer piece

Exercise 1

1 *Students' own answers*

2 No

3 *Students' own answers* (It should be typical of the region.)

4 a general introduction to the area, why visitors will enjoy the typical place to eat

5 readers who are thinking of visiting your country; quite informal but enthusiastic and informative

Exercise 2

1 F – it has a general introduction to the area, but no conclusion.

2 T

3 *Students' own answers*

Letters

Exercise 1

1 *Students should underline*: pop festival, bad review in an international music magazine, explain how much you and your friends enjoyed the festival, how you feel about the review, *the four extracts from the review*

2 informal

3 *Students' own answers*

Exercise 2

1 Yes

2 informal, enthusiastic, colloquial

3 Yes: the final paragraph – this is to round off the letter on an enthusiastic note.

CAE model paper from Cambridge ESOL

Paper 1   Reading

Part 1
1 A   2 B   3 D   4 C   5 A   6 D

Part 2
7 C   8 F   9 G   10 D   11 E   12 A

Part 3
13 D   14 C   15 B   16 C   17 B   18 A   19 D

Part 4
20 A   21 F   22 B   23 E   24 E   25 A   26 C   27 D
28 B   29 D   30 C   31 A   32 B   33 D   34 F

Paper 2   Writing

Part 1

Question 1

CONTENT

For Band 3 or above, the candidate's proposal must:

- explain which two facilities should feature on the website
- describe contrasting benefits
- justify choices.

More able candidates will focus more effectively on the target reader's requirements.

ORGANISATION AND COHESION

Clear organisation into paragraphs with suitable linking devices. Headed sections may be an advantage.

RANGE

Language of explanation and suggestion. Vocabulary related to learning facilities.

REGISTER

Formal to unmarked.

TARGET READER

Would be informed.

Part 2

Question 2

CONTENT

For Band 3 or above, the candidate's guidebook entry must:

- describe at least two animals (NB: maximum Band 3 for farmyard animals, maximum Band 2 for pets; no penalty for misspellings of names / use of L1 names)
- specify where the animals can be seen (NB: place name(s) need not be specified; 'natural surroundings' may be addressed as part of the general introduction; inclusion of zoo is acceptable as long as 'natural surroundings' are also addressed).

ORGANISATION AND COHESION

Clear organisation with appropriate paragraphing. Letter format is acceptable.

The contribution may be two distinct paragraphs.

RANGE

Language of description.

REGISTER

Any register, as long as it is consistent.

TARGET READER

Would be informed.

Question 3

CONTENT

For Band 3 or above, the candidate's letter must:

- give early reason for writing
- explain why they are suitable for the job
- describe at least two local issues.

ORGANISATION AND COHESION

Letter format with appropriate opening and closing formulae. Clear organisation with appropriate paragraphing.

RANGE

Language of explanation and description.

REGISTER

Formal or semi-formal – must be consistent.

TARGET READER

Would be informed.

Question 4

CONTENT

For Band 3 or above, the candidate's article must:

- describe their house or flat
- outline at least two desirable changes
- explain the improvements these changes would make.

NB: the second and third points may be embedded in the first.

ORGANISATION AND COHESION

Clear organisation into paragraphs with suitable linking devices.

RANGE

Language of description and explanation. Vocabulary relating to homes and decorating.

REGISTER

Any register, as long as it is consistent.

TARGET READER

Would be informed.

Question 5 (a)

CONTENT

For Band 3 or above, the candidate's review must:

- explain which character in the book they find most unpleasant
- comment on whether they would or would not recommend the book to other students.

ORGANISATION AND COHESION

Clear organisation into paragraphs with appropriate linking devices.

RANGE

Language of description, opinion and recommendation. Vocabulary related to describing character and giving opinions.

REGISTER

Generally consistent but may mix registers if this is appropriate to the approach taken by the candidate.

TARGET READER

Would be informed both about the character and about *Lucky Jim* in general.

Question 5 (b)

CONTENT

For Band 3 or above, the candidate's report must:

- briefly outline the plot of *The Pelican Brief*
- explain whether it will interest students in the candidate's class
- comment on whether it will help students with their language learning.

Given the wording of the task, it is probable that candidates would recommend the book for class study. However, they would not be penalised for saying that it would be an unsuitable choice provided that they justify their opinions.

ORGANISATION AND COHESION

Clear organisation into paragraphs with suitable linking devices. Headings may be an advantage.

RANGE

Language of narration, recommendation and evaluation. Vocabulary related to studying *The Pelican Brief* and to language learning.

REGISTER

Formal to unmarked – must be consistent.

TARGET READER

Would be informed as to whether or not *The Pelican Brief* would be an appropriate choice for study in the candidate's class.

Paper 3   Use of English

Part 1

1 B   2 B   3 A   4 A   5 B   6 C   7 D   8 A   9 C
10 C   11 C   12 B

Part 2

13 for/over   14 in   15 although/though/while/whilst
16 and   17 it   18 like   19 the   20 which   21 were
22 is   23 that   24 without   25 to   26 not
27 but/except/beyond/ besides

Part 3

28 environmental **29** endangered **30** enable
31 willingness **32** permission **33** offence
34 inappropriate **35** preferable **36** erosion
37 destruction

Part 4

38 point **39** shot **40** run **41** hard **42** carried

Part 5

43 A *great/good deal of work is* required to make a
good documentary film.
44 'Please take immediate *action/steps/measures to
find a solution / an answer* to this problem!' said
the Managing Director.
45 Concerns are *being expressed with/in* regard to the
poor quality of the water.
46 Students with an ID card *are / will be admitted free*
of charge.
47 I am really *grateful to you for* sending me the
information about voluntary jobs abroad.
48 I don't think *you will / you'll have much difficulty /
trouble (in/with)* learning to drive an automatic car.
49 The lift has *been out of order* for a week.
50 Fatima's marriage *came as no surprise* to Paul.

Paper 4 Listening

Part 1

1 B **2** A **3** A **4** B **5** B **6** A

Part 2

7 east **8** ash(es) **9** bell **10** port/harbour **11** oak
12 factory **13** (plently of) cream **14** plastic (foods)

Part 3

15 C **16** D **17** A **18** C **19** D **20** B

Part 4

21 D **22** B **23** G **24** E **25** F **26** A **27** B **28** F
29 G **30** H

Model paper

Recording script CD3 Track 2

This is the Cambridge Certificate in Advanced
English, Listening Test.

I'm going to give you instructions for this test.

I'll introduce each part of the test and give you
time to look at the questions.

At the start of each piece you will hear this
sound:

***

You'll hear each piece twice.

Remember, while you're listening, write your
answers on the question paper. You'll have
five minutes at the end of the test to copy your
answers onto the separate answer sheet.

There'll now be a pause. Please ask any
questions now, because you must not speak
during the test.

PART 1 CD3 Track 3

Now open your question paper and look at
Part One.

You'll hear three different extracts. For
questions one to six, choose the answer (A,
B, or C) which fits best according to what you
hear.

There are two questions for each extract.

Extract One

You hear part of a radio programme in which a
recent prize-winning book is being discussed.
Now look at questions one and two.

***

Man:	Now, what makes a good science book? Is it one that satisfies an appetite for knowledge or maybe one that restores a sense of wonder in the world? Maggie, you were one of the judges – what criteria were you using?
Woman:	Well, the factual content has to be up to the mark of course. But, as so often is the case, it's the dynamism of the writing. Interestingly, our top choice this year was about the sea and though none of the judges were experts in that field, we were just bowled over. <u>We really felt we were there with the divers.</u>
Q1	
Man:	Yes, but there was also a lot about jellyfish.
Woman:	But they're extraordinarily beautiful, aren't they?

Man:

Q2 It's incredible – how is it that someone comes to spend his or her life studying jellyfish and I think, to me, that's one of the pluses of good science writing. While scientists are completely like the rest of us in some ways, <u>they're also remarkable in how they choose to spend their time – totally focused on something most of us give no thought to at all.</u>

***

REPEAT

Extract Two

You hear a man called Ian telling a friend about learning to play the piano.

Now look at questions three and four.

***

Woman: I hear you're quite an amateur musician, Ian. So what made you take it up?

Ian: I'd had a very worrying time, trying to hold work together and stave off redundancy, so when it all came to a head and I lost my job, I felt a sense of release. We'd inherited an old piano, and a neighbour started teaching me to play. <u>You get an incredible feeling of learning to do something you couldn't do before</u> – pretty **Q3** unusual these days! And then I nurture the probably vain hope that I may be able to join a string quartet one day!

Woman: You say your music teacher is your neighbour. How does that work?

Ian: Well, just like any other pupil–teacher relationship. Just because I might occasionally bump into her in the street doesn't mean I should take her for granted. She hasn't got a degree in music, but <u>wow, is she gifted when it</u> **Q4** <u>comes to playing!</u> And nobody could be more creative in thinking up ways of appealing to the musical side of me. She does sometimes get irritated with me, but I owe her so much. Without her I'd never have got this far.

***

REPEAT

Extract Three

You hear part of a radio discussion about the work of the nineteenth-century writer, Charles Dickens.

Now look at questions five and six.

***

Interviewer: People disagree about Dickens' work. Some love him while others find him overpowering. Which side are you on, Alan?

Alan: The thing about his work is that it's ridiculously uneven. This makes it hard to choose one novel and say this is *the* masterpiece. Within **Q5** his huge output <u>there's so much daring stuff. Also what's attractive is that he didn't spend months pondering about the structure and the plot. He just went for it. I admire his nerve</u> and the way he pulled it off against the odds.

Interviewer: Dickens started his career as a writer very young, didn't he?

Alan: He had a few false starts – the law, and he worked in parliament – then his first success came when he was twenty-four. I can relate to his desire to find the right path. I was under pressure to follow a proper profession and the fact that I wanted to go into journalism took ages for my parents to come to terms with. They thought I'd never make any money. <u>I</u> **Q6** <u>can sympathise with his restlessness and his fear of settling down to being a banker, for example, as that would have been so limiting.</u>

***

REPEAT

That's the end of Part One.

PART 2   CD3 Track 4

Now turn to Part Two.

You'll hear the food historian Nina Travis talking about the tradition of smoking fish in the Scottish town of Arbroath. For questions seven to fourteen, complete the sentences. You now have forty-five seconds to look at Part Two.

***

Nina Travis: Today I want to discuss the tradition of fish-smoking and one particular type of smoked fish that's experiencing a revival. Smoked fish, particularly salmon and mackerel, are regularly eaten in the UK and around the world. Salmon farms have grown up in the west of Scotland, especially around the islands. Another great and less well-known fish delicacy is smoked haddock. It's called the 'Arbroath smoky' as it was produced in Scotland in a town called **Q7** Arbroath, situated on the <u>east</u> coast. This is the smoked fish I want to focus on.

today. Historians tell us that the tradition of fish-smoking was brought to Scotland by Scandinavian seafarers over a thousand years ago.

There's also a less reliable but more homely folk tale in Arbroath itself. Haddock used to be salted to preserve it and kept in wooden barrels. According to this tale, an old house burned down and when people were digging through the ashes to see if there was anything left, they came across some salted haddock that had been smoked in the fire. They tasted it, found it delicious and that's how smoked haddock started! Whatever the origin, when the trade was at its height in Arbroath, fishermen would go out to sea early in the morning and bring the haddock back. A man would be sent round the town with a bell to tell people that the boats were in, the equivalent of today's loudspeaker, I suppose. People would rush down to the port, where the fish was auctioned off, rather than being sent by lorry to the big cities as would be the case today. The traditional process was to clean the haddock, remove the heads and fasten the fish together in pairs before leaving them in salt overnight. The fish were then hung on sticks and suspended over the fire in the smokehouse.

They were smoked over a hard wood such as oak, rather than the more available pine, for reasons of flavour. Most small family-run businesses have faded out but a company has recently relaunched the 'smoky' in its traditional home – Arbroath. They've built a state-of-the-art factory there to produce the smoked fish in large enough quantities to sell to supermarkets. But what can you do with smoked haddock? In fact it's a very easy fish to handle. You just remove the backbone and the fish can be eaten cold or hot. My favourite method is to put the fish in a dish with, for example, onions and mushrooms, cover it with plenty of cream, bake it and serve it hot with potatoes or as a filling for pancakes. Let's hope the relaunch succeeds. Throughout Britain now, so many people are eating what I call 'plastic' foods which are mass-produced and taste horribly bland, while here's a traditional regional product which tastes delicious. Good luck to the smoky!

Q8

Q9

Q10

Q11

Q12

Q13

Q14

Now you'll hear Part Two again.

***

REPEAT

That's the end of Part Two.

PART 3   CD3 Track 5

Now turn to Part Three.

You'll hear a radio interview in which a composer, Sam Tilbrook, is talking about his life and work. For questions fifteen to twenty, choose the answer (A, B, C or D) which fits best according to what you hear.

You now have one minute to look at Part Three.

***

Interviewer: In the studio with me today is Sam Tilbrook, whose recent work has confirmed him in most critics' eyes as one of the foremost Canadian composers. Let's go back to your musical beginnings for a moment, and the thing that triggered your musical career – your mother insisting you should start learning the clarinet.

Sam Tilbrook: Well, she didn't have to insist. Because I was singing in a choir, I'd already been taught to read music, and that gave me the urge to write music – it was a purely instinctive thing, the next step, if you like. So I loved the idea of the clarinet and I've composed a lot for it over the years, even as a student.

Q15

Interviewer: So, did you know about music when you started studying at the Toronto Music College?

Sam Tilbrook: I knew nothing about the rules of composition, and when I was confronted with official tuition, I found it difficult to make it tally with my own feelings about composing.

Interviewer: It was very brave of you to say, 'I know what the sound of my music is, and although my elders and betters are applying these incredibly persuasive systems, that's not for me, because it won't allow me to reveal what I can hear inside my head.' That's your approach, isn't it?

Sam Tilbrook: It's more complex than that. What I do when composing is improvise a chord I like, then break it down to see if I can produce more of a similar type of sound. I add to it over time, so it's hardly like a bolt from the blue.

Q16

Interviewer: You've never had any impulse to follow the classical disciplines, have you?

Sam Tilbrook: I wouldn't say that exactly. But I do have a problem with music that imitates classical forms, and then fails to deliver the goods.

Interviewer: I think you've said that as soon as you started composing, you were profoundly affected by the French composer Olivier Messiaen. What did he do for you?

Sam Tilbrook:
Q17
It wasn't so much the way he composed, it was what he *did* that gave me hope. Funnily enough, to listen to him – not that I ever met him – you'd think he was steeped in tradition from the beginning of time! But in fact he invented a new sort of music in one go …

Interviewer: Like including birdsong in some of his pieces …

Sam Tilbrook: Which I considered putting in one of my symphonies, and then thought better of it – yeah!

Interviewer: Now let's talk about theatre, and the huge role it's played in your composing.

Sam Tilbrook: Well, it was pretty important to me. I used to act in an amateur dramatic society at school.

Interviewer:
Q18
And that ignited your feeling for drama – when someone stepped on the stage, it was magic?

Sam Tilbrook: That sort of thing. It was extraordinary, having to learn your lines by heart and then deliver them under a spotlight. You're on your own out there! Acting or playing an instrument in public – it's quite a challenge.

Interviewer: Your latest work took you a long time to write. Do you enjoy the whole process of composing?

Sam Tilbrook: I find it incredibly painful, sometimes terrifying, although I don't have an artist-must-suffer syndrome. I totally believe in what I'm doing, in the moment. So it's pretty hard, in the context of my work, to lay off for a while.
Q19
And very often if I come up with an answer to a problem, I'll just walk away from it – it's too easy.

Interviewer: The moment you have some sense of certainty, you think, 'Forget it!'

Sam Tilbrook: Unpredictability certainly appeals to me more.

Interviewer: You talk a lot about art versus music. Maybe you envy modern artists who can put their intuition directly onto canvas, which is something composers can't do?

Sam Tilbrook:
Q20
There's no equivalent in music to taking a big brush, making a gesture, completely unplanned, and seeing what the effect is. *My* work is intensely practical – it's slowly constructed out of tiny carefully-chosen elements. Painting can be more spontaneous, less considered, but that kind of art means the public may not get much out of it after their first encounter with it.

Interviewer: Sam Tilbrook, thank you for being with us.

Now you'll hear Part Three again.

***

REPEAT

That's the end of Part Three.

PART 4   CD3 Track 6

Now turn to Part Four.

Part Four consists of two tasks. You will hear five short extracts in which people are talking about education. Look at Task One. For questions twenty-one to twenty-five, choose from the list A to H each person's occupation. Now look at Task Two. For questions twenty-six to thirty, choose from the list A to H what each person is doing when they speak. While you listen you must complete both tasks.

You now have forty-five seconds to look at Part Four.

***

Speaker 1: You can do all sorts of courses at college nowadays, get qualifications in things you never even knew existed. It's marvellous really.
Q21
What we really need to know is how hard to push her. We neither of us went to college ourselves, and
Q26
we don't really know how much work they have to do. Is she doing enough homework? It seems like a lot to us, but as I say, we can't tell.

Speaker 2:
Q27
The thing that concerns me is that higher education is not fitting young people for the world in which they are going to find themselves. It's no use their dreaming up fancy policies if they produce too many teachers and not enough mechanics. They should be more in touch with the real world – turning out people to fit jobs we want done in the manufacturing
Q22
industries. We can't be expected to turn in a profit if we can't get the labour with the right skills.

Speaker 3:   When I started, I thought they'd be difficult to handle, wandering about, trying to fiddle with

Q23   things, <u>touching the things on display.</u> Actually, they're usually very well behaved. And they're much better informed than most members

Q28   of the public. <u>It's often a visit that ties in with a history project and sometimes I help the teacher prepare worksheets.</u> They ask some difficult questions, too, sometimes. It's quite challenging, in a pleasant sort of way.

Speaker 4:   Well, we do sometimes get a youngster coming in from his school with glowing reports about how many junior records he's broken and so on. But we don't take too much notice of that.

Q24 & Q29   <u>What we do is, we put everyone through three months of intensive training, mainly to get rid of all the bad habits they've picked up, and see they're really fit, and then we start selection and specialisation after that.</u> We find it works really well.

Speaker 5:   I know you've all been wondering about <u>the</u>
Q30   <u>details for next week.</u> Well, I can now tell you that the Education Minister herself will be <u>on</u>

Q25   <u>the campus for most of the day on Wednesday, and she will be spending part of the morning in this faculty, looking in on some lectures</u> and having coffee with us here in the common room. I myself will be lunching with her along with other department heads and the senior administrative staff.

Now you'll hear Part Four again.

***

REPEAT

That's the end of Part Four.

There'll now be a pause of five minutes for you to copy your answers onto the separate answer sheet. Be sure to follow the numbering of all the questions. I'll remind you when there's one minute left, so that you're sure to finish in time.

You have one more minute left.

That's the end of the test. Please stop now. Your supervisor will now collect all the question papers and answer sheets.

Acknowledgements

We offer our warmest thanks to the editors for their guidance, support, feedback and general hard work during this project: Nik White and Niki Donnelly at CUP; Diane Hall and Meredith Levy for their painstaking hard work and enthusiasm; Kevin Brown (picture researcher); John Green (audio producer); Tim Woolf (audio editor) and Marcus Fletcher (proof reader). Particular thanks also go to Steve, Rebecca and the team at Wild Apple Design.

Guy Brook-Hart would also like to thank his CAE students at the British Council, Valencia, from 2007–2008 for working on and trialling materials later used in the book. Also, special thanks to Liam Carolan for the interview he gave for Unit 6 and for supplying his self-portrait and a portrait of one of his sitters (p. 61). He especially thanks his family, Paz, Esteban and Elena, for their support, enthusiasm and good humour throughout the project. He dedicates his part in this book to Paz, with love.

Simon Haines would also like to thank his family, Val, Laura and Jo for their occasional advice and continuous support.

Guy Brook-Hart, Valencia, Spain

Simon Haines, England

March 2009

The editors are also grateful to the following for participation in the recording scripts: Fran Matthews and Sally Oliphant for the recording scripts on pp. 215–216, pp. 217–218, pp. 231–232; Liam Carolan for the recording script on p. 223; Hannah Bethia Thomas for the script on p. 212; Sam Taylor and Hannah Bethia Thomas for the recording script on pp. 238–239; Sara Harden and Chris Willis for the recording scripts on p. 245; Sara Bennett and James Dingle for the recording script on p. 252; for participation on the *Complete CAE* CD-ROM: Alyson Maskell, Nikalaos Kovaios, Ian Collier and Nick Robinson; for reviewing early drafts of the material: Dennis Akers, IH Mataro; Maggie Baigent; Christine Barton; Jane Coates; Rachel Connabeer; Rosie Ganne; Joanna Kazmierczak; Laura Matthews; Karyl Mueller-Pringle; Brendan Ó Sé, University College Cork; Luiza Wojtowicz-Waga, Warsaw Study Centre.

The authors and publishers acknowledge the following sources of copyright material and are grateful for the permissions granted. While every effort has been made, it has not always been possible to identify the sources of all the material used, or to trace all copyright holders. If any omissions are brought to our notice, we will be happy to include the appropriate acknowledgements on reprinting.

For the Student's Book: Little, Brown Book Group Limited for the extract on p. 11 from *The Bookseller of Kabul* by Åsne Seierstad. Reproduced by permission of Little, Brown Book Group Limited; Hodder & Stoughton Limited and Random House Inc. for the extract on p. 12 from *Mr Commitment*. Copyright © 1999 Mike Gayle. Reproduced by permission of Hodder & Stoughton Limited & Broadway Books, a division of Random House Inc.; Hodder & Stoughton Limited and Stuart Krichevsky Literary Agency, Inc. for the adapted extract on p. 12 from *The Hungry Ocean*. Copyright © 1999 by Linda Greenlaw. Reprinted by permission of Hodder & Stoughton Limited and the Stuart Krichevsky Literary Agency, Inc.;

The Economist for the adapted text on p. 16 'Kenneth Hale, Master Linguist' from *The Economist*, November 2001, for the adapted text on p. 118 'Alex the African Grey' *The Economist* 20 September 2007, for the text on p. 139 'When talent goes abroad' from 'Emigration: outward bound' *The Economist* 26 September 2002, for the audio recording and recording script on pp. 213–214 adapted from 'About Face, Prosopagnosia' from *The Economist* 13 December 2004. Copyright © The Economist Newspaper Limited, London; Cambridge University Press for the adapted text on p. 22 from *The Cambridge Encyclopedia of Language*, 2nd edition by David Crystal. Copyright © Cambridge University press, 1997. Reproduced by permission of the author and Cambridge University Press; BBC.co.uk for the text on p. 28 from www.bbc.co.uk/science/leonardo/thinker_quiz/allresults.

shtml. Reproduced with permission from bbc.co.uk; NI Syndication for the adapted text on p. 32 'The next step in brain evolution' by Richard Woods from *The Sunday Times* 9 July 2006, for the adapted text on p. 42 from *The Times* 20 October 2005, for the text on p. 58 from The Times online 13 May 2007, for the text on p. 90 'Bugatti Veyron' by Jeremy Clarkson, *The Sunday Times* 23 July 2007. Copyright © NI syndication Limited; About.com for the text on p. 34 from http://genealogy.about.com/cd/geneticgenealogy/a/nature_nurture.htm. ©2008 by Kimberly Powell Used with permission of About, Inc., which can be found online at www.about.com. All rights reserved; *The Guardian* for the adapted text on pp. 38–39 'Is there an architect in the house?' by Tom Dyckhoff, *The Guardian* 19 June 2001, for the adapted text on pp. 70–71 'How to get the life you really want' by David Smith, *The Observer* 9 July 2006, for the adapted text on p. 116 'Island Wanted' from 'Meet the tribe' by Simon Orr, *The Observer* (Travel) 25 March 2007, for the audio recording and recording script on pp. 237–238 adapted from 'Life Swap' by Amy Smith and Hodka Baraka, *The Guardian* 21 January 2006. Copyright © Guardian News & Media Limited; Random House Group Limited for the text on p. 52 from *Cal* by Bernard MacLaverty, published by Jonathan Cape. Reprinted by permission of The Random House Group Limited; The Orion Publishing Group for the text on p. 53 from *Himalaya* by Michael Palin. Reproduced by permission of Weidenfeld & Nicholson, a division of The Orion Publishing Group (London); Random House Inc., Random House Group Limited and Random House of Canada Limited for the adapted text on p. 53 from *A Walk in the Woods* by Bill Bryson, copyright © 1997 by Bill Bryson. Used by permission of Broadway Books, a division of Random House, Inc., The Random House Group Limited and Doubleday, Canada; Adapted text on p. 64 from 'Offices down to a fine art' by Caroline Palmer, *The Observer* 13 May 2001; Media Ethics for the adapted text on p. 79 from 'The Ethics of Reality Television Producers' by Richard Crew from *Media Ethics* Magazine, vol. 18, No. 2 (pp. 10 & 19); *NowPublic* for the audio recording and recording script on pp. 239–240 from http://www.nowpublic.com; Professor Greg Philo for the adapted text on p. 83 from *The Guardian* letters, 23 July 2007. Reproduced by kind permission of Professor Greg Philo; The Committee for Economic Development of Australia (CEDA) for the adapted text on p. 103 from CEDA – Lifelong learning: How to pass the test by Professor Louise Roland, www.ceda.com.au; Penguin Books Limited for the text on pp. 112–13 from *Dark Star Safari: Overland from Cairo to Cape Town* by Paul Theroux (Penguin Books 2002) Copyright © Cape Cod Scriveners Co., 2002. Reproduced by permission of Penguin Books Limited; Environmental News Network (ENN), Inc. for the headlines on p. 117 'China to Build Offshore Wind Power Complex', 'BUS Fish and Wildlife Service to Consider Black-footed Albatross for Protection', 'Pollutant linked to bronchitis in toddlers', 'Britons top table of carbon emissions from planes'. Reproduced by permission of ENN, Inc.; *New Scientist* for the headline on p. 117 'Is the bio fuel dream over?' From *New Scientist* 15 December 2007; National Geographic Society for the headline on p. 117 'Arctic Melt Opens Northwest Passage' from *National Geographic News* 17 September 2007; Reuters for the adapted text on p. 120 from 'Endangered China tiger caught on camera after 30 years', 12 October 2007. Copyright 2007 Reuters. Reprinted with permission from Reuters. Reuters content is the intellectual property of Reuters or its third party content providers. Any copying, republication or redistribution or Reuters content is expressly prohibited without the prior written consent of Reuters. Reuters shall not be liable for any errors or delays in content, or for any actions taken in reliance thereon. Reuters and the Reuters Sphere Logo are registered trademarks of the Reuters group of companies around the world. For additional information about Reuters content and services, please visit Reuters website at www.reuters.com. License #REU-4913-MES; Australian Associated Press Pty Limited (AAP) for the adapted text on p. 127 from 'Alarm over mantling of Arctic Ice Cap'. Copyright © AAP 2003; Random House Group Limited for the text on p. 138 'The Atlantic Passage' from *Hunting Mister Heartbreak* by Jonathan Raban, published by Harvill. Reprinted by permission of The Random House Group Limited and Aitken Alexander Associates on behalf of the author;

'Immigration New Zealand for the text on p. 139 'Getting a Student Visa or Permit' from www.immigration.govt.nz; Alex Clark for the adapted text on p. 179 from 'Prize fighting' *The Guardian* 19 January 2002. Reproduced by permission of Alex Clark; David Nokes for the adapted text on p. 180 from Adaptations. www.clearingtakings.org. Reproduced by permission of David Nokes; Antony Harwood Limited for the extract on p. 181 from a *Vicious Circle*. Copyright © Amanda Craig 1996; Independent Newspapers for the adapted article on p. 182 from 'How we met' by Esther Oxford, *The Independent* 4 October 1992. Copyright © Independent News & Media Limited; Penguin Books Limited and Abner Stein for the text on pp. 184–185 from *Revolution in Time* (Penguin Books, 2000). Copyright © David Landes 2000. Reproduced by permission of Penguin Books Limited and Abner Stein on behalf of the author; *Cosmopolitan* for the adapted text on p. 187 from 'Women on a winning streak'. *Cosmopolitan*, September 1991. Reproduced by permission of *Cosmopolitan*; Adapted text on p. 193 from 'Responsible tourism' www.raptoradventures.co.uk/raptor; *The Washington Post* for the audio recording and recording script on pp. 243–244 adapted from 'Signs of Thaw in a Desert of Snow' by DeNeen L. Brown, *Washington Post* Foreign Services, 28 May 2002. All rights reserved. Used by permission and protected by the Copyright Laws of the United States. The printing, copying and redistribution, or retransmission of the Material with express written permission is prohibited.

For the CD-ROM: Jobs.ac.uk, University of Warwick for the adapted text 'How your personality affects your work' by Neil Harris, Reading Units 3–4, www.jobs.ac.uk/careers; Fran Molloy for the adapted text 'Magnificent Obsessions', Reading Units 7–8 from *Sydney Morning Herald*, 16 November 2006. Reproduced with kind permission of Fran Molloy; *Nanyang Chronicle* for the adapted recording and recording script, Listening Units 9–10 'Self education, a manifesto' written by Jared Tham, *The Nanyang Chronicle*, July 2000; BBC News Online for the text 'Virgin Galactic: the logical next step' by Paul Rincon, Reading Units 11–12, from www.bbc.co.uk/bbcnews. Reproduced by permission of bbc.co.uk; *The Independent* for recording and recording script Listening units 11–12, loosely based on article 'Too cool for school: Britain's most eco-friendly building' by Esther Walker, *The Independent*, 10 April 2008. Copyright © Independent News & Media Ltd, 2008.

Key: l = Left, r = Right, t = Top, bk = Background, b = Bottom, c = Centre, u = Upper, w = Lower, f = Far.

For permission to reproduce photographs: © 20th Century Fox / Everett / Rex Features p. 77 (r); Action Plus p. 88 (2), p. 132 (1); © ADAGP, Paris and DACS, London 2008 p. 29 (r) *Son of Man*, 1964 (oil on canvas) by Rene Magritte, (1898–1967) / The Bridgeman Art Library; Alamy/ p. 9(7) (Henry Owen),/ (Sam Toren) p. 12,/ (Callas) (Content Mine International) p. 29,/ (Sally & Richard Greenhill) p. 35 (tl),/ (Joe Foxx) p. 35 (bl),/ (Stan Gamester) p. 39 (r),/ (Betty LaRue) p. 44 (cl),/ (powietrzynski) p. 49(tr),/ (Mike Booth) p. 58,/ (Marwood Jenkins) p. 63 (cl),/ (Ted Foxx) p. 63(br),/ (vario images GmbH & Co.KG) p. 64 (sculpture),/ (Stephen Power) p. 69 (5),/ (Lou Linwei) p. 84 (bl),/ (Peter Bowater) p. 88(1),/ (DBURKE) p. 88 (3),/ (Mikael Karlsson) p. 94 (tl),/ (Alibi Productions) p. 95(b),/ (Bubbles Photolibrary) p. 97 (cr),/ (Sigrid Dauth) p. 98 (tr),/ (travelib) p. 98(b),/ (Dennie Cody) p. 99 (cr),/ (Arch White) p. 100,/ (student group) (David R. Frazier Photolibrary, Inc.) p. 103,/ (whiteboard) (Patrick Eden) p. 103,/ (Craig Lovell) p. 108 (1),/ (imagebroker) p. 108 (2),/ (Les Gibbon) p. 111,/ (Rolf Richardson p. 116(t)) ,/ (Skyscan Photolibrary) p. 116 (b),/ (Kevin Schafer) p. 120 (t),/ (Steve Mansfield-Devine) p. 128 (tl),/ (Robert Clare) p. 129,/ (avatra images) p. 131(cl),/ (www.gerardbrown.co.uk) p. 131 (tr),/ (Colin Woodbridge) p. 132 (2),/ (Photolocation Ltd) p. 137 (t),/ (Penny Tweedie) p. 137 (ct),/ (Sally & Richard Greenhill), p. 140 (t) / (Bubbles Photolibrary) p. 204 (br); Art Directors & TRIP p. 49 (b),62 (tr), 63 (cr), 74 (t), 75 (l), 94 (b), 97 (tl), 137 (b), 178 (bl); Sibelius 5 Sibelius Software – A part of Avid from the website http://www.sibelius.com/press/sibelius.html p. 69 (2); Martyn Chillmaid / photographersdirect.com p. 204(cl); Corbis/ (Catherine Karnow) p. 8 (5),/ (Simon Jarratt) p. 17(cr),/ (Elke Van De Velde/zefa) p. 17(bc),/ (Larry Hirshowitz) p. 21,/ (Sergio Gaudenti/Kipa) p. 23(b),/ (Matthias

Kulka/zefa) p. 28,/ (Bourgeois) (Christopher Felver) p. 29,/ (Acheba) (Frank May/epa) p. 29,/ (FURGOLLE/Image Point FR) p. 35 (tr),/ (Toby Melville / Reuters) p. 35(cl),/ (Manuel Blondeau/Sygma) p. 39(l),/ (John Henley) p. 43,/ (Ted Levine/zefa) p. 48 (br),/ (Kim Eriksen/zefa) p. 49 (tl),/ (Roger Ball) p. 54 (tl),/ (Stephen Hird / Reuters) p. 54(cl),/ (Bob Krist) p. 63 (bl), / (fishtank) (DK Images) p. 64,/ (Atlantide Phototravel) p. 84 (tr)/, (Justin Lane/epa) p. 84 (br),/ (Chen Xiaogen/ Xinhua Press) p. 88 (4),/ (Luis Orteo/Hemis) p. 88 (bl), p. 102,/ (Waltraud Grubitzsch/epa) p. 103 (lecture hall),/ (Kennan Ward) p. 108 (4),/ (Ryan Pyle) p. 117 (t),/ (JLP/Jose L. Pelaez) p. 128 (br),/ (Anne-Marie Weber) p. 131 (br); Dharma Productions / The Kobal Collection p. 73; Disney / Ronald Grant Archives p. 89 (r); Mark Duffin p. 68, p. 77 (l); Enigma / Goldcrest / Warner Bros / Ronald Grant Archive p. 52; Getty Images/ (Stephen Alvarez / National Geographic) p. 8 (2),/ (Spencer Platt) p. 11,/ (Johannes Kroemer) p. 13,/ (arabianEye) p. 17 (br),/ (David Young-Wolff) p. 23 (c),/ (Cameron Davidson) p. 24 (l),/ (Catherine Ledner) p. 24 (c),/ (Darwin) (Time & Life Pictures) p. 29,/ (Rand) p. 29,/ (Commercial Eye) p. 31, p. 35 (bl),/ (Jetta Productions) p. 37 (2),/ (Siri Stafford) p. 37 (3),/ (Angela Wyant) p. 37 (4),/ (Darrin Klimek) p. 45,/ (Roberto Mettifogo) p. 48 (tr),/ (Martin Barraud) p. 54 (br),/ (Emmanuel Faure) p. 63 (tl),/ (a███████ ██s) p. 69 (3),/ (Kazuhiro Nogi /AFP) p. 88 (5),/ (Stu Fors███ ██/ (Ian Murphy) p. 112 (br),/ (Ryan McVay) p. 132 (c),/ p. █ 178 (t); M. Harvey / NHPA / Photoshot for p. 112(tr);██████ ██or pp. 63(tr), 74(b); International Photobank p. 177 (t); i█████ ██ 9 (6), p. 64 (plant, painting, bearings); Benji Lanyado/C█████rs & Media Limited 2007 for p. 115; Lebrecht Arts & Mus███ ██p. 29(Gaudi) (Interfoto); Mary Evans Picture Library p. 1███ ██e/ (artist) (David Mendelsohn) p. 64,/ (Sherman Hines) ████████ Morzinelets.com p. 48(l); Musicpictures.com/ Redferr██████ana Scrimgeour); PA Photos/ (Polgár) p. 29, p. 55, p. 120 (l███; Photolibrary.com/ p. 8 (1), p. 54(tr, cr), p. 62(br), p. 7███, p. 113(t), p. 123(5), p. 128(tr), p. 145, p. 204(tr); NI Sy████ the photographs on p. 57 Self Portraits at Tate. *The Times*████ Copyright © NI Syndication Limited; *NowPublic* for the█████n p. 81 from http://www.nowpublic.com; Punchstock/ (█████8 (4),/ (Creatas) p. 15 (l),/ (Digital Vision) p. 9 (8), p. 1███p. 32, p. 37 (5), p. 74 (c), p. 99 (tl), p. 123 (4, 6), p. 131 (t██/ (moodboard) p. 17 (tl) p. 62 (cr),/ (Blend Images) p. 1██ (r), p. 35 (cr),/ (Bananastock) p. 23 (t), p. 37 (1),/ (Im██ (tl, ctr), p. 62(bl),/ (Thinkstock) p. 44(tr), p. 62 (cl),/ (Co██████ p. 84 (tl, cr), p. 108 (3), p. 137 (cb),/ (Uppercut) p. 95 (tl██████d), 103(girl with laptop) 130 178(tl) 204(tl) (Image Source███████) p. 177(c),/ (Polka Dot) p. 177(b), / (Comstock) p. 204 ██ Features/ (Olycom Spa) p. 8 (3), (Pete Oxford / Nature██████ry) p. 20,/ (Sipa Press) (Richard Young) p. 22, p. 29(Zidan██p. 44 (cbr),/ (Daneli Krolls/WestEnd61) p. 44 (bl),/ (G█████ Mountain Light) p. 53,/ (Sipa Press) p. 54 (bl),/ (Burg██ 62(tl),/ (Sipoa Press) p. 70,/ ITV p. 78 (t),/ (David Fish██ (Beretta/Sims) p. 83, (Richard Jones) p. 84(cl),/ (Etien██ pp. 90–91, p. 94 (tr),/ (Alix/Phanie) p. 97 (tr),/ (Rober██ 97(br),/ (Nils Jorgensen) p. 98(tl),/ (Bader-Butowski/V███ p. 99(tr),/ (boy & teacher) (John Powell) p. 103,/ (class███ ██ Ehlers/Stock Connection) p. 103,/ (Sipa Press) p. 109 █████ian Press) p. 112(l), 117(b),/ (Garald Davies) p. 118(t),/, (S██████ 123 (1),(3),/ (Corey Hochachka/Design Pics Inc) p. 123 (2)██████tis) p. 131(bl),/ (Brett Jorgensen) p. 131(cr),/ (Clive Dixon██████. 140 (b),/ (Per Lindgren) p. 178 (cl),/ (Design Pics Inc█████ Science Photo Library (Daniel Sambraus) p. 178(cr); J██████3; Shutterstock p. 44(br), p. 99(cl, br); Still Pictures/ (C█████ p. 121 (t); Barry Tessman / National Geographic Image██████109 (6); www.alexfoundation.org, Brandeis University, P████████e Levin-Rowe p. 118 (b); www.britainonview.com p. 7█████ ██e Walker).

Commissioned photography: p. 142 (Sophie Clarke█████

Illustrations: Martina Farrow: p. 10, p. 93, p. 206; M██████4, p. 81; Bruno Drummond: p. 36, p. 51, p. 82, p. 135; Mar███████p. 77

Cover design by Wild Apple Design Ltd

Designed and typeset by Wild Apple Design Ltd